UNCIVIL WARS

Political Campaigns
in a Media Age

D1413769

UNCIVIL WARS
Political Campaigns
in a Media Age

Second Edition

Thomas A. Hollihan

Annenberg School for Communication
University of Southern California

Bedford / St. Martin's
Boston ♦ New York

For Bedford / St. Martin's

Executive Editor for Communication: Erika Gutierrez
Editor: Noel Hohnstine
Developmental Editor: Betty Slack
Senior Production Supervisor: Dennis J. Conroy
Production Associate: Samuel Jones
Marketing Manager: Casey Carroll
Project Management: Books By Design, Inc.
Cover Design: Billy Boardman
Cover Photo: Senator and Democratic Presidential Candidate Barack Obama
    (D—Illinois) Takes a Street Walk while Campaigning in Downtown Concord,
    New Hampshire, February 2, 2007. © Brooks Kraft/Corbis.
Composition: Achorn International
Printing and Binding: R R Donnelley & Sons Company

President: Joan E. Feinberg
Editorial Director: Denise B. Wydra
Editor in Chief: Karen S. Henry
Director of Development: Erica T. Appel
Director of Marketing: Karen Melton Soeltz
Director of Editing, Design, and Production: Marcia Cohen
Assistant Director of Editing, Design, and Production: Elise S. Kaiser
Manager, Publishing Services: Emily Berleth

Library of Congress Control Number: 2007943426

Manufactured in the United States of America.

3 2 1 0 9 8
f e d c b

For information, write: Bedford / St. Martin's, 75 Arlington Street, Boston, MA
02116   (617-399-4000)

ISBN-10: 0-312-47883-6
ISBN-13: 978-0-312-47883-4

Acknowledgments

Mike Royko. Excerpt from "The Long Campaign." From *The Los Angeles Times*,
May 9, 1984, p. D7. © Tribune Media Services, Inc. All Rights Reserved.
Reprinted with permission.

Preface

Uncivil Wars: Political Campaigns in a Media Age undertakes a systematic and comprehensive examination of recent political campaigns, including the 2008 presidential race. The book discusses how campaign strategies and media practices influence people's attitudes and confidence in their political leaders and civic institutions. Since the book's first edition, many dramatic events have impacted politics in the United States: the terrorist attacks of 9/11, the wars in Afghanistan and Iraq, the devastation of Hurricane Katrina, and others. In addition, our political practices have been altered by new technologies such as the exponential growth of Internet usage, online video sharing, new social networking sites, and mobile phone text-messaging. As increasing numbers of people access, create, and share political information online, we have seen a sharp decline in the audience for traditional forms of media and also a restructuring of the media industry. These changes have significantly shaped our politics and influenced the second edition of *Uncivil Wars*.

THE SECOND EDITION

The second edition of *Uncivil Wars*, like the first edition, argues that citizens make their political judgments both rationally and emotionally, and it offers insights into a wide range of relevant topics and theories. Early chapters consider the role communication plays in politics, the development of campaign strategies, and the formation of candidate images. Later chapters discuss how the media cover campaigns, the use and impact of political advertising, and the strategic use of contemporary polling to identify possible voters and to create campaign messages. The text also includes topics rarely considered by traditional political communication scholarship. For example, there is coverage of political socialization—how people acquire their foundational political beliefs and understandings—and the role of money in politics.

The new edition also includes the most recent examples and legislative developments, providing students with timely and relevant information. New sections in Chapter 1, "Campaigning during the Iraq War," and Chapter 2, "Gender Politics," discuss issues specific to the 2008 presidential race. New material in Chapter 4 explains how politicians create their image in the media and how our image-dominated campaigns affect voting behavior. Chapter 8, "The Impact of New Communications Technologies on Political Campaigns," is thoroughly revised from the first edition and includes coverage of online fund-raising, e-mail campaigns, and the candidates' use of YouTube and MySpace. New coverage on campaign finance reform in Chapter 10 includes a discussion of the Bipartisan Campaign Reform Act of 2002 (the McCain-Feingold Act) and the 527 and 501(c) political organizations. Finally, the book makes new arguments about how current campaign practices have contributed to the creation of a cynical and polarized public that has led some citizens to withdraw from politics and has made it more difficult for elected officials to govern. In response, the last chapter suggests possible solutions and strategies to rehabilitate and reform our political system and to encourage citizens to become politically engaged.

INTRODUCTION: SETTING THE STAGE FOR 2008

Uncivil Wars explains many facets of political campaigns using examples from local, state, and national elections. However, it is important to take a moment and reflect on the remarkable moment in time that will determine our 44th president. The 2008 presidential contest has been one of the most unusual and dramatic election campaigns in our nation's history. The Democratic Party's two finalists for the nomination were both "firsts": Senator Hillary Clinton (D – New York), the first female candidate and the first former first lady, and Senator Barack Obama (D – Illinois), the first African American. The Republican Party nominated Senator John McCain (Arizona), whom all the political pundits had declared hopelessly far behind only weeks before the primary season began. The choices were narrowed to these candidates only after the longest and most expensive campaign in our history. Because no incumbent president or vice president was running, a large field of candidates — nine Democrats and ten Republicans — originally competed for the nominations. The results of the early caucuses and primaries produced many surprises. Presumptive early favorites such as former governor Mitt Romney (R – Massachusetts), former mayor Rudy Giuliani (R – New York), former senator Fred Thompson (R – Tennessee), and former senator John Edwards (D – North Carolina) did worse than expected and dropped out of the race before the voters in many states had an opportunity to express their choices. At the same time, former governor Mike Huckabee (R – Arkansas), who was relatively unknown nationally and considered an underdog by most pundits, surprisingly won the first showcase event of the season, the Iowa caucuses, and several states on Super Tuesday in early February. Polls the week before the New Hampshire primary reported that Obama enjoyed a double-digit lead, yet Clinton won a decisive victory in the contest. Clinton came back with a strong performance on Super Tuesday (winning in California, New York, and New Jersey), only to then see Obama claim a string of twelve straight wins to regain momentum.

Public interest in these campaigns was significantly higher than it had been in recent primary elections. To fully understand why the public was more engaged in the 2008 campaign we need to look back to the 2000 presidential election and the polarizing presidency of George W. Bush.

The 2000 presidential campaign between Vice President Al Gore and Texas governor George W. Bush was an especially bitter and closely fought contest, and the election was so close that the winner of the Electoral College vote was determined by the outcome in a single state — Florida. After weeks of dispute, Bush was declared the winner in Florida by a margin of 537 votes, out of more than 5.8 million cast. The Gore campaign appealed and demanded manual recounts. The case was argued before the state courts and the Florida Supreme Court, and ultimately found its way to the United States Supreme Court, which in a 5-4 decision (one of the five justices siding with the majority had been appointed to the Supreme Court by Bush's father, President George H. W. Bush) ordered an end to the manual recounting of ballots. The Court's action was considered troublesome because the Court's written opinion strangely asserted that "our consideration is limited to the present circumstances" and thus would not establish clear legal precedent (Toobin, 2007, p. 173).

The 537-vote Bush margin of victory was permitted to stand and Bush was declared the winner. Allegations of voter fraud in Florida and in other states in the 2000 election were rampant. Bush had failed to win the national popular vote (Gore won the popular vote by more than 500,000 votes), and he had seemingly been awarded the office by a Supreme Court tainted by charges of cronyism. President George W.

Bush began his first term in what could be considered a weakened position. Although it is often difficult for candidates elected after divisive campaigns to win unified public support, President Bush faced an especially skeptical public, for he was actively disliked by large numbers of the American people and considered by many to have been an illegitimate choice.

The nation rallied around its president, however, following the terrorist attacks of September 11, 2001. Bush called the attacks an intentional act of war and likened them to the attack at Pearl Harbor. He promised to hunt down the terrorist enemies. That October the United States invaded Afghanistan and toppled the Taliban fundamentalist government that had given refuge to Al Qaeda, the group responsible for the terrorist attacks. The president then began calling for military action against Iraq. Bush claimed that Iraq's dictator, Saddam Hussein, was a "gathering threat" who either already possessed weapons of mass destruction or was intent on developing them. Although many traditional U.S. allies declined to support the invasion of Iraq, the Bush administration won the support of Britain and a handful of other nations that agreed to send at least token forces to Iraq. At first, the March 2003 invasion seemed to go as planned. The Hussein regime was quickly overthrown, but instead of winning a peaceful settlement the United States soon found itself confronting a violent insurgency. No weapons of mass destruction were found, and military scandals, such as the photos of U.S. troops humiliating captives in a prison, further intensified the violent resistance in Iraq and increased the opposition to the war both within the United States and around the world.

The 2004 presidential campaign and election thus occurred while the nation was in the midst of an increasingly unpopular war. This campaign was every bit as divisive as the one in 2000. Democratic candidate Senator John Kerry railed against President Bush's purported deceptions about the claims of weapons of mass destruction and his failed leadership in the Iraq war. The Republicans thundered that Kerry was a "flip-flopper" who lacked the strength of character and conviction to lead the United States in a time of war. In addition to serving as a referendum on the war, eleven states gave voters the opportunity to vote on whether the state should permit gay marriages. This sharply divisive issue seemed designed to motivate conservatives to vote. The 2004 election was remarkably close, but this time, it was Ohio that decided the Electoral College outcome. President Bush ultimately won Ohio by a margin of approximately 118,000 votes and was elected to a second term. Yet rumors of election fraud quickly surfaced, with many Democratic partisans claiming that the election had again been stolen, this time by computerized voting machines, which sometimes reported either conflicting or obviously inaccurate counts and which supplied no paper record (for example, see Kennedy, 2006).

As the violence in Iraq continued, the public became increasingly disenchanted by the war, and Bush's popularity plummeted. The situation in Afghanistan also worsened as the Taliban resurfaced. Meanwhile, Osama bin Laden continued to elude capture and release videotaped threats of more violence. As if the continuing violence in Iraq and Afghanistan were not enough to contend with, in 2005, Hurricane Katrina wiped out much of the city of New Orleans and large sections of the Mississippi and Alabama Gulf Coast. The local, state, and federal response to the tragedy was woefully inadequate, uncoordinated, and slow. Viewing the destruction and suffering, television audiences around the world were shocked that such conditions could be experienced in one of the most powerful and wealthy nations on earth.

Consequently, the Republicans lost control of both the U.S. Senate and the House of Representatives in the 2006 midterm elections. Although the Democrats now controlled Congress, they lacked the sixty votes in the Senate necessary to end a Republican filibuster. As a result, the Republicans were able to prevent the passage of legislation that would set a firm timetable for the withdrawal of troops from Iraq. Thus, as the 2008 campaign began, the war in Iraq continued to concern American voters.

All these events and issues set the stage for the 2008 presidential election, when voters will decide who will lead this country next. My hope is that this book not only helps to increase students' knowledge about politics, campaigns, and elections, but that it also inspires and motivates them to become politically involved. The United States has long proclaimed its commitment to democracy abroad; now it is time to rehabilitate our democratic practices at home.

ACKNOWLEDGMENTS

I want to thank my colleagues in the Annenberg School at the University of Southern California who provided me with their insights in countless conversations about politics. I am especially fortunate to have had the opportunity to interact on a daily basis with people such as Rebecca Avila, Sandra Ball-Rokeach, Geoff Baum, Manuel Castells, Geoff Cowan,

Pat Dean, Walt Fisher, Larry Gross, Tom Goodnight, Ed Guthman, Marty Kaplan, Judy Muller, Bryce Nelson, Randy Lake, Stephen O'Leary, Michael Parks, Phil Seib, Ken Sereno, and Peter Vorderer.

I would also like to thank several others with whom I regularly discuss politics, including Kevin Baaske, Pat Ganer, Robert Leventer, Bob Powell, and Takeshi Suzuki.

I also want to acknowledge my students. I have worked with such wonderful students at both the undergraduate and graduate level at USC that I can honestly say that I have never taught a class where I did not feel that I learned more from them than they could possibly have learned from me. It is a true delight to be in the company of such smart and ambitious people.

This edition greatly benefited from the helpful suggestions of several reviewers, including Peter Andersen, San Diego State University; David Henry, University of Nevada–Las Vegas; Jenifer L. Lewis, Western Kentucky University; Timothy Francisco, Youngstown State University; Clifford Manlove, Pennsylvania State University–McKeesport; Jeff McCall, DePauw University; Mitchell McKinney, University of Missouri–Columbia; Rozilyn Miller, University of Central Oklahoma; Beth Ann Rosenson, University of Florida; and Jay Self, Truman State University.

I also really appreciated the support and assistance provided by the outstanding team at Bedford/St. Martin's. I would specifically acknowledge Joan Feinberg, President; Denise Wydra, Editorial Director; Erica Appel, Director of Development; Erika Gutierrez, Executive Editor; Betty Slack, Developmental Editor; and Noel Hohnstine, Editor. I would also like to thank Nancy Benjamin of Books By Design for her assistance in the editing and production.

Finally, and most significantly, I want to thank my family. Our dinner table conversations are often about politics. Patti Riley is my fiercest critic and warmest advocate, and I benefit from both, sometimes in equal measure. My children, Alexandra and Sean, are sharp, compassionate, and engaged citizens. I am confident that they will go out into the world inspired to try to make a difference. Like their mother and me, they have strong political opinions and are not shy about sharing them. I am proud of them both.

                                                            Thomas A. Hollihan

Contents

Preface v

CHAPTER 1: **Politics *Is* Communication** **1**

    Campaigning during the Iraq War 3
    Politics and Political Power 4
    The Role of Communication 9
    The U.S. Presidency 22
    The Outline for This Book 25
    My Goals for This Book 26

CHAPTER 2: **The Long Campaign** **28**

    The Role of Political Parties 30
    The Role of Special Interest and Lobbying Groups 42
    Gender Politics 44
    An Expanded Role for Political Consultants 44
    Mass-Mediated Politics 50

CHAPTER 3: **Political Socialization** **54**

    The Role of the Family 54
    Schools and Civic Education 60
    The Relationship of Church and State 66
    The Mass Media 69
    The Formation of Ideology 71

CHAPTER 4: **Crafting Political Images** **75**

    Creating an Image 76
        Conflicting Images 76
        Image-Dominated Campaigns 79
        Images and Voting Behavior 83

Dimensions of Image   85
  Homophily   85
  Redefining an Image   88
  Political Images and Personal Images   91
  Appearance and Nonverbal Behaviors   94
  Age   96
  Charisma   98
The Power of Public Discourse   99

CHAPTER 5:   **How the News Media Shape Political
              Campaigns   102**

The Primary Sources of Political News   104
  Newspapers   104
  News Magazines   107
  Television   108
  Radio   114
  The Internet   115
The Agenda-Setting Function of the News Media   116
The Campaign News Environment   124
The Content of Campaign News   128
Planting Seeds of Cynicism and Doubt   132

CHAPTER 6:   **Political Advertising   136**

Parades, Banners, and Buttons   136
Newspaper Display Advertisements   139
The Advent of Radio   140
The Television Campaign   143
Direct Mail Advertising   147
Telephone Advertising   149
Advertising Strategies   150
What Political Advertising Can Achieve   152
Negative Attack-Style Advertisements   155
The Consequences of Negative Advertising   160

CHAPTER 7:   **Telling the People What They Want to Hear:
              The Importance of Public Opinion Polls   167**

The History of Political Polling   170
The Polls and Campaign Strategy   172
Let the Consumer Beware   173
  Sampling   173
  Constructing the Survey   175
  "Push Polling"   177

Conducting the Polls   180
   Mail Surveys   180
   Telephone Interviews   181
   Internet Polls   184
   Personal Interviews   185
   Tracking Polls   187
   Focus Groups   188
   Exit Polls   189
Interpreting and Reporting the Results   192
The Costs of Anonymity   194
The Mandate of Public Opinion   195

CHAPTER 8:   **The Impact of New Communication Technologies
                on Political Campaigns   198**

The Internet   199
The Internet and Political Campaigns   201
Accessing News Online   209
Cyberspace and the Public Sphere   215

CHAPTER 9:   **Televised Campaign Debates   222**

Are Televised Debates "Real" Debates?   227
The Effects of Debates on Voter Knowledge and Voting
   Behavior   230
The "Spin"   234
The "Appearance of Rationality"   237

CHAPTER 10:   **Financing Campaigns: The Relationship between
                 Money and Politics   240**

Campaign Contribution Controversies in Recent
   Campaigns   245
The Bipartisan Campaign Reform Act of 2002   253
Politics as Usual   263
Only the Wealthy Need Apply   269
Campaign Finance Reform   271

CHAPTER 11:   **Campaigning and Governing   274**

Campaigns Breed Cynicism   277
Contemporary Political Practices May Result in Flawed Policy
   Making   283
Divisive Political Discourse Undermines Attempts to Achieve
   National Unity   290

Lobbyists and Special Interest Governance   293
The Politics of Character and the Search for Scandal   295
The Legacy of the Politics of Scandal   303
Conclusion   305

CHAPTER 12:   **The Crisis in American Democracy   306**

Political Cynicism Is Common   309
The Causes of Political Cynicism   311
Liberty, Civility, and Trust   314
Reinventing Politics in America   316
Finding Your Voice   317
    Schools   318
    Revitalizing the Political Parties   321
    Political Action Groups   322
    All Politics Are Local   323
    Civic and Community Groups   324
    Democratizing the Workplace   325
Suggested Political Reforms   326
    Campaign Finance Reform   327
    Free Airtime   328
    Voting Made Easier   329
    Revitalized Public Forums   330
Conclusion   331

Works Cited   332

Index   381

UNCIVIL WARS

**Political Campaigns
in a Media Age**

CHAPTER 1

Politics *Is* Communication

The 2008 presidential campaign broke new ground. First, consider the diversity of the candidates. One can scarcely imagine how an American citizen in 1958 would have reacted had he or she been told that in five decades the candidates for the Democratic nomination would include a former first lady, an African American, and a Hispanic American, and that throughout most of the campaign the female candidate, Senator Hillary Clinton, and the African American candidate, Senator Barack Obama (who faced the additional handicap of having a distinctly foreign-sounding name), would be considered the front-runners. Although the Hispanic American candidate, Governor Bill Richardson (who had a distinctly non-Hispanic-sounding name), trailed in the polls throughout most of the campaign and dropped out of the race after finishing fourth in Iowa and New Hampshire, he was often mentioned as a leading candidate for vice president. The Democratic field also included some more traditional candidates: the white male senators or former senators Joe Biden, John Edwards, Chris Dodd, and Mike Gravel, Representative Dennis Kucinich, and Governor Tom Vilsak (who became the first announced candidate to drop out of the race). The Republican field was far less diverse, as it was made up exclusively of white, male candidates: senators John McCain (a former war hero) and Sam Brownback, former senator and Hollywood actor Fred Thompson, representatives Duncan Hunter, Ron Paul, and Tom Tancredo, and former governors Mitt Romney, Tommy Thompson, and Mike Huckabee, as well as former New York City mayor Rudy Giuliani.

Second, this was without question the longest presidential campaign in the nation's history. The votes in the 2004 election had scarcely been tallied before the candidates were jostling for media attention to position themselves for the 2008 campaign. This was the first presidential race in more than half a century that did not include an incumbent president or vice president as a candidate. Furthermore, a number of states, including the delegate-rich states California, Illinois, and New

York, moved up their presidential primaries earlier into the spring in an attempt to have greater influence on the selection of the parties' nominees. This action prompted Iowa, New Hampshire, and South Carolina, the states that by tradition have hosted the earliest presidential contests, also to move up their elections. The need to pursue campaign cash and public recognition thus prompted candidates to declare their interest in the office earlier than ever before. Perhaps this urge to declare early was also inspired by the fact that the current administration of George W. Bush was sinking in popularity as the public became increasingly disenchanted with its failure to find a way to end the costly and tragic conflict in Iraq. At any rate, the 2008 campaign was approximately twice as long as those conducted in the 1980s. Before the end of January 2007, a full year before the Iowa caucuses that were the first important event in the campaign season, virtually all of the declared candidates had already visited the state (Senator Edwards alone had been to Iowa on sixteen separate trips), and most had already established campaign organizations in Iowa and New Hampshire (Broder & Healy, 2007).

Third, the candidates in this campaign faced the closest public scrutiny in history. Not only would these candidates be under review by the traditional media in newspapers and magazines and on television, but now they were also likely to be captured on film by ordinary citizens with cell phone–sized video cameras and able to instantly post their homemade productions on Internet sites such as YouTube.

Fourth, the 2008 campaign was the most expensive in the nation's history. For the past sixty years almost every presidential election has been much more expensive than the one that came before it, but this one was expected to be almost twice as costly as the 2004 election. Experts predicted that before it was over, the two major party candidates who reach Election Day will have spent more than $500 million each. Candidates very quickly needed vast sums of money, as Michael Toner, chair of the Federal Election Commission, noted: "Top tier candidates are going to have to raise $100 million by the end of 2007 to be considered a serious candidate. . . . We are looking at a $100 million entry fee" (cited by Kirkpatrick, 2007, p. A16). Anticipating that such vast sums of money would be necessary and eager to raise funds, most of the front-runners quickly announced that they would not be accepting government funds because they came with a $150 million expenditure ceiling. Clearly this could only be considered "chump change" in this election environment.

CAMPAIGNING DURING THE IRAQ WAR

The 2004 and 2008 presidential elections and the 2006 midterm election took place as the nation was at war. Although the country has gone to the polls in the midst of war in many previous elections—for example, Lincoln was reelected in 1864 during the Civil War, defeating General George McClellan, an officer whom he had relieved of command of the Union Army—there is strong evidence that campaigns undertaken during time of war are unique. In these recent elections, all the candidates for national office were challenged to explain or defend their votes and/or positions in support of or opposition to the war, a task that seemed to become more difficult as the battles waged on without clear prospects for success and as the public support for the war, and for the Bush administration's conduct of the war, waned. Every candidate pledged to protect the security and vital national interests of the United States, every candidate argued that he or she was committed to supporting the people of Iraq as they sought to develop their young democracy, and every candidate expressed support for the U.S. armed forces and their families, who were making great sacrifices to wage the fight. Beyond these points of agreement, however, much of the discourse in these campaigns revealed sharp differences in how the war should be prosecuted and how the interests of freedom might be best protected. In the very crowded presidential primary field in 2008, for example, candidates were forced to distinguish their positions on the issue from one another and from the war policy of the Bush administration. Although it was essential that candidates address the issue of the war, it was also apparent that this issue was fraught with danger for candidates because passions ran high, and events or facts on the ground—either battlefield successes or failures in Iraq or new terrorist incidents elsewhere around the globe—could quickly and dramatically change the situation and public opinion.

The 2006 midterm and the 2008 presidential contests continued some other recent trends in American politics. One was that politics is a family business. Certainly this trend had been affirmed earlier with the Bush dynasty. But the trend increased. In 1986, twenty-four U.S. senators and representatives were closely related to governors or other members of Congress. Twenty years later there were more than fifty. In addition to Elizabeth Dole, wife of former Senate majority leader Bob Dole, and Hillary Rodham Clinton, wife of former president (and Arkansas governor) Bill Clinton, the group included two sets of siblings, four widows, and dozens of offspring. In the 2006 elections, two children of retiring House members ran to succeed their fathers; two governors' sons ran for Senate seats (in Pennsylvania and New Jersey); and in Nevada, Jack Carter, the son of former president Jimmy Carter, ran for the Senate, and Dawn Gibbons, the wife of a retiring member of Congress, ran for her husband's seat (Lawrence, 2006).

The success of already well-known, wealthy, and celebrity political candidates should not surprise us. We live in an era in which brand names are increasingly important. Thousands and thousands of television commercials strive to help us as consumers to discriminate among the myriad of choices of beers, soft drinks, automobiles, laundry detergents, and even toilet paper. Advertisements for prescription drugs, fad diets, and plastic surgeons promise that we can remake ourselves into healthier, happier, slimmer, and more beautiful people. Product placements crowd their way onto movie screens, and billboards now dominate sports stadiums, race cars, and even player uniforms. Even the stadiums themselves are now advertisements. Otherwise, who would have ever considered naming their new sports complex Petco Park?

Critics of campaign politics in the United States have long complained that candidates are merchandised in much the same way that commercial products are sold. This complaint is neither fair nor accurate. I believe that the marketplace does a far better job of helping us recognize the intrinsic differences in products such as soaps or skin lotions than it does political candidates. At least with soaps and lotions we usually get what we pay for, and we have the opportunity to pay a little bit less for a generic brand. If the cheaper generic brand performs to our satisfaction, we can save money by purchasing it instead of the more expensive name brand. In politics, though, there is no guarantee that we will get what we pay for or that the better-known "brands" will perform as well as, let alone better than, the unknowns. Indeed, as more and more money is spent on political campaigns, it sometimes seems that the candidates selected are less and less to our liking. In this book we examine why we market and select political candidates as we do and consider the implications for the American political system.

POLITICS AND POLITICAL POWER

Political activity engages people in attempts to acquire, maintain, and exercise power and control over others. Any governmental structure creates hierarchies of power. In a democracy, people surrender voluntarily to elected officials the power to create laws governing aspects of their lives ranging from the mundane (e.g., how fast cars may be driven and where they may be parked) to the more substantive (e.g., compulsory school attendance for children, control over the curriculum, demands for taxes, and military conscription). Elected officials limit what people may do with their private property (e.g., by enacting building codes or by controlling development) and even with their bodies (e.g., by restricting a woman's decision to terminate a pregnancy or by passing laws prohibiting assisted suicide). Politics, and the outcome of the political campaign process, matters in people's lives. The issues at stake have consequences that affect war and peace, the health of the environment, the vibrancy of the national and global economy, and the protection of our civil liberties.

By participating in the political process—by casting our votes, paying our taxes, and serving on juries—we affirm our support for democratic government and imply our willingness to see the existing government continue. If a substantial percentage of a nation's citizens begin to doubt the legitimacy of the political system—if they decide to withhold their taxes, refuse to serve on juries, or cease to vote—then the democratic government will unravel. History teaches that when democratic governments fail, the result usually is movement toward anarchy, fascism, despotism, or revolution.

Political campaigns and elections are thus important public rituals that are vital to the preservation of democratic government. Elections give citizens a measure of control and power over their own lives, conveying the impression that their elected officials are the citizens' public servants (unlike political systems in which citizens are the subjects of their rulers, as might be the case, for example, in monarchies or in totalitarian dictatorships).

American democracy is based on the principles of equality under law—the Constitution promises a system of color-blind justice—and of one person, one vote. The poorest citizen's vote counts just as much as that of the wealthiest citizen. To an extent, this notion of equality is an illusion—or, in the terms of prominent literary and rhetorical critic Kenneth Burke (1937/1959, pp. 162–163), a "mystification" that conceals the fundamental inequalities of society, but it is still an important illusion. By celebrating a language of equality, our democratic governmental system commits itself to a principle of political inclusion.

Political practices in any nation may, of course, differ from the promises offered in the sacred texts. As mentioned, the U.S. Constitution promises that all votes are supposed to count the same, and faith that all votes will be counted is necessary if the political system is to maintain legitimacy. Allegations that some votes were left uncounted in Florida in the 2000 presidential election, and the narrow 5–4 decision of the U.S. Supreme Court to block an attempted hand-recount of ballots, left many people quite bitter that the Court's ruling had ignored the will of the voters (since Vice President Al Gore won the greatest number of popular votes) in awarding the victory to Republican candidate George W. Bush. President Bush was reelected in another very close race in 2004, and again there were significant complaints about the accuracy and legitimacy of the outcome. This time the complaints primarily focused on Ohio, the closely contested state whose electoral votes tipped the contest to the Republicans. For example, former representative Robert F. Kennedy Jr. argued that some 350,000 people in Ohio were either wrongly prevented from voting or voted but did not have their votes correctly tallied (Kennedy, 2006). The Bush administration was also among the most polarizing in American history, no doubt at least in part because of the persistent questions about the legitimacy of Bush's election (Jacobson, 2006). Trust is a vital and necessary ingredient in any democracy, and the 2000 and 2004 presidential elections have notably diminished the reservoir of trust and confidence in our political institutions, a point that will be revisited and developed in greater depth in later chapters.

Recent experiences in other nations also help illustrate the importance of public trust in the maintenance of political stability. For example, the 2006 presidential election in Mexico resulted in many angry protests when the supporters of the more liberal candidate claimed that thousands of votes for their candidate were never recorded. When the losing candidate failed to concede defeat, the government of Mexico was for a brief time paralyzed by public protests. In some cases public concerns over the fairness of an election have even been sufficient to bring down a government, as occurred in what has become known as the "Orange Revolution" in Ukraine in 2004. Because public protesters became convinced that the ballots were not counted fairly and that the opposition was denied the opportunity to develop its campaign issues and to get them discussed by the media, thousands of citizens took to the streets. Unwilling or unable to suppress the street protests, the supposedly elected government fell, new elections took place, and the opposition candidate was elected.

Although the fundamental principle of democracy is that all votes are to be counted as equal, it is readily apparent that in any democracy some citizens possess far more political influence and power than do others. For example, if you or I pick up the phone to call the president of the United States, it is unlikely that we will get through. The president is too busy to accept phone calls from most ordinary citizens. If, on the other hand, Bill Gates, the founder of Microsoft, picks up the phone to call the president, we can surmise that the president will probably be made available to accept his call in fairly short order. Many wealthy and influential citizens ensure their continuing access to political leaders by contributing generously to their campaigns. Often such contributions are offered even though the contributor and the candidate disagree on important issues. Indeed, many contributors offer money to both candidates in a race, guaranteeing that they will have access regardless of who wins the election.

Despite the inequalities in political power and influence, members of the public must be made to feel that the government is concerned about their welfare. No democratic government can maintain the trust and respect of its citizens if they believe that government is insensitive to their needs or interests. Democratic government must be based on respect for law; citizens must believe they have a stake in the continuation of the system of law; and citizens must trust the political officeholders who pass legislation, the police and other officials who enforce the law, and the judges who administer it. Much evidence exists, however, that significant numbers of American citizens lack confidence in their political system or their elected officials. For example, "barely a third (34 percent) agree with the statement 'most elected officials care what people like me think,' nearly matching the twenty-year low of 33 percent recorded in 1994 and a ten-point drop since 2002" (Trends in political values, 2007). There is also evidence that many people express little interest in politics, feel themselves to be politically impotent, and do not have confidence that their elected officials look out for their interests. These attitudes have been blamed for depressing voter turnout, increasing public skepticism about politics, and diminishing the political efficacy of our citizenry (Patterson, 2002; Vanishing voter, 2004).

Compared to many other nations, however, the United States has enjoyed a relatively stable political democracy. Preserving respect for governmental authority has seldom been a problem. The most notable exception occurred following the 1860 election of Abraham Lincoln as president when the southern states decided to secede from the union because they became convinced that the federal government sought to trample their state power and thwart their interests. Hundreds of thousands of lives were lost on the battlefield before this conflict ended. We have also endured the assassination of four presidents and the rampant development of conspiracy theories to lay blame for these assassinations, the impeachment of two presidents, and the forced resignation from office of another. Yet, somehow our fragile democracy and public confidence and trust in our leadership and our civic rituals and institutions have survived. During the past forty years attacks on the government's legitimacy have come from extremists on both the political left and the right. During the 1960s some protesters against the Vietnam War claimed that the government lacked the moral authority to govern, and they openly preached anarchy and active resistance. Most opponents of the war did not go this far; they may have opposed the right of the government to conscript citizens and compel them to serve in an undeclared war, but they continued to vote and work within the system by trying to elect antiwar candidates to achieve policy changes. In recent years fringe groups have also sought to reshape environmental policy by engaging in acts of "eco-terrorism" aimed at blocking new developments in wilderness areas or the cutting down of mature old-growth forests. Such radical actors have mostly been confined to the margins of American politics, however, as most pro-environmentalists have devoted their energies to attempting to influence public policy through more conventional means.

Likewise, some extremely conservative citizens have attacked the legitimacy of governmental authority and have proclaimed that the real enemies of American freedom are bureaucrats and government agents. Such remarks commonly occur on "talk radio" call-in shows or on Internet Web sites. In some instances this rhetoric has become dangerously extreme. Some people contend that such comments provoke radical fringe elements, such as militia groups who stockpile arms. The increasingly strident antigovernment rhetoric can have very serious consequences. Such radical views, for example, may have been responsible for the actions of Timothy McVeigh, who was convicted and executed for his leadership role in the 1995 bombing of the Alfred P. Murrah Federal Building in Oklahoma City. Although most experts concede that the number of such right-wing extremists is small—estimates range from approximately 10,000 to 100,000—they still worry that such feelings of alienation pose a genuine threat to our pluralist democratic political system (Foster & Levinson, 1995; Kaplan, 1996; Michael, 2003; Mulloy, 2004). Following the terrorist attacks of September 11, 2001, Tom Metzger, the leader of a fringe group known as the White Aryan Resistance, praised the terrorists for their commitment to their cause and expressed his view that this incident created an example of what a successful citizen effort against the U.S. government could look like. Mark Potok, a spokesperson for a group called Klan Watch that monitors right-wing extremist organizations, declared, "Today, these people despise America, they despise capitalism, they despise globalism and racial and religious diversity. What was essentially a restorationist movement, like the Klan wanting to restore Southern apartheid . . . is an utterly revolutionary radical right today" (cited in Nesbitt, 2001).

Political anger and alienation can pose a major threat to our democratic government, especially when people believe they have become victims of other powerful or destructive forces. Democratic governance is a fragile human creation, and sustaining it requires the continuous attention not just of elected officials but also of ordinary citizens. The maintenance of democratic government requires a dynamic and open climate for political communication and the discussion of differences. A healthy democracy is also based on a set of shared interests. An elected government must be responsive to the needs of all citizens if it is to win their allegiance and support. Maintaining these shared interests within a political system that emphasizes voters acting to protect their own interests is a challenge facing all democracies.

During political campaigns citizens form dramatically different—and sometimes incompatible—ideological factions, each committed to the election of a candidate (or slate of candidates) who best reflect their worldviews. Following the election, citizens are expected to put aside their differences and to acknowledge the system's legitimacy and the winner's rightful authority to govern.

THE ROLE OF COMMUNICATION

Politics is fundamentally a communicative activity. Because people and their governments organize and maintain connections to each other through communication, the process of democratic rule centers on the ability to create and preserve a system of mutual trust and respect through communication. Candidates for public office communicate their values, goals, and objectives through their actions, public speeches, press statements, public mailings, and advertisements. These communications begin during the campaigns for elected office and continue even after the victorious candidates have been sworn into office. Because political officeholders need the support of the public at large, they must continually communicate with their constituents to explain their actions, clarify their goals, claim credit for their achievements, account for their failings, and gain support for new policy initiatives. The communication that sustains democracy is not only that which flows from political candidates and officeholders to voters and constituents; citizens, in turn, must express their concerns and desires to those holding power or aspiring to power. Citizens express their values, goals, and objectives through public opinion polls, donations to and participation in political campaigns, letters to the editor, votes, postings on Internet Web sites, and, if necessary, public marches and/or protests.

Political communication is therefore the means by which people express both their unity and their differences. Through communication we petition our government, plead our interests, rally those who agree with us to our causes, and chastise those who do not share our views. The messages that shape political dialogue in the United States give insight into the values, beliefs, attitudes, and aspirations of our society. These messages reflect the current conditions under which we live, our sense of history and traditions, and our dreams for the future. To a certain extent all these messages have a continuity. Some issues recur from one election to the next, and the messages created to address these issues are remarkably similar. In other aspects, however, our political communications are directly responsive to the particular demands of the period in which we are living. Some issues burst into the public consciousness in a dramatic way that cannot be ignored, as occurred with the attacks of September 11, 2001. Other issues gain public awareness only after many years of discussion and media attention and when the problem seems to become so severe that it can no longer be ignored, as may now be happening with the issue of global climate change.

People are understandably preoccupied by the problems of the moment. If we are insecure about employment prospects, worried about health insurance, or fearful of neighborhood crime, we talk about those issues and expect candidates for public office to talk about them too. Candidates who fail to address those issues in a convincing way not only fail to win voters' attention and respect but appear to be so out of touch that voters are likely to consider them unqualified for public office. Candidates often create campaign messages that emphasize their similarities to voters to illustrate that they understand their problems and share their concerns. In the 2000 presidential campaign both

George W. Bush and Al Gore emphasized their small-town rural origins and not the fact that they had grown up in the midst of very privileged and powerful Washington-insider families. In the 2004 campaign, vice presidential candidate Senator John Edwards of North Carolina described himself as the "son of a mill worker" who came from a small town and not as a successful and wealthy personal injury lawyer. Incumbents who spend too much time in Washington and who do not make sufficient efforts to keep in close contact with the voters at home can be vulnerable to the charge that they are out of touch with the people who sent them to Congress. In 1996, for example, Republican presidential candidate Patrick Buchanan disparagingly referred to his opponent, Senate majority leader Robert Dole, as "Beltway Bob" and "the guy who sold out American workers for the benefit of his corporate friends" (Rosenbaum, 1996, p. E3). Such a message of anticorporate populism gained significant public attention and support because many voters were worried about becoming unemployed as manufacturing companies were closing their American factories and moving jobs overseas. Dole, an outspoken advocate of the North American Free Trade Agreement (NAFTA), which Buchanan strongly opposed, was deemed especially vulnerable to such an attack (Bennet, 1996; Molyneux, 1996).

People communicate through shared symbols, which are the primary building blocks of our language system. These symbols allow us to name objects, emotions, and actions and to share our thoughts and feelings with others. Using shared symbols enables us to organize collective activities and to form societies and communities. Through symbols we learn about our history, express our discontents, and strive for solutions to our problems. As symbol users, humans seek to improve the quality of their lives. Kenneth Burke argued that humans are "rotten with perfection," always seeking to improve their circumstances and their conditions (Burke, 1966, p. 16).

People experience their world through communication. This is not to say that material reality does not exist, but rather that even material reality is given shape and character through our symbolic capacity. For example, most Americans believe that large cities such as New York, Los Angeles, and Chicago are rife with crime and that the problem of crime worsens every year. This belief persists despite the fact that statistics compiled by the U.S. Department of Justice suggest that these large cities in fact have lower crime rates than do many smaller cities. In addition, statistics suggest that violent crime rates in the United

States have actually been falling over the past fifteen years, indeed down 32 percent between 1994 and 2004 (Crime and victims statistics, 2006). Despite the falling crime rates, however, public fears about crime continue to increase. Public opinion polls have suggested that most people believe that the crime rate is increasing and that criminals are eluding punishment, even though it is a fact that the crime rate is falling, arrest and conviction rates are increasing, and convicted felons are serving longer sentences (Sourcebook on criminal justice statistics, 2002).

The fear and anxiety that people feel about crime are understandable. When they watch or listen to the evening news, they are assaulted with stories of urban violence. When they open the newspaper, they read still more stories about violent crime. Movies, television programs, novels, and video games all heighten public awareness of the dangers lurking around us. People do not need to personally experience a crime to believe that criminals are out there preying on innocent victims. Crime sparks fear in us because we identify with those victims. When children are kidnapped, we think of our own children and how we would react to their loss. When a motorist is hijacked at gunpoint, we recall the last time we traversed that same street. Despite the actual relative infrequency of violent crime and the fact that a very large percentage of violent crimes are between family members and not directed toward strangers, those crimes still have the power to penetrate our consciousness because they lead the evening news. Each incident of violent crime seems to suggest a failure of government in its responsibility to protect its citizens. Events such as the school massacres that have taken place at Virginia Tech University and at high schools in Littleton, Colorado; West Paducah, Kentucky; Jonesboro, Arkansas; and Red Lake, Minnesota, spark intense media coverage that puts people on edge. That so many violent acts take place, and that they take place in small towns and not just in large cities, only serves to further frighten people about the danger of crime. News stories that report actual crime statistics and trends are tucked into the inside pages of the newspaper. News of sensational episodes of school violence in seemingly safe suburban or small-town high schools, on the other hand, is splashed across the front pages of newspapers and leads the evening newscasts. Such news stories fuel public perceptions that our society is at risk and even that it has produced a generation that includes hordes of young sociopaths who are little more than ticking time bombs, well armed and capable of exploding into unthinkable violence.

The realities that we construct are also shaped in large part by our own interests. We attend to those issues and concerns that affect us, and we neglect those that do not. Parents with school-age children are naturally concerned about safe schools. Media coverage of school violence sends shivers down the spines of all parents. Even if one can intellectually understand that such school massacres are rare events, they seem to occur with enough frequency and are sufficiently horrendous that they provoke deep fear and a sense of helplessness in the face of such random and unpredictable violence.

It is not only parents who carefully attend to the news and to events that affect them most directly. All citizens pay attention to issues that personally affect them. For example, elderly citizens worry about proposed cuts in Medicare or Social Security, programs that are essential to their financial security and the quality of their daily lives. Students fret about proposed changes in federal assistance for college financial aid. Farmers attend to news about government price supports for agriculture. People can be easily persuaded that government spending should be reduced and that many currently funded programs are wasteful. Yet, they can become very concerned when cuts are proposed that might close down the military base in their hometown that helps sustain the local economy. An old saying suggests that it is a recession when your neighbor loses his job, but it is a depression when you lose yours.

The situations that we experience, both directly and through the media, acquire meaning according to how we interpret them. These differences are expressed subjectively as differences in our assignment of motives. Thus, as Burke (1954/1965, p. 109) has noted, "We call *obstinacy* in an enemy what we call *perseverance* in ourselves."

The language used to give voice to political messages and opinions is significant. Sociologist Hugh Dalziel Duncan (1965) observed the following:

> Words are not merely "signs"; they are names whose "attachment" to events, objects, persons, institutions, status groups, classes, and indeed any great or small collectivity, soon tends to determine what we do in regard to the bearer of the name. War on poverty has recently been declared. Yet, no matter how much money is voted for the eradication of poverty, the first battle that must be won is the symbolic battle over how to *name* poverty. Are the poor *lazy, degenerate, shiftless, sick, evil, childlike, cunning, ignorant, proud, humble, victimized,* or *unfortunate*? The name that we give to poverty largely determines how we fight the war against it. (p. xv)

The observations that Duncan offers about the language used to describe the conditions of the poor were most apt in recent public debates over reforms to public assistance and welfare programs. Does our current system of welfare feed, clothe, and sustain America's desperately poor until they can get themselves back on their feet and become self-sufficient? Or does welfare destroy people's self-concept, inhibit their ability to become self-sufficient, and lock them into a culture of dependency? Which claim is true? Whose account of reality is most compelling? To what extent can both views be valid? How can we overcome the prejudices contained within the language that we use to frame our discussions of such complex problems?

The language used to construct and name a problem acts to assign blame and praise, and it suggests appropriate solutions for the problem. Such language also vests authority in certain kinds of people who can claim expertise for solving such problems. The following are political scientist Murray Edelman's (1988) observations:

> If poverty stems from individual inadequacies, then psychologists, social workers, and educators have a claim to authority in dealing with it; but if an economy that fails to provide enough jobs paying an adequate wage is the source of poverty, then economists have a claim to authority. Military threats, crime, mental illness, illiteracy, and every other problem yield claims to authority, though the claim is disputed in each case because diverse reasons for the problem compete for acceptance. (p. 20)

The rival stories about welfare and those who receive it acquire persuasiveness because they seem credible and believable, because they agree with our experience, because they confirm our sense of ourselves and the "truths" we believe, and because they serve our interests.

In 2006 the Bush administration promised to overhaul U.S. immigration policies to stem the influx of illegal immigrants. Arguments quickly emerged about whether immigrant workers contributed to the growth and well-being of the U.S. economy by reducing the price of goods and services and by doing jobs that other Americans were unwilling to perform or if, instead, illegal immigrants depressed wages and contributed to persistent and chronic rates of unemployment for other groups already in the United States. Advocates on both sides of the debate could muster empirical and anecdotal evidence to support their cases. Workers who have been displaced from their jobs by immigrants or who are locked in low-paying jobs might naturally be expected to have strong worries about the impact of illegal immigration. Those who benefit from low-wage workers—for example, farmers who depend on immigrant workers to harvest their crops—can be expected to have very different opinions, experiences, and understandings of the nature of the problem. In this particular case, it is noteworthy that the strongest voice for a very strict immigration policy that would criminalize illegal immigrants and send even long-term U.S. residents back to their homelands was Representative F. James Sensenbrenner (R—Wisconsin), who represented a district with almost no illegal immigrants. Even his housekeeper in his hometown of Appleton, Wisconsin, Sensenbrenner explained to the *New York Times*, had been born in Wisconsin (Leibovich, 2006). Sensenbrenner especially thundered against any proposal that might give amnesty to illegal aliens who could prove that they had been in the United States for a fixed period of time. He declared that such a policy would merely reward lawbreaking (Seper & Dinan, 2006).

Members of Congress whose districts include substantial numbers of Hispanics—and whose housekeepers might not have been born in Wisconsin—understandably opposed the legislation that might send illegal aliens back to their native lands and deny those who have been living in the United States for several years, working jobs, and paying taxes the right to petition for citizenship. These legislators were no doubt listening to constituents who constructed their world differently from those in Mr. Sensenbrenner's mostly rural Wisconsin district. They might also have been reacting to poll data that indicated that Latinos, the fastest-growing segment of future voters, indicated that they were far more likely to vote in the next election because of their interest in this issue. One poll indicated that 54 percent of Latinos surveyed believed that they had seen an increase in discrimination due to the immigration policy debate; 75 percent of respondents indicated that they would be more likely to vote in the next election because of this issue; 63 percent thought that this debate would spark a lasting immigrant rights social movement; and most held the Republican Party responsible for what they saw as the negative consequences of the immigration debate (Suro & Escobar, 2006).

The noted communication theorist and critic Walter R. Fisher (1987) argued that people reason by telling and evaluating stories, a process he calls "narrative rationality." Fisher claims that people access arguments by evaluating their narrative probability and narrative fidelity. Narrative probability relates to a story's coherence. Is the argumentative structure of the story satisfying and complete? Does the chronology of events seem to make sense and explain the movement of action in the story? Does the story account for the material facts of the situation?

Do the heroes behave in ways that are appropriate? Do the villains behave as expected?

Narrative fidelity relates to a story's consistency with other stories that people have heard before and have already accepted as true—stories that explained their past experiences. When President George H. W. Bush argued for the need for the United States to commit military forces to thwart Iraq's aggression against Kuwait in 1990, he used rhetoric that emphasized the similarities between Iraq's leader, Saddam Hussein, and Adolf Hitler. Bush was certainly not arguing that Hussein was a reincarnation of the German dictator, nor was he asserting that Iraq was Germany. He was, however, asserting that Hussein was the moral equivalent of Hitler and that Iraq's aggression against Kuwait was the moral equivalent of Hitler's aggression during World War II.

There is, in fact, a useful symbolic elasticity in the Hitler persona. The same Hitler references that helped convince people that the action against Saddam Hussein was justified were also used to justify the U.S. invasion in Panama in 1989 to unseat Manuel Noriega and the NATO bombing campaign against Serbia in 1999. Both Noriega and Slobodan Milosevic, the Serb leader, were depicted as villains capable of unthinkable cruelties, thoroughly untrustworthy, and willing to retreat only if confronted by the far superior U.S. or NATO forces (Solomon, 2005). Noriega was described as a narcoterrorist and Milosevic as a beyond-reason extremist committed to ethnic cleansing (Clark, 2006).

Former secretary of defense Donald Rumsfeld also drew a close parallel between the Nazi leader and the head of the Al Qaeda terrorist network, Osama bin Laden. Rumsfeld warned that Americans would have to accept that a battle against the terrorist network that wants to rule the world would be long and hard fought and that they would have to "prepare for a battle of wills that could stretch for years" (cited by White & Tyson, 2006, p. A08). Rumsfeld also used the Hitler analogy in an attempt to rebut critics of the Iraq war when he warned that those who favored a phased withdrawal from Iraq "seem not to have learned history's lessons," and alluded to those in the 1930s who advocated appeasing Nazi Germany (Cloud, 2006).

The Hitler analogy has also been applied to North Korean dictator Kim Jong Il. Not only is the reclusive despot intent on building nuclear weapons and testing missiles capable of striking the West Coast of the United States, but prominent Republican leaders declared that he has run his entire nation as if it were a concentration camp aimed at starving its citizens into submission and blind obedience to his maniacal rule (Steve Forbes and Jim Michaels, cited by Karlgaard, 2006).

The application of the Hitler analogy in each of these cases is of questionable argumentative value. Noriega, Hussein, Milosevic, bin Laden, and Kim Jong Il may indeed be evil, but none of them had the ability to command the same type of military and industrial forces as did Hitler in Germany. Nor can one assert that Panama, Iraq, Serbia, North Korea, or Al Qaeda had the same clear territorial ambitions as did Nazi Germany. The analogy nonetheless has power as a narrative, in that it can be used to justify an assertive and interventionist military policy. All who use the Hitler analogy are familiar with the historical narrative of Hitler's coming to power in Europe and thus know from this experience that dictators cannot be appeased. In 1938 Prime Minister Neville Chamberlain of Great Britain took steps to appease Hitler and succeeded only in enabling him to gain more power. Thus, it seems the appropriate response in the face of aggression is to crush aggressors before they acquire so much power that they cannot be easily defeated.* This lesson has become part of the shared historical knowledge of World War II. It resonates with American audiences because it tells a story that most people believe to be true (Hollihan & Baaske, 2005, pp. 26–27).

Public audiences are exposed to a barrage of experiences, events, and messages that they must attempt to explain and understand. People acquire their political attitudes and information through these experiences and through their interactions with others. The media play a role in these events, as do conversations with friends, relatives, neighbors, and colleagues. People recall the lessons from their formal schooling and the precepts from any religious training that they may have had. People actively create their understanding of the messages they receive by drawing on these resources when they seem appropriate. Constructing one's opinion on a social issue is therefore an active rather than a passive process. This perspective helps explain how different people can experience the same event and hear the same arguments yet come away with very different understandings and interpretations. Because people actively create their own meanings for observed events, they also have different interpretations for what constitutes evidence to support their arguments. As Delia and Grossberg (1977) pointed out, facts do not merely exist outside of experience. Instead, they are abstractions

---

* President Clinton was perhaps most explicit in developing the narrative when in a 1999 speech he likened Serbia's Slobodan Milosevic to Hitler. Clinton declared, "And so I want to talk to you about Kosovo today but just remember this—it's about our values. What if someone had listened to Winston Churchill and stood up to Adolf Hitler earlier?" (cited in Solomon, 2005, pp. 67–68).

from that experience; they are generative and help shape the construction of reasons that are part of an ongoing process of "interpretive understanding."

Nimmo and Combs (1990, pp. 3–4) lent further support to this view when they observed that "(1) our everyday, taken-for-granted reality is a delusion; (2) reality is created, or constructed, through communication, not expressed by it; (3) for any situation there is no single reality, no one objective truth, but multiple subjectively derived realities."

This perspective, however, does not suggest that all interpretations or understandings have equal value or credibility, for this is assuredly not the case. As mentioned earlier, some radicals during the Vietnam War saw their opposition to that conflict as an argument against the legitimacy of the entire U.S. government. Some reactionaries today regard the federal government as so powerful that they are ready to speak openly of armed resistance. These constructions of political events and issues, however, are held only by those on the political fringes. Most Americans consider such views absurd because they do not jibe with their own experiences or interpretations of events. Communication scholars Hinds and Windt (1991) declared:

> To a substantial degree the rhetoric that accompanies any event comes from an a priori rhetoric, based on values that have come to be regarded as basic beliefs, on preexisting language that is always present exerting its influence in shaping our consciousness, on previous interpretations of past events that may or may not be similar to current events. In such ways we are both liberated and imprisoned by language. Government officials and others do not construct a language or a rhetoric out of thin air; they inherit it from the past and modify or adapt it to meet current or future concerns. (p. 8)

Thus, the political arguments that create public discourse in our democracy shape and are shaped by the central values held by citizens. These values are embodied in the symbols by which we communicate. Through symbolic choices we construct the stories that give meaning to our lives, and these stories are populated with heroes and villains acting out roles in accordance with our expectations. Characters who fail to live up to our expectations violate our understanding of the stories and may thus undermine their roles in the dramas in which they are cast.

We sometimes discover that our heroes behave in ways that are less than heroic, or our villains may reveal a side to their character that we find commendable, and on occasion their performance of their roles may undercut the coherence of the entire drama. For example, in his pursuit of the 2000 Democratic presidential nomination, former senator Bill Bradley attempted to portray himself as someone who was above politics as usual. He was not the typical candidate who would resort to name calling or using negative messages. His unwillingness to attack Vice President Gore, however, caused some political pundits to speculate that perhaps Bradley was not "tough enough" to be a strong contender against the Republican candidate in the general election. Perhaps Bradley did not have the "fire in his belly" that would be required for the race. Even Bradley's closest aides urged him to become more aggressive and to go on the offensive (Dao, 2000). When Bradley's ratings began to slip behind Gore's in the days before the New Hampshire primary, he finally did become much more aggressive, accusing the vice president of lying when Gore claimed to have always been a supporter of abortion rights (Gerstenzang & Gold, 2000). The strategy entailed risks, however, for in making the attack Bradley no longer seemed to be a candidate who rose above politics; he was instead just another player in the game of politics.

A similar problem faced California Governor Arnold Schwarzenegger, who defeated Governor Gray Davis in a recall election in 2003. Schwarzenegger's campaign emphasized that he was not a fierce partisan political warrior, focused on raising money for future elections, but instead a consensus builder who could reach across the aisles and get the state of California moving forward. Schwarzenegger was no ordinary candidate but a world-renowned bodybuilder, the holder of the Mr. Universe title, a true "A-list" Hollywood superstar, and a live-action hero poised to take office and remedy all the problems of politics as usual in California. Yet, after taking office, Schwarzenegger immediately began to solicit donations for a huge campaign war chest. Furthermore, he called the Democrats in the legislature "girly men," and then he qualified four sharply partisan propositions for the ballot. The measures sought to significantly reduce the power of labor unions, curb state spending, limit the power of the Democrats in the legislature to control redistricting, and lengthen the amount of time required before a public school teacher would qualify for tenure. The labor unions (especially those of teachers, nurses, and firefighters) responded with a barrage of television ads attacking Schwarzenegger for his partisanship and lack of concern for working people. All four ballot measures were soundly defeated, and Schwarzenegger's popularity sharply declined (Finnigan & Saladay, 2005). Schwarzenegger apparently learned from his mistake: Within a few months he was attempting to rehabilitate his reputation as a moderate centrist by proposing a huge bond initiative to finance stem cell research and the building of new roads, bridges, and other improvements to the state's infrastructure— programs that were extremely popular with California moderates and even liberals (Herrera, 2006). Of course, Schwarzenegger now had the problem that these new expenses alarmed his Republican supporters and made them wonder exactly what the governor believed (Spillman, 2006). The governor's problems with his fellow Republicans persisted over the next year, as members of his own party refused to approve his proposed budget that would fund his new initiatives (Steinhauer, 2007). In this case, leading Republican senators had noticed that although voters may not always pay close attention to politics, they do attend to how faithfully and coherently the actors in the political dramas around them perform their roles (Fisher, 1987). As Schwarzenegger became more appealing to liberals and moderates, he became less appealing to conservatives, giving them greater incentive to challenge his authority.

Observers of the same political events and of the same political actors often make sense of them by devising very different dramas that often invest the actors with very different views of their character. When asked to describe why he voted for the reelection of President George W. Bush, for example, one respondent replied:

> President Bush is a true defender of the American people, a stalwart, often stubborn, always determined, man of his word. He is a straight shooter who loves this country and is willing to defend it, regardless of whatever opinions may be expressed around the world. I admire him greatly, and feel much more secure knowing that he will be in office four more years. (Russell Herbst, cited in Why did you vote for Bush? 2004)

Another respondent offered a contrasting view of the same character traits:

> The tragedy of George Bush is ultimately one of his own making, and one that he cannot readily extricate himself from, because rigid absolutism and an overly simplistic worldview seem deeply embedded in his character. It is meant to be tough. It is meant to show resolve. It is meant to project national strength and purpose. But, no, the too often utopic aspirations instead lead to myopia. It is actually stubborn, actually short-sighted, actually too often negatively impacting the American national interest. (Djerejian, 2006)

Milton Rokeach (1968), a sociologist who was deeply interested in the formation of human values, argued that by the time human beings reach adulthood they have formed thousands of beliefs concerning what is true or not true, beautiful or not beautiful, and good or evil. Although these beliefs might not be organized in an easily discernible and coherently logical form, they are structured into belief systems. From such belief systems emerge our attitudes. Rokeach (p. 112) defined an attitude as "a relatively enduring organization of beliefs around an object or situation predisposing one to respond in some preferential manner." Attitudes are thus made up of beliefs and have three components: a *cognitive* component, which represents a person's knowledge; an *affective* component, which suggests positive or negative feelings that vary in intensity; and a *behavioral* component, because a belief must lead to some action when it is suitably activated.

People's beliefs and attitudes may ultimately come to be identified as an *ideology*. An ideology is an organization of beliefs and attitudes—which may be religious, political, or intellectual—that has been more or less institutionalized so that it can be shared with others; thus, it derives external authority as a means for synthesizing worldviews or opinions (Rokeach, 1968, pp. 123–124).

Political rivals often espouse—and even come to embody—different political attitudes, beliefs, and ideological positions. They seek votes by communicating their positions, their ideologies, and their worldviews to the electorate. In a campaign, candidates attempt to create arguments that will appeal to voters. Although most candidates "stand for something" and do not create positions on issues that merely tell voters what they want to hear, successful candidates do adapt to what voters seem to desire from their elected officials. Thus, candidates construct their positions on issues both on the basis of their own symbolic constructions of reality and in accordance with their understanding of the issues that motivate and shape their constituencies. The process of campaigning for public office is therefore fundamentally a persuasive exercise of matching voters, ideas, and candidates to one another.

The messages generated during political campaigns give important insights into the values shaping our culture. These messages express the hopes, frustrations, anxieties, and aspirations of the voters at that point in time. There is a sense of continuity and change in these messages. Some political arguments reappear in election after election, and our position on these issues comes to reflect how we conceive of ourselves both as individual voters and as a nation. Other issues appear for the first time as voters confront problems that had not previously aroused their concerns. Attention to the issues raised in political campaign communications thus represents an important way to study our nation's history, our cultural identity, and our goals for the future. As Hinds and Windt (1991) argued:

> Political language and arguments—in sum, political rhetoric—create political consequences, define political settings, create national identity, stimulate people to act, and give sense and purpose to these actions. Political reality is a persuasive description of "things as they are," and once situations are so described, certain responses are eliminated and others seem right. Decisions are discussed and debated within the rhetorical description, ever with an eye toward action. (p. 7)

Over time citizens and political leaders develop patterns for the conduct of political discourse. Such patterns are visible in the use of recurrent symbols, often repeated stories, and historical accounts and explanations retold so often that they are accepted as common knowledge. According to Hinds and Windt (1991), such habitual uses of language and rhetoric create a unified understanding of national being, a discernible pattern of national identity, and a shared sense of purpose. These patterns of rhetorical interaction are heightened by the need to interpret the present in light of the nation's shared sense of its past.

THE U.S. PRESIDENCY

Although elections at all levels are important public rituals that shape our nation and preserve our democracy, campaigns for the presidency attract the most public attention. Presidential races are far more likely to receive substantial media coverage, and citizens are far more likely to vote in presidential elections than in any others. A strong presidential candidate can even influence the outcomes of other elections, as others seek to attach themselves to the president's "coattails." In some cases a political era even becomes known by the impact of a particular president's style, public personality, and public discourse. As the essayist Richard Stengel (2006, p. 8) noted, "Being an American is not based on a common ancestry, a common religion, even a common culture—it's based on accepting an uncommon set of ideas." It is, of course, U.S. presidents who are most forcefully communicating and articulating these ideas. Presidential elections are thus the most important moments in our election rituals. They mark the time when the ideological divisions that identify the two major political parties and that most sharply define our sense of purpose and commitment and that chart the course for our future will be most sharply revealed.

Because of the wealth and power of the United States, the entire world watches U.S. presidential campaigns and elections with interest. During the 2004 campaign, the left-leaning London newspaper the *Guardian* lamented that the outcome of the U.S. presidential election affected British subjects every bit as much as an election in Britain, and yet they had no vote to cast. The newspaper thus launched a campaign urging their readers to send e-mails to individual citizens in Ohio—a critical swing state—to persuade them not to vote to reelect President Bush (My fellow non-Americans, 2004). More than 11,000 *Guardian* readers responded and sent e-mails. The plan seemed to backfire, however, when many Americans—especially more conservative Americans—objected to the British intervention in a U.S. election. The *Guardian* reprinted some of the Americans' responses in a column headlined "You Limey Assholes." Among the more colorful replies was the following:

> Have you not noticed that Americans don't give two shits what Europeans think of us? Each e-mail someone gets from some arrogant Brit telling us why to NOT vote for George Bush is going to backfire, you stupid, yellow-toothed pansies. . . . I don't give a rat's ass if our election is going to have an effect on your worthless little life. I really don't. (Cited in Bowers, 2004)

The president is not only the "commander in chief" of the world's most powerful nation, but he (and someday she) also represents how we conceive of ourselves as a nation. Our presidents are the embodiment of our national identity, in no small part because they have an opportunity to shape and sometimes reshape that identity. Thus, through the lives, achievements, and failures of our presidents, we gain insight into the different aspects of our national character. The writer Michael Novak (1974, p. 3) argued that when Americans elect a president, they elect a "king, a high priest, and a prophet." As king, the president represents our national power; as priest, he enacts the rituals of our "civic religion"; and as prophet, she interprets and shapes our goals and guides our destiny. The presidency is a symbolic institution, and the president's actions affect the daily lives of U.S. citizens and people throughout the world. With broad authority to project American power, the president also projects our values and represents us to the rest of the world (Denton, 2006).

Communication scholar S. F. Schram (1991, p. 214) argued that "the electronic political age has led to the creation of the 'postmodern president,' whose first task is to symbolize what the nation represents before 'the people' have even decided what that is." In times of crisis or calamity, this presidential role becomes even more significant. For example, in the immediate aftermath of the terrorist attacks of September 11, 2001, the American people, and indeed people around the world, waited in anticipation for a statement from President Bush that would lend some meaning to the events and suggest a course of action. In the days that followed, the nation, at least temporarily, put aside its sharp partisan divisions and responded to the president's call to come together both to express our shared grief and to face the challenge of a war against terrorism.

When voters assess candidates for the presidency, then, they are doing more than deciding whom they would prefer to have administer and execute power in their government. They are also deciding who they believe might best speak for them. The president has, as communication scholar Mary Stuckey (1991, p. 1) declared, "become the nation's chief story-teller, its 'interpreter in chief.'" As Roderick Hart (1987), an expert on presidential discourse, argued:

> When most ordinary Americans speak, they speak in behalf of themselves or, at most in behalf of their friends, families, and work associates. Presidents, in contrast, represent the viewpoints of abstract entities—their party, the administration, government itself, the Western alliance. (p. 6)

Giving someone the right to speak for you is significant. Most of us would hesitate to give this privilege to a parent or spouse, let alone to a political candidate whom we know only through the mass media. Yet, there is also a sense in which knowing someone through the media, and especially through television, is in some ways more real than knowing that person through face-to-face contact. Knowledge gleaned through television represents a kind of "behind the scenes" hyperrealism in which voters meet candidates through intimate conversations conducted by professional interviewers (e.g., Katie Couric, Matt Lauer, or Larry King). These interviewers can often ask personal questions in such a skillful manner that even the most jaded of candidates let down their guard and speak from their hearts—or at least this is how it appears. Intimate personal interviews on television thus seem much more informative than stump speeches, and they also demand less of us as listeners. Mediated processes such as televised interviews or news programs convince us that we genuinely know our political leaders (Hart, 1999). Thus, during the past twenty-five years we have watched Ronald Reagan chop wood, Bill Clinton jog and eat greasy fast food, and George W. Bush drive around his Crawford, Texas, ranch in his pickup truck.

The sense that we know our political leaders through a mediated presence may also contribute to our inevitable frustrations and disappointment with them. Communication scholars Betty Winfield and Barbara Friedman (2003, p. 548) wrote, "Twentieth-century coverage of the president as the symbolic head of state has extended to his wife. They together become the First Family, an ideal couple for the nation, with the wife a model for upper-middle-class women." When, however, presidential candidates construct media images of their perfect family lives—attentive spouses; obedient, disciplined, and successful children; harmonious marriages—they may create an expectation for perfection that they cannot live up to once they are in office. The public may feel betrayed when their elected officials disappoint them, just as people might if their own spouses or children failed to live up to their expectations.

Knowing their political leaders and feeling comfortable with their televised presence are important for most citizens because voters seek candidates who seem to share their worldviews, understand their problems, and represent their interests. We want our presidents to, as former President Clinton was known to gush, "feel our pain." We expect our presidents to be intellectually and morally sound, wise and able to lead, yet willing to listen and to reflect our will. We want presidents who are like us and who share our worldview but who also possess strengths and attributes that we ourselves may not.

THE OUTLINE FOR THIS BOOK

This book explains how political campaigns in the United States have developed and changed throughout history. The book discusses the development of campaign strategies beginning in the early 1800s up to the 2008 election campaign. The increased emphasis on image-based politics, the declining power of the political parties, recent developments in the media (including the application of new communication technologies such as the Internet to campaigns), the increased emphasis on public opinion polling, the increased reliance on paid political advertising, and the emphasis on winning the game of politics are all covered. In addition to providing extensive examples drawn from recent campaigns, the book considers how scholars in communication, journalism, political science, and other related fields have studied political campaigns, and it discusses some of the theories and research findings that scholars have advanced to explain the dynamic process of political electioneering in the United States.

The book also addresses political conditions in the United States today, examining such issues as public apathy, low voter turnout, voter alienation, distrust of politicians and elected officials, and political fragmentation and polarization, and identifying the factors that contribute to these problems. My argument is that many of these conditions are in fact created by the strategies employed by candidates when they run for office and by the campaign fund-raising process that has been developed to pay for the campaigns. I also argue that the manner in which campaigns are conducted and officials are elected has also influenced, in a profoundly negative fashion, candidates' ability to govern once they assume office.

Finally, the book considers how the conduct of campaigns has led to an increased cynicism on the part of the American people, lessened respect for elected officials and faith in government, and fostered a politics of scandal and character assassination. I argue that the style and content of political campaigns in the United States have undermined the possibilities for citizens' full, fruitful, and rewarding political participation. I also suggest some strategies for reinvigorating and rehabilitating the democratic process.

MY GOALS FOR THIS BOOK

I hope that this book appeals to students of politics and communication. Readers will be introduced to important theories drawn from several different academic disciplines and will examine the dynamics of the electoral process in the United States through examples drawn from current and past campaigns. The political system in the United States has many positive attributes, but I argue that it also suffers from serious problems that threaten to undermine its vitality and even its legitimacy. The United States has long proclaimed itself as a beacon of democratic freedom, and notions of "American exceptionalism"—that we are unique among all nations in the world because of our unique democratic system—have long infused our cultural self-identity (Zarefsky,

2006). We have actively sought to export our political values to other nations through modeling democratic behaviors, through civil society development projects, and even through military intervention. We loudly proclaim our commitment to democracy before international bodies such as the United Nations (Cronin, 2001). But what precisely have we exported? Political candidates in Europe, the Middle East, and Asia have begun retaining the services of U.S. political consultants and are increasingly seeking office through media-dominated campaigns that emphasize public opinion polling, spot television advertising, and candidates' images. Is this the best we have to offer? I believe it is time for us to develop strategies to reinvent our political system and to engage and empower our citizens so that they may better be able to respond to the global problems facing our nation.

We have, I fear, become a nation of political "couch potatoes." I want to encourage readers to get up off their couches and take direct political action. I hope that this book will motivate readers to become engaged citizen activists. If we can improve the conduct of politics in the United States—if we can enliven our political conversations, demand more substantive media coverage of complex issues, achieve greater voter participation, and foster a deeper sense of mutual respect and shared purpose and commitment among citizens—then we will have an opportunity to create a democratic system that truly merits our best efforts to export it abroad.

CHAPTER 2

The Long Campaign

When Abraham Lincoln accepted the presidential nomination of the newly formed Republican Party in 1860, he was a relatively unknown, one-term former congressman from the western frontier. Lincoln was eager to hit the campaign trail and to meet prospective voters, but his advisors urged him to stay at home in Springfield, Illinois, and to make no public speeches. It would, they declared, be unseemly for him to campaign openly for office, and it might signal that he was desperate and lacked confidence in his chances for victory in November. Lincoln subsequently commented that the time between his nomination and the general election was the most boring period in his adult life (cited in Donald, 1995).

Things did not change all that much for most of the remainder of the nineteenth century. The 1896 presidential campaign, however, marked a change as candidates became more involved in their own campaigns. Republican candidate William McKinley spent the entire 1896 campaign at his home in Canton, Ohio. McKinley was not quite as circumspect as Lincoln had been; he did meet potential voters and members of the press while sitting in his rocking chair on his front porch (Jamieson, 1996). In contrast to McKinley, the Democratic candidate in 1896, William Jennings Bryan of Nebraska, adopted a bold new strategy. In the 1896 presidential campaign, Bryan traveled 18,000 miles, made over 2,500 speeches, and sometimes spoke as many as twenty-five times in a single day (Cornelius, 2007). Bryan's efforts were to no avail: He was soundly defeated (Jamieson, 1996). It was not until 1912 that the modern presidential campaign was born. In 1912 Woodrow Wilson, a Democratic candidate who prided himself on his abilities as a speaker, openly campaigned for the presidency in a hard-fought campaign against Republican candidate and incumbent president William Howard Taft, former president and Progressive Party candidate Theodore Roosevelt, and Socialist Party candidate Eugene Debs. This extraordinary election campaign captivated the American people and forever changed the nature of presidential campaigns in the United States (Chace, 2004). Wilson's triumph may have been in part a result of his effectiveness on the campaign trail, but it was also a result of the fact that the Republicans split their votes between Taft and Roosevelt. Nonetheless, the fact that all of the major candidates in this election actively campaigned on their own behalf established a new presumption that future candidates would also be expected to likewise speak and campaign from that time on (Jamieson, 1996).

The nature of presidential campaigns in the United States, and the nature of most campaigns that were not distinctly local, changed dramatically during the twentieth century and has continued to evolve during the first decade of the twenty-first century. From a period in which presidential candidates were too modest to advocate their own election (Lincoln, for example, refused to cast a ballot in the presidential race so no one could accuse him of the ungentlemanly act of voting for himself; Donald, 1995), we now see candidates relentlessly traversing the country to woo potential voters.

The first state to help choose the Democratic and Republican presidential nominees is Iowa. The Iowa caucuses traditionally take place in January.* Yet, in the single month of October 2005, less than a year after the 2004 presidential election and more than three years before the next general election, ten prospective presidential candidates visited Iowa to campaign (Candidates start early in Iowa, 2005). By late June 2006, Republican candidate Senator Sam Brownback of Kansas had been to Iowa eight times, New York Governor George Pataki seven times, Governor Mike Huckabee of Arkansas seven times, Senator George Allen of Virginia twice, former House Speaker Newt Gingrich of Georgia four times, and Massachusetts Governor Mitt Romney four times (Zito, 2006). The Democrats did not intend to be outdone in Iowa, as former senator and 2004 vice presidential candidate John Edwards of North Carolina, Indiana Governor Evan Bayh, New Mexico Governor Bill Richardson, Wisconsin Senator Russ Feingold, and retired General Wesley Clark of Arkansas also found a reason to visit the state. In addition, Iowa's own Governor Tom Vilsak campaigned across the state, informing his constituents that he too would be interested in moving to a mansion in Washington, D.C. (Iowa politics.com report, 2006). Certainly, these many visits represent a lot of attention lavished on a state

---

* Iowa state law directs its parties to schedule their caucuses at least eight days before any other state's selections (Raney, 2007). Because several other states have moved up their primaries, as was discussed in Chapter 1, the Iowa caucuses were moved up and held on January 3, 2008.

that ranks thirtieth in total population, has fewer than 3 million residents, and has only seven electoral votes.

Today, most elected officials are always in campaign mode, demonstrated by the attention that candidates and officeholders pay to public opinion polls, their concern for managing their image, their focus on securing campaign funds for their next election, and their attempts to maintain a very public presence. In this chapter we explore how and why the nature of the American political process has changed in the twentieth and twenty-first centuries and consider how to account for the impact of these changes on the communication dynamics of campaigns.

THE ROLE OF POLITICAL PARTIES

The U.S. Constitution created a republic based on a system of limited suffrage and indirect elections. In the nation's early years, the vote was limited to free men who could meet the requirements that they owned real property and that they paid taxes. The Constitution also determined that the nation's president was to be chosen not by direct ballots cast by citizens but by the Electoral College. In the nation's early years, members of the House of Representatives were elected by direct ballot, but members of the Senate were elected by the state legislatures. The limits on direct elections signaled a cautious approach to democracy that sought to protect the interests of social and economic elites (Sorauf, 1984).

The U.S. Constitution does not mention political parties; indeed, the Founders likely did not envision the formation of parties. The first parties emerged in the United States as caucuses of like-minded members of Congress, but even rudimentary party organizations did not develop until about 1800. Political parties did not become significant factors in U.S. elections until the electorate was expanded by the removal of restrictions limiting the franchise to those who owned property (Sorauf, 1984). These property requirements were gradually dismantled state by state until all had been eliminated by 1850.

When new voters acquired the ballot, they were understandably suspicious of the ways in which the elites—typically affluent planters and merchants—got together to select candidates from within their ranks for public office. The movement toward genuine popular democracy inspired a search for alternative ways by which ordinary citizens could achieve political influence. Political parties not only drew together like-minded citizens, but they helped identify candidates who shared a set of opinions and interests, and they helped shape positions on public policies (Sorauf, 1984).

The first mass political party to gain great influence was the Democratic Party. In 1828, President Andrew Jackson drew together the frontier and agrarian wings of loosely connected groups known as the Jeffersonians to form the national Democratic Party. Meanwhile, Senator Henry Clay helped to merge disparate factions of Whigs into a national party, and a two-party system was created. By 1840, both the Democrats and the Whigs were active in all states and were fielding candidates for state and local races (Sorauf, 1984).

Political parties came to be especially important because the American electorate was composed of large numbers of voters who were not politically sophisticated. Many voters were poorly educated and lived in areas where there was little access to political information. In many cases, voters were recent immigrants to the United States who did not have experience with democratic governance in their native countries.

The meetings of political parties provided citizens with a forum in which to debate political issues and to propose legislation that would serve their interests. In short, they provided essential opportunities for public deliberation and discussion, for disagreements to be expressed and agreements to be forged. From these arguments, the parties shaped political platforms that identified what the party stood for and suggested what its candidates might be counted on to enact into legislation should they win election. Because political candidates were selected by party committees, they tended to be drawn from the ranks of the parties' most committed members, generally the well-known figures within the party hierarchy. Such a system presumed that the candidates nominated for public office would be reasonably loyal to the party platform and committed to its enactment. Party affiliation meant that political partisans could be depended on to turn out and vote for the candidates nominated by their party, and few voters engaged in ticket splitting by voting for candidates of the opposite party. Political parties thus lent stability and predictability to the political process.

Even though political parties are continually evolving organizations (e.g., the Whig Party disappeared in the late 1850s, and out of its ashes emerged the Republican Party), they have also been a source of continuity and ideological consistency in American politics. Although one can easily be guilty of overgeneralization in any attempt to identify the likely constituents of a given political party, historically certain groups of voters have aligned with particular parties. It is also important to recognize, however, that party membership is not always fixed in the United States. Most people do not pay dues to a party, attend formal party functions, or carry a membership card. In most states citizens declare their party affiliation when they register to vote, entitling them to vote in the party's primary election, but people are increasingly willing to cross party lines when they cast their ballots.

Over the past sixty years or so, the following groups have tended to vote Democratic: African Americans, Jews, Catholics (especially Catholics of Irish, Polish, Hispanic, and Italian descent), labor union members, teachers and other academics, social workers, those who reside in central cities, and blue-collar workers. The following groups have tended to vote Republican: business executives, small business entrepreneurs, suburbanites, and white Anglo-Saxon Protestants (especially persons of Scandinavian, British, and German descent). Republicans have tended to have higher incomes, more prestigious occupations, and better educational opportunities than do Democrats (Greenberg, 2004; Wayne, 1980). The reasons that particular groups align with particular parties are complex and difficult to analyze. In some cases they may be a result of perceived economic interest, whereas in others it may be due to feelings of social and cultural identification. We will discuss this topic in greater detail in Chapter 3.

There have been some dramatic shifts in party identification. African Americans tended to vote Republican when first given the franchise in 1865; this was, after all, the party of Abraham Lincoln. They did not vote Democratic in large numbers until the 1930s, when President Franklin Delano Roosevelt won them over with his massive public works programs during the Great Depression. African Americans now constitute the single most reliable group of Democratic voters (Greenberg, 2004). The movement of large numbers of African Americans into the Democratic Party was countered by (indeed, it may have even provoked) the movement of many southern whites from the Democratic to the Republican Party. The major impetus for this transformation was the national Democratic Party's support—particularly the support of President Lyndon Johnson and many northern Democrats in Congress—for the passage of civil rights legislation. These migrations from the Democratic Party to the Republican Party were hastened by such issues as forced busing to achieve racial integration in public schools and by anxieties that emerged following the urban unrest of the 1960s. President Richard Nixon and his advisor Kevin Phillips developed what was known as the Southern Strategy to deliberately exploit these anxieties and to reach out to southern white Democrats and convince them to vote Republican (Phillips, 1969).

More recently, some Roman Catholics have moved from the Democratic Party to the Republican Party to protest the Democrats' support for abortion rights. Also, some union members have abandoned the Democrats, complaining that the party was too devoted to protecting the interests of minorities and gays (Greenberg, 2004). For the most part, however, throughout American history party membership has been reasonably constant and predictable, and major realignments have occurred infrequently and only over periods of many years (Campbell, Converse, Miller, & Stokes, 1960; Kamieniecki, 1985; Maisel, 2007).

The political parties seemed to enjoy their greatest power from roughly the 1870s until the 1920s. This was also the period during which American cities grew and rapidly industrialized. Many Americans left their small farms and moved into the cities to find work. Hundreds of thousands of immigrants also poured into the cities. Both the Democrats and the Republicans sought to attract these voters, but the Democrats were especially successful at gaining new members. The Democratic Party formed what has sometimes been labeled a "city machine," which assumed responsibility for providing services to its members. In many cities the party apparatus became indistinguishable from the city bureaucracy (Ackerman, 2005).

Many large American cities were controlled by political machines, with New York, Chicago, and Kansas City especially dominated by machine politics and powerful city bosses. Urban politics during this period were very personal. Party members came to know their local party officials and counted on them for favors. Likewise, the party understood that maintaining party loyalty meant meeting the needs of its constituents. Although many people complained that this system inevitably became corrupt, as bribes, graft, and the selling of political influence were all too common, urban political machines became firmly entrenched, and it was difficult for candidates and/or voters to oppose the machine and maintain any real influence within the party. Because many cities were thoroughly dominated by voters who belonged to a single party, that party's leaders and elected officeholders were almost impossible to unseat (Ackerman, 2005).

Urban political machines were at the height of their power between 1880 and 1940, but they strongly influenced both the Democratic and Republican presidential nominating conventions from 1836 to 1968. Probably the most powerful, and arguably the most corrupt, of the urban political machines was New York's Tammany Hall. Under the direction of the notorious William "Boss" Tweed, the Tammany Hall machine controlled New York City politics, often dominated politics in New York State, and heavily influenced national elections (Ackerman, 2005). As Ed Flynn, a Bronx County, New York, Democratic Party boss, boasted in 1948, "Less than one hundred men in any convention . . . really dictate what occurs" (cited in Pious, 1996, p. 123).

Such dominance was possible because the bosses of the state delegations that were sent to participate in the national conventions would pack those delegations with loyal followers. The leaders would hold the proxies of the rank-and-file members. In many cases a "unit rule" required that the delegates to the conventions meet to select which candidate the entire state delegation would support. Such rules effectively prevented individual delegates from defecting to support candidates of their own choosing. In 1932, for example, only 15 percent of the state delegations at the national party conventions cast divided ballots (Pious, 1996). Delegations often went to the national conventions uncommitted, nominally supporting a favorite son (typically a governor or senator from the state) whom the delegations backed until their bosses had negotiated deals and were prepared to throw their support to a serious contender for the nomination (Pious, 1996). Party bosses did not usually seek ideologically pure or deeply partisan candidates for office; instead, they sought candidates who were most likely to win the election and thereafter be in a position to dispense patronage in the form of political favors (e.g., appointments to office, public works projects, or favorable legislation) back to the machine.

Perhaps the most persistent of the urban political machines was the organization in Chicago. Newspaper columnist Mike Royko (1984), who acquired his reputation largely through his biting yet humorous attacks on politics "Chicago-style," provided the following description of how the Chicago Democratic Party maintained its hold over the city's electorate:

> Under the system used in most cities . . . you dial City Hall for a broken curb or some other problem. You talk to an anonymous bureaucrat, a functionary, a faceless voice on the phone who takes down your name, address and tells you to "have a nice day."
>
> You don't know this person, and that person doesn't know you or really care if you have a nice day or a disastrous day. You are just a voice on the phone, a name and address on a complaint form.
>
> But the Chicago system has always been different. In the Chicago way you saw that your curb was crumbling, so you walked down the

street and rapped on your precinct captain's door and said: "Tony, I've got a broken curb."

He would say, "I'll see what I can do." The precinct captain now had an opportunity to do something for you, which is what he lived for, and why he had a patronage job as a city earthquake inspector. He would then tell the alderman that you had a broken curb, thus demonstrating to the alderman that he was keeping right on top of problems in the precinct. And the alderman would say: "I'll see what I can do."

So now the alderman had an opportunity to do something for you. The alderman would then call his wife's brother, an assistant supervisor in the Department of Streets and Sanitation, and tell him about your curb. The assistant supervisor, who owed his job to the alderman, would now have an opportunity to show his gratitude. . . . He would call a crew foreman, who also owed his job to the alderman, and ask him to fix your curb. . . . Then the precinct captain would come to your house and point at the curb and say, "I took care of it." Later he would drop by and say, "The alderman is running for reelection, you know. I'd appreciate it if you would give him your vote." . . . We call it participatory democracy. (p. D7)

The urban political machine especially thrived on the opportunity to deliver patronage jobs and vital services to its members, but even in rural areas the political parties sought to form close and personal relationships with constituents. The progressive reform movement sought to weaken the power of the political bosses. By the 1920s the movement had secured the creation of civil service requirements for public jobs at the national level. Eventually these reforms gained greater influence at the state and local levels. Such reforms greatly reduced the patronage power that political parties formerly used to reward party service and loyalty, and no doubt played a role in diminishing the power of the political parties. This is not to suggest that political patronage is a relic of another era, however, for it still persists. Whenever a new administration takes over in Washington, in a state capital, or in city hall, the moving vans are kept busy as the supporters of the outgoing officeholders leave their posts and are replaced by the appointees of the incoming elected officials. Indeed, one of the most significant controversies in 2007 was the claim that the Bush administration fired eight U.S. Department of Justice prosecuting attorneys because they were not sufficiently loyal to the Republican administration (Eggen & Solomon, 2007).

Other factors also helped to decrease the power of political parties in the United States. First, beginning in the 1950s, many large cities began to lose population as residents moved to the suburbs. The ease of commuting by automobile, the lure of the single-family home with an attached garage, the opportunity to find peace and quiet along shaded streets with expansive green lawns—all of these represented the idyllic American dream of prosperity. The large-scale movement to the suburbs as American cities sprawled out from their formerly compact centers significantly changed the dynamics of electoral politics. The political parties had less and less influence over voters in their new neighborhoods. Once voters moved to the suburbs, they were less likely to be beholden to party figures for jobs, the performance of services, or political information. In fact, politics in the suburbs was less personal. Suburban voters, who were no longer served by urban political machines, experienced fewer campaigns that were conducted door-to-door and thus had less face-to-face contact with candidates. Instead, more campaigns were waged through the mass media. As this shift occurred, voters had less direct contact with their political party, and eventually their feelings of party loyalty weakened.

Second, the class and cultural markers that signaled party identification were often diminished in the wake of the profound economic changes occurring in America. More and more Americans graduated from high school, attended college, and found employment in white-collar professions. Families, helped largely by the fact that women were entering the workforce in record numbers, now earned incomes far beyond those of their parents. In the late 1940s and through the 1950s and 1960s, labor unions played an important role in creating higher wages, improved standards of living, health insurance benefits, and greater employment and retirement security for members. Since then, however, union membership has declined and organized labor has lost much of its political clout. The power of labor unions and the numbers of U.S. citizens residing in union households have sharply declined as manufacturing industries that were previously dominated by organized labor have employed fewer workers (Immigrant union members, 2004). In addition, economic developments in the United States during the 1960s and thereafter had the effect of reducing class consciousness, formerly an important dimension of party affiliation. Party allegiance came to have less meaning when it was no longer assumed that individuals would follow in the footsteps of their parents and grandparents toward patronage employment, life on the family farm or in a job at the local mine or factory, or membership in a particular party. There are also more people today who see themselves as independents (unaffiliated with any political party) or as members of a third party (Saad, 2007).

Third, new regulations and operating procedures changed political parties themselves. Historically the party leadership had wide latitude in the selection of candidates, and political candidates tended to be selected in smoke-filled backrooms or in boisterous convention halls. In response to the outcry that these nominating procedures diminished the opportunities for political participation by the citizenry at large, however, these electoral procedures were refined and altered. The civil rights movement of the 1960s brought pressure to ensure that the processes used to select delegates for party conventions did not discriminate against minorities. This change was, of course, more significant in the Democratic Party than it was in the Republican Party, because most minorities tended to register as Democrats. Additional pressure to "democratize" the Democratic Party came during the Vietnam War. Following extensive public protests against the party regulars at the 1968 Democratic National Convention, the party nominating processes were opened up to ensure that the selection of convention delegates and the numbers of ex officio and uncommitted delegates who could be controlled by the party leadership were reduced (Epstein, 1986).

The creation of direct caucuses and state-sponsored primary elections has also enhanced direct popular citizen participation in the nominating process. Whereas most party candidates were formerly selected by delegates in conventions held at county, state, and national levels, now most candidates are selected by voters participating in state-sponsored primary elections. These changes have diminished the power or control that the party and especially party leaders have over candidates. Because candidates are no longer so dependent on winning approval from party leaders, they can appeal directly to voters for support. This has diminished the ability of the party leadership to force candidates to adhere to the party platform. It has also meant that prior party activity, experience, endorsements, and faithfulness to party ideology are no longer important predictors of who will or will not seek or eventually win a party's endorsement.

The suggestion that political parties are not as important as they once were does not imply that parties are unimportant. Most voters do identify with one of the two major political parties, most voters do vote for candidates nominated by their parties, and the parties do provide ideological coherence to the American electoral process. On occasion, party membership and adherence to party values get sorely, and often very openly, tested. For example, Senator Joe Lieberman, Democrat from Connecticut and a candidate for vice president in 2000, was challenged for the nomination in his own party in the 2006 primary because his outspoken and vocal support for the Bush administration's policy to invade Iraq had become so profoundly unpopular among Connecticut Democrats (Lieberman losing ground, 2006). After Lieberman was defeated in the Democratic Party primary in Connecticut, he declared himself to be an independent. As an independent he was able to gain reelection by defeating both the Republican and Democratic parties' nominees. The Lieberman victory was achieved because he was able to draw votes from both registered Democrats and Republicans. Once elected, however, the newly independent Senator Lieberman continued to vote with the Democrats for the election of the presiding officer of the Senate. Lieberman's independence was also visible, however, when he endorsed Senator John McCain for the Republican presidential nomination in 2008.

Judging from recent surveys of younger Americans, however, the future of U.S. political parties may hold even more uncertainty. "Generation Xers" and other younger Americans are more likely to feel alienated from both politics and their elected officials. Studies suggest that they are far less likely to vote, call or write elected officials, attend candidate rallies, or work on political campaigns than are members of any other voting age group of citizens (Attitudes towards politics and public service, 2000; Freyman & McGoldrick, 2000). This is not to say that youth do not vote, but they vote in much lower numbers than older citizens. Forty-two percent of U.S. citizens between the ages of 18 and 24 voted in 2000, whereas 64 percent of those aged 25 and older voted (A guide to reaching young voters, 2004). There was a marked increase in the deeply polarizing election of 2004, when 47 percent of 18- to 24-year-olds voted, but the number of those over 25 who cast ballots also increased from 64 to 66 percent (Youth voting trends, 2004). One note of optimism, however, is the fact that the number of young voters also increased in the 2006 midterm elections, when the youth share of the electorate went from 10 percent in 2002 to 12 percent, the largest gain for any age group (America goes to the polls, 2007).

Those young people who do not vote can be presumed to be somewhat disinterested in supporting either the Democratic or the Republican party. Those who did vote in the 2000 and 2004 elections, however, were more likely to declare themselves to be independents than were older voters (A guide to reaching young voters, 2004). This may now be changing, however, for in recent polls the Democratic Party has been gaining much more support from younger voters than has the Republican Party. For example, a New York Times/CBS News Poll conducted in June 2007 found that "54 percent of young voters indicated that they intend to vote for a Democrat for president in 2008." This poll attributed these results to the fact that younger voters expressed strongly negative views of President Bush (who had a 28 percent approval rating with this group) and of the Republican Party. The poll also found that "young Americans appear to lean slightly more to the left than the general population: 28 percent described themselves as liberal, compared with 20 percent of the nation at large. And 27 percent called themselves conservative, compared with 32 percent of the general public" (cited by Nagourney & Thee, 2007, p. 7).

Despite the earlier arguments offered about the diminished influence and power of the political parties, it is clear that the Democratic and Republican parties are by no means relics of the past. Research suggests that party labels convey most of what voters come to know about candidates' ideologies. Party differences help voters distinguish between liberals and conservatives (Snyder & Ting, 2002). The major parties continue to nominate candidates for public office, and it is almost impossible for independents or third-party candidates to gain election in partisan races. The participation by third-party candidates has, however, helped decide recent presidential races. The highest vote total ever achieved by a presidential candidate not affiliated with one of the two major parties was when Reform Party candidate Ross Perot received more than 19 percent of the popular vote in 1992. In that election, Perot was able to overcome at least in part the obstacle of raising the vast sums of money necessary to gain name recognition because he was independently wealthy and able to fund his campaign with his own money (Perot launches third-party presidential bid, 1996). Some have argued that Perot captured more votes from incumbent Republican President George H. W. Bush than he did from the Democratic challenger, Bill Clinton, and thus Perot's participation in the campaign decided the outcome of the 1992 election (Derbyshire, 2003). Perot made a second attempt at the presidency in 1996, but his share of the vote fell to less than 9 percent (Popular votes, 1996). In the 2000 presidential campaign, third-party candidate Ralph Nader, running on the Green Party ticket, earned less than 3 percent of the nationwide popular vote, and yet his participation was sufficient to tip the election to Governor George W. Bush over Vice President Al Gore. Nader received 97,488 votes in Florida, a state where the margin between Bush and Gore was 537 votes. The Voter News Service national exit poll showed that had Nader not run, 47 percent of his voters would have cast their ballots for Gore, while only 21 percent said they would have voted for Bush. Thirty percent said they would not have voted (Cook, 2004). Like Perot, Nader also made another attempt at the presidency, running in the 2004 campaign. Again, like Perot, Nader's vote total was cut almost in half in his second attempt, as he earned only 1.6 percent of the votes cast (President results, 2004).

The primary obstacle that seems to have limited the formation of successful third-party efforts in the United States is the Electoral College. The Electoral College is designed so the winner of a state captures that state's electoral votes.* The vast majority of American voters have fairly consistently demonstrated that they are unwilling to spend either their votes or their campaign contributions on political candidates representing parties that do not have a realistic prospect for getting elected. Third-party candidates and third-party movements have, however, often helped spark political activism because they provide new opportunities for citizens to express their opinions and to exercise their voices.

Leaders of the Democratic and Republican parties continue to wield significant financial influence in political campaigns, and because money matters more than ever in contemporary politics, this also helps to keep candidates and elected officials somewhat loyal to party principles. Party leaders are often in a position to raise vast sums of cash for campaigns and to dispense those funds to candidates in the best position to win office. As we shall discuss in greater detail in Chapter 10 on the financing of political campaigns, party leaders solicit campaign donations from lobbyists and others eager to guarantee themselves access to those in power. Party leaders are often able to pass those funds

* "Only two states, Nebraska and Maine, do not follow the winner-takes-all rule. In those states, there could be a split of electoral votes among candidates through the state's system for proportional allocation of votes. For example, Maine has four electoral votes and two congressional districts. It awards one electoral vote per congressional district and two by the statewide, 'at-large' vote. It is possible for Candidate A to win the first district and receive one electoral vote, Candidate B to win the second district and receive one electoral vote, and candidate C, who finished a close second in both the first and second districts, to win the two at-large electoral votes. Although this is a possible scenario, it has not actually occurred in recent elections" (U.S. Electoral College, 2007). Republican Party activists in California were pushing for a statewide ballot initiative that would use this same system to assign California's electoral votes in the 2008 presidential campaign. Many noted that if this proposition qualified for the ballot and was approved by the state's voters, it could easily tip a close election to the Republican candidate (Yamamura, 2007).

directly to candidates who are unable to raise such sums on their own. This "power of the purse" gives party leaders some measure of control over their colleagues that can be used to help ensure party discipline (Drew, 1999b; Dwyer, 1999). The relationship between campaign donations, party leadership, and strategies to enforce party discipline was played out in a very public drama involving former House Majority Leader Tom DeLay (R—Texas). DeLay was especially adept at raising campaign funds, directing them to needy House colleagues, and enforcing discipline in the ranks. Indeed, DeLay's nickname was "the Hammer" because he was so effective in keeping fellow members in line and in winning their support on controversial votes. Ultimately, however, DeLay was indicted on charges that he had conspired to violate campaign fund-raising laws. He resigned his seat in Congress in April 2006 (Weissman & Cillizza, 2006).

The political parties suggest strategies for candidates to follow and even provide workshops and clinics for citizens contemplating a run for public office. In these workshops, prospective candidates have the opportunity to meet with party leaders and interact with professional campaign consultants and pollsters. These meetings also allow prospective candidates to meet with one another, with party donors, and with party activists. Such meetings are no doubt helpful in shaping the parties' central messages and in making sure that most of the candidates seeking election under the parties' banners remain faithful to those central messages.

Party leaders are often very actively engaged in attempting to set the tone for the party. The president and the governor of a state naturally are in a position to serve as leaders for their party. The party that is out of power at the moment, however, may have a somewhat more difficult task in gaining media and public attention for their party's positions. The selection of an outspoken party leader may be an important means to provoke public confrontations with the incumbent party. For example, in February 2005, the Democrats selected former governor and presidential candidate Howard Dean of Vermont as chairman of the Democratic National Committee because he had been such an effective voice in mobilizing the progressive wing of his party in the 2004 presidential campaign.

The maintenance of a semblance of party discipline is important to the creation and protection of a party's label as an indicator of core beliefs and values to guide voter decisions—but only to the extent that the candidates who run under those labels live up to those values (Snyder & Ting, 2002). Despite the importance of measures such as those mentioned to create and enforce party coherence and discipline, however, it is clear that today's candidates have more control over their own campaigns than they did formerly. Candidates can now bypass the party leaders and go directly to the voters to secure their support and to gain a party nomination for public office. The diminishing influence of the political parties has had a dramatic effect on how campaigns are conducted and on the nature of campaign communications.

THE ROLE OF SPECIAL INTEREST AND LOBBYING GROUPS

Partially as a result of the importance of access to sufficient funds to conduct a successful campaign for public office, and partially as a response to the decline of conventional party authority, alternative sources of influence and control have begun to play a more important role in the selection of candidates for public office. Well-organized citizen activist groups and special interest lobbies are often able to secure the nomination and even the election of candidates favorable to their interests. Such groups include environmentalists (e.g., the Sierra Club), Christian fundamentalists (e.g., the Christian Coalition), feminists (e.g., EMILY'S List), gay rights activists (e.g., ACT UP), and gun owners (e.g., the National Rifle Association), to name just a few representative examples.

These groups solicit contributions from members who share their political concerns and goals, and then the groups offer financial contributions, volunteer efforts, and other forms of direct political assistance to candidates who support their legislative agendas. One interesting result of such efforts is an increasing effect of "nationalizing" local or statewide races. For example, in 2004, Senate Minority Leader Tom Daschle (D—South Dakota) was locked in an extremely tight race for reelection against Republican challenger Representative John Thune. The race drew interest and contributions from across the country. More than $26 million, or approximately $50 per South Dakota voter, was spent on the race, with liberal special interest donors contributing to Daschle's campaign and conservative special interest donors pouring their money in to help Thune. Conservatives also spent millions of dollars on "issue" ads that especially targeted Daschle because of his support for abortion rights. In the end, Daschle was narrowly defeated, becoming the first Senate minority leader in history to lose in a bid for reelection (GOP tightens hold on Senate, 2004).

Citizens who are active in special interest groups are significantly more likely to engage in political discussions and to write letters to candidates and/or elected officials, at least with regard to those issues that most matter to them. These activists are also more likely to donate money to campaigns and to vote. As a result, activists have far greater influence on the selection of candidates and on the formation of public opinion than their numbers might warrant. Activists tend to favor one party over the other (e.g., feminists, environmentalists, and gay rights activists typically support the Democrats; and Christian evangelicals, anti-abortionists, and citizens opposed to gun control tend to ally with the Republicans). Such activists may be so focused on the one issue that most concerns them, however, that they actually have less party allegiance than do other voters. In short, if they feel that their preferred party or favored candidate abandons them on their special issue, they may in turn vote against that candidate or party. For example, even though most observers would characterize President George W. Bush as very devoted to conservative issues and causes, members of his own Republican Party criticized him for his interventionist and "Wilsonian" foreign policy and his tolerance for big government and the growth of deficit spending (Bandow, 2003; Bryk, 2004). The criticisms of activists may also disproportionately affect the actions of elected officials. As already noted, activists often represent the loyal base of party supporters. They are the donors and volunteers for party activities as well as the most likely party voters. If they do not enthusiastically support a party's candidate, they may not become engaged in the campaign, and suddenly even a powerful incumbent may be left vulnerable.

In 2004, many argued that evangelical Christian political activists decided the outcome of the presidential election. One important objective in any election is to make certain that the most partisan and committed voters turn up at the polls on Election Day. The Republicans helped motivate their core conservatives by qualifying ballot initiatives that would prohibit gay marriages in eleven states. The strategy clearly worked. These measures were approved in every instance, and Republican turnout was sharply up. Even though the final outcome in the election between Bush and Kerry was very close, and in fact came down to one state—Ohio—in the Electoral College voting, Bush won almost 60 million votes overall. The only other successful candidate to win that many votes was Ronald Reagan in 1984, in an election where he carried forty-nine states (Green, 2007). The increased turnout of conservative activists in Ohio alone might have been sufficient to tip the election toward the Republican candidate, President George W. Bush (Cooperman, 2004).

GENDER POLITICS

In recent presidential elections, going back at least to 1992, there has been a distinct "gender gap" in the American electorate. Women have tended to favor the Democratic candidate over the Republican candidate. A woman has appeared on a major national party presidential ticket only once in our history, when Representative Geraldine Ferraro (D—New York) ran as a candidate for vice president in 1984. Of course Ferraro was not elected, but her participation did help spark a long-term movement to increase the number of women in public office and to enhance their political influence. Despite the fact that more women tend to vote Democratic than Republican, both parties have seen an increase in the number of women candidates. For example, in 1992, Senator Elizabeth Dole sought to win more women voters over to the Republican ticket by explicitly encouraging women voters to "make history" by supporting her bid to break the ultimate glass ceiling. Many Democratic Party consultants worried that their party faithful would have been willing to cross over and vote for this Republican to do just that (Brownstein, 1999). Senator Dole may have been unsuccessful in securing the GOP nomination, but her efforts no doubt helped empower other women to enter politics. Both the Republican and Democratic parties have been successful in significantly increasing the number of women holding elective office. In 2007, eighty-six women served in Congress (sixteen in the Senate and seventy in the House), another seventy-six women served in statewide elective executive positions, and women composed 23.5 percent of the membership in state legislatures (Women officeholders, 2007). The most dramatic news on the issue of women in politics, of course, is that Senator Hillary Clinton is, as this chapter is being written, a strong contender for the presidential nomination of the Democratic Party for the 2008 election.

AN EXPANDED ROLE FOR POLITICAL CONSULTANTS

When political parties dominated the electoral process, citizens motivated by their ideological passions volunteered their time and effort to help the party elect its candidates to public office. Citizens were rewarded for their efforts when they were given positions of leadership in their party or perhaps even considered as potential candidates in future races. The party leadership played an active role in identifying candidates, choosing from among competing candidates, and providing direction for campaigns.

The role formerly played by the party leader is now increasingly undertaken by the paid political consultant. Campaign consultants are often public relations specialists who advise candidates on how to organize and fund their campaigns, identify issues to discuss in the campaign, prepare their speeches and advertisements, and conduct public opinion polls. Sydney Blumenthal (1982), an author and former advisor to President Clinton, likened consultants to the political bosses of old, declaring that it was now consultants who controlled the institutional memory of the parties.

The increased use of political consultants reflects two fundamental changes in American politics. First, the increasing dependence on the mass media to get candidates' messages to the voters has heightened the importance of advertising and public relations while simultaneously driving up the cost of running for public office. Second, advances in social scientific research techniques have increased awareness of how public opinion can be understood, formed, and manipulated by candidate messages (Friedenberg, 1997).

Party professionals tend to be committed to the advancement of their ideology. Political consultants, on the other hand, may be as much influenced by the pursuit of profits and a healthy income. The impact of political consultants on the conduct of American campaigns was already evident decades ago. As Larry Sabato (1981) argued:

> Political professionals and their techniques have helped homogenize American politics, added significantly to campaign costs, lengthened campaigns, and narrowed the focus of elections. Consultants have emphasized personality and gimmickry over issues, often exploiting emotional and negative themes rather than encouraging rational discussion. They have sought candidates who fit their technologies more than the requirements of office and have given an extra boost to candidates who are more skilled at electioneering than governing. They have encouraged candidates' own worst instincts to blow with the prevailing winds of public opinion. (p. 7)

Whereas political parties used to recruit candidates to run for public office, now potential candidates seek to recruit high-profile and successful consultants to manage their campaigns. The ability to hire a well-known and visible consultant to manage a campaign sends a clear message to other potential candidates, to the press, and to party activists that the contender is a serious candidate for office. A candidate's hiring of the right "big name" consultant creates an immediate buzz that affects fund raising as the party's special interest group elite leaders (for example, in the Democratic Party this might mean union leaders; in the Republican Party it might mean evangelical Christian leaders) take notice (Klein, 2006). Potential campaign contributors, reporters, and political activists know who the most successful consultants are and assume that these consultants will hire on with candidates who they believe can wage successful campaigns (or at least raise sufficient campaign funds to pay for the consultants' services!). Political consultants have thus become preselectors in the nominating processes, encouraging and dissuading candidacies, often with the mere announcement of their clients in a given race.

Prior experience in public life, service to the party, knowledge about public issues, intense ideological commitment—all these attributes might be desirable in potential candidates, but they seem to matter much less than having deep pockets. Consultants want to work for candidates who can raise the vast amounts of money now necessary in any campaign for public office. A candidate such as Mitt Romney, Steven Forbes, Ross Perot, Michael Bloomberg, or Arnold Schwarzenegger, who is personally wealthy and willing to spend vast sums of a personal fortune to campaign for public office, can become a significant player in a campaign. Candidates who do not possess personal wealth must be able to demonstrate that they can attract campaign contributions from influential donors or from organized political action committees. Thus, money, name recognition, and a telegenic personality that lends itself to campaigning in a mediated age have more to do with a candidate's ability to become a factor in an election than that candidate's leadership abilities or political acumen. Texas governor George W. Bush, for example, was proclaimed by some to have already clinched the 2000 Republican presidential nomination before a single primary vote was cast because he was able to raise more campaign money than any other candidate had ever raised in the nation's history (Fineman, 1999). Likewise, in the 2008 campaign, Senator Hillary Clinton was a presumptive front-runner for the presidential nomination long before she had actually formally announced her candidacy because she had strong name recognition, the support of her still-popular husband, and access to the long list of donors developed by President Bill Clinton. Senator Clinton's strongest rival in the 2008 campaign was Senator Barack Obama, a handsome, youthful, and charismatic figure who was able to raise large sums of money from small donors.

Some political consultants are motivated to do whatever it takes to win elections. Many consultants, for example, focus on digging up as much potential dirt as they can against their opponents and then leaking such dirt to the media (Perloff, 1998). Consultants are often willing to use attack-style negative political advertisements, they may spread rumors and use innuendo to undermine an opponent, and they may willingly distort or oversimplify issues and arguments in a campaign (Ansolabehere & Iyengar, 1995; Jamieson, 1992; Sabato, 1981; Scully, 2007).

In an interview with the *Los Angeles Times*, Richie Ross, one of the best-known political consultants in California, explained his views of negative campaigning and of the responsibilities of consultants toward their candidates and toward the political system:

> If it's going to help the candidate I've been hired to help elect, I'm going to do it. If I think it would backfire, I'm not going to do it. I'm going to run a positive campaign if I'm ahead. I'm going to run a very negative campaign if I think I'm very far behind. . . . Those of you who are more interested in the system can debate its values. I don't have a particular interest in the system. I don't wake up in the morning and feel as though my job is to fix the system. (Cited in Skelton, 1996, p. A3)

One of today's more controversial political consultants is also one of the most successful and well known. Karl Rove, who worked to elect President George W. Bush in 2000 and to reelect him in 2004, has been called "Bush's brain." During the Republican primaries in 2000, Rove was accused of sparking a rumor that Senator John McCain, who was challenging Bush for the presidential nomination, was mentally unstable because of his experiences decades earlier as a prisoner of war in Vietnam (Dubose, 2001). This was not the first time that Rove had been accused of starting rumors about his opponents. In the Texas gubernatorial race in 1994, Rove was running George W. Bush's campaign against incumbent Governor Ann Richards. The Bush camp began telephoning voters to ask, "Would you be more or less likely to vote for Governor Richards if you knew her staff is dominated by lesbians?" Most recently, Rove became embroiled in a felony criminal case when he was reported to have been the source of a strategically planned "leak" of a CIA undercover agent's name designed to silence Bush administration critics. Rove is alleged to have made calls to Washington journalists identifying a CIA undercover agent, Valerie

Plame, who was married to Joseph Wilson, a former ambassador who had called into question the administration's claims about Iraq's alleged attempts to acquire nuclear weapons. Rove is reported to have told the journalists that Plame was "fair game" because her husband had gone public with his criticism (Borger, 2004). Although the Justice Department chose not to prosecute Rove in the case, his reputation was badly sullied by the affair, particularly when Vice President Cheney's chief of staff, I. Lewis "Scooter" Libby, was convicted of lying to the FBI (Lewis, 2007).

Political consultants operate in an environment in which no formal rules of evidence or enforceable standards for ethical and appropriate conduct exist. Even contemplating such rules or standards for how to conduct campaigns is problematic because our nation is committed to the principles of free speech granted in the First Amendment.

Even if one assumes that most consultants are ethical, however, and not actively attempting to mislead people with their messages, one can argue quite convincingly that the impact of political consultants on the conduct of modern campaigns has been negative. As political journalist Joe Klein (2006, p. 20) argued, "Rather than make the game more interesting, they have drained a good deal of the life from our democracy. They have become specialists in caution, literal reactionaries—they tend to react to the results of their polling and focus groups, they fear anything they haven't tested." As an example, Klein says that he asked several of the consultants who advised Al Gore in the 2000 presidential campaign why Gore, who was deeply committed to the issue of the environment and who later was featured in an Oscar-winning and critically acclaimed documentary about the environment, did not discuss the environment during the campaign. Gore's leadership on the environment eventually resulted in his winning the Nobel Prize, yet Klein reports that the consultants said they advised Gore not to talk about the environment because it would not help him win the election. Klein (2006, p. 21) notes that throughout the campaign, Gore was criticized as "stiff, phony, and uncomfortable in public. The stiffness was, in effect, a campaign strategy: Every last word he uttered had been market tested in advance." Klein goes on to wonder whether "Gore might have been a warmer, more credible and inspiring candidate if he'd been able to talk about things, like the environment, that he'd really wanted to talk about."

The dominant role that consultants now play in a campaign also affects how elected officials govern. Consultants condition candidates to pay attention to polling data and public opinion. Consultants also emphasize strategies whereby candidates are encouraged to target special interests and craft messages designed to appeal to those interests. Once elected, however, candidates face the delicate task of trying to meet the needs of disparate groups of voters, needs that may be incompatible or directly in conflict. Political parties provided opportunities to hammer out and reach compromises. Consultants do not focus on compromises; they seek to clarify and make stark the choices before voters. Governing is different from campaigning, but many modern candidates have difficulty moving beyond the campaign stage. Even after taking office they conduct themselves from within the perspective of the ongoing campaign, ever sensitive to the day-to-day vagaries of public opinion. For example, when the scandal involving President Clinton's improper relationship with White House intern Monica Lewinsky first surfaced, Clinton reportedly asked his pollster to conduct a survey to determine whether he could tell the truth and admit to having had an improper sexual relationship with a young subordinate and still maintain the public's support. Supposedly, the poll suggested that he could not do so and that the public would neither forgive nor forget such a distasteful lapse in judgment and moral conduct. Armed with this advice from his consultant, the president continued to weave a web of misleading, if not directly perjurious, denials of improper conduct, which ultimately led to his impeachment by the House of Representatives (Isikoff, 1999).

The preceding discussion may have convinced readers that I see political consultants as such a destructive force in contemporary campaigns that they should be purged so that the nation can return to a more pure and wholesome democratic system. This is not my argument, and in the spirit of full disclosure, I must concede that I have served in the role of consultant and advisor, sometimes as a volunteer and sometimes for pay, to several political candidates and elected officials. I would also concede that the past in American politics was far from perfect; it was often an era where political decisions were made by a handful of unelected elites behind closed doors. Certainly much political corruption was a direct result of these practices. Now that candidates have come to recognize the contribution that political consultants can make to their campaigns and have come to appreciate their expertise, there is little likelihood that candidates will ever attempt to run their campaigns by themselves. Why would any candidate choose to place his or her own campaign at a disadvantage by not having a trained professional on the team?

Political consultants have considerable expertise in polling, advertising, direct-mail fund raising, telephone canvassing, issue selection, message construction, scheduling, and speech performance — all tasks that are vital to the success of a modern mediated political campaign. Consultants are almost certain to remain important players in the political process. They must, however, be made to recognize the consequences of their activities for the health and vitality of the political process. The public must hold the candidates, and thus indirectly the consultants, accountable for the strategic choices they make in the conduct of campaigns. We need to continue tinkering with laws and regulations on issues related to campaign funding, and we need to develop strategies by which we can demand "truth in advertising" standards for political campaigns, much as we do in product advertising. The public, the media, and, most important, the candidates for whom they conduct their work must demand that consultants establish and live up to ethical standards for their profession. Consultants who fail to live up to these expectations, as well as the candidates who retain their services, should be punished when voters go to the polls on Election Day.

MASS-MEDIATED POLITICS

One important reason for the development of political parties was that the parties supplied political information to voters and synthesized that information into useful political positions on issues. Voters learned of this political information in conversations with friends and neighbors, by attending political rallies and listening to speeches, or by reading newspapers slanted toward the political views of a particular party. Beginning in the 1920s and 1930s, Americans increasingly turned to the radio for political information.

Originally, the radio primarily served to extend the audience for the candidates' speeches from those present in the auditorium to those listening at home (Jamieson, 1996). Soon, however, candidates were purchasing advertisements on the radio, and radio stations were moving into the news business, assigning reporters to cover political campaigns and to discuss political issues.

During the 1950s and thereafter, television served as a dominant source for political information. Although large numbers of Americans report that they read a newspaper daily or at least several times a week, the numbers have been declining for decades. According to the Newspaper Association of America, more than 80 percent of American adults read a newspaper each weekday in 1964. By 2003, only an estimated 54 percent read a newspaper each weekday. Experts predict that this decline will continue in the years to come and that fewer than half of adults will read a paper every day by the end of this decade (Crosbie, 2004). Indeed, a study released in 2007 found that only 16 percent of young adults (age 18 to 30) and 9 percent of teenagers surveyed read a newspaper on a daily basis (US: Study finds, 2007). As newspaper readership has declined, television has become a ubiquitous part of American life. According to recent surveys, 99 percent of American homes have at least one television. The average number of TVs in each home is 2.73, 66 percent of U.S. homes own three or more TV sets, and the TV is on for an average of six hours and forty-seven minutes each day in the typical American home (Herr, 2001; State of the news media, 2006). Of course, many Americans are now accessing news, including political news, on the Internet, but as we will discuss in Chapter 8, this does not necessarily mean they are developing media usage habits that will enable them to make informed political choices.

As television came to dominate other sources for political information, political candidates had to respond and develop strategies appropriate for communicating in this medium. As Ansolabehere, Behr, and Iyengar (1993) argued:

> Politics is Darwinism in action. Those who best adapt to new surroundings survive; those who cannot become extinct. Before the advent of the modern political age, political debate and communication was the province of political parties, and politicians were required to conform to the views expressed by party leaders. Today, however, the influence of party leaders has been reduced, and the mass media cover politicians as individuals, not as party members. Candidates must thus fend for themselves, and the survivors are those who can most effectively carve out their own identities in the media jungle. (p. 3)

Because candidates—and, of course, their professional consultants— are acutely aware of the importance of television in political campaigns, the rhythms of campaigns are increasingly shaped by television news coverage. Hart (1999, p. 4) argued that television not only makes us see politics in a certain way, "but it also makes us see seeing in a certain way. Television tells us, a bit at a time, that politics can be reduced to pictures."

Candidates who have an attractive image, who can create memorable sound bites, and who can demonstrate that they are media savvy are likely to make the best impressions on viewers. Unfortunately, the skills of political governance and the talent for making a positive impression on television may not be the same thing.

We might learn more about political candidates and how they would govern if we could get candidates to talk in detail about their positions on complex issues such as the federal budget deficit and tax reform. Instead, candidates make pithy sound-bite statements such as "Read my lips, no new taxes" or "I promise a middle-class tax cut," and the public gets little in the way of real information as to whether the candidate will be able to meet this commitment.

Many critics of media practices have complained that the news media emphasize the negative side of American political life and as a result have actually increased public cynicism about elected officials and even about democracy (Cappella & Jamieson, 1997; Shaw, Critics of, 1996). As an example, for years *NBC Nightly News* included a special feature entitled "The Fleecing of America," which investigated examples of wasteful government spending. The message, delivered night after night, was that the government was not only ineffectual and incompetent, it was often downright corrupt. Government leaders and bureaucrats were depicted as callously acting out of personal greed and as trying literally to loot the nation's treasury. The stories suggested not that there might be differences of opinion regarding the benefit of certain government programs or that there might have been more efficient ways for the government to conduct its business but rather that the government was out to rob us blind. Is it any wonder that many have suggested that Americans have become increasingly distrustful of their elected officials and are losing hope that government can find solutions to the problems that they face (Cappella & Jamieson, 1997; Dionne, 1996)?

The public's trust and confidence in government has especially been challenged by the invasion of Iraq. The Bush administration justified the invasion on the basis of arguments that Saddam Hussein was somehow linked to the terrorist attacks of 9/11 and that he had an arsenal of weapons of mass destruction that he was willing to use. Yet, increasingly, the evidence that came to light after the invasion demonstrated that the alleged links between Iraq and the Al Qaeda terrorist network were at best exaggerated and at worse an out-and-out attempt to deceive the public. Furthermore, no weapons of mass destruction or any clear evidence of a plan to attempt to produce such weapons were ever discovered (Rampton & Stauber, 2006). As a result, over time, public support for the war and for President George W. Bush began to decline rapidly. Bush, who had enjoyed very strong public support in the days immediately following 9/11, came to be seen as an increasingly unpopular and polarizing figure (Broder & Balz, 2006).

As we saw in Chapter 1, faith and trust in government are essential to maintaining high levels of political participation, and political participation is essential to the preservation of democratic governance. This chapter suggests that the public's faith may be declining in large part because of the ways in which political campaigns are now being conducted. In the next chapter we shall explore how voters are socialized to develop particular political attitudes and opinions.

CHAPTER 3

Political Socialization

The term *political socialization* refers to those processes by which individuals are taught, and come to internalize, the values that shape their political opinions and beliefs. These values, taken collectively, also form a nation's political culture. Political socialization takes place at home, in school, in interactions with peers, and through consumption of the mass media (Viale, 2001). We acquire our political beliefs as we acquire a vocabulary of symbols that carry ideological meaning. Because many of these words are learned from those we trust, such as our parents and teachers, we are conditioned to accept their political values as they are "fed to us" (Hahn, 2002). A citizen socialized into a political culture has not only developed certain attitudes but also is capable of functioning as an effective, although not necessarily compliant, member of that society (Sherman & Kolker, 1987).

To remain vital and healthy as nation-states, all countries must succeed in socializing their citizens into the political culture. The norms of loyalty to one's nation and respect for civilian authority are transmitted to people as they become aware of the political beliefs and values of their political culture (Dawson, Prewitt, & Dawson, 1977; Viale, 2001). The transmission of knowledge from one generation to the next is "predominantly tacit" and therefore is taking place even when it is unintended and the participants may be unaware that it is occurring (Polyani, 1983, p. 61). No generation, let alone each member in it, can test all the knowledge to which it is exposed. It must accept much as a given. Research suggests that societies likely exert more influence on "what the youth think about than on what they think" (Kuran, 1995, p. 187).

THE ROLE OF THE FAMILY

The family plays a major role in determining a child's initial political opinions and attitudes. The influence of the family, although reduced somewhat as the child matures, continues to be significant in shaping political attitudes and convictions well into adulthood (Neimi & Jennings, 1991).

Many factors account for the significance of the family in shaping political values and orientations. A starting point for many scholars is the issue of trust. Children learn to depend on and trust their primary caregivers. The more stable and secure the relationship between children and their primary caregivers, the more trusting children may become. Children also seem to be highly sensitive to the cues that signal how secure and trusting the adults who care for them are. Caregivers who seem uncertain, fearful, anxious, or hostile may well pass on those feelings to the children who rely on them. On the other hand, caregivers who seem contented, trusting, well adjusted, and friendly toward others pass on those feelings. Such attitudes may not by themselves shape children's political beliefs, but they may influence children's self-identity and values (Brotherson, 2006; Markus, 1979; Searing, Schwartz, & Lind, 1973).

An individual's capacity to trust others has implications in shaping political opinions and values. To illustrate the importance of trust, consider how children form opinions of people who are different from them. The way children respond to those of different races, religions, and socioeconomic classes, or to individuals with different sexual preferences or different beliefs, may be largely influenced by their own sense of security and their capacity to trust others. Children imitate the behaviors, both positive and negative, of their parents and important caregivers, so these significant adults predispose children to behave in certain ways (Dohmen, Falk, Huffman, & Sunde, 2006; Riccards, 1973).

Children as young as age 3 or 4 begin to develop a sense of racial self-identification (Hirschfeld, 1997). Ethnic preferences have been detected among children almost as soon as they become aware that the important adults in their lives exhibit racial and/or skin color preferences. Studies suggest that by age 5, children can attribute an individual's talents or abilities according to the racial grouping in which they supposedly belong. Perhaps what is more revealing is that "white children tend to insist that an individual's lack of ability or ability is race specific, even in the face of evidence that disproves or contradicts their assertions" (Marable, 2004). By age 7 or 8, a child may have developed a bigoted personality, although research suggests that such attitudes are almost certainly reversible if addressed by alternative educational messages (Stacey, 1977). It may be difficult to undermine racist attitudes once they are firmly entrenched, however, since social psychologists have argued that racism has become institutionalized in the United

States because it is so often and so easily expressed in everyday language and social practices (Van Ausdale & Feagin, 2001).

As discussed in Chapter 2, significant gender and racial differences play a part in how people may choose to cast their ballots (e.g., at the present time, women and minority voters are more inclined to vote for Democrats). The research has suggested that these differences in political beliefs and voting behaviors may also be strongly influenced by parental attitudes and beliefs. For example, researchers have noted that men and women, and majority and minority culture voters, respond differently to cues about how much empathy or compassion candidates seem to have for vulnerable social groups (Hutchings, Valentino, Philpot, & White, 2004). These differences in perceptions and values may reflect the differences in how people experienced their early political education. Because women and minorities may feel that they have historically lacked political power and influence, they may be more inclined to hold political views that are sympathetic to other powerless individuals and groups (Atkeson & Rapoport, 2003; Hutchings et al., 2004).

One of the most important characteristics of a healthy democratic society is that the citizens have developed and "buy into" a shared social contract in which they acknowledge and value their connections to one another. This shared social contract and these perceptions of social connectedness are a product of our political socialization and are also influenced by our parents. As psychologists Laura Wray and Constance Flanagan (2006) wrote, "Parents and other family members are critical for helping youth understand the elements of the social contract—how they view the world and others in it." In further exploring the role that parents play, they cited research that suggested the following:

> Asking American youth about their definitions of democracy directly illustrates how values impact their perceptions of the way society is organized. Youth who gave an individual rights definition of democracy had families who emphasized values of social vigilance, while youth who defined democracy as civic equality reported hearing values of social responsibility from their parents, and were also less likely to report personal values of materialism. (p. 1)

Flanagan et al. (2005) developed a similar argument. This research also suggested that "adolescents who hear self-enhancing values emphasized by their parents hold individuals more accountable for problems such as homelessness, poverty and unemployment. . . . On the other hand, adolescents hearing messages of compassion from parents tend to endorse more situational causes for these three social issues" (Wray & Flanagan, 2006, p. 1; also citing Flanagan & Tucker, 1999).

Another dimension related to the issue of trust involves attitudes toward authority. Positive attitudes toward the police are essential if the police are to function effectively in any society (Webb & Marshall, 1995).* Children develop their opinions about the police from their parents as they observe their parents' behaviors. Through the observation of police cars, behavior at traffic lights, parking meters, and traffic signs, children both learn about the role of the police in society and develop attitudes about the legitimacy of police authority and the role of the police in political life. These attitudes help shape a child's acceptance of the legitimacy of the legal and political system that embodies the essence of governmental authority. Parents or caretakers who talk disrespectfully about the police or who openly disregard laws in the presence of the child who looks to them for guidance send a message about authority that may have significant consequences in the child's later life. The attitudes and behaviors connected with adolescent rebellion against authority, for example, may have been planted by the interactions with parents or other significant adults from a child's formative years (Stacey, 1977).

Researchers have also reported that attitudes juveniles have toward the police are similar to the attitudes they hold about other authority figures, including their teachers and their parents (Nihart, Lersch, Sellers, & Mieczkowski, 2005). Thus, parents who speak disrespectfully about the police may end up encouraging anti-authoritarian attitudes in their children, and these attitudes may both undermine their academic performance at school and lead to family conflict. On the other hand, parents who are very trusting and deferential to police authority may produce children who are more likely to be willing to trade their civil liberties protections—for example, to tolerate wiretapping without a court order to protect themselves from terrorism. The point

---

* Some of the most acute moments of social unrest in the United States have come about as a result of public perceptions that the police were unfair, discriminatory, or abusive. As examples one might cite the 1965 civil disturbances in South Central Los Angeles, which were sparked when onlookers believed that the police were responding too harshly in arresting a drunk-driving suspect. In March 1991 a bystander videotaped Los Angeles police officers beating motorist Rodney King, whom they had stopped for speeding and drunk driving. The following year, another uprising erupted in Los Angeles when the officers were acquitted of charges of police brutality.

is, of course, that there is no "right" answer as to how much trust of the police is justified or warranted. Each case must be decided on its own merits, and individuals will differ on whether they trust and respect the authorities based on their own political convictions.

Political distrust, which is also a product of one's political socialization in the family, may also be a significant factor in the development of feelings of political alienation (Hill & Luttbeg, 1983). Distrust or political cynicism often results in a negative evaluation of government, a lack of faith in political institutions, and a sense of personal powerlessness. The implications for widespread feelings of such discontent could be profound and could fundamentally undermine the legitimacy of a government (Abramson & Finifter, 1981; Patterson, 2002).

Families also give their children a social identity and a place within the social structure. Attitudes regarding social class, self-esteem, racial or ethnic pride, religious commitment, and civic identity, for example, are communicated to children in their formative years, and they are developed and tested as children mature (Glass, Bengston, & Dunham, 1986; Goldberg, 2000; Sigel & Hoskin, 1981). Children develop an awareness of social and economic class at a fairly young age, and this awareness may help shape their attitudes about what is expected of them as adults, what rights and privileges they may be entitled to, and their appropriate place in society (Sherman & Kolker, 1987; Waters, Hamilton, & Weinfield, 2000).

Interest in politics develops through social interactions. Children in third and fourth grades often express interest in political issues and are eager to discuss the significant political questions of the day with their parents (Hyman, 1969). By age 12, almost two-thirds of children in the United States have developed and can articulate political party preferences. As might be expected, these early partisan preferences generally reflect the opinions expressed by the children's parents (Stacey, 1977). Parents may not so much mold their children's beliefs as instead place them in a sociopolitical context that serves to reinforce those parental views (Austin & Pinkleton, 2001; Connell, 1972; Verba, Burns, & Schlozman, 2004).

Mothers seem to have more influence in determining the political attitudes of children than do fathers (Cassel, 1993), perhaps because mothers spend more time caring for children. With the greater level of social contact, it may be that mothers simply have more opportunities to pass on their opinions. Research on this topic has not been extensive, however, and may now be somewhat dated in that in contemporary societies mothers may be more likely to work outside the home and fathers may be somewhat more involved in the everyday lives of their children. It is also possible that mothers have somewhat more political influence over their children because of differences in the way men and women communicate (Tannen, 1990). Mothers may express more interest in the children's opinions—they may listen more carefully and talk less—thereby facilitating more extensive and substantive dialogues that aid children in the formation of opinions on political issues.

Young people who grow up in homes with politically active and well-educated parents are more likely to become interested in politics. Researchers suggest that this is because such homes are more likely to also be sites for lively and engaging political discussions that challenge children to develop and test their own political opinions (Verba, Burns, & Schlozman, 2004). Furthermore, the more politically partisan the parents, the more likely their children are to develop intensely partisan attitudes. The parents' political impact is also stronger when they are in political accord and are loyal to the political party that is most often supported by voters sharing the family's socioeconomic characteristics. More intense partisan values and feelings of political engagement and empowerment seem to develop in families and neighborhoods of the upper socioeconomic classes (Kamieniecki, 1985; Stacey, 1977; Verba, Burns, & Schlozman, 2004). This may occur because U.S. citizens of the upper classes tend to be more politically active, and a high degree of political involvement seems to promote political partisanship (Verba, Burns, & Schlozman, 2004).

Likewise, if parents are political independents, their offspring are likely to be independents (Mattei and Neimi, 1991). Ascending in social class is also accompanied by an increase in political independence (Kamieniecki, 1985). Some scholars have suggested that as people come to feel more economically secure, they may be less motivated by their traditional political loyalties or party affiliations based on their economic needs and interests and more inclined to consider political candidates who can address their concerns regarding other issues that they now may deem as more relevant to the quality of their lives (Radcliff, 2005). This may explain why voters who are anxious about the security of their jobs may be more focused on pro-growth and pro-development candidates, whereas voters who become more financially secure may become more interested in candidates who are talking about the need to protect the environment (Shaw, 1996).

Thus, it is clear that partisan attitudes are not permanently fixed by parental political attitudes, but political opinions develop and change as children age (Kinder, 2006). Researchers have argued that as people age, their experiences of voting and living in the midst of the political controversies that shape everyday life may affect their degree of partisanship. Some studies have suggested, for example, that people may be somewhat independent (or loosely partisan) in their twenties, more firmly partisan in their forties, and very partisan by age seventy. These lifecycle changes in political partisanship suggest that the behavior of endorsing a candidate or the platform of a particular political party is itself reinforcing and becomes increasingly important as a means of identifying who we are and what we believe (Cassel, 1993; Converse, 1976).

Some researchers argue that adolescent children are not only receptive to political information, but they also have the power to transform patterns of family communication in ways that benefit their parents. McDevitt and Chaffee (2002) referred to this as a "trickle-up influence," in which child-initiated discussions prompted by school civics courses prompted parents to increase their own civic understanding and competence. The researchers speculated that parents may have wanted to maintain their leadership role in the family and therefore felt the need to become more informed about politics so they could make useful contributions to discussions with their children.

SCHOOLS AND CIVIC EDUCATION

Political socialization also occurs through structured and unstructured educational experiences. Governments establish curriculum standards with an eye toward teaching students to be loyal and patriotic citizens. Students also participate in ritualistic activities aimed at shaping their political attitudes and values. For example, elementary school students in the United States learn the Pledge of Allegiance and salute the flag. The flag is regarded as a symbol of American nationhood, and the Pledge of Allegiance is offered as an expression of loyalty, commitment, and shared national purpose. The Pledge functions as a civic prayer. It not only expresses political loyalty, but its very recitation is a ritualistic and symbolic embodiment of community that binds children to the national identity.

The required school curriculum also teaches a shared history of the national experience. It introduces students to national heroes, celebrates and explains important national holidays, and teaches about the privileges and obligations that accompany democratic life. Sacred institutions and loyalty oaths, stories of personal sacrifice and heroism, and accounts of notorious villains all communicate a shared sense of national purpose. Students are not only taught about the mechanics of political institutions but are inculcated with an attitude that coaches civic piety. "Doing one's duty for God and Country" cements civic loyalty, religious commitment and purpose, and the notion of nationhood as an extension of family and community that establishes a firm emotional identity in our citizenry.

Most U.S. states have very specific content standards regarding precisely what students should be taught with regard to civic education at each grade level. Increasingly, school districts, often at the prompting of both the state and federal governments, have begun to emphasize specific assessment criteria and standards to evaluate the effectiveness of civic education (Civic education of American youth, 1999). Recent research calls into question the success of current civics education programs. A Zogby International poll found that in 2006, three-quarters of Americans could correctly identify two of the seven dwarfs in *Snow White*, but only one-quarter of respondents could name two U.S. Supreme Court justices. Twice as many respondents knew Taylor Hicks was the 2006 winner on the television talent show *American Idol* than were able to identify Supreme Court Justice Samuel A. Alito Jr., whose appointment to the Court was confirmed in January 2006 (We know Bart, 2006).

Low rates of voting and political participation by young people suggest that civics education is not meeting its goal of increasing political interest and efficacy. Recently, however, there has been a significant increase in the amount of attention paid to civics education. Several organizations have emerged that encourage data sharing and provide a forum for the discussion of "best practices" in teaching modules and curricula, as well as for the best way to articulate state standards. For example, the National Conference of State Legislatures has created a project aimed at improving civics education across the nation (see Civic and policy engagement of youth, 2006). In addition, many private foundations have stepped forward with creative projects aimed at enhancing civics education.*

Elementary school students learn about the nation's Founders, the struggles for freedom from Great Britain, the U.S. Civil War, the immigrants coming ashore with their dreams of freedom and prosperity, and the heroic sacrifices made in defending the nation's liberty in overseas

* For example, see the Constitutional Rights Foundation (http://www.crf-usa.org/) and the Student Voices Project (http://studentvoices.org).

wars. This education tends to be a view of the nation that is replete with heroes and villains, and who gets classified as hero or villain is sometimes controversial. Much of this history is designed to bring these figures, both historical and current, to life so that students can see parallels to their own lives. As a fascinating example, I was given a copy of a first-grade picture book entitled *Let's Read about George W. Bush*. In this book students are invited to "follow his story, and learn how he became the leader of our country." The book has illustrated drawings of the president as an infant, as a preteen astride a pony and dressed as a cowboy, in a Little League baseball uniform, as a college student, as a military pilot, standing next to an oil well, as a father holding his twin daughters, and dressed in a suit and cowboy hat as an elected official. The printed text describes how the president was very friendly, very popular in school, loved baseball, worked in Houston with poor children, started his own oil business, owned the Texas Rangers, was a good governor of Texas, and was elected president following a recount of the ballots (no mention of the intervention by the Supreme Court to halt another recount). The book ends by declaring that Bush "pledged to make the United States a better, stronger nation" (Fry, 2003). I do not know how many school districts across the United States adopted this book for their students' use, but I do know that it was used in at least one Republican-dominated Orange County, California, district.

In middle and high school, students are encouraged to participate in elections for class officers and members of the student council. Such activities provide opportunities for students to engage in political activities and develop attitudes of acceptance toward self-government and civic participation. Schools also design civics course materials to address topics such as racial justice, tolerance, and social and political acceptance of minorities and their viewpoints. This type of education is a cornerstone of preparation for life in a pluralistic society. One can also look at textbooks for insight into how a nondemocratic society educates its youth. As an illustration, much discussion occurred in the United States recently regarding how Saudi Arabian youth were told about their religion, their nation, and the world beyond their borders. Many Americans, including many members of Congress, were appalled to learn that our supposed allies in the Middle East were teaching schoolchildren anti-Christian, anti-Jewish, and anti-American messages in required textbooks and classes. The Bush administration coerced and cajoled the Saudi ruling family into a commitment that they would "tone down" these messages (Shea, 2006).

Civic education does not stop in primary school or high school; colleges and universities continue to play a role in teaching students about politics and inculcating political values. One ongoing public controversy in recent years has centered on the claim that colleges and universities have been slanting that education in favor of a liberal perspective. Conservative activists worry, for example, about the "political correctness" movement. As one such activist named Bill Lind (2000) warned:

> The totalitarian nature of Political Correctness is revealed nowhere more clearly than on college campuses, many of which at this point are small ivy-covered North Koreas, where the student or faculty member who dares to cross any of the lines set up by the gender feminist or the homosexual-rights activists, or the local black or Hispanic group, or any of the other sainted "victims" groups that PC revolves around, quickly find themselves in judicial trouble. Within the small legal system of the college, they face formal charges— some star-chamber proceeding—and punishment. That is a little look into the future that Political Correctness intends for the nation as a whole.

The critic of the "PC" movement is correct in his claim that college and university educators—like teachers at the elementary and secondary levels—have made a conscious and deliberate effort to teach students to value political pluralism, to have respect for the opinions of others, and to be accepting of persons different from themselves. This type of instruction clearly represents an overt effort in political socialization. This educational focus was developed out of an openly expressed conviction that such an education was necessary to promote a more harmonious society. There is also evidence to suggest that such efforts have been successful and have produced noteworthy changes in opinion and increased levels of tolerance for women's rights, minorities, and gays (Otis & Loeffler, 2005; Trends in political values, 2007). This educational agenda, and especially the evidence that it is successfully changing students' opinions, concerns those citizen activists who view homosexuality as morally wrong, who may not want to see more women working outside the home, or who may be anxious about interracial dating. On the other hand, those who advocate this liberal instruction worry that society has not done enough and that even more must be done to change student attitudes and values. These liberal activists go so far as to cite examples of violent interracial or antigay incidents to support their belief that schools should do even more to address this topic.*

Civic education has many purposes in addition to coaching attitudes of human compassion and civility. First, it increases students' level of political knowledge. They learn about the nation's history, the Constitution and the Bill of Rights, the obligations of citizenship, and the role that the nation has played in world affairs. Second, political education enhances students' skills in critical thinking and political analysis. They learn how to evaluate and consider alternative solutions to problems, and in so doing they learn how to create, evaluate, and select from among competing policy alternatives. Third, students learn the life skills for participation in a democratic society. They learn how to get along with peers, how to advocate their own ideas, how to register and vote, how to communicate with elected officials, and how to express themselves in a letter to the editor of a newspaper. Finally, students ultimately acquire an awareness of the importance of political values. They shape and refine their moral and ethical foundations, and they apply those values to the political issues they encounter (Patrick, 1977; Pratte, 1998).

Schools are important to the political socialization process because so many levels of communication are involved in this setting. Students learn through interpersonal communication when interacting with teachers, who often serve as surrogate parental figures and are thus accorded a great deal of credibility. Students also interact with peers, whose values they generally mirror. Finally, students are exposed to texts and supplemental classroom materials that shape their level of political awareness and their political attitudes. Because students encounter so many message sources at school, it is difficult to determine which source has the greatest effect on the formation of political attitudes and opinions (Meadow, 1980). Research does suggest, however, that an effective civic education program can stimulate children and their parents to become more interested in politics even if they come from homes that have not previously been politically active. A focus on civic

---

* Liberal activists have argued that several of the recent school shooting tragedies, as well as acts of racially or homophobic-inspired violence, reveal the dangers that arise when some students feel isolated or alienated from the mainstream community. Eyewitnesses reported, for example, that minority students were especially targeted by the shooters in the Columbine High School incident in Littleton, Colorado, (Moehringer, 1999). Incidents of violence against gays and transgendered people continue to be common in the United States. One study reported that there were more than 2,100 victims of such violence in 2004 (Anti-gay, bisexual, and transgender violence, 2005).

education and political awareness may provide these students and their parents a "second chance" at citizenship (McDevitt & Chaffee, 2000).

One of the most significant issues in the United States in recent years has been young people's decline in political participation and decreasing interest in politics. Recent studies have shown that young Americans are less politically or civically engaged, exhibit less social trust, have less confidence in government, have a weaker alliance to their country, and are more materialistic than were previous generations. Experts attribute this situation to the failure of the educational system's current approach to civic education, the antigovernment and anti-Washington campaign themes of recent years, and the decline of the traditional nuclear family (Halstead, 1999; New Millennium Survey, 2006). There was some evidence that in the 2004 campaign, young adults were significantly more interested and engaged than they had been in other recent presidential elections, but a large gap still remained based on education level. Young people who had attended a college or university were far more likely to vote than their less-educated peers (Patterson, 2004).

That somewhat more young people (18- to 24-year-olds) cast ballots in the 2004 presidential election and the 2006 midterm elections may have been due to the increased efforts to build political awareness, interest, and patriotism previously discussed. There have also been many new civic education programs created in recent years to encourage young people to become more politically aware; programs such as Kids Voting USA encourage children in grades K through 12 to go to official polls, with parents and guardians in tow, to cast ballots in their own voting booths on the same issues that adults do. "Rock the Vote" and similar programs seek to increase young people's political participation by inserting messages into MTV and radio music programs, often using young celebrity spokespersons.

Although educators agree that civic education is important to the formation of public values, there are significant disagreements regarding what such education should include. The curriculum for civic education is itself a frequently disputed political issue. Nationalistic political values tend to permeate the curriculum. Courses in American history, for example, tend to cover issues selectively, and episodes that celebrate our national accomplishments seem to receive the most emphasis (Dawson, Prewitt, & Dawson, 1977; Merry, 2007).

The emphasis on patriotic history has not satisfied critics from either the political left or right. Many years ago, Patrick J. Buchanan, who has been a White House staff member, conservative political columnist, and even a presidential candidate, lamented:

> Americans have the right to have their tax-supported schools teach their children not only to revere the great men [*sic*] of America's past, but to understand, respect, appreciate, and defend the society and systems in which Americans have chosen to live. . . . The mythology, the shared beliefs, the heroes of American history are part of the cement that binds together this diverse society. They are part of the common heritage of all Americans, which every citizen should know. (Cited in Dawson, Prewitt, & Dawson, 1977, p. 152)

More recently, critics from the left have protested that the heroes who are praised in our schools' curricula are too often white, male, and European oppressors, whereas women, persons of color, and non-Europeans are ignored. These controversies have turned issues such as the selection of civics and/or history textbooks into full-scale culture wars (Gitlin, 1995).

The fear that seems to emanate from political activists both on the left and the right is that the education students receive in school can and will have a lasting effect on their political attitudes. The research is less than convincing on this issue, however, because most studies suggest that a person's political identity lies somewhere within a more complex belief and identity system (Beck & Jennings, 1991).

THE RELATIONSHIP OF CHURCH AND STATE

Many researchers have investigated how a person's religious beliefs or convictions shape the acquisition of political attitudes. The role of religion in political expression has a long and disputed history in the United States. The Bill of Rights emphasizes the importance of free religious expression and the separation of church and state, but this separation usually has been expressed in the company of arguments identifying the United States as a Protestant nation created with God's blessing. A long tradition in American political discourse celebrates the notion of "American exceptionalism"—the belief that the United States is unique among nations because of our core democratic and moral values, including our respect for human liberty. Those professing such a view of American exceptionalism often argue that the United States has prospered because it has been singled out for divine favor and thus has a special role to play in the world (Zarefsky, 2006).

A central tenet of the notion of American exceptionalism—one that has existed from the founding of the nation—is the freedom to worship as one chooses. As vice presidential candidate Joe Lieberman declared in a speech at the University of Notre Dame during the 2000 campaign, however, "Freedom of religion is not freedom from religion. We are after all not just another nation, but 'one nation under God'" (Lieberman again claims, 2000). At various points in history, Americans' tolerance for religious freedom has been severely tested. The anti-Catholic movements of the mid-1800s, the forced exile of Latter-Day Saints (Mormons) to Utah, and the persecution of Jews all demonstrate the challenge of living up to the nation's commitments to religious tolerance. Perhaps nothing in our history has challenged these principles as deeply as the terrorist events of September 11, 2001, and the anxieties about Islamic fundamentalists who continue to threaten our well-being.

Most scholars of political socialization acknowledge the potential impact that organized religion can have on political values, but they disagree over the way different religions shape the attitudes of believers. These differences largely reflect the fact that (1) some faiths may have far greater influence over their adherents than others, (2) the intensity of religious conviction varies greatly from one person to the next, and (3) different faiths have very different interests and commitments to effecting political change through the electoral process.

Citizens live in a variety of social worlds, all of which may have important political consequences. For example, people are socially rooted in neighborhoods, churches, workplaces, clubs, and associations. Which of these social worlds exerts more or less influence in shaping political attitudes differs from one person to the next (Gimpel, 2003; Huckfeldt, Plutzer, & Sprague, 1993). Research suggests, however, that conservative or fundamentalist churches that regard the church as the principal source of authority in people's lives are likely to have more impact on the formation of their members' political preferences than do liberal churches (Wald, Owen, & Hill, 1990).

Protestants who claim that their religious convictions are a very important part of their lives tend to vote Republican and to be strongly partisan. On the other hand, Catholics who assert that their religion is an extremely important part of their lives do not seem to be more intensely partisan than other citizens (Kamieniecki, 1985; Yamane, 2003). There have, however, been issues on which the Catholic Church has sought to motivate its members to take political action—for example, opposition to nuclear weapons in the 1980s (Bjork, 1992; Hogan, 1989a) and long-standing opposition to legalized abortion (Vanderford, 1989)—but even in these areas the results have been somewhat mixed, at least in comparison to the success that many Protestant churches have had in mobilizing congregants for political activity.

Research also suggests that churches have more influence over the partisanship behaviors and beliefs of persons of lower social status than they do over those of higher social status. Low-social-status believers may not only be more open to guidance from their religious leaders but may find that their religious activities compensate for their perceived status inferiority and induce them toward political involvement (Wald, Owen, & Hill, 1990).

Religious partisans are not necessarily members of one major party or the other. Although many religious fundamentalists favor the conservative wing of the Republican Party, other religious activists are drawn to the liberal Democratic concerns for the environment or on behalf of welfare programs for families and children. Since the presidency of Franklin Delano Roosevelt, Catholic and Jewish support for the Democratic Party has been reasonably dependable, although this party attachment seems to be weaker today than it used to be. As Catholics have become more affluent and have moved into the professional classes, and in response to social issues such as abortion, more Catholics are voting Republican. Similarly, Jewish voters have become more conservative, perhaps in response to the strongly pro-Israel positions taken by recent Republican presidential administrations.

Religious political activists, especially those drawn from conservative and evangelical Protestant faiths, have been much more actively involved in political campaigns in recent years. Polls suggest that perhaps as many as 45 percent of U.S. residents consider themselves to be "born again," "evangelical," or "very religious." About 14 percent of the U.S. electorate in 2000 self-identified as members of the "Christian right" (Berlet, 2003).

In 2004 President Bush received 78 percent of the vote among white evangelicals, up 10 percent from 2000 (Religion and the presidential vote, 2004). Many analysts have argued that the decision to place state initiatives banning gay marriage on the ballot in thirteen states in 2004 dramatically increased the conservative voter turnout in those states and ultimately contributed to Bush's reelection (for a thorough discussion, see Campbell & Munson, 2005). Their success in 2004 inspired conservative activists to focus even more strongly on using churches as sites for political mobilization. James C. Dobson, the founder and head of the group known as "Focus on the Family," has used a variety of methods, including information inserted in church publications and booths placed outside worship services, to recruit new conservative voters (Wallsten, 2006).

Much evidence supports the notion that American voters tend to see moral and cultural issues as increasingly important in how they cast their votes (Page, 2004). One might question whether this is a "chicken or egg" issue. Do voters focus on these issues because candidates introduce them as important themes in their campaigns? Do candidates talk about these issues because they know voters are interested in them? Do voters harbor these concerns because they are religious partisans? Or are voters becoming more interested in religion because of their anxieties and concerns about the great moral issues of our time? It does seem clear that U.S. citizens are among the most religious people found in any Western democracy (as measured by church attendance). Americans are far more religious than our European allies, and political campaign discourse in the United States is also far more likely to focus on religious and moral issues (Religious practices in the U.S., 2000). The impact of religion on politics is not simply felt at the ballot box; it also affects public policy issues, as was made evident in the recent public controversy over the availability of federal research funds for studies of fetal stem cells for medical treatments (Gertzen, 2006).

Thus, what is clear is that the choices people make with regard to the churches they join, the neighborhoods in which they live, and the schools where they send their children all have consequences in shaping political attitudes and values. According to political scientists Robert Huckfeldt, Eric Plutzer, and John Sprague (1993):

> People locate themselves in neighborhoods, churches, workplaces, clubs, and associations. They make these locational choices for good reasons on rational grounds, but in the process they also define—even if indirectly and unintentionally—the dimensions of their social experience. This social experience has relevance far beyond the basis of the original choice. In particular, it defines the composition of political preferences to which the individual is exposed. (p. 380)

People tend to associate with other people who share their values and worldviews, which are in turn reinforced by their increased interactions with those people. This may explain why people seem to become increasingly partisan as they age (Kinder, 2006).

THE MASS MEDIA

The mass media are extremely important in forming the political views of today's citizens. The most significant early influences in children's political attitudes are the adults around them—parents, caregivers, and teachers. All these people receive their day-to-day political information from the media, and by the time children are toddlers, they too are "plugged in" to television sets. As the media columnist Jeanne Sather (2006) noted, "The average U.S. household has at least one TV set turned on for about seven hours a day; the average school-aged child spends twenty-seven hours per week watching TV (some preschoolers watch much more); and, over the course of a year, children spend more time watching TV than they spend in school or participating in any other activity except sleep."

From television, people not only learn about political issues but also observe the institutions and rituals that characterize the operations of the political system. Ample evidence suggests that news coverage significantly shapes people's political awareness (Chaffee, Ward, & Tipton, 1970; Kiousis, McDevitt, & Xu, 2005; Meadow, 1980; Roberts, Hawkins, & Pingree, 1975). Young children may acquire much of their early political knowledge from television glimpsed while their parents are viewing a news program (Meadow, 1980). Although the size of the network TV news audience is shrinking, and these statistics may be somewhat misleading, a 1994 national poll found that 65 percent of 11- to 16-year-olds reported that they had seen a TV news program the day before they were interviewed (cited by Smith & Wilson, 2002). People today may also be increasingly exposed to news from cable television networks, talk radio, or Internet sites. Studies have suggested that exposure to TV news has a significant and unique impact on children. Exposure to stories about war and violence, for example, may leave children feeling sad, angry, frightened, and worried (Smith & Wilson, 2002). As might be expected, older children are more likely to better understand complex news issues and to comprehend information that is explained verbally, whereas younger children might focus more on the visual images in news programming (Smith & Wilson, 2002).

Television has an impact on how political campaigns, elections, and policy making are understood and valued. The communication scholar Roderick Hart (1999, p. 23) argued that "television's nature as a visual, electronic medium reduces the scale of politics." Thus, politics as viewed on television may be less intense, less emotional, more orderly, and less ambiguous than it is in real life. Perhaps to compensate and to attract audiences, broadcasters may emphasize emotional and intense moments with television news programs that feature conflict and clashes between candidates, reporters, and the public. We will examine this aspect of television campaign coverage in greater detail in Chapter 5.

Although voters receive political information from a wide variety of media, including the newly emergent role of the Internet, television is especially important because it requires minimal effort to watch, is easiest to understand, and is the medium that brings people much of their daily entertainment (Chadwick, 2006; Meadow, 1980; Owen, 1991).

The mass media not only supply information about the candidates and the issues but suggest appropriate ways to evaluate candidates and political parties, not only during campaigns but also during periods between campaigns (Weaver, McCombs, & Spellman, 1975). A significant body of research suggests that (1) Americans are somewhat poorly informed about politics, (2) those who are better informed usually hold political opinions that are different from those who are least informed, and (3) exposure to misinformation or distorted media messages will negatively affect a person's political efficacy (see Delli Carpini, 2005). Access to an effective and honest press is essential to the preservation of our democracy because the media provide the starting points for deliberative political conversations among attentive citizens. As the foreign policy scholar B. C. Cohen (1963, p. 13) declared, the press "may not be successful much of the time in telling people what to think, but it is stunningly successful in telling its readers what to think about."

The power of the press to shape public attention and awareness has been labeled "agenda setting" (McCombs & Shaw, 1972). The theory of agenda setting is that the media play an important role in determining which issues merit public attention, in evaluating how effective certain elected officials have been in the conduct of their duties, and in shaping public attitudes. Through media coverage of certain issues, people learn how their circumstances and situations relate to others. This theory will be discussed in greater detail in Chapter 5.

THE FORMATION OF IDEOLOGY

One outcome of exposure to the various sources of political information and socialization that have been discussed in this chapter is that some people—perhaps especially those who develop a strong interest in politics and who may thus become more partisan in their convictions—will develop a synthesized and organized set of political opinions and ideas that give coherence to their beliefs. These organized opinions may be referred to as an ideology. The term *ideology* is similar to the

German term *Weltanschauung* (*welt* is the German word for "world," and *anschauung* is the German word for "view" or "outlook").*

The notion of ideology was developed by the French philosopher Destutt de Tracy at the end of the eighteenth century as he sought to "scientifically" purify ideas from the distortions created by authorities in the church and state to achieve objective truth and correct thought (Bell, 1962). The pejorative term *ideologue* was soon coined by the Emperor Napoleon when he banished such teachings as irresponsible speculations. Napoleon understood that religious orthodoxy was crucial to the maintenance of the French state and could be undermined by these ideas.

Karl Marx then transformed the term by linking ideology to philosophical realism. Marx characterized ideologies as products of social and political relationships. According to Marx, ideologies evolved from the life processes of individuals "not as they may appear in their own or in other people's imaginations, but as they really are; i.e., as they operate, produce materially, and hence as they work under definite material limits, presuppositions and conditions independent of their will" (Marx, cited in Tucker, 1978, p. 154). For Marx, ideologies not only represented false ideas, but they masked particular interests. Although ideologies claimed to represent the truth, they instead reflected the needs of specific interest groups (Bell, 1962). For example, Marx attacked the notion of "natural rights," similar to the concept of the inalienable human rights identified in the U.S. Declaration of Independence—the freedom to worship or the freedom to own property— as "bourgeois rights" that made a false claim of universal validity (Bell, see p. 396).

Today the term *ideology* is used in two ways: One describes a worldview held by a social group that is declared for some set of reasons to be morally "right." It is in this sense that political beliefs begin to congeal into what may be known as a secular religion. The other is ideology as praxis—the conversion of ideas into social levers (Hollihan & Riley, 1993). One example of such a synthesizing ideology was the

---

* For example, consider a discussion of the term *Weltanschauung* and its meaning and significance by Sigmund Freud (1932). Freud declares, "By *Weltanschauung*, then, I mean an intellectual construction which gives a unified solution of all the problems of our existence in virtue of a comprehensive hypothesis, a construction, therefore, in which no question is left open and in which everything in which we are interested finds a place. It is easy to see that the possession of such a *Weltanschauung* is one of the ideal wishes of mankind. When one believes in such a thing, one feels secure in life, one knows what one ought to strive after, and how one ought to organize one's emotions and interests to the best purpose."

declaration made by Charles E. Wilson, then secretary of defense under President Eisenhower and at one time the president of General Motors, that "what is good for the United States is good for General Motors, and vice-versa" (cited by Bell, 1962, p. 399). This statement, Bell declared, expressed "the view that economic policy should be geared to the needs of the business community, since the welfare of the country depended on the health of business."

Ideologies can be distinguished by their relative coherence, internal consistency, and the degree to which they can be used to rationalize actions taken by those who most devoutly cling to them. An ideology might also encompass a statement of the desired ends that advocates a wish to attain or defend (Sherman & Kolker, 1987). Examples of competing ideologies might include differing views on the pursuit of a color-blind society, the equality of women, the sanctity of marriage (should the right to marry be extended only to heterosexual couples, or is it an inalienable right that should be available to all persons?), or on governmental obligations to provide care for its citizens (should we move toward a welfare state, or should government pursue the libertarian ideal of minimal governmental intrusion in daily life?).

The tension between the conflicting values of freedom and equality provides an interesting example by which to discuss the concept of ideology (White, 2004). Both *freedom* and *equality* are key terms in the hierarchy of American values. Both terms frequently appear in the nation's historical texts, in court decisions, public conversations, and classroom discussions. These terms acquire meaning through the historical narratives that describe the beliefs, actions, and sacrifices of the patriots who gave life to the American democratic experiment. Yet, these terms are often in conflict with each other. For instance, the freedom to associate with those of your own choosing (which is legally argued as part of the First Amendment right of freedom of assembly) may conflict with the obligation to treat all people equally. Thus, the government has intervened to pass laws restricting the freedom of landlords—for instance, to refuse to rent apartments to tenants on the basis of their race, religion, or sexual orientation. Negotiating such disputes between conflicting values is an inevitable dimension of politics as a process of civic engagement.

The intensity of ideological commitments, and the degree of confidence or certainty with which those commitments are expressed, varies greatly. Some citizens hold strong partisan positions on issues; others are much more tentative or moderate in their political opinions. As we have discussed in this chapter, the sources of information, opinion, and attitudes that shape our ideologies are multiple and complex. Our ideologies stem at least in part from our ever-developing self-identity. Our self-identity may be shaped by our awareness of our position in the social and governmental hierarchy, our sense of our racial identification, our social and economic class, our education, our religious or moral convictions, and our fears and dreams. Because we are political creatures living within a democratic system and experiencing the day-to-day uncertainties of life, however, our political values and beliefs change as we process new information, acquire new perspectives, and confront new realities.

Political candidates attempt through discourse to motivate people to action, but as the noted literary critic and social theorist Kenneth Burke (1954/1965, p. 25) argued, "A motive is not some fixed thing, like a table, which one can go and look at. It is a term of interpretation, and being such it will naturally take its place within the framework of our *Weltanshauung* as a whole." Our political convictions therefore are best understood as a product of our lived experience—our interactions with our parents, teachers, classmates, spiritual leaders, and the media as we have come to apply them in the task of creating meaning in our lives. We must acknowledge that, from a political standpoint at least, we are never fully formed human beings. We are always in the process of becoming.

CHAPTER 4

Crafting Political Images

All human beings experience their world by creating images of the objects, events, and people that surround them. These highly subjective images both reflect and create a person's self-identity. The images that we hold give meaning and purpose to our lives. They help us organize our experiences, and they give form to the dramas that become our life stories. These dramas also constitute our motives for action. Noted economist Kenneth E. Boulding (1961) observed the following in a landmark study on the image:

> The image is built up as a result of all past experience of the possessor of the image. Part of the image is the history of the image itself. . . . From the moment of birth if not before, there is a constant stream of messages entering the organism and the senses. . . . Every time a message reaches him [*sic*] his image is likely to be changed in some degree by it, and as his image is changed his behavior patterns will be changed likewise. (p. 6)

Political scientist Dan Nimmo (1974, pp. 5–6) described an image as a "subjective representation of something previously perceived. It is an interpreted sensation or, in other words, a meaningful impression, appearance, semblance, or similar mental representation of our perceptions."

The images we hold to be true are always being subjected to new information, which suggests that they must be continually evaluated and re-created. Yet, our images are not easily altered; once formed, they may prove quite resistant to change. As Boulding (1961) observed:

> Suppose, for instance, that somebody tells us something which is inconsistent with our picture of a certain person. Our first impulse is to reject the proffered information as false. As we continue to receive messages which contradict our image, however, we may begin to have doubts, and then one day we receive a message which overthrows our previous image and we revise it completely. The person, for instance,

whom we saw as a trusted friend is now seen to be a hypocrite and a deceiver. (pp. 8–9)

Although all humans participate in the creation of their own images, these images are not painted on a blank canvas. As communication scholar Pamela Benoit (1997, p. 1) observed, "Self-presentations are fundamental to interpersonal communication. Individuals construe and negotiate their identities with others and give meaning to their discursive behaviors. Relational outcomes, like social approval, are contingent on self-presentations."

CREATING AN IMAGE

We are continually exposed to images created by others for our consumption. Advertisers assure us that if we use their soap, we will become more beautiful, smell better, and perhaps have greater sex appeal. Similarly, political candidates market themselves by emphasizing their strength of character, humble origins, knowledge, experience, and compassion. Because very few of us ever get to know well the candidates who are seeking our support—few of us actually hear the presidential candidates speak in person—we develop impressions of them through the images that they and their advisors, the media, and we ourselves create of them. These images are, of course, highly contested because candidates are not only trying to construct their own image, but they are also trying to define the image of their opponents.

Conflicting Images

By way of example, consider the contested images of Republican candidate George W. Bush when he first sought the presidency in the 2000 election. Richard Berke, a political reporter for the *New York Times* (Bush is the man, 1999, p. 1), contemplated the conflicting images of the Texas governor:

Governor George W. Bush is appealingly self-confident. Or is he arrogant? He is engaging and fun loving. Or is he immature? He is, refreshingly, an ordinary guy who has not plotted his whole life to end up in the White House. Or is he too cavalier about the office? He is decisive and sees the big picture. Or is he shallow, impulsive, and impatient, not willing to sweat the nitty-gritty of policy?

No one's personality can fairly be described in black-and-white terms, for people are more complex than that. But such questions are not merely matters of curiosity. All candidates face the challenge of persuading the public that they have the appropriate temperament and maturity to serve in office. As Berke (Bush is the man, 1999) noted, Bush sometimes behaved in ways that were appealing to some and off-putting to others. He mugged for the camera, winked at reporters, and teased reporters and others in the audience about being old or ugly. Bush's behavior prompted Marilyn Quayle, the wife of former vice president Dan Quayle, to describe her husband's rival as a "party frat-boy type" (cited in Berke, Bush is the man, 1999, p. 5). (This was a somewhat ironic criticism because the same complaint was frequently leveled at her husband.) While Bush's strategists sought to allay concerns about his image and to communicate that the Texas Republican was experienced, wise, compassionate, and moral, his opponents openly questioned his maturity, hinted at his problems with alcohol and illicit drugs, and claimed that he regarded the presidency as his birthright (Dowd, 1999). It was not just candidate Bush's opponents, however, who judged his image negatively; even conservative political columnist George F. Will criticized Bush for operating in "an atmosphere of adolescence, a lack of gravitas—carelessness, even a recklessness, perhaps born of things having gone a bit too easily so far" (cited in Berke, Bush is the man, 1999, p. 5).

A documentary film made during Bush's 2000 presidential campaign emphasized what it was like to travel on his campaign plane and attend his events. The film, *Journeys with George*, revealed all of the preceding attributes of his personality and permitted viewers to see the candidate in both scripted and unscripted moments. I have shown the film to different groups of students many times and have been most interested to discover that both my conservative and my more liberal students often comment on the same behaviors and personality characteristics that they see in the candidate, and yet they evaluate and assign meanings to them very differently and in accordance with their own political perspectives. The liberal students are shocked to find a candidate who seems at times to resemble a smirking, hard-partying "frat-boy" engaged in banter with the reporters on his plane. The conservative students, on the other hand, praise the fact that Bush seems so genuinely relaxed, informal, and good-natured.

In the 2000 campaign, Vice President Al Gore and his advisors also attempted to establish a favorable public image. Their goal was to reveal Gore as sober, serious, experienced, dedicated, and responsible.

Gore's opponents, on the other hand, portrayed the vice president as a person of questionable ethics—based on concerns about his fund raising in the Asian community—and, worse (perhaps the most damaging complaint that can be made in the media age), as stiff and boring (Ayres, Of hay, 1999).

Senator John Kerry, when running for president in 2004, also had to create an image that would refute the public perception that he was somewhat stiff and unfriendly. His goal was to define himself as a warm, passionate, engaged, principled, and empathetic war hero. His opponents instead depicted him as a distant New England patrician who was also an insincere "flip-flopper" who frequently changed his position on issues (Harris, 2004).

The contrasting images constructed by the candidates of themselves and their opponents are designed to reveal more starkly the perceived differences between the candidates and thus to guide voters in making their choices. Perhaps no political candidates have ever more sharply divided voters than have former president Bill Clinton and his wife, Senator Hillary Clinton. To his supporters, President Clinton was principled, warm, caring, and compassionate. His opponents, on the other hand, saw him as ambitious, unprincipled, waffling, and lacking a moral compass. Her supporters admired Senator Hillary Clinton as a strong, assertive, smart, accomplished, and conscientious woman who stood by her husband during very difficult times. Opponents characterized her as abrasive, insensitive, cold, and putting her own political goals above all else. A *Time* magazine poll taken in the summer of 2006 found that 53 percent of those surveyed had a positive impression of her, whereas 44 percent held negative views. Only 3 percent had no opinion of Senator Clinton. Karen Tumulty (2006) concluded her report on the survey in *Time* with the following observation:

> She is the inkblot test of a polarized electorate. In the *Time* poll, Democrats overwhelmingly describe her as a strong leader (77 percent) who has strong moral values (69 percent). Republicans by and large see an opportunist who would say or do anything to further her political ambitions (68 percent) and puts her political interests ahead of her beliefs (60 percent). (p. 29)

Concerns about Senator Clinton's ability to overcome these deeply divided public views prompted many to declare that even though she would be the clear front-runner for the Democratic presidential nomination in 2008, she would have a very difficult time in the general election (Tumulty, 2006).

The images that we observe in political advertisements and in news coverage of candidates and issues, as well as those we actively create as we develop our understandings of social issues, meld together and serve as an important means to connect our strategic understandings of complex policy issues (Jacobs & Shapiro, 1994). These images become embedded within our ideology; they give us the power to comprehend what is going on and to explain ourselves to others.

It is not just candidates and their advisors who seek to control their images; political parties are also very concerned with the images that voters may form of the party. For several years the Democrats have battled the image that Republicans saddled them with as "tax and spend liberals." The very term *liberal* has become imbued with a deeply negative connotation that has disadvantaged Democratic candidates (Katz & Baldassare, 1992). Republicans, on the other hand, have tried to overcome the image that the Democrats have attributed to them as being the party of wealthy elites and uncaring toward minorities. President Bush acknowledged the power of this image when he told a friendly audience at an $800-per-plate GOP fundraiser, "This is an impressive crowd—the haves and the have-mores. Some people call you the elites. I call you my base" (Harp, 2006). All jokes aside, the leaders of both parties have been extremely sensitive to the negative baggage of unfavorable images. For example, the Democratic Leadership Council has actively encouraged Democratic candidates to rebut the image that they are not supportive of family values or religion by attempting to find ways to openly discuss their faith (Sullivan, 2003). Democratic leaders were very concerned that the party's candidates might be badly damaged if the Republicans were able to claim that theirs was the only party concerned about moral values. The Republicans, on the other hand, have sought to soften their party's image as insensitive to the needs and interests of minorities, especially so they could reach out and capture the ever-growing Hispanic vote (Lambro, 2003).

Image-Dominated Campaigns

Some critics of American electoral politics have lamented the fact that images have supplanted the meaningful discussion of issues in contemporary campaigns. Image-dominated campaigns are faulted for oversimplifying issues and confusing voters. Nimmo and Combs (1990, p. 58) added their concern that presidential candidates too often act like "beauty contestants [who] introduce themselves, offer standardized statements, explain their vision for America, wear costumes appropriate to the setting (hard hats outside factories, billed caps on the farm, Stetsons in the Southwest) . . . and endeavor not to offend." Political reporter Joe Klein (2006) complained that image campaigns trivialized politics and treated people as if they were too stupid to evaluate complex political arguments or to assess candidates' positions on issues.

Others have argued, however, that the distinction between an issue-oriented campaign and one dominated by images is much harder to draw and that the images and issues in a campaign must be blended into a unifying whole (Davis, 1981; Jacobs & Shapiro, 1994). In some elections the candidate's image becomes the central, defining issue in the campaign (for a discussion, see Hellweg, 1995, especially p. 15). In the wake of the Watergate scandal of the 1970s, for example, Americans were disgusted with professional politicians and Washington insiders. A relatively unknown southern governor, Jimmy Carter of Georgia, won the presidential election by telling voters that he was not a polished "inside the Beltway" politician but a peanut farmer and an engineer. More recently, following the tragedy of September 11, 2001, President George W. Bush repeatedly emphasized that he should be reelected in 2004 because he was a staunch antiterrorist who was absolutely certain about his core beliefs and values and would doggedly pursue the terrorists wherever they might hide.

Another contemporary political figure whose personal image is integrally tied to his style of governance is Rudolph W. Giuliani, the combative mayor of New York City from 1994 to 2001. As a candidate for the Republican presidential nomination in 2008, Giuliani's message was that he was tough enough to govern in a time marked by danger from terrorists. He frequently referred to his leadership in New York City during the 9/11 tragedy and to how quickly he personally made his way to "Ground Zero" to take charge of the rescue efforts. He even let it be known that he, like many of the firefighters and police officers on the scene, had reason to be anxious about his health given his exposure to toxic chemicals released from the collapse of the Twin Towers (Barrett, 2007).

The carefully crafted image of "toughness" did not begin with Giuliani's presidential campaign. This image had long been an essential element of his political life. The former mayor was a federal prosecutor who first established his reputation by his dogged pursuit of high-profile organized crime cases. As mayor he had his own radio talk show, which he used as a way to speak directly to citizens who were frustrated with politics, urban bureaucracy, crime, and city life. The talk show gave him a platform to preach and moralize about how to change life in the Metropolis, including a long-running campaign aimed at urging New Yorkers to treat each other and tourists with a higher degree of civility. Through his own tough language and sharply honed image, he took on rude taxi drivers, corrupt landlords, and dog owners who failed to clean up after their pets. While previous mayors had failed, Giuliani's message was that he was "tough enough" to clean up New York City (Goodnough, 1999). Giuliani also kept his name alive for the Republican faithful when he served as a keynote speaker at the 2004 GOP convention and repeatedly invoked the terrorist attacks of September 11 as a reason to reelect President Bush (Grieve, 2004).

"Toughness" is not always an asset for a political candidate, of course. Political figures should also be able to demonstrate that they are kind and compassionate. Giuliani withdrew from the hotly contested New York Senate race against Hillary Clinton in 2000, explaining that he needed all of his energy to battle his recently diagnosed prostate cancer. His decision was probably also influenced, however, by all of the negative publicity he had faced as a result of his very public divorce from his wife, Donna Hanover, and his affair with another woman. Indeed, it seems that Giuliani told reporters about his plans to divorce Hanover before he told her. The press conference at which Hanover berated her husband for his duplicity and lack of sensitivity may have made for good television, but it did little to enhance the candidate's image (Lipton, 2000). The Giuliani family discord also made its way into the 2008 presidential campaign when it became known that neither of his children from his marriage to Hanover would support his candidacy for president. Giuliani's son, Andrew, age 21, declared that he was intent on becoming a professional golfer and thus had no time to devote to the campaign (Buettner & Perez-Pena, 2007). A few weeks later, it was revealed that his 17-year-old daughter, Caroline, had written on her Facebook page that she considered herself to be a liberal and was endorsing Democratic candidate Senator Barack Obama (Caldwell, 2007). Thus, the "toughness" that may help a candidate in some contexts may become a most unappealing character trait in other contexts—especially for a candidate trying to run as a "family values" conservative.

Candidate images are carefully constructed and nurtured, but they may also genuinely reflect the candidate's personality. For example, Senator John McCain (R—Arizona) has gained a reputation as a fiercely independent, outspoken, accessible, and even somewhat volatile figure who is willing to break ranks with members of his own party. The former

Navy pilot and Vietnam prisoner of war has worked with Democrats in the Senate to cosponsor landmark campaign finance reform legislation (the Bipartisan Campaign Finance Reform Act, popularly known as the McCain-Feingold Act, will be discussed in detail in Chapter 10) and to focus on immigration and welfare reform. As a candidate in the 2000 presidential campaign, McCain attacked religious conservatives within his own party. McCain's reputation as a maverick caused him to make enemies within the Republican ranks even as he appealed to independents and possibly also to Democrats. As a candidate for the 2008 Republican presidential nomination, McCain faced real difficulties attracting supporters and financial contributions from the GOP faithful. To gain more support from Republican conservatives, he sought to make peace with evangelical Christian leaders, even agreeing to give the commencement address at Reverend Jerry Falwell's Liberty University in 2006 (Herman, 2007). Voters also look for consistency in a candidate's image, however, so many were left to question who exactly McCain was. Was he the political maverick and moderate candidate he appeared to be in 2000? Or was he merely another candidate who would tell voters whatever they seemed to want to hear just to gain his party's nomination? Although the other GOP candidates questioned McCain's conservative credentials, he surprised the pundits and gained significant support as the campaign went on.

Another of the more interesting image campaigns in the 2008 presidential race involved Senator Barack Obama (D—Illinois). Obama, a youthful (born in 1961) African American candidate, was elected to the U.S. Senate in 2004 after a relatively short term of service (1997–2004) in the Illinois State Senate. Obama first gained national visibility when he delivered the keynote address at the Democratic National Convention in 2004 while still serving as a state legislator. Obama was well educated (a graduate of Columbia University and Harvard Law School) and had already enjoyed significant career success, including an appointment to the faculty of the prestigious University of Chicago School of Law. Obama authored two books, *Dreams from My Father* and *The Audacity of Hope*, both of which made the best-seller lists. In both books Obama developed very personal narratives intended to introduce himself to the American people. Obama attracted so much attention following his well-received keynote speech in 2004 that he was almost immediately discussed as a likely candidate in 2008. Yet, despite all of his early successes, it became evident that it was difficult for a relatively unknown candidate to establish an effective public image. His campaign sought to emphasize his youth, intellect, energy, and creativity and attempted to turn his lack of extensive Washington experience into an asset by arguing that he would bring fresh perspectives to the White House. His adversaries, on the other hand, publicly fretted about his lack of experience, particularly in foreign policy, and especially at a time when the nation was at war (for example, see Gitel, 2007).

As the first African American presidential candidate who had emerged as a front-runner for his party's nomination, Obama also received significant attention regarding his racial heritage and identity. The senator's campaign sought to avoid too much emphasis on the fact that he was African American, perhaps motivated by the belief that to do so would be to potentially marginalize his candidacy and possibly provoke a backlash from those voters not yet open to the idea of a minority president (Obama downplays, 2007). The response to this strategy in some quarters of the African American community, however, was an ongoing public discussion about whether Obama was sufficiently or genuinely African American (The Obamas are tired, 2007).

Images and Voting Behavior

Studies have consistently demonstrated that candidate images are very important predictors of how people will vote (Boyd, 1969; Druckman, 2003; Natchez & Bupp, 1968) and that candidates seek to convey both a positive image for themselves and a negative one for their opponents (Sniderman, Glaser, & Griffin, 1990).

As the power of political parties has decreased, more voters are likely to express themselves as independents, to engage in ticket splitting, and to trust their own judgments in choosing between competing candidates (Epstein, 1986; Fiorina, 1992; Hillygus & Shields, 2007; Sorauf, 1984). The fact that voters now are more likely to make their own choices between candidates has been cited as at least partly to blame for the increasing dependence on image-dominated political campaigns. Such campaigns are appealing because images (1) enable voters to personalize their choices and (2) are generally easier for voters to process and understand than are complex issues (Kendall & Paine, 1995; Sears, 1969).

Political scientists Pamela Johnston Conover and Stanley Feldman (1984, p. 96) offered perhaps the most cynical view of image politics when they asserted that people may be best understood as "cognitive misers." As such, voters have a "limited capacity for dealing with information, and thus must use cues and previously stored knowledge to reach judgments and decisions as accurately and efficiently as possible."

Samuel Popkin (1994), also a political scientist, advanced a similar theory, suggesting that voters are motivated to use "low information rationality." Popkin claimed that most voters are not motivated to find substantial information on political issues and instead seek shortcuts that do not require their careful attention to complex issues. Specifically, he argued that voters make heavy use of the day-to-day information they acquire from lived experience, the media, and interactions with peers. Furthermore, Popkin asserted that voters often rely on "pseudocertainty principles" when making choices among candidates and when faced with conflicting data. He referred to this process as a "Drunkard's Search" (p. 92). The term refers to the drunk who looks for his lost car keys under the lamppost not because that is where he dropped them but because the light is better there. As Popkin (1994) explained:

> The Drunkard's Search, as the very name implies, is a shortcut to easier information acquisition. Here I am referring to a decision about how to compare candidates, about the criterion on which to compare candidates and make a choice, because a decision about where to look or a decision about which information to retrieve becomes a decision about how to decide. People are particularly likely to use one-dimensional searches, focusing on a single issue or attribute, when there is no dominant alternative. Such a procedure avoids mental strain and produces a compelling argument. (pp. 92–93)

Popkin illustrated the Drunkard's Search by discussing how a voter might consider candidates in a primary race by first analyzing the front-runner:

> Front-runners can be a reference point for voters and for other candidates. At the beginning of the primary season, voters will not know anything about many of the candidates and will consider information about only a few from the whole field. If there is a front-runner, the voter is likely to consider that candidate when evaluating other candidates, both because the front-runner is likely to be known and because the front-runner is likely to be considered viable. . . . The features of the front-runner which other candidates will discuss become focal points of candidate comparison. . . . When the front-runner is well-enough known so that voters know his [sic] warts and blemishes, these faults can be magnified in the primaries. (p. 93)

The decreasing role of the political parties, the use of direct primary elections for selecting candidates, the condensed primary season (due to the fact that more and more states have moved their primaries up in the calendar in the hope that they will have a greater role to play in the selection of the eventual nominees), the increasing tendency of voters to rely on television news rather than on newspapers for political information, and the dominance of spot political advertising all suggest that the reliance on the Drunkard's Search may become even more common in the years ahead.

DIMENSIONS OF IMAGE

Research into candidate images has provided significant insight into how images shape voter decisions. Even though the process of evaluating and forming candidate images is rational—after all, voters do seem to deliberate over their choices—there is no denying that emotions play a very important role in shaping images. Asking people to articulate their feelings toward candidates has been found to be roughly the equivalent of ascertaining the disposition of their votes. Indeed, emotions are predictive of attitudes. If voters are made angry, uneasy, fearful, or disgusted by a candidate, they will likely vote against him or her. If, on the other hand, they are sympathetic to, hopeful about, or proud of a candidate, they will vote for him or her (Marcus, 1988).

Homophily

One important factor in predicting a positive emotional evaluation of a candidate's image is homophily, or the natural tendency of people to bond with others like themselves. In fact, research suggests that people may choose a political candidate in the same way they choose friends. They evaluate the candidate's personal qualities, beliefs, and attitudes, and they seek to determine how close these characteristics are to their own (Andersen & Kibler, 1978; Kendall & Yum, 1984).

For example, candidates routinely try to demonstrate their similarity to voters by emphasizing their small-town roots. Bill Clinton emphasized that he came from Hope, Arkansas; Robert Dole from Russell, Kansas; George W. Bush from Midland, Texas; and Al Gore described summers on the family farm in Carthage, Tennessee, omitting the fact that he spent the rest of the year living in a lavish hotel suite in Washington, DC. Sometimes they brag about their blue-collar origins. Again, Al Gore talked about that family farm, John Edwards described himself as the son of a mill worker, and Dick Cheney mentioned that his grandfather was a cook on a railroad. Virtually every candidate discusses the love and devotion of their families (this often includes grandparents, parents, spouses, and, of course, their children). Increasingly, candidates are also trying to learn at least a few words in Spanish so that they can communicate with the growing number of Hispanic voters in their own language.

In the 1996 race, Clinton and Dole used their hometowns of Hope, Arkansas, and Russell, Kansas. Both candidates described how their small-town origins had instilled in them core American values while they endured economic and familial hardships and struggles.* The Dole story emphasized the candidate's lower-middle-class origins and his life in a hardscrabble prairie town. He told how his family had to move into the basement and rent out the upstairs of their home to survive the Great Depression. The Dole narrative crafted an image of a gifted high school athlete who worked as a soda jerk at the local drugstore and who then made heroic sacrifices during World War II. Dole's life-threatening injury required a long period of recovery and recuperation and left him with a badly damaged arm that never fully recovered. All of these experiences were described as powerful forces in forging Dole's identity (e.g., see Cooper, 1996; Maraniss, 1996).

The Clinton materials in 1996 emphasized that the president hailed from Hope, Arkansas, a bucolic southern town. In his 1992 campaign, Clinton employed Hollywood filmmakers to produce a campaign video of his boyhood experiences to be shown at the Democratic National Convention. The film depicted Clinton's grandfather, a local grocer, as an exceptional person because of his many acts of kindness toward local blacks. It was thus reasonable to presume that Clinton would have been heavily influenced by his grandfather's spirit of respect for all citizens, so obviously Bill Clinton was not the stereotypical southern white politician. The fact that Clinton spent much more of his youth in the wild and wide-open resort town of Hot Springs, where gambling, prostitution, and hard drinking were more the order of the day, was not the focus of the Clinton image creators. The Clinton story did, however, emphasize that he had a very close relationship with his mother, that he stood up to his alcoholic stepfather to protect his mother from physical and emotional abuse, and that he went on to become a model student. Videotapes were shown over and over again throughout the campaign

* The competing narratives of Russell, Kansas, and Hot Springs, Arkansas, and the images of Dole and Clinton are beautifully and fully recounted in the PBS *Frontline* documentary entitled "The Choice '96." It is available on the Web at http://www.pbs.org/wgbh/pages/frontline/shows/choice/. Retrieved on August 29, 2006.

of a teenaged Bill Clinton shaking President John F. Kennedy's hand at a White House gathering for outstanding high school students. Obviously, this was a youth who was destined for greatness (see *Frontline*, 1996)!

The 2004 race between incumbent President George W. Bush and challenger Senator John Kerry drew a striking contrast between the military records of the candidates. In 2004, the United States was engaged in a two-front war, with troops deployed in Iraq and Afghanistan. Both candidates were intent on establishing that they were tough enough to wage the war successfully. President Bush emphasized his leadership in the days after the September 11, 2001, attacks and his unwillingness to compromise with the terrorists. Senator Kerry emphasized his heroic service as commander of a "swift boat" (a Navy vessel used in counterinsurgency operations) on the Mekong River during the Vietnam War. Indeed, upon accepting the Democratic nomination at the party's national convention in 2004, Kerry approached the podium, stood at attention, and saluted the delegates (and, of course the television cameras) declaring, "I'm John Kerry, and I'm reporting for duty." He then went on to state, "I defended this country as a young man and I will defend it as president" (Wilkinson, 2004). This decision to wrap himself in the flag by emphasizing his military service seemed intended to encourage voters to contrast his heroic active-duty service in Vietnam with President Bush's in the Texas National Guard, service, it was suspected, that Bush had in fact not completed (Bush fell short on duty, 2004; Wilkinson, 2004).

The contrasting service records of President Bush and Senator Kerry sparked a huge public controversy during the campaign. A quasi-independent GOP activist group that called itself the Swift Boat Veterans for Truth produced a series of television ads aimed at discrediting Senator Kerry's war record and undermining his achievements in Vietnam. Kerry sought to rehabilitate his image by appearing on stage with several of the men who served with him on his boat (Zernike, 2006). Meanwhile, CBS News ran a series of stories claiming to have found definitive documents that President Bush did not report to duty as a National Guard officer as required. When the documents proved to have been forged, the controversy further heated up, ultimately ending in demands that Dan Rather, the long-serving anchor of the network's nightly news program, step down (Kurtz, 2004).* The fact that the

---

* The Swift Boat Veterans for Truth and their impact on the 2004 campaign will be discussed in greater detail in Chapter 10 on campaign funding.

nation's voters and the media would devote so much attention to refighting the battles of who served and how they served during the Vietnam War, which had ended almost thirty years earlier, certainly testifies to the power of narratives about character and image.

Redefining an Image

Although candidates often choose to focus on past events and historical narratives in defining their own and their opponents' images, there is also a continuing effort during a campaign at rehabilitating and "freshening" images. One of the most direct acknowledgments to this notion of "branding" a candidate, just as companies "brand" products, came from an advisor to former presidential candidate Steve Forbes. The publishing heir ran in the 1996 campaign on the issue of advocating a "flat tax," an income tax rate that would be the same for all taxpayers. Forbes proved to be an awkward and somewhat unattractive candidate whose message became somewhat monotonous. As a result Forbes never really connected with voters. When Forbes decided to run again in 2000, he hired William Eisner, the head of a Milwaukee advertising agency, to freshen his image. The goal was to remake public perceptions of Forbes so that he would be seen as a scintillating and witty man with the personality to sit in the Oval Office. Eisner declared, "We're trying to resuscitate brands all the time that lost their luster with consumers; we're doing the same with Steve. . . . The first, most important fact is having people see Steve in the position of president, which they have trouble seeing right now" (Berke, Fitting Forbes, 1999, p. 1). The image that Eisner tried to create for Forbes was of a wise businessman, a sage investor, a good listener, and, most important, an outsider. Clearly the goal was to turn Forbes's lack of experience in elected office into an advantage (Berke, Fitting Forbes, 1999).

If a candidate's advisor is willing to talk so openly about managing the image of a client, it seems only fair that the media should be allowed to criticize the efforts at image making. *New York Times* columnist and media pundit Frank Rich was brutal in his assessment of Forbes's efforts to refashion his image and offered a not-so-subtle dig at the superficiality of contemporary image-dominated campaigns:

> Surely, though, the most spectacular geek show is that of Steve Forbes, who has spent $60 million of his own money to act out his delusions on the public stage. No one will say the poignant truth about this

guy—that even if he were a better speaker, or less of a hypocrite (how can the billionaire owner of *Forbes* magazine inveigh repeatedly against the "media elites"?), there would still be the insurmountable problem of his giggly Peeping Tom grin and pop-eyed spectacles. The most virulent, if least acknowledged, bigotry in this country—far more widespread than sexism or racism and practiced by all genders and ethnic groups—is looksism. Even in the pre-HDTV era, no one is going to be elected president who doesn't meet the minimal physical standard required of a game-show host. (Rich, 2000, p. A29)

Sometimes candidates fail in their efforts to redefine their images. For example, in 1996 former governor and former secretary of education Lamar Alexander of Tennessee sought the Republican nomination for president. To distinguish himself from his opponents, he showed up at events and appeared in TV commercials wearing a plaid shirt. Soon he became known as the "plaid" candidate. Although it may have seemed like a good idea at the time, when Alexander again sought the Republican nomination in 2000, he abandoned his trademark plaid shirt in favor of a dark business suit. However, Alexander withdrew from the 2000 race following the Iowa straw poll and before a single vote had been cast. Upon withdrawing, he protested that the media never permitted him to overcome the image of a "loser" who could not be elected and as "used goods" because he was unable to freshen his image (Brownstein & Barabak, 1999).

Candidates' images are also influenced by "non-news" programs. When comedian Jay Leno teased Bill Clinton for his inexhaustible libido or Hillary Clinton for her supposed frigidity, his comments made those images stick in viewers' minds. Leno declared that Vice President Gore was so boring that "when he painted a self-portrait it was a still life" (Weinraub, 2000). Comedians had an especially good time with Vice President Dick Cheney after he accidentally shot and wounded a companion while on a quail-hunting trip. Jon Stewart and Stephen Colbert attract large audiences with their faux news programs on the cable network Comedy Central that subject candidates and elected officials to ridicule. Baumgartner and Morris (2006) found that those who were exposed to jokes about candidates George W. Bush and John Kerry on Stewart's *The Daily Show* were more likely to rate both candidates more negatively, even when the study controlled for partisanship and other demographic variables. They also found that the program's viewers were more cynical about politics than those who did not view such programs. What troubled these researchers even more was that the viewers of such programs may think they are getting genuine news. Respondents in this study who watched *The Daily Show* expressed more confidence in their understanding of politics than other television viewers. The researchers concluded that although some have argued that these programs are beneficial because they reach an otherwise inattentive public, they may also undermine democratic citizenship and further diminish support for our political institutions and elected officials.

The ability of such humor programs to define a candidate's image is terrifying to both candidates and their advisors. Dan Schnur, a campaign advisor to Senator John McCain in 2000, declared, "Their impact is incredible and it's growing. . . . During the campaign season you're often cowering at 11:30—what are these guys going to say? They often reflect what voters feel, and their observations have a tremendous effect on how voters view the candidates, much more so than the evening news shows" (cited in Weinraub, 2000, p. A16). Former vice president Dan Quayle never recovered from the fact that he was an intellectual lightweight and became the butt of jokes because he misspelled the word *potato* when visiting an elementary school. As we shall discuss in Chapter 8 on new communication technologies, the power of these comedic depictions is further enhanced now that viewers can quickly e-mail them to friends or post them on Web sites such as YouTube, thus dramatically expanding the size of the viewing audience.

Candidates sometimes face specific challenges when attempting to rehabilitate their images. For example, Senator Joe Biden (D—Delaware) had to drop out of the 1988 contest for the Democratic presidential nomination when it was revealed that he had plagiarized passages from a speech by British Labor Party leader Neil Kinnock. Further press investigations revealed that Biden had been found guilty of a serious plagiarism incident during his law school years and that he had exaggerated his academic achievements in speaking at a New Hampshire campaign event (Joseph Biden's plagiarism, 1998). The image of Biden as an intellectually dishonest and conniving politician seemed to persist in the public's mind. Nearly twenty years and many significant political achievements later, many people continued to define his image by their recollections of these events. Perhaps this public memory was reinforced in part by the fact that Biden's plagiarism was featured on university Web sites to serve as a warning to students about how a reputation for plagiarism could devastate a person's long-term career goals (Harvey, 2003). When Biden announced that he intended to seek the Democratic presidential nomination again in the 2008 elections, the stories about his past resurfaced. Type the words *Biden* and *plagiarism* into a Web search engine, and you will see the degree to which it may be difficult for him to ever alter this public image.

President George W. Bush has also faced the challenge of trying to alter his public image—in his case the perception that he is not especially bright or intellectually curious. A March 2006 poll conducted by the independent Pew Research Center found that the three most frequently mentioned adjectives that came to people's minds when they were asked to describe the president were "incompetent," "idiot," and "liar" (Bush approval falls, 2006). Even conservatives in the media began to question the president's mental agility. MSNBC's conservative TV talk show pundit Rick Scarborough did a ten-minute segment on the president's lack of intelligence, accompanied by graphics on the bottom of the screen that asked, "IS BUSH AN IDIOT?" (caps in original text). Attempting to alter this perception, the White House press office launched a campaign to depict the president as a voracious reader. Press Secretary Tony Snow released President Bush's summer reading list, which included Albert Camus's existentialist novel *The Stranger*. Other White House aides claimed that the president was in a book-reading competition with his advisor Karl Rove and that the president was currently in the lead, having read sixty books to date, ten more than Rove (Benen, 2006). The White House Press Office further sought to bolster the impression that the president was a serious man of letters by releasing to C-SPAN a list of more than two dozen titles that Bush had recently finished. The list included works on the great flu epidemic of 1918, studies of the lives of Islamic women, several books on baseball, and the Shakespearean classics *Macbeth* and *Hamlet* (Benen, 2006).

Political Images and Personal Images

Candidate images fall into two broad categories. First is the candidate's political image, which might include the candidate's identification with a particular party, discernible ideological commitments, positions on issues, and linkages to other known political figures or interest groups. The second category is the candidate's personal image. Candidates possess a set of traits and characteristics such as age, intellectual abilities, speaking style, and so on that become known to voters (Husson,

Stephen, Harrison, & Fehr, 1988). Candidate images are thus evaluations that link together ideological, value, appearance, and job performance dimensions, all interacting with each voter's own characteristics
and predispositions (Kaid & Chanslor, 1995).

Senator Biden's image problems are further magnified by the fact
that even though different voters place different emphasis on particular
characteristics of candidate image, research suggests that voters are
especially interested in the issue of trust and in the honesty of the candidate. Scott Keeler (1987) reported that trust was the most important
predictor of how well voters liked a candidate. It may well be that most
people pride themselves on being fairly good judges of character, and
consequently evaluations of trust become the classic example of Popkin's "low information rationality." This finding is also consistent with
Walter Fisher's (1987) "narrative paradigm," which suggested that
issues of character consistency shaped people's evaluations of competing stories. Noting that trust was even more important to voters who
reported obtaining most of their political information from television
than it was for the general population, Keeler (1987) theorized that television may enable voters to feel especially close to the candidates and
thus may seem uniquely helpful to them in their search for a candidate
whom they feel they can trust.

President Bush's image problem is similarly difficult to refute
because even though the White House was eager to convince the public that the president was knowledgeable, well-read, and smart, TV
comedians such as Jay Leno, David Letterman, Conan O'Brien, and
Jon Stewart openly ridiculed both the book lists and the transparent
public relations campaign. Attempts at image manipulation may do little to alter a deeply and firmly rooted public perception, especially
when that impression is reinforced by the media.

During the 2008 presidential campaign, Senator Hillary Clinton
was intent on making efforts to "soften" her image, perhaps to reduce
the negative public perceptions mentioned earlier (Lambro, 2006). Campaign commercials filmed her in softly lit domestic settings, and news
photographers took pictures of her shopping with daughter Chelsea. In
speeches she frequently referred to her role as a mother, and she even
changed her wardrobe to appear more feminine (Sherwell, 2007). The
wardrobe change was noticed by the fashion police and prompted an
intense public discussion about whether it was appropriate for a female
presidential candidate to reveal a bit of cleavage. Robin Givhan (2007),
the fashion columnist for the *Washington Post*, set off the controversy
when she wrote the following:

With Clinton, there was the sense that you were catching a surreptitious glimpse at something private. You were intruding—being a voyeur. Showing cleavage is a request to be engaged in a particular way. It doesn't necessarily mean that a woman is asking to be objectified, but it does suggest a certain confidence and physical ease. It means that a woman is content being perceived as a sexual person in addition to being seen as someone who is intelligent, authoritative, witty, and whatever else might define her personality. It also means that she feels that all those other characteristics are so apparent and undeniable that they will not be overshadowed. (p. C01)

The column produced a firestorm of protest about gender, femininity, and politics. Deborah Howell (2007, p. B06), the ombudsman for the *Washington Post*, acknowledged that she received thousands of letters and phone calls about the column, with many calling the column "sexist and demeaning of both women and the seriousness of issues needing to be addressed." The Clinton campaign was reported to be upset by the column, so upset that they used it as a basis for a fundraising letter directed to core supporters (Howell, 2007, p. B06). The letter called the column "insulting to every woman who has ever tried to be taken seriously in a business meeting." The letter urged readers to "take a stand against this kind of coarseness and pettiness" (cited by Howell, 2007, p. B06). For what it is worth, the fashion columnist defended her original column by noting that she had frequently criticized the hairstyles and clothing choices made by male candidates as well (Howell, 2007).

Senator Clinton's presidential candidacy demonstrated sharp gender differences. A New York Times/CBS Poll conducted during the summer of 2007 suggested that "among all registered voters, 46 percent of women have a favorable view of Mrs. Clinton, while 33 percent have an unfavorable view. The rest are undecided. The numbers are opposite for men, with 34 percent having a positive view of her and 47 percent holding a negative one" (Seelye, 2007). These differences may have been due to the power of her political image, since studies suggest that women and men evaluate images differently (Harrison, Stephen, Husson, & Fehr, 1991). Senator Clinton's surprising win in the New Hampshire primary provided further evidence of the power of gender differences in voting behavior.

Roberts (1981) reported that liking or disliking a particular candidate, as indicated by a measure of trustworthiness, seemed to precede the adoption of the candidate's stance on specific issues. This finding suggests that candidates who earn the voters' trust can use that positive image to persuade voters to accept their positions on issues. Hellweg (1979) asked voters to identify the characteristics of an ideal political candidate. She reported that honesty, which is closely related to the ability to trust the candidate, was the most important factor. This finding was confirmed by another study that surveyed voters across presidential elections from 1988 to 2000. That study found that trust and the willingness to talk about those issues deemed most important to the respondent were the key factors in identifying "ideal" traits for candidates (Trent et al., 2001).

Kendall and Paine (1995) suggested that voters may judge candidates in two stages: first the issues of trust and character (looking, for example, at a candidate's sincerity, honesty, and caring qualities) and then the candidate's competence and effectiveness. This view is consistent with that expressed by Tannenbaum, Greenberg, and Silverman (1962), who argued that voters seek candidates who are wise, fair, experienced, strong, active, deep, and calm. The three adjectives that emerged most frequently when respondents were asked to identify desired traits in presidential candidates were *honesty*, *intelligence*, and *independence*.

Appearance and Nonverbal Behaviors

Asserting that voters seem to care most about integrity and competence is useful, but it does not explain how they determine who can be trusted or who is competent. With regard to trust and integrity, research suggests that voters are very sensitive to a candidate's physical appearance. For example, studies demonstrate that subjects are very responsive to how often political candidates smile. Likewise, candidates are rewarded for their wit and their ability to demonstrate grace and charm. Voters respond much more favorably to candidates who have a sense of humor and who can laugh at themselves, but they tend to dislike candidates whose wit is too sarcastic or biting (Ostrom & Simon, 1989). Many pundits claimed that in the 1996 campaign Senator Dole's wit was too abrasive and his demeanor too sour compared to President Clinton's (Fineman, 1996). During the 2000 campaign, Vice President Gore sought to overcome his image as a bore by using ample amounts of self-deprecating humor. Another interesting move by the Gore campaign was the lingering kiss he shared with his wife during the Democratic convention. Any man who would display such public emotion for his wife in front of the media was clearly not lacking in passion. It was also a sign that unlike his predecessor in office, this was a man who was unlikely to violate his marriage vows.

Voters also appear to be sensitive to a candidate's nonverbal behaviors. A candidate who has shadowy or furtive eyes, for example, may send cues that cause viewers to judge him or her as less than honest. Likewise, someone who perspires heavily, mops his or her brow, has poor posture, or makes inappropriate gestures or head nods might create a poor self-image (Friedman, Mertz, & DiMatteo, 1980). President Richard Nixon, for example, was troubled throughout his career by his thick growth of beard (even though he is said to have shaved twice a day) and by the fact that his upper lip frequently glistened with perspiration when he spoke on television. Caricatures of President Jimmy Carter emphasized his overly toothy grin, while President George W. Bush was often criticized for his inability to control his smirk.

Selecting different photographs of the same person has been shown to influence the candidate's image. Rosenberg and McCafferty (1987) found that a candidate's perceived fitness for public office, competence, trustworthiness, and likability could be influenced by different presentations of the candidate's appearance. It is common practice for rival campaigns to select especially unflattering photographs of the opposing candidate for use in their own advertising appeals. During the 1996 campaign, for example, Dole ads often showed photographs of President Clinton that made him appear to be conniving and untrustworthy. In the 2000 campaign for mayor of Los Angeles, city attorney James Hahn defeated Hispanic candidate Antonio Villaraigosa with the help of a television ad that used a grainy, darkened black-and-white photograph of the swarthy, dark-skinned Villaraigosa juxtaposed with images of a graffiti-covered wall, a crack cocaine pipe, and other assorted drug paraphernalia while a narrator questioned whether Los Angeles could trust Villaraigosa. The ad reminded voters of the growth in the number of illegal Hispanic immigrants in Los Angeles and also of the link between Hispanics and youth gangs (Hollihan, 2006; York, 2001).

Candidates may damage their images through simple missteps or awkward moments that could happen to anyone. President Gerald Ford was perhaps one of our nation's most fit and active officeholders, yet his public image was that he was clumsy and perhaps not very smart (Roberts, 1981). Ford had the misfortune of slipping in full view of the television cameras when deplaning from *Air Force One*. His image as a bumbler was further fixed in the public mind when the comedian Chevy Chase impersonated him on the popular television program *Saturday Night Live*. Ford's own press secretary, Ron Nessen, even appeared on the program and participated in skits poking fun at his boss

(Gold, 1978). During the 1988 presidential campaign, Democratic candidate Michael Dukakis, attempting to show that he was not "soft on defense," appeared in videotaped footage wearing an army helmet and riding in a tank. The attempt backfired when Bush campaign ads played the tape to mock Dukakis for trying to appear like a warrior when he was actually soft on support for national defense. A few years later, President George H. W. Bush found that his image as a smooth, experienced, and polished statesman was damaged when he became ill at a formal state dinner in Japan and vomited on the shoes of his host, an image that was replayed over and over again on the nightly news.

Age

Evidence suggests that voters may be keenly sensitive to a candidate's age as an important dimension of political image. Age especially matters if one candidate is particularly young or old, or if the age gap is especially large. Perhaps the most dramatic moment in a contemporary campaign when age became an issue was in the contest between President Ronald Reagan and former Vice President Walter Mondale in 1984. In his second televised debate with Mondale, Reagan was asked this question:

> "Mr. President, I want to raise an issue that I think has been lurking out there for two or three weeks and cast it specifically in national security terms. You already are the oldest president in history, and some of your staff say you were tired after your most recent encounter with Mr. Mondale. I recall, yet, that President Kennedy . . . had to go for days on end with very little sleep during the Cuban missile crisis. Is there any doubt in your mind that you would be able to function under such circumstances?"
>
> [Reagan replied] "Not at all, Mr. Trewhitt. And I want you to know that also I will not make age an issue in this campaign. I am not going to exploit, for political purposes, my opponent's youth and inexperience." (Cited in Germond, 1999, p. 163)

Reagan's quick and witty retort to the question about his age, even though it had no doubt been scripted in advance of the debate, suggested that he was still in command of his faculties. The statement also became the sound bite that was rebroadcast in every radio and television news story about the debate. The comment put to rest the age issue and any doubts that Reagan would be reelected to a second term (Germond, 1999). Many years later, of course, President Reagan was diagnosed with Alzheimer's disease, and many stories and accounts offered by those close to him acknowledged that his mental decline was evident even early in his first term. Indeed, Reeves (2005) argues that there is significant evidence that Reagan began losing ground after the assassination attempt in 1981, during the first year of his presidency, and that the intellectual decline continued each year. Near the end of Reagan's second term in 1988, Reeves provides evidence that there might have been a truly frightening deterioration in the president's mental health:

> Office gossip about the President's drifting attention and little naps at big meetings was merging into eyewitness accounts of decline in his mental capacity. One involved a British television crew invited into the Oval Office for a short question-and-answer session on Margaret Thatcher's long service as Prime Minister. The President was already wearing a small microphone on his lapel, and the British technicians heard the conversation between a young press assistant and Reagan. The young man was telling the 77-year-old President where he was: "You're in the Oval Office, Mr. President. These people are British and they will ask you for a short comment about Prime Minister Thatcher." (p. 452)

The issue of age also emerged as a factor in the 1996 presidential contest between Clinton and Dole because the age gap between two candidates had never been greater and because both men seemed to reflect so thoroughly the experiences and values of their own generations — Dole as a decorated World War II veteran and Clinton as a pot-smoking baby boomer and member of the anti–Vietnam War student movement. To counter images of Clinton as too youthful and inexperienced to be the commander in chief, his campaign emphasized his achievements as a statesman and made heavy use of photographs in which he appeared with other world leaders. Clinton even brought along a Hollywood producer on his Middle East tour to shoot video footage for later use in political spot advertisements (Broder, 1996). To counter images that he was "old, tired, and worn-out," the Dole campaign made heavy use of photographs showing the trim 72-year-old senator working out on his treadmill (Berke, Is age-bashing, 1996). It is not clear that the photographs were all that helpful to Senator Dole, however, because they showed him doing his workout in a white dress shirt! Schubert (1988) suggested that voters are aware that a candidate's age might affect his or her leadership style. Consequently, voters seeking a more active president might be inclined to seek a younger candidate, whereas voters seeking a less active role for the commander in chief might be more inclined to prefer an older and more mature leader.

Charisma

The term *charisma* is frequently tossed about in discussions of candidate image. Although most people would have difficulty defining the term or identifying precisely what attributes made a candidate charismatic, scholars generally agree that charisma is strongly associated with the ability to project confidence, enthusiasm, optimism, goal-orientation, inspirational leadership, and compassion (Bligh, Kohles, & Pillai, 2005; Emrich, Brower, Feldman, & Garland, 2001; Pillai, Williams, Lowe, & Jung, 2003; Shamir, 1994). It is not enough for candidates to merely exhibit such traits; they must be perceived by audiences as appropriate given the demands of the current context or situation (Merolla, Ramos, & Zechmeister, 2007). In short, charisma exists when charismatic leaders convince others to follow and trust them (Pillai & Williams, 1988).

A sense of charisma may be projected in a candidate's image, most often through the communication of campaign discourse. A charismatic candidate may also be one who conveys a warm and friendly image, who seems genuine and personable, who is comfortable speaking, and who has the capacity to speak from his or her heart—or at least can make us so believe (Friedman, Mertz, & Dimatteo, 1980). Even though the ability to speak without notes or to read easily from a teleprompter may not be the litmus test of political competence or integrity, for many voters this capacity is an identifiable leadership quality consistent with the very public nature of electoral politics.

Hart (1999, p. 27) has argued that one of the most significant implications of politics in the age of television is that the medium succeeds in bringing "persons of great magnitude into our own very modest living rooms. They share themselves with us, persons whom they have never met, persons whom they will never meet." Television thus creates an intimacy among candidates and voters that favors the development of image or personality politics. Hart's concern is that this devotion to the candidates causes voters to become sentimentally attached to certain images and increases the likelihood that political cynicism will be provoked when the candidates disappoint us, as they almost inevitably will in due time.

Schram (1991) argued that in this electronic age, voters often analyze candidate images in a futile attempt to find out what real substance may exist below the polished public surface. He referred to this as the search for the nonexistent "real leader." Schram claimed that voters seem to be aware that campaigns have become phony and filled with gimmicks, and in response they search for the real thing, the genuine candidate underneath the polished surface. In response, campaigns emphasize the vague concept of leadership, but leadership is difficult to express in concrete terms, thus resulting in even more artificial images that seek to convey leadership skills. Schram cited political debates as an example. The debates were intended to give candidates a forum to discuss complex policy issues, but instead they have become important primarily because they allow candidates to craft and show their presidential images, their "real character," their sense of humor, and their grace under pressure (Schram, 1991).

THE POWER OF PUBLIC DISCOURSE

The most powerful tool that political candidates have to help shape their public images and to express their views is their ability to speak directly to the public. Most candidates have difficulty being heard. Senators, for example, may speak on the floor of the Senate almost at will, but they typically speak to an almost empty chamber, and seldom are their remarks televised. For the most part, they are speaking only to have their remarks printed in the *Congressional Record*, which is seldom if ever read by most ordinary citizens. Likewise, mayors, governors, city council members, school board members, and other public officials may find it difficult to draw an audience for their speeches. I worked on a campaign on behalf of a candidate for mayor of Los Angeles, America's second largest city, but during the campaign he often spoke to audiences of fewer than two dozen people, and his speeches were seldom given any significant attention by the local news media. One of the most powerful political figures in the United States, for example, is the Speaker of the House of Representatives. Should both the president and vice president die in office, the Speaker of the House would assume the presidency, yet when Representative Nancy Pelosi was named the first female Speaker of the House, 67 percent of respondents polled in a survey reported that they did not know enough about her to express an opinion (Somin, 2006). Representative Pelosi should not feel too bad about this lack of public recognition; her predecessor, Dennis Hastert, held the same position for the previous eight years, and 55 percent reported that they had no opinion about him either (Somin, 2006). Because it is unlikely that the major television networks would grant the Speaker free air time to make a significant public speech, it is also unlikely that the Speaker will have much opportunity to speak directly to the public.

The power of public discourse is readily apparent, however, when one examines the opportunities for rhetoric that are accorded to the president and often to those who are candidates for that office. Whenever significant public events occur, the media and the public look to the president for comments and opinions. When Israeli troops attack terrorist strongholds in Lebanon, the president is asked to comment. When an air traffic controller is identified as being at least partially responsible for the crash of a commercial jetliner in Lexington, Kentucky, the president is asked for his opinion. Even the celebration of Mother's Day becomes a topic for the president to comment on, as his memories of his mother contribute to our collective experience in honoring our own mothers (Clinton, 1996).

As Hart (1987, p. 46) observed, "Rhetoric may now be the primary means of personal assertion, the primary means of performing the act of presidential leadership." Hart noted that it is through their speeches that presidents address important issues, define the terms in public debates, and lead and shape public opinion. Presidents today are speaking more often than before (although giving far fewer press conferences where they can be subjected to tough questions from the national press corps), and they are speaking before increasingly diverse audiences on very diverse topics, both great and small (Hart, 1987, pp. 7–14). As Hart argued:

> Clearly, presidents no longer use speech merely to get elected. Instead, they increasingly balance their workday on the fulcrum of public discourse, discourse both weighty and silly, and many Americans have come to believe that government occurs only when their presidents talk to them. What used to be a natural "seam" between election and nonelection years no longer exists. Depending upon one's perspective, the reelection campaign never begins or it never ends. Presidents are out among us constantly. (p. 15)

As we have entered the electronic media age, the presidency has become more important as a rhetorical office, and the president has increasingly become our chief spokesperson and the symbolic advocate for our nation's political system and our way of life. Effective rhetorical leadership means utilizing the power of public speaking to craft a favorable public image. This is, of course, easier said than done. A candidate's accent, inflection, delivery skills, gestures, and eye contact can all have a favorable or unfavorable impact on potential voters (Harden, 1996). A southern accent, a Boston accent, or a foreign accent, for example, will appeal to some voters and likely turn off others. Certainly some candidates, and indeed some of our recently elected presidents, have been more rhetorically skilled than others. Few, for example, would claim that President George W. Bush is an especially effective speaker; in fact, he has often been the subject of very rude jokes because of his tendency to mangle the English language. Yet, for many people, President Bush does effectively communicate his sincerity and good nature. What is suggested therefore is that—as mentioned in the discussion of charisma—it is not just that candidates possess certain traits or abilities, but it is also how they are perceived by audiences, given the demands of the current situation. Likewise, it is not just how a message is packaged or delivered that is important to voters; it is the message itself and whether the content of that message resonates with voters' interests and concerns.

The challenge to the notion of image is that professional speechwriters can and do draft most of the texts that professional politicians deliver, and speech coaches and consultants work with the candidates to polish and improve their delivery. As Hart (1987, p. 212) lamented, "Presidential speech-making—perhaps presidential communication in general—has now become a tool of barter rather than a means of informing and challenging the citizenry." Many voters and campaign consultants alike see the demand for presidential leadership as a demand for presidential symbol making and for the image of the president as a primary actor and a heroic persona in our political dramas.

CHAPTER 5

How the News Media Shape
Political Campaigns

Communities are born out of common experiences, and one important dimension of common experience is a shared understanding of the world. This understanding is shaped, in part, from shared sources of news about public events. News, both local and international, gives us a sense of ourselves and our world. Conversations give us a sense of where we have been and where we seem to be going, and "by marking and legitimizing the conversational commons, journalism contributes to communication links among people, groups, and places that were previously disconnected" (Anderson, Dardenne, & Killenberg, 1994, pp. 10, 11). This view of the role of the press suggests that it actively "forms" and does not merely "inform" an engaged public capable of democratic participation (Grimes, 1999, p. 5). News organizations "not only serve but create their communities by providing raw materials for collective social and political life" (Fuller, 1996, p. 228).

As the political scientist W. Lance Bennett (2005, p. 3) observed, "Information is so basic to democratic government that it is easy to take for granted. Yet, without a free flow of accurate, timely, and useful information, people cannot participate effectively." Thus, access to reliable sources of information is essential to democratic life. The news not only informs but also comforts by affording us the means to preserve our sense of identity and to celebrate our culture (see Anderson, Dardenne, & Killenberg, 1994, p. 164; Carey, 1975). News both reflects and orders the rituals of ordinary life; it unites us in "fellowship and commonality" (Carey, 2002, pp. 18–19). As we discussed in Chapter 3, the news media also play an important role by helping to socialize citizens into the political system.

In a democratic society, the media must accomplish more than simply serving as a conduit of information. Raw information is made useful when citizens can understand it, structure it, transform it, and use it as a resource in their interactions with other citizens. Without access to basic facts and a framework for understanding how these facts fit together, people begin to feel civically isolated from one another (Schmuhl, 1998). They may begin to nurse personal grievances and prejudices whether or not these feelings are well founded. Information is useful when it enriches and sustains effective, deliberative decision making. The distinguished American philosopher and educator John Dewey argued the following (cited in Anderson, Dardenne, & Killenberg, 1994):

> Systematic and continuous inquiry into all the conditions which affect association and their dissemination in print is a precondition of the creation of a true public. But it and its results are but tools after all. Their final actuality is accomplished in face-to-face relationships by means of direct give and take. Logic in its fulfillment recurs to the primitive sense of the word: dialogue. Ideas which are not communicated, shared, and reborn in expression are but soliloquy, and soliloquy is but broken and imperfect thought. (p. 21)

The press, Dewey declared, must not only be free, but it must participate in the creation of a broad social conversation by trusting and creating its own constituent audiences. He suggested an agrarian analogy: "Dissemination is something other than scattering at large. Seeds are sown, not by virtue of being thrown out at random, but by being so distributed as to take root and have a chance of growth" (cited in Anderson, Dardenne, & Killenberg, 1994, p. 22). What is grown by this careful planting of information and ideas? The answer is, an articulate and organized populace that is capable of self-government and aware of its members' mutual interest and interdependence. Jurgen Habermas, the German philosopher and social critic, argued that a free press provides the information for the reflexive circulation of public opinion and creates the foundation for a vibrant public sphere (Habermas, 1991).

The news media thus play a vital role in politics, because the news media shape the perceptions that are pieced together to form the social reality that motivates political action. As Graber (1993, p. 292) declared, "Media do more than depict the political environment; they *are* the political environment. Because direct contact with political actors and situations is limited, media images define people and situations for nearly all participants in the political process."

Although the standard dictum of the beat reporter is an emphasis on ferreting out and reporting the facts, the actual business of reporting is more complex than merely providing information. As Carey (1989, p. 21) observed, "News is not information but drama. It does not describe the world but portrays an arena of dramatic focus and action." The drama of news provides us a glimpse into the world beyond our own immediate experience. The news is itself a construction of reality, however, as Fisher (1970) noted:

> Although its aim is to express a reliable guide to belief and action for one's daily needs, it ultimately is a fiction, since its advice is not, in the final analysis, susceptible of empirical verification. The fiction is not hypothetical; its author wants and intends that it be accepted as the true and right way of conceiving of a matter; and if he [sic] is successful, his fiction becomes one of those by which men [and women] live. (p. 132)

The "real fictions" constructed by reporters, and salable to editors, are thus communicated to those using the media, who in turn draw upon these dramatic accounts to form their own view of the world and of the primary actors on the public stage.

THE PRIMARY SOURCES OF POLITICAL NEWS

Citizens gain access to political news from a variety of different sources, including newspapers, news magazines, television, radio, and the Internet. In this section we will briefly consider each of these sources.

Newspapers

There are approximately 1,500 daily newspapers in the United States, with an estimated combined circulation of 57 million readers (Newspaper Association of America, 2006). Newspapers provide the most thorough reporting of local news stories, including political stories, of any news source. For national political news, the most thorough, comprehensive, and substantive political information regarding political campaigns, political issues, and public policies is available to readers of comprehensive large city daily newspapers. The nation's leading papers—the *New York Times, Washington Post,* and *Los Angeles Times*—assign several reporters to cover political campaigns, and the volume and quality of their coverage are impressive. Much of the work of these reporters is shared with other media outlets through their news services (although many stories are exclusives to the major newspapers, and few smaller newspapers print as many political stories as do the three big dailies). In addition, the wire services—the Associated Press and Reuters—assign reporters to cover politics, and their stories are shared with subscribing media outlets. Finally, a few other strong regional newspapers—for example, the *Chicago Tribune*, *Boston Globe*, *Atlanta Constitution*, *Baltimore Sun*, and *Dallas Morning News*, to name just a few—assign their own reporters to cover political campaigns, usually during their own state primaries or during the final days before a general election.

The volume of political or governmental coverage in daily newspapers is impressive. Peer and Nesbitt (2004) reported that 24.4 percent of weekday news coverage and 21.8 percent of Sunday news coverage focused on politics. Furthermore, they reported that approximately 45 percent of front-page news stories concerned politics.* Another content analysis study, however, suggested that the volume of governmental and political news had slightly fallen in recent years, while there was a slight increase in the amount of soft-news or lifestyle coverage. This same study also reported that large-circulation newspapers provided more political and governmental news coverage than did smaller local papers (State of the news media, 2004). This finding confirms what earlier scholars had reported. For example, Stempel (1994, p. 42), in a study of the 1988 presidential campaign, found that the *Washington Post* ran 695 stories and more than 450,000 words on the campaign. He also noted that the *Baltimore Sun*, *Los Angeles Times*, and *New York Times* each had more than 500 stories and 300,000 words about the campaign between September 5 and November 7, 1988. To achieve this level of coverage, the *Post* averaged more than ten stories a day and the other papers more than seven stories a day. Smaller-circulation newspapers no doubt may run fewer and shorter stories because they have a smaller news hole (they can sell fewer display ads), but nonetheless, a significant amount of political news coverage appears in daily newspapers.

Studies suggest that the percentage of Americans who claimed to read the newspaper every day has been dropping since the late 1940s and the advent of television. In 1950, there were 1.23 newspapers sold per household (thus indicating that many households purchased more than one each day). By 1990, only 67 percent of households purchased a newspaper each day. By 2000, the number had fallen to 53 percent (State of the news media, 2004). Today, approximately 54 percent of

---

* Peer and Nesbitt (2004) also noted that the page 1 stories tended to be substantive, with an average length of 87 square inches and that 86 percent of these stories also included a jump to an inside page.

Americans read a daily newspaper, and approximately 62 percent read a newspaper on Sundays. As a result of declining circulation, the number of daily newspapers has also declined, dropping almost 1 percent each year for the past two decades (Kovach, Rosenstiel, & Mitchell, 2006). Most of the decline in the number of newspapers has been in the afternoon dailies, perhaps as a result of changed reading and commuting habits.

The newspaper circulation declines have also led many newspapers, large and small, to sharply reduce their reporting staffs. As these staff reductions have taken place, they have affected the types of stories likely to be reported. Reporters may have less time to investigate complex stories about public policy and political issues and may instead be drawn to stories that are somewhat easier to research and that may gather bigger headlines. Thus, crime, scandals, and entertainment stories are crowding more substantive political stories out of many daily newspapers (Klinenberg, 2005).

To understand the full impact of the dramatic drop in newspaper readership, we must also consider who constitutes today's newspaper audience. Studies suggest that readership is declining in every age bracket with the exception of those over age 65, that few immigrants are reading newspapers, and that readership is dropping across all education levels. Furthermore, the deepest drops are among young people aged 18 to 24, where only 40 percent claim to read a daily newspaper and 48 percent read a Sunday newspaper (State of the news media, 2004). Certainly, there is some evidence that more Americans, and especially more young Americans, are reading news online (a topic we will explore more deeply in Chapter 8), but nonetheless, there is also reason to believe that that online news experience may be less information rich, at least with regard to political news, than the daily newspaper (Raine, Cornfield, & Horrigan, 2005).

Exposure to political news coverage in a daily newspaper does not necessarily equate with actually reading these stories. Many newspaper readers skip over the political stories and turn directly to the sections that focus on sports, entertainment, local news, or the classified ads. More than 40 percent of newspaper readers admit that they usually do not read the entire paper (Ansolabehere, Behr, & Iyengar, 1993). Interest in political news coverage also seems to be diminishing. For example, in a 2006 poll conducted by the Pew Research Center, only 17 percent of respondents said they follow news about political figures and events in Washington, DC, down from 24 percent two years earlier. The decline occurred across the political spectrum, with the exception of self-declared liberal Democrats. Approximately 34 percent of liberals said that they followed political news from the nation's capital very closely. This figure represented no change from 2004 and also was a much higher percentage than for any other political group (Online papers modestly boost, 2006).

News Magazines

Americans also have access to extensive political information from the three major weekly news magazines. *Time, Newsweek,* and *U.S. News & World Report* boast a combined circulation of approximately 9.5 million, but this figure represents a fairly steep decline in readership over almost two decades (State of the news media, 2006). The circulation declines have negatively affected reporting budgets at the news magazines as well. To attract new readers, the news magazines have sought to broaden their focus with more features on health, new technologies, and entertainment, but nonetheless, the quality of political reporting in these news weeklies continues to be reasonably impressive. The nature of the coverage in all three magazines is similar. All offer fairly long and descriptive summaries of the events in political campaigns, and they all come out with new editions on Mondays. Often these magazines can have an especially important agenda-setting effect. For example, in October 2006, *Newsweek* featured a cover story and a large excerpt from the noted *Washington Post* reporter Bob Woodward's book *State of Denial: Bush at War, Part III* (2006). The book was sharply critical of the Bush administration's handling of the war in Iraq. The *Newsweek* article helped not only drive up sales of the book but also ensured that the book received sustained public discussion in other outlets.

Perhaps the greatest power of these news magazines is not the content of their stories but the impact of their decisions regarding which candidates they will feature on their front covers. A favorable cover photo (one that does not portray a candidate as tired, haggard, old, worried, etc.) can have a dramatic impact on the candidate's viability and credibility. Research suggests that the covers are the most memorable part of any issues when readers are surveyed (Scott & Sieber, 1992). One can imagine how pleased Senator Barack Obama (D—Illinois) must have been when he was pictured on the October 23, 2006, cover of *Time* with the caption "The Next President." The late Democratic political consultant Bob Squier (cited in Colford, 1996, p. A20) once declared that "getting on the covers of these magazines is like winning a primary" because it gives a candidate instant credibility.

Television

Despite the depth, variety, and wealth of political campaign information available through daily newspapers and news magazines, most people report that they get the bulk of their political news from television. In a sense, this is not surprising. Watching television now takes up more of the typical American's waking hours than almost any other activity, including interpersonal communication. A Nielsen Media survey reported that in 2006 Americans, on average, spent four hours and thirty-five minutes each day watching television, which represented an increase of 10 percent over the past four years (cited in Medved, 2006). The same study reported that "for the first time, the average American home now contains more television sets than people. The typical household accommodates only 2.55 people but 2.73 televisions. An astonishing 50 percent of all homes boast three or more TVs, and only 19 percent contain just one. In 1975, by contrast, 57 percent of households owned only one television, and only 11 percent contained three or more." Most television viewers are not spending their many hours in front of their sets watching political news programs, of course, but the estimated audience for the ABC, CBS, and NBC nightly newscasts is some 27 million people, a significant number but nonetheless a significantly smaller audience than it was only a decade earlier (State of the news media, 2006). One recent study claimed that network TV news has lost half of its audience over the past twenty years, and the current average age of the network TV news audience is 60. Television news skews more toward older viewers than any other segment of television programming (State of the news media, 2006). This skewing toward elderly viewers is clearly revealed in the advertising that accompanies news programs, which typically includes such products as prescription drugs (especially for sexual impotence, high cholesterol, arthritis, incontinence, and something called "restless leg syndrome").

More respondents claim to watch their local TV news than the national news programs. Although the audience size for local TV news has dropped slightly for early-morning and early-evening news programs (there is speculation that changing commuting patterns likely mean that people leave home earlier for work and get home later in the evening), the audience for late-night news (in the 10 and 11 P.M. time-slots) is either remaining stable or perhaps even growing slightly (State of the news media, 2006). What is less clear, however, is how much actual political news content these viewers are getting. Content studies of local TV news suggest that these programs are often filled with stories about crime, lifestyle features, sports, and weather but offer scant coverage of political campaigns or issues. Crime stories constituted 42 percent of coverage, whereas government and elections coverage accounted for only 11 percent of local news stories in 2005 (State of the news media, 2006). An even more detailed glimpse at local TV news coverage was available for 2002. The communication scholar Martin Kaplan (2003) conducted a content analysis study of more than 10,000 local TV news broadcasts and reported that only 44 percent contained any campaign coverage whatsoever, and that most stories that did air were played during the final two weeks of the campaign. Research has also suggested that local TV newscasts offer especially brief coverage of state, city, or local politics. Kaplan (2003) reported that state and local politics was the subject of only 14 percent of all campaign stories on local news. Kiolbassa (1996) found that even local TV stations focused on presidential campaigns rather than on state, city, or local political candidates or issues.

Local newspapers do a much better job of providing information on political candidates and issues, but such newspapers may rely heavily on national news syndicates for their national news, and they may have a subtle bias in favor of regional economic growth that can shape their coverage on local stories. Because a local newspaper is frequently identified with the city, it is understandable that reporters and editors may be tempted to view the growth of the city in positive terms (Perloff, 1998; Schudson, 1978; Schudson, 2003).

Thus, although it is clear that newspapers provide more detailed and extensive news coverage of politics, television news programs seem to be more appealing to viewers. Television news programs may appeal to viewers because they ask so little of them. Many television viewers are no doubt only partially tuned in to the broadcasts. The news serves as a background while they prepare or consume meals, tend to household chores, read, or engage in other pastimes. Television does not require careful or complete attention. It does not challenge viewers by introducing them to very many difficult words or complex analysis of issues. Instead, television news provides viewers with dramatic and intimate images of candidates and political events. Indeed, the intimacy of candidate images may be one of the greatest advantages that television news has for many viewers. Television permits viewers to glimpse candidates in action-oriented scenes that help them develop feelings and attitudes regarding their leadership potential, trustworthiness, and warmth (Pfau, Diedrich, Larson, & Van Winkle, 1995).

Television news is essentially a headline service, and it does not provide the thorough and detailed discussions of public issues that are common in the print media. The nightly network newscasts are thirty minutes long, but only about twenty-two minutes of this time is used for stories, with the remainder of the time going to commercials, introductions, and credits. A study of the 2000 presidential primary campaign conducted by the Alliance for Better Campaigns indicated that during the first two weeks of February, while the New Hampshire presidential primary was dominating the news, the networks devoted an average of less than five minutes per day to news of the presidential campaigns. Of the three major networks, NBC offered the most time to the campaign, ABC the second most, and CBS the least (By the numbers, 2000, p. A12). Most network coverage emphasizes brief stories with simplistic and episodic event-dominated reporting.

Anchor: "The candidate appeared at a rally today, where he had this to say:"
   [cut to videotape]
Candidate: "I am the candidate of change, and in November we are going to reclaim the White House for the American people!"
   [back to the anchor]

Critics of television news have labeled such coverage "sound bite" journalism. There is support for their criticisms. In a study of how television news reporters covered presidential campaigns from 1968 to 1988, Hallin (1992) discovered that the length of the average sound bite shrank dramatically—from more than forty seconds in 1968 to fewer than ten seconds in the 1980s. In a 2004 study of how local television news stations cover politics—significant because more people claim that they get their political information from local TV news than from any other source—the researchers found that "a typical half hour of news contained three minutes and eleven seconds of campaign coverage. An average campaign story was eighty-six seconds long, and an average candidate sound bite (which appeared in just 28 percent of the stories) was twelve seconds long" (Kaplan, Goldstein, & Hale, 2005, p. 3). This study also reported that local TV news broadcasts emphasized coverage of the presidential campaign (55 percent of the broadcasts analyzed mentioned the national race) at the expense of coverage of state or local politics (only 8 percent of the broadcasts mentioned any election race other than that for president). As a result, any citizen who in 2004 was depending on local TV news to be informed about races for the U.S. Senate, House of Representatives, gubernatorial campaigns, mayoral campaigns, and so on was very poorly served (Kaplan, Goldstein, & Hale, 2005, p. 3).

The nature of television coverage of politics has changed significantly over time. In the early days of television, election coverage was dominated by the words of the candidates themselves. Today, reporters view the candidates' words as "raw material to be taken apart, combined with other sounds and images and reintegrated into a new narrative. Not only are speeches and other statements chopped into brief sound bites, but visuals, including both film and graphics, are used much more extensively" (Hallin, 1992, pp. 9–10). In the early days of television news, the delivery of information more resembled "talking heads" reading scripted news stories to the public, almost as if they were reading from the daily newspaper. When candidates appeared, they were typically given the opportunity to make fairly complete statements outlining their positions. Today, however, TV news producers have decided that their broadcasts must be more dramatic and entertaining if they are to capture busy viewers. This means more engaging and even confrontational conversations, more use of videotape excerpts of speeches or events — often selected either to highlight gaffes or mistakes or to show surprising, sometimes angry, encounters with audiences. Today's broadcasts are also more likely to include discussions with "experts," who may be political consultants or advisors, academics, or even other reporters. The broadcasters see their task as not merely the reporting of news but the active attempt to explain the news and put it into context so viewers will be better able to comprehend it.

Television news coverage of politics tends to be sparse. A content analysis study of television coverage of the 2000 presidential primary campaign, funded by the Project for Excellence in Journalism, found that during the Iowa and New Hampshire campaigns, television news programs averaged less than one political story per show each day, compared to roughly five stories per day in the newspapers studied. The television stories were also more likely to focus on the candidates' personalities, less likely to discuss policy topics, and more likely to be superficial. In addition, television news stories were found to be substantially more subjective in their analysis than was printed news. Fully 40 percent of television stories involved press analysis, whereas only 18 percent of print stories did. Finally, television news stories were more likely to be framed around political tactics and strategies (13 percent) than were print stories (8 percent; TV versus print, 2000, p. 1).

As the national networks have lost audience share, more Americans have turned to cable news outlets such as CNN, Fox News, and MSNBC for national news. As Tom Rosenstiel (2004) argued, however, there are substantial differences in the nature of news coverage:

> Network news was built around the carefully written and edited story, produced by correspondents and vetted in advance to match words and pictures. On the network evening newscasts, 84 percent of the time is taken up by such packages, according to content analysis by the Project for Excellence in Journalism's annual State of the News Media study.
>
> Cable news is a live and extemporaneous medium built around talk. Only 11 percent of the time is devoted to edited stories. Eighty percent is given over to in-studio interviews, studio banter, "anchor reads," and live reporter stand-ups, in which correspondents talk off the top of their heads or from hasty notes.
>
> What is lost in the cable obsession with "live" is the chance to double-check, to rewrite, to edit—and often to even report. What is lost with the passing of network TV, in other words, is the journalism of verification. It is gradually yielding place to a journalism of assertion.

Political discussion shows on cable are often conducted in an interview form where the hosts ask questions and frequently challenge the answers provided by their guests. Often the hosts are openly opinionated themselves and are sharply critical of alternative points of view. Typical of such political news program hosts are Sean Hannity and Alan Colmes on Fox, Keith Olbermann on MSNBC, and Lou Dobbs on CNN. Anyone who has heard Lou Dobbs express his strongly held opinions on the subject of U.S. immigration policy, for example, would immediately notice the difference between this kind of program and the more neutral and objective reporting that dominates network news programs.

Network television news reporting tends to emphasize action. Discussions of policy proposals or political platforms are often presumed to be too dry to hold the viewer's attention, as are speeches delivered from platforms in stuffy auditoriums. Candidates are thus often shown boarding or leaving airplanes, meeting workers at factory gates, confronting angry protesters, or kissing babies when surrounded by cheering supporters. Indeed, fully cognizant of the nature and tone of much of the television reporting, the Bush campaign in 2004 limited attendance at the president's speaking events to those who were already committed to the president's reelection (Milbank, 2004). Bush's advisors understood that those "live" public events were of little value in actually converting people to vote for the president; their value was in creating the kind of television news coverage that suggested that the president was warmly loved everywhere he went. The more action, color, and excitement a candidate can create for the pursuing cameras, the more likely the candidate is to garner vital moments of airtime on the evening news.

Candidates, elected officials, and their consultants carefully craft their video images because they know that they can be either helped or hurt by the news clips. For example, the warm grin that President Reagan gave from his hospital bed as he recovered from the attempt on his life in 1981 no doubt struck a chord with many viewers as an example of his plucky courage. Richard Reeves (2005), the former political reporter for the *New York Times*, in his biography of Reagan, makes the case that the president's health and vigor were badly diminished by the unsuccessful attempt on his life, but his actual condition was known to very few people because there was such a concerted effort to project visual images of a healthy man who was quickly on the mend. An unfortunate visual image can wreak havoc on a campaign or even a sitting president. In 2003, President George W. Bush's advisors were going for an out-of-the-park symbolic moment when they crafted a news conference following the toppling of the Hussein regime in Iraq. They contrived to have the president land in a jet fighter on the deck of the *Abraham Lincoln*, an aircraft carrier off the Pacific coast, wearing a leather flight jacket. Before an enthusiastic audience of sailors, with a huge banner behind him proclaiming "Mission Accomplished," the president declared the war to be all but over. When the violence in Iraq not only continued but quickly escalated, this video image was frequently cited as evidence of a president and an administration that had lost their grip on reality.

Candidates and their consultants have adapted to the changes in the way television reporters cover political campaigns, and the reporters have adapted to changing viewer tastes and advances in broadcast technologies. In addition to satellite up- and down-link technologies that facilitate broadcasting from remote sites such as an aircraft carrier at sea, reporters and editors now have access to complex graphics generators, electronic editing units, and "morphing" technologies. The news broadcasts from the mid-1960s, with the longer candidate sound bites and more substantive issue discussions, would look boring and old-fashioned now given how accustomed viewers have become to these new modes of storytelling.

Radio

Although Americans today have many possible sources for news and public information, radio remains one of the most widely used media formats. Arbitron, the national radio ratings company, claims that "more than 90 percent of Americans aged 12 or older listen to radio each week, a higher penetration than television, magazines, newspapers, or the Internet. Although listening hours have declined slightly in recent years, Americans listened on average to nineteen hours of radio per week in 2006" (Halpin et al., 2007). Radio has many benefits for news audiences: Most notably, even more than television, it does not require one's undivided attention. Radio wins its largest audiences during peak commuting times when people are listening in their cars, and many people listen to radio while at work. As a source for news, radio is especially useful when people are seeking breaking stories about rapidly developing events. Most radio stations devote a substantial portion of their broadcasts to music or sports programming, and for them, news primarily consists of short news programs with prepackaged segments that can be frequently repeated. Many large cities, of course, have all-news radio stations that give news, weather, sports, and traffic reports throughout the day. Typically, such reports consist of headlines with little attention devoted to details.

Radio has been a source of news and political information since it was developed in the 1920s. Recently, however, the radio audience for political news has become increasingly polarized. Two developments in radio news and public information programming merit discussion.

The first significant development was the emergence of National Public Radio (NPR). Founded in 1970, NPR is both the producer and distributor of noncommercial news, talk, and entertainment programming. NPR, a nonprofit organization, is privately supported (both by foundation grants and individual listeners). NPR claims to serve an audience of 26 million Americans each week who tune in to one of more than 800 independently operated public radio stations (What is NPR?, 2007). Unlike most commercial radio stations, NPR operates a full-service news-gathering bureau to investigate and research stories and to provide detailed, nuanced, and well-researched news broadcasts. The network tends to tell stories in longer segments and with more complex narratives. The network also employs a team of political analysts who interview guests about current political topics. A 2004 study found that 16 percent of Americans regularly listen to NPR and that this audience was "fairly young, well-educated, and Democratic."

Fully 41 percent of regular NPR listeners are Democrats, and 24 percent are Republicans (News audiences increasingly politicized, 2004).

The second significant development was the emergence of commercial talk radio. If NPR appeals disproportionately to liberals, commercial talk radio appeals to conservatives. Studies suggest that Republicans are significantly more likely than Democrats to access political information via the radio and that these differences are even greater when it comes to interactive talk radio. Fully 24 percent of Republicans regularly listen to radio shows that invite listeners to call in to discuss current events, public issues, and politics. Only about half as many Democrats (13 percent) regularly listen to these types of shows, and the partisan gap in the talk radio audience has grown in recent years (News audiences increasingly politicized, 2004). As an example, "Rush Limbaugh's radio show attracts a disproportionately conservative audience: 77 percent of Limbaugh's regular listeners describe themselves as conservative. This compares with 36 percent of the general public who describe themselves in these terms" (News audiences increasingly politicized, 2004). Although Limbaugh may be the best known of the conservative radio personalities, he is not alone. One recent content analysis study claimed that 91 percent of the content on political talk radio programs skewed toward conservative positions and only 9 percent toward liberal or progressive positions (Halpin et al., 2007). Concerned that the conservative message was so thoroughly dominating the talk radio airwaves, a group of liberal activists organized a new radio network that promised programs slanted toward progressive positions. The Air America network began broadcasting in 2004. Among the early radio hosts on the network was the well-known comedian Al Franken. It seems, however, that the network failed to catch on with the public, and it has consistently struggled to find an audience. Although it is still broadcasting in several media markets, the network filed for bankruptcy and was reorganized in 2006 (Air America Radio files, 2006).

As we will discuss in greater detail in Chapter 11, the increasingly polarized character of contemporary media does have consequences on the formation of public opinion, the conduct of political campaigns, and on how elected officials govern once they are in office.

The Internet

A relatively new source of political news is the Internet, which offers a rich and wide variety of news about political issues and campaigns.

Those who go online for their news can choose from conventional mainstream news sources (major newspapers, magazines, and television and radio networks all have Web sites), as well as from blogs, or activist group Web sites. The key issue to remember with regard to online news, however, is that those seeking information must go to the Web and actively search for information that interests them or meets their needs (they may, of course, set their Web browsers to tailor the news that they receive to topics that they already know interest them). This fundamentally changes the nature of the conversational commons about news and leads to a series of other complex questions regarding who is exercising editorial news judgment and even about how skilled consumers are in evaluating the quality of the sources in an online news environment. We will discuss the Internet as a news source in greater detail in Chapter 8, which focuses on new communication technologies.

THE AGENDA-SETTING FUNCTION OF THE NEWS MEDIA

The power of the press to shape public attention and awareness has been labeled "agenda setting." As mass communication scholars Maxwell McCombs and Donald Shaw (1993) defined this concept:

> Both the selection of objects for attention and the selection of frames for thinking about those objects are powerful agenda-setting roles. Central to the news agenda and its daily set of objects—issues, personalities, events, etc.—are the perspectives that journalists and consequently members of the public employ to think about each object. These perspectives direct attention toward certain attributes and away from others. (p. 62)

The media play an important role in determining which issues merit public attention, evaluating how effective certain elected officials have been in the conduct of their duties, and shaping public attitudes. Through media coverage of certain issues, people learn about how their circumstances and situations relate to those of others. Someone may not perceive some problem as more important to him personally just because he has seen news coverage of it, but that person will very likely see that the issue is important to others and thus regard it as a key social problem (Hawkins & Pingree, 1982). For example, the stories about political corruption involving members of the U.S. Congress that dominated the news in 2006 may not have stimulated that much interest from most citizens, who are much more concerned about other issues such as their own financial well-being or the war in Iraq. However, when the press continues to focus on the story, the public does begin to notice.

Even when the public seems not to care very much about an issue, persistent day-after-day press coverage sends an unambiguous message that others see this as an issue that merits attention and that therefore you *should* probably care about it as well. Diana Mutz (1994) argued as follows:

> It is through media coverage that the unemployed worker learns she is one of many thousands nationwide, and the crime victim learns that his robbery was not an isolated incident, but rather part of a pattern of increasing drug-related crime. . . . Media coverage legitimizes a problem as something for which national leadership can fairly be held accountable. (p. 692)

Research suggests that the media are especially important in guiding voters' evaluations of candidates who are relatively unknown, especially during primary campaigns (Pfau et al., 1995). Studies further suggest that those who seek the most information during campaigns (in short, those who make the greatest use of the mass media) are far more likely to participate in political activity, are more likely to vote, and are more politically effective, more opinionated, and more fiercely partisan than those who do not (Delli Carpini & Keetzer, 1993).

The power of the media to set an agenda of public issues also serves to project an image of reality that confers a certain status on individuals and issues. Consumers select certain media to fulfill their needs or gratify their self-seeking motives. The strengths of their needs, motives, expectations, and convictions are thus shaped by the media they select and are reinforced by their exposure to the messages conveyed in the chosen media (Lin, 1993). Indeed, as we noted in Chapter 1, we seek out information that confirms our identity, validates our experiences, and expresses truths that we already believe.

The media have profound power to shape public conversations about social issues. Journalists and editors decide what stories will be covered as they judge what will constitute the news. Some stories demand coverage. When there is a disaster—for example, a hurricane in Florida or Louisiana, a tornado in Oklahoma, or an earthquake or fire in California— public curiosity drives news decisions. The press must be responsive to the interests of its audience, and the public's thirst for information must be quenched. Media coverage of the 9/11 terrorist attacks drove virtually all other news stories off the air for several days. Likewise, news coverage of the 2003 invasion of Iraq dominated media coverage for several days. After a time, however, the public seems to tire of news that seems repetitive. As the car bombings and assassinations in Iraq continue, it seems to become more and more difficult to get the American people to pay attention to the daily reports of carnage and atrocity.

Some issues never seem to gain the attention of the media and thus never really get reported to the public. As McCombs (1976, p. 3) noted, "If the media tell us nothing about a topic or event, then in most cases it simply will not exist on our personal agenda or in our life space." A classic example from American history of a story that might never have sustained the public's attention without persistent press coverage was the break-in at the Democratic Party headquarters at the Watergate Complex in 1972. At first glance, the incident hardly seemed to merit more than a brief paragraph inside the newspaper. Thefts and burglaries are hardly front-page news stories in Washington, DC. Yet, the reporters and editors from the *Washington Post* relentlessly pursued the story day after day. They turned up evidence linking those arrested in the break-in to U.S. intelligence agencies and to members of the White House staff. With each new report more information dribbled out, and this information seemed to deepen public interest in the story and to justify the continued expenditure of the paper's resources for still more investigations. Eventually, the reporters—most notably Bob Woodward and Carl Bernstein—uncovered a trail of responsibility for the break-in and its cover-up that led directly to President Richard Nixon and his closest advisors. As a result, Nixon was forced to resign.

More recently, the press became very interested in undertaking research that would link donations and gifts from Washington lobbyists to members of Congress in return for their votes on key issues. The persistence of the press investigations brought to light the very close and cozy relationships that had developed between lobbyist Jack Abramoff and Representative Tom DeLay (R—Texas), the House majority leader, and Robert Ney (R—Ohio). Even though this story might not have constituted the kind of very dramatic news events assured of winning public attention, the public did begin to take notice as a result of the continuing press attention. Ultimately, both DeLay and Ney surrendered their offices under the taint of the corruption scandal (Weisman, 2006). The ethics scandals, which ultimately came to involve additional elected officials from both parties, will be discussed in greater detail in later chapters.

Decisions about which news stories will receive attention reflect the images and impressions that journalists have about the topics that they believe will interest their readers or viewers and the professional norms regarding what they believe constitutes significant "news." In the early 1980s, for example, AIDS activists complained that the disease did not become a major news story until it struck and killed prominent celebrities and threatened heterosexuals. It was perceived that the deaths of thousands of gay men were insufficient to motivate reporters and editors (and, by implication, the public and their elected officials) to realize that this disease merited significant public attention (Shilts, 1987).

By choosing to focus on certain stories while ignoring others, and by identifying some stories as deserving of front-page attention while relegating others to small columns inside the paper (or the television equivalent—leading with some stories and not others), the media cue us as to how significant they believe certain stories are and how much attention they believe these stories merit. These media decisions inevitably begin to shape public attitudes regarding what issues are significant and deserving of attention. In the United States, for example, there has been a lack of press attention to reporting complex issues involving science or the environment, and as a result, it has been quite difficult to motivate public policy action regarding issues such as global warming. Without significant media coverage of this issue, the melting polar ice caps seem very far away and the impending ecological crisis far removed from everyday concerns. The issue of global warming is now beginning to attract somewhat more media and public attention than it did earlier. Perhaps this is due to former vice president Al Gore's Academy Award–winning documentary, *An Inconvenient Truth*. The destruction of New Orleans and the Mississippi Gulf Coast by Hurricane Katrina also created significant media attention and an ongoing public discussion of the scientific theory that the increased ferocity of hurricanes in the region was likely a result of global temperature increases.

Research suggests that the agenda-setting function of the media can have a significant effect on the outcome of elections. If the media focus more attention on issues that favor one candidate over another and thus help the more successful candidate tell his or her story and give credibility to that story with either negative or positive coverage, that media attention can help determine how people will vote (Fico & Freedman, 2001; Miller, Andsager, & Reichert, 1998).

Communication scholars have argued that one of the most important implications of the agenda-setting function of the media is "priming" citizens in the selection of issues. Such media "priming" serves to bring certain issues to the public's attention by planting the seed of an idea in their minds. Research suggests that people prefer to rely on simple rules of thumb in evaluating political candidates. When they have seen certain stories over and over again in the press, they will likely come to view the issues discussed in those stories as significant elements to consider in making their voting decisions (Perloff, 1998). Thus, if "character" stories dominate the press coverage of a particular candidate, then voters may be more likely to regard character as an important electoral issue. This is not to suggest, however, that the media are always able to shape the public sense of what issues are important, for experience suggests otherwise. Sometimes the relationship between media stories and the impact of those stories on voter behavior is more complex. For example, despite a daily drumbeat of news stories about President Clinton's relationship with a White House intern, most of which were intensely critical of the president, the public was willing to forgive and forget. Shah, Watts, Domke, and Fan (2002) argued that this may have been because many people came to view the persistent stories about Clinton's sexual conduct as evidence not of his moral failings but evidence of an explicit attempt by conservative elites to undermine the president. Shah et al. thus asserted that "this confirms our expectation that Clinton's strong approval ratings were, in part, the result of a counterresponse by citizens—that is, a reaction against conservative efforts to disparage and remove a popular president over what may have seemed to be private, highly personal indiscretions" (p. 366). They further asserted that this response may have been triggered by the fact that the public is increasingly exposed to, and no doubt influenced by, press coverage that explicitly focuses on political "strategy" more than substance.

Media coverage can frame an event in such a way as to document its significance and scope, suggest alternative solutions, and present some persons as experts while belittling the roles or contributions of others. The more dramatic, vivid, or creative the story, the more salience it can have in shaping the public agenda (Gitlin, 1980).

The 2000 Democratic presidential primary campaign pitted Vice President Al Gore against New Jersey senator Bill Bradley. Gore led in the polls from the earliest days in the race. Bradley sought to compete by focusing his message on bold new initiatives in the areas of education and health. He talked about these issues in every speech, released position papers and updates on his proposed policies every few days, and made them the focus of his advertising campaign. A study of how the media actually reported on the Bradley campaign in the days leading up to the New Hampshire primary, however, suggested that coverage of these issues was scant. When the media did cover the Bradley campaign, a majority of the stories were devoted to his personality and his health (he suffered from repeated bouts of an irregular heartbeat) and not to his policy proposals. Indeed, 36 percent of the stories in which Bradley was the dominant figure focused on his health (In the public interest?, 2000). One reason for the predominance of this coverage is that the networks have made a heavy investment in health reporting and often maintain doctor-reporters on their staff. Even though the medical community seemed to agree that Bradley's health problems amounted to little more than a nuisance, the media's interest in health issues caused the topic to be regarded as a substantive issue and thus helped to place it on the public's agenda (In the public interest?, 2000).

Studies of media coverage of the 2004 campaign revealed that just 13 percent of stories concentrated on explaining the policy proposals of the candidates or their differences on a wide range of foreign and domestic matters, including Iraq, the war on terror, taxes, the economy, jobs, stem cell research, and healthcare. The media instead focused on the politics of campaigning, which accounted for more than half of the coverage (The debate effect, 2004).

The public's focus on strategy in politics should not be surprising because there is strong evidence that the way the media frame an issue can have measurable behavioral effects and can shape public opinion (Gitlin, 1980; McCombs & Shaw, 1993). Entman (1993) defined *framing* as the ability to select some aspects of a perceived reality and make them seem more significant than others in the news accounts. Framing, then, promotes a particular definition of a problem, offers an interpretation of likely causation, possibly suggests a moral evaluation, and perhaps recommends a certain policy to respond to the problem. The way the media frame the issues in campaigns has an impact on what issues voters see as most important, who is considered deserving of praise or blame for current conditions, and which candidates are regarded as credible and able to address those conditions (Devitt, 1997; Gamson, 1996; Golan & Wanta, 2001; Graber, 1987; Iorio & Huxman, 1996; Iyengar, 1996; McLeod & Detenber, 1999). The impact of media framing was further explained by Weaver, McCombs, and Spellman (cited in McCombs & Shaw, 1993):

> For persons with a high need for orientation about politics, mass communication does more than merely reinforce preexisting beliefs. In fact, the media may teach these members of the audience the issues

and topics to use in evaluating certain candidates and parties, not just during political campaigns, but also in the long periods between campaigns. (p. 63)

An interesting example of alternative media frames of an unusual political issue involved the stories that surfaced just before the 2006 midterm elections about Representative Mark Foley (R—Florida), who wrote a series of e-mails attempting to seduce high-school-aged congressional pages. The dozens of messages that Foley sent to boys under the age of 18 included not-so-vague sexual advances and invitations to the boys to join him over the weekend in his home for drinking parties. One series of instant message exchanges seemed to suggest that Foley and the teenaged boy he was messaging may both have been masturbating while online. Foley ended the e-mail exchange by explaining that he needed to go to the House chamber to cast a vote (Ross & Sauer, 2006). Once the news stories became public, Foley resigned his office and agreed to check himself into a treatment facility to address his alcoholism and related problems. The story, as might be expected, produced a flurry of media attention that lasted for several days. Mainstream media outlets in the earliest days of the controversy focused on the unfolding facts in the case as more e-mails were released and as other pages came forward to talk about their experiences where Foley made inappropriate advances. In other accounts, pages explained that Foley's interest in young males was an open secret on the Hill and that they had been warned by other congressional staff members to stay clear of him (Sauer & Schecter, 2006). Broadcast news stories showed Foley presenting a public speech expressing his strong support for the page system in Congress and praising the efforts of the youthful congressional aides. Other stories focused on his hypocrisy by citing his strong support for legislation to protect children from sexual predators and his criticisms of President Clinton during the Monica Lewinsky scandal and the impeachment hearings (Crowley, 2006; Wallace, 2006).

Meanwhile, in the days immediately following the release of the e-mails, President Bush's press secretary, Tony Snow, seemed to downplay the significance of the story, dismissing it as mere partisan politics when he told an interviewer on CNN that the sexual and graphic e-mails that Foley had sent to several teenage pages were "simply naughty e-mails." Snow stated, "Look, I hate to tell you, but it's not always pretty up there on Capitol Hill, and there have been other scandals as you know that have been more than simply naughty e-mails" (cited in Tony Snow labels Foley's sex messages, 2006). Other media stories also sought to frame the story as being only about politics. For example, one Internet news column raged, "If anything, the episode reveals the Democrats' hypocrisy about their own behavior. The fact that Foley resigned virtually within minutes of being told that ABC News had copies of his salacious e-mails and text messages indicates he at least felt shame for his actions. Can the same be said for Democrats?" (Did Democrats page Mark Foley?, 2006).

The invitation to frame the story as primarily about politics did not necessarily help Republicans, however, for not only did it not seem to attract much public support, but it also invited reporters to consider how the furor over the Foley e-mails might damage Republican Speaker of the House Dennis Hastert of Illinois. Hastert had been told about the inappropriate e-mails almost a year earlier but took no action to prevent future contact between Foley and the pages. Stories began to question whether Hastert would have to surrender his leadership position in the House to demonstrate that the GOP got the message and understood that this was a real problem. Reporters also focused on the political consequences of the story, questioning whether the scandal would undermine the Republican Party's pro-family and conservative message and perhaps cost it control of the House of Representatives in the 2006 midterm elections (Hook & Brownstein, 2006; Hulse & Zeleney, 2006).

In the meantime, Foley's attorney sought to absolve his client's personal responsibility for the inappropriate e-mails and perhaps also to create a possible line of argument to be used in his defense against possible criminal charges. The attorney explained that Foley had never had any actual sexual contact with minors, that the congressman's addiction to alcohol impaired his judgment, and that as a teenager Foley himself had been sexually abused by a male clergyman (Levey & Schmitt, 2006). The press coverage and political responses thus provide a very clear example of the way different frames focus our attention on individual acts, the responsibilities of political leaders, party motivations, and even possible election outcomes.*

*Still another story about a Republican legislator and gay sex surfaced during the summer of 2007. Senator Larry Craig (R—Idaho) was arrested and pled guilty to disorderly conduct on a charge that he solicited an undercover police officer for sex in a men's room at the Minneapolis–St. Paul airport. Craig argued that he was not gay and that he should not have pled guilty because he was misunderstood and committed no offense. The Republican leadership in the Senate, already smarting from the Foley scandal, convinced Craig to resign his seat rather than cause further embarrassment to the party (Kane & Murray, 2007). Senator Craig sought to retract his guilty plea, but the court rejected this request. He did, however, decide not to resign his Senate seat, although he also indicated that he would not seek reelection in 2008.

Even the most dramatic news stories become repetitive over time, and public attention to them wanes. Thus, the news media may often reframe an event, either deliberately or unconsciously, as they seek to keep a story fresh and interesting and as they uncover new facts or interview new sources that present alternative perspectives (Chyi & McCombs, 2004).

Probably more social scientific research studies of the agenda-setting and framing functions of the media have been conducted than of any other mass-communication topic. Rogers, Dearing, and Bregman (1993) identified 223 academic publications that were explicitly or implicitly concerned with the topic, and even a cursory glance at the scholarly journals suggests that the number increased even further in the years following. These researchers suggest that the primary benefit of agenda-setting studies is that they demonstrate that it is insufficient for scholars to focus on the immediate short-term effects of mass-mediated messages. To fully comprehend the ways the mass media shape social values, political discussions, and, ultimately, public policies, one must consider the long-term longitudinal effects of the media (Rogers, Dearing, & Bregman, 1993, p. 73). As media scholars have long recognized, the members of the media are not omnipotent. They do not always set the public agenda, and even when they do, their influence is not always felt in the same way. Furthermore, audiences are exposed to a variety of different media, and thus messages often counteract each other. As Perloff (1998, p. 219) argued, "The news does not inject viewers with perspectives; it suggests that certain issues are more important than others, and people (some more than others) come to accept these interpretations and adjust their political priorities accordingly."

THE CAMPAIGN NEWS ENVIRONMENT

We have entered the age of celebrity journalists. Network news anchors, and even many local news anchors, earn huge salaries. For example, Katie Couric, anchor of the *CBS Evening News* since September 5, 2006, was reportedly paid $15 million a year, or $60,000 per evening newscast. Peter Jennings, anchor of ABC's *World News Tonight* from 1983 until his death in 2005, earned $10 million a year. Even cable TV compensates its anchors well, with Larry King pulling in $7 million each year and Anderson Cooper earning $2 million (Belenkaya, Huff, & Siemaszko, 2006). These reporters can also supplement their incomes with generous fees for speaking engagements. Even though print reporters are not so well paid for their work, they too can become celebrities by getting their bylines into major city newspapers or news magazines. Once they are well known, they may be invited to appear on television news discussion programs (e.g., the *McLaughlin Group*), where their celebrity reputations are enhanced. To maintain their star status, these reporters must attract significant audiences. They must also demonstrate to audiences that they have access to important news makers. Thus, the reporters and the campaigns they are assigned to cover are mutually dependent on each other. Reporters need meaningful access to candidates to develop their stories and stay ahead of the competition. If they cease filing interesting and informative stories, they will not get their time on the nightly newscast or their stories into their papers. Having their reports from the campaign trail published "above the fold" on the newspaper's front page or as lead stories on the nightly news is a sign of achievement in the profession. Candidates, of course, also want to see the news accounts of their campaigns highlighted in the media. The result is a press–candidate relationship with consequences for how campaigns are covered. This interdependent relationship is hardly new; it was already in place and well documented in the classic study of the Nixon-McGovern race known as *The Boys on the Bus* (Crouse, 1972). For example, to improve his relations with the press covering his campaign in 2000, Al Gore upgraded the quality of the food and wine served on his campaign plane. Gore apparently recognized that the national press corps—like an army—traveled on its stomach. Did the increased attention lavished on the press influence the coverage that Gore received? It is difficult to determine, but it certainly did not hurt (How Gore caters, 2000). The film *Journeys with George*, which provided an inside glimpse into the George W. Bush campaign in 2000, demonstrated the camaraderie and close relationship between reporters and the candidate. Even when the reporters are shown to be openly skeptical of Bush's public statements and perhaps even of his qualifications for office, the film seems to suggest that many reporters came to like Bush personally.

Berkowitz and Beach (1993) argued that the sources that reporters talk to in forming their stories have a significant influence on the nature and content of the news that gets reported. They further argued that more than half of all campaign news stories originate from the sources' deliberate efforts to have their voices heard in the mass media. Reporters frequently interview "experts," who are asked to comment not just on the issues discussed in political debates and campaigns but also on the dynamics of the race itself. Most often the experts will be academicians, pollsters, or political consultants (Freedman & Fico, 2004), but some-times the experts for these "horse race" stories—stories that seek to handicap the race by focusing on who is ahead, who is trailing, or who may have momentum—will be other reporters covering the same cam-paigns. The use of other reporters as experts certainly complicates the source-candidate-reporter relationship. It may lead to increased pres-sures toward "group think" in assessing a campaign.* It may also be a way for reporter bias to creep into news stories. Some critics have sug-gested that when reporters interview other reporters or express their opinions, even of the dynamics of the "horse race" coverage of a cam-paign, they must be careful to inform their audience that they are now being exposed to "opinion" or "analysis" (Carter, Fico, & McCabe, 2002).

The news business is fiercely competitive. Violence (crime stories, wars, and revolutions), disasters, conflicts, crises, controversies, and scandals (especially sex scandals) make great news stories. In-depth studies of complex issues of public policy (e.g., the implications of changes in welfare eligibility requirements on the poor) do not make very exciting stories. With television networks, major newspapers, and news magazines all competing with one another for an audience, it is not surprising that these complex and unexciting issues garner little media attention. Berkowitz and Beach (1993) commented:

> Because media organizations are profit-making enterprises, journalists must learn to select and gather news that will draw a large audience. At the same time, journalists must learn to do their jobs efficiently, apply-ing strategies that virtually assure their efforts will bring back a story. One of journalists' common strategies is to rely on source-originated news about planned events, events that present predictable news at an expected time through prearranged sources. (p. 5)

As a result of this interdependent relationship between campaigns and reporters, most campaign coverage is remarkably homogeneous, influenced by the interests and values of reporters, candidates, and campaign managers, who are all social and economic elites (Parenti, 1993). Parenti argued that this elite domination heavily shapes news content and influences the tenor and the scope of campaign coverage.

In the nineteenth century, American newspapers were openly par-tisan and favored one party over the other. In fact, an 1850 census

* "Group think" refers to the tendency for group members to reinforce each other's observations and beliefs to minimize disagreement. The result is a situation where new ideas tend not to be heard and alternative explanations or perspectives are not considered.

classified a mere 5 percent of American newspapers as "neutral and independent." These biases were also reflected in the coverage of political candidates. For example, during the campaigns of 1824 and 1828, newspapers called Andrew Jackson an "adulterer," an "ignoramus," and a "Southerner, who feared neither God nor man" (Jamieson, 1986, p. 7).

Contemporary newspapers are likely to adhere to professional norms that encourage fairer, if not more objective, reporting. There are, of course, exceptions. One study by Kenney and Simpson (1993) suggested that when newspapers endorsed a candidate on their editorial pages, the papers' news coverage did sometimes favor that candidate. Examining coverage of the 1988 campaigns in the *Washington Times*, the conservative newspaper owned by the Korean Reunification Church, Kenney and Simpson (1993) declared:

> Those readers who relied upon the *Washington Times* for their news received an incomplete account of important events during the campaign, and both stories and headlines were frequently biased. It ignored events favoring the Democrats and highlighted events favoring the Republicans. More than one-third of its headlines and stories were biased, and each time, they were biased in favor of the Republicans. (p. 353)

It seems far more common, however, that even newspapers that are published by ideologically committed owners permit their opinion page editors and reporters considerable autonomy in expressing their own points of view (Kapoor & Kang, 1993). For example, the *Wall Street Journal*, which most would consider a very conservative newspaper based on an evaluation of its masthead editorials, is nonetheless frequently praised for the objectivity of its news reporting.

Graber (1993) observed that even though most broadcast networks and newspapers were owned by pro-business and pro-Republican conservatives, only a small percentage of the working press in prominent news organizations were Republicans. Yet, Graber also noted that the fact that most reporters were male, affluent, well educated, and urban unquestionably influenced what issues they reported and how they related to the candidates or elected officials they were assigned to cover (see especially pp. 101–109).

Sabato (1992) argued that what was surprising, given the competitive journalistic environment, was that most journalists, editors, and producers move forward together in essentially the same story direction. This phenomenon has been called "pack journalism" (Crouse, 1972). To illustrate the concept, Sabato (1992) cited a statement by George Skelton, a political reporter for the *Los Angeles Times*:

> When you're covering the White House and twenty reporters are listening to the president's speech, someone comes up to the most senior reporter and says, "What's the lead?" And several reporters say, "Yeah, that makes sense to me." And pretty soon . . . eighteen of the twenty reporters [are] using the same lead. That's pack journalism. (p. 131)

Frank (2003) offered a strong argument that reporters more often resemble, and frequently see themselves, more as members of a "docile herd" that is led from story to story by public relations experts and political campaign consultants than they do as members of an "aggressive pack" eager to uncover a story.

THE CONTENT OF CAMPAIGN NEWS

Despite the fact that the reporters who cover political campaigns depend on the goodwill of the candidates and their staff for access to good news stories, and despite the fact that much of the news that gets reported about politics is heavily managed by campaign consultants and public relations experts, when the herd sniffs the scent of scandal, they quickly become an aggressive pack. The competitive journalistic environment is about selling stories, and sex and scandal certainly sell better than dispassionate discussions about complex policy issues. In 1998 the big news story was about married Democratic senator and presidential candidate Gary Hart's liaisons with model and actress Donna Rice aboard the aptly named yacht *Monkey Business*. The *Miami Herald* first broke the story, but soon many other media outlets were picking it up. The story refused to die down, and eventually Hart was hounded from the race (Shogan, 1999).

In the 1992 presidential campaign, the hot story was Governor Bill Clinton's alleged affair with nightclub singer Gennifer Flowers, which blurred the line between serious campaign coverage in the mainstream press and tabloid "trash for cash" television shows such as *Hard Copy* and *A Current Affair*. This story culminated in two marvelous media moments: Flowers baring her story in the pages of *Penthouse* and Bill and Hillary Clinton appearing on the CBS program *60 Minutes* to affirm that even though their marriage had not been perfect, they continued to trust and love each other (for a discussion of these events, see Auletta,

1993). Although Bill Clinton survived this scandal and went on to win the election, Hillary Clinton did serious damage to her relationship with many traditional family values voters when she declared that it was not as if she was the kind of woman who was willing to stay home and bake cookies. She further declared, "I'm not sitting here as some little woman standing by my man like Tammy Wynette. I'm sitting here because I love him." The comment caused such a heated uproar that it helped keep the story alive for many days. Ultimately, Clinton publicly apologized to the country-western singer Tammy Wynette and also to those women who did stay home and bake cookies (Hillary Clinton is first First Lady, 2000).

Reporters have succeeded not only in convincing themselves that this kind of coverage is popular with audiences—and thus increasingly important in an era when many people are not actively seeking news about politics but may be interested in entertaining or titillating gossip—they also seem to have come to believe that this kind of news is somehow significant. Auletta (1993) reported the following:

> An astonishing 46 percent of the more than four hundred journalists surveyed by the *Times-Mirror* poll in May 1992 concluded that questions about Clinton's character was [*sic*] the most important event of the contest; 20 percent said Gennifer Flowers's press conference was the most significant event of the entire campaign. (p. 74)

The media fascination with sex scandals has certainly not diminished since this 1992 poll. The gay sex scandal involving Florida Republican Representative Mark Foley and teenage congressional pages amply illustrates this point. Some have claimed that public interest and ultimately disgust over this case and the failure of the House Republican leadership to protect these children may have helped cost the GOP the control of Congress in the 2006 midterm elections (Grunwald & Cillizza, 2006).

Most major news organizations in the United States do not allow journalists to pay for interviews, citing the possibility of sources embellishing on or even inventing facts to make their stories more salable. The tabloid press, however, has a different philosophy. This was illustrated during the 1996 campaign when President Clinton's campaign advisor, Dick Morris, was forced to resign after the national weekly tabloid the *Star* reported that Morris had sex with a $200-an-hour prostitute and discussed campaign strategies with her. The *Star* reportedly paid the woman $150,000 for her story and for compromising photographs taken of her and Morris at a posh Washington hotel. The moral scruples of the mainstream press did not prevent them from reporting the story at length once it had been published in the tabloid. The reporting of the event was timed to coincide with the Democratic National Convention so that it would have maximum effect. As it turned out, the story was on the front page of almost every newspaper in the country, alongside news reports of President Clinton's speech accepting the Democratic presidential nomination (Randolph & Boyarsky, 1996, p. A19).

Online news sources such as the *Drudge Report* often print stories that mainstream newspapers or networks would not touch. But once the story is reported in the online source, the mainstream reporters refer to the Web stories and thus frame their own coverage as being about the news story as reported online. This point was illustrated in January 2007 when an obscure Web site called *Insight*, edited by Jeffrey T. Kuhner, published a story that claimed that Senator Hillary Clinton was preparing an accusation that Senator Barack Obama had studied at an Islamic religious school in Indonesia when he was six years old. Kuhner refused to name his sources or provide proof for his claim, and the story was quickly discredited. This did not, however, prevent the Fox news network, the *Drudge Report*, Rush Limbaugh, or the *Washington Times* newspaper from running with the story (Kirkpatrick, 2007).

Even when reporters are not focused on scandals, they are often focused not on issues but on the "horse race" or the strategic elements of the campaign. Which candidate has the best chance of winning? Who does or does not have momentum? Who is raising the most money? Who is winning key endorsements? How has the campaign been organized? What are the candidate's media strategies? Studies of campaign coverage suggest that as much as 70 to 80 percent of news stories in recent presidential campaigns have been focused on campaign strategies and tactics (In the public interest?, 2000; Weaver & Drew, 2001). Some have complained that this media obsession with reporting who is ahead or behind in the race can produce a "bandwagon effect," wherein voters begin to favor one candidate over another just because it appears that others are beginning to lean that way. Studies also suggest that voters are very reluctant to support a candidate whom they perceive as having little chance of winning (Fico & Freedman, 2001; King, 1990; Lichter, 1988; Skalaban, 1988).

Momentum coverage may be most important during the primaries, when voters know the least about the candidates and are actively seeking cues to help them decide how they should cast their ballots. Johnson (1993b) observed:

A candidate's standing not only determines amount of coverage, but also tone of coverage. Candidates who are treated as also-rans receive "death-watch coverage"—stories that monitor the health of their campaign. Contenders, especially ones who do better than expected, can anticipate largely favorable coverage. (p. 312)

Johnson (1993b) further noted that those given extensive coverage usually show improved standing in the polls, whereas those candidates who are denied coverage usually sink. This preoccupation with who is ahead or behind has led to a proliferation of media organizations conducting public opinion polls and a dramatic increase in campaign coverage of the polls (Johnson, 1993a).

A relatively recent development on polling is the phone-in poll. Clearly intended as a vehicle to encourage the active participation of TV viewers or readers on an Internet news site, the poll invites people to weigh in by expressing their opinions, often for a modest charge (if it costs a caller to participate, it is reasonable to assume that at least a token amount of income flows back to the media outlet promoting the poll). Such phone-in polls are notoriously inaccurate, however, because those who hold strong opinions are far more likely to phone in. One can also expect that people with more disposable income are likely to phone in. In recent years political campaigns and political parties have actively sought to influence these polls by encouraging their partisans to register their opinions. One study (Bates & Harmon, 1993) suggested that there might be as much as a 23-percentage-point discrepancy between the results reported in a phone-in poll and those gleaned from conventional public opinion survey techniques. Nonetheless, when the results of these phone-in polls are reported in the media, they have the effect of influencing voter attitudes regarding what their fellow citizens believe. Following the 2007 State of the Union Address, for example, the Fox News network encouraged viewers to phone in to register their opinions regarding the effectiveness of President Bush's speech. Throughout the evening, approximately 85 percent of callers reported that they found the president's speech to be either effective or very effective. Yet, most political commentators were unimpressed with the speech and did not give it high marks.

Jamieson (1993) argued that this emphasis on reporting who is ahead, as well as the focus on poll results, has trivialized the issues in political campaigns. Jamieson (1993) also made a compelling argument about how the languages of sports and war are inappropriate to mobilize an electorate to active political participation:

The language through which the press reports on politics assumes that the American electorate selects a president through a process called a "campaign" seen as a "game" or "war" between a "frontrunner" and an "underdog" in which each "candidate's" goal is "winning." Candidates' words and actions are seen as their choice of what they presumably consider a means to victory. So enmeshed is the vocabulary of horse race and war in our thoughts about politics that we are not conscious that the "race" is a metaphor and "spectatorship" an inappropriate role for the electorate. Press reliance on the language of strategy reduces candidate and public accountability. (p. 37)

PLANTING SEEDS OF CYNICISM AND DOUBT

Media critics and reporters alike have become aware that political campaign reporting has become increasingly negative and cynical. Sabato (1992, p. 128) argued that this evolution toward more negative reporting originated with the Vietnam War and Watergate. From approximately 1941 to 1966, Sabato said, journalists engaged in "lapdog" journalism. They reported the news in ways that reinforced the political establishment. Then, from 1966 to 1974, as reporters came to believe that politicians and elected officials were actively seeking to deceive and mislead them, the reporters engaged in "watchdog" journalism. This style of journalism, according to Sabato, was marked by reporters carefully scrutinizing the words and behaviors of the political elites by making independent investigations of their statements. Since 1974, Sabato declared, journalists have been more like "junkyard" dogs; their reporting has become increasingly aggressive, intrusive, negative, and cynical, often focusing on gossip and rumors.

Patterson (2002, p. 70) argued, "Perhaps even more so than Vietnam, Watergate made a deep impression on reporters. Watergate quickly became the prevailing myth of journalism. Reporters believed that the press had saved American democracy and that it had a continuing responsibility to protect the public from lying, manipulative politicians." Patterson went on to observe that George W. Bush's media coverage was 63 percent negative in tone when he was campaigning in the 2000 presidential election, and he also noted that Al Gore fared about the same, with 60 percent of his coverage on the nightly news being negative. These findings prompted Patterson (2002) to argue:

The news media were showing their bias, but it was not a liberal or a conservative one. It was a preference for the negative. Often the more highly charged the subject, the more one-sided is the portrayal. A good deal of Bush's coverage during the 2000 election suggested that he was not too smart. There were nine such claims in the news for every contrary claim. Gore's coverage was dotted with suggestions that he was not all that truthful. Such claims outpaced rebuttals by seventeen to one. (p. 64)

Patterson also noted that this negative coverage is not limited to presidential candidates; it also applies to elected presidents and to candidates seeking other offices. Cappella and Jamieson (1997, pp. 31–32) argued that the media seem to be preoccupied with conflict and that this type of framing contributed to cynical reporting. They further noted that studies of both congressional and presidential campaigns indicated a rise in negative coverage.

Cappella and Jamieson (1997) discussed the significance of such negative message framing:

The central goal of campaigns, candidates, and elections is winning. When actions are placed in this interpretive frame, the motivation for action (of any sort, whether a policy or personal choice) is reduced to a single, simple human motivation—the desire to win and to take the power that elected office provides. In such an interpretive frame, all actions are tainted—they are seen not as the by-product of a desire to solve social ills, redirect national goals, or create a better future for our offspring but are instead viewed in terms of winning. Winning is equivalent to advancing one's own agenda, one's own self-interest, so the actions stand not for themselves but for the motivational system that gives rise to them—narrow self interest. (p. 34)

Cappella and Jamieson (1997) and Patterson (2002) argued that the real consequence of such negative framing is that it is infectious and contributes to public perceptions that politicians are self-interested, sometimes corrupt, and really do not care very much about the concerns of their constituents.

These cynical public attitudes may also be affected by the fact that political news is now often discussed in forums that have become increasingly argumentative, confrontational, and often one-sided. While political news programs such as *Meet the Press* and *Face the Nation*, which feature reasonable and informative panel discussions between reporters and the politicians they cover, still exist, they have now been joined by programs such as *Hardball*, *Hannity and Colmes*, and *The O'Reilly Factor*. On these programs the emphasis is not on calm discussion of political issues, campaigns, and controversies with an eye

toward finding common ground. Instead, the hosts and panelists inter-
rupt one another and yell and shout, with each participant attempting
to say something more controversial, outrageous, or biting than what
the others said. Certainly this form of political media coverage encourages a perception of politics as a game or, even worse, as ideological
warfare.

Another factor that may be increasing the level of cynicism about
politics is the proliferation of humorous programs that mock politicians. For many years now, late-night TV hosts Jay Leno (of NBC's
The Tonight Show) and David Letterman (of CBS's *The Late Show with
David Letterman*) have directed their very sharp humor at political figures. In 1992, former president Bill Clinton appeared on the *Arsenio Hall
Show*, playing the saxophone and discussing his preference for briefs
over boxers. In 2003, Hollywood celebrity Arnold Schwarzenegger
announced that he was running for governor of California on *The Tonight
Show*, and he has been a frequent guest on the program since his election. Now, however, these late-night programs have been joined on the
air by faux news shows that have taken political humor a step further.
The most popular of such shows are *The Daily Show with Jon Stewart*
and *The Colbert Report*, both broadcast on cable TV's Comedy Central
channel. These programs have attracted large audiences and are especially appealing to younger viewers. They have also become "musts"
on the campaign circuit for almost every presidential candidate. For
example, on the day that Senator Joseph Biden announced his intention
to seek his party's nomination in the 2008 presidential contest, he committed a flagrant gaffe when he referred to fellow candidate Senator
Barack Obama as "the first mainstream African American candidate
who is articulate and bright and clean and a nice-looking guy." Not
surprisingly, the Reverends Jesse Jackson and Al Sharpton and former
senator Carol Moseley Braun took strong offense to being considered
inarticulate, dim, or unclean. Sure enough, that same night Biden appeared on *The Daily Show* to express his regret at having been misunderstood (Nagourney, 2007). Where better to attempt to make such a
slip seem nothing more than an innocent communication misstep than on
a widely watched comedy program?

In their study of viewers of *The Daily Show*, Baumgartner and
Morris (2006) discovered that study subjects who were exposed to
this program and to the steady stream of jokes about George W. Bush
and John Kerry tended to rate both candidates more negatively, even
controlling for their own political and ideological biases. Perhaps
what was even more alarming about the results from this study was

that these subjects not only exhibited increased cynicism about the electoral system and about governmental leaders, but they also reported an increased confidence in their own ability to understand the complicated world of politics. The scholars noted that the lasting consequence of such programming may be that it dramatically decreases voters' political efficacy—the ability to exercise political power and influence to serve their own interests.

The continuing impact of exposure to cynicism in media accounts about politics sparks worry that today's cynics will produce future generations that are even less interested or concerned about participating in political life. As Austin and Pinkleton (2001, p. 221) pointed out, "Cynical citizens may produce disaffected children who never participate in public affairs."

Despite the many concerns and complaints that have been raised regarding how the American media cover political campaigns and political issues, there are a few signs that merit optimism about the future. For example, journalists seem to be more reflective and conscientious about self-improvement than are members of almost any other profession. The topics of journalism ethics and professional responsibilities are important components of the curriculum of virtually every journalism school in the United States. These issues also receive significant attention at meetings of the Association for Education in Journalism and Mass Communication, the American Society of Newspaper Editors, and the Society of Professional Journalists. Through peer pressure; the promotion of high professional standards; improvements in the way in which journalism schools prepare future reporters, editors, and producers; and vigilant public interest and media watch groups, there are continuing pressures on the news profession to improve its products.

In addition, a number of foundations, such as the Pew Charitable Trusts, the Annenberg Foundation, and the Poynter Institute, to name just a few, have undertaken journalism ethics, political campaign coverage, and related topics as important areas of focus for their efforts to reform news coverage. Many of these projects seek to develop new strategies for reporting that would invite increased civic engagement, be less conflict oriented, concentrate more on issues, contain less focus on poll results, and encourage more minority voices in newsrooms. Although the pressures of the new economic marketplace in which newspapers, broadcasters, and online journalists compete for audiences inevitably complicate any attempts to improve the media coverage of politics, the hope remains that the continuing public conversation will result in some benefits to citizens and the nation's fragile democracy.

CHAPTER 6

Political Advertising

Political candidates and elected officials are continually engaged in efforts to communicate with voters and constituents. They give speeches, show up at public events, grant interviews, hold press conferences, appear on television and radio news programs, and advertise their candidacies through yard signs, newspaper displays, Web sites, radio and television spots, and direct mail. Television advertising is now the primary means by which most national and statewide candidates try to reach potential voters (Goldstein & Ridout, 2004). Paid media or political advertising is the only form of communication that is completely controlled by the candidate and/or the campaign staff. Advertising often consumes between 50 and 75 percent of the budget in a campaign for major public office. Although expenditures on all forms of campaign advertising have increased in recent years, broadcast advertising predominates and is the most expensive. Candidates will often spend vast sums of money on broadcast ads even when the races in which they are running are not especially competitive (DHinMI, 2005; Morris, 1998; Taylor & Ornstein, 2002).

PARADES, BANNERS, AND BUTTONS

American political candidates have always used advertisements of varying kinds to win votes. President George Washington is said to have promoted support for his candidacy by supplying potential voters with rum, punch, wine, cider, and beer (Jamieson, 1986). Once the voters were in the mood for celebration, it may have been easy to get them into the streets and organized into torchlight parades. The drinking parties and parades remained the primary form of campaigning throughout the nineteenth century. It is said, for example, that as many as ten thousand participants marched in torchlight parades to support the candidacy of Abraham Lincoln (Lincoln campaign, 2007). It is quite likely that such political parades inspired the noisy demonstrations that are routine today at the national party conventions.

It was common in the early campaigns for a candidate's supporters to join together to sing songs that celebrated the candidate's achievements and linked them to important political phrases. Thus, the supporters of John Adams bellowed out the song "Adams and Liberty," and those backing Thomas Jefferson sang "Honored Son of Liberty." Often these songs linked the preferred candidate to earlier patriots; for example, the supporters of Civil War general George McClellan, the Democratic nominee for president in 1864, sang "We'll Have Another Washington, McClellan Is the Man." Sometimes the songs offered brutal attacks on the opponent. In a campaign in which Grover Cleveland admitted he might have fathered an illegitimate child, his opponents took up the chant "Ma, Ma, where's my pa? Gone to the White House, ha, ha, ha" (Jamieson, 1986, p. 5).

Even today, candidates work to identify songs that will best communicate the campaign's message and that will attract and motivate potential voters. In the 2008 campaign, for example, Senator Hillary Clinton announced a contest so that supporters could help choose which song they wanted to hear during the candidate's public appearances and in her advertisements (Hillary Clinton's campaign song, 2007).

As campaign parades became more carefully staged events, marchers were encouraged to carry flags and banners bearing the candidates' likenesses. These banners often had slogans printed on them as well. The marches and parades were useful campaign devices because they mobilized the electorate in festive celebrations that demonstrated broad public support for the candidate. They also helped foster public understanding of electioneering as an important public ritual in a young democracy. The slogans the marchers yelled often succinctly expressed central messages or themes for the campaign. Some of the better-known slogans from past presidential campaigns include the following (Presidential campaign slogans, 2005):

William H. Harrison	1840	"Tippecanoe and Tyler too"
Abraham Lincoln	1864	"Don't swap horses in the middle of a stream"
William McKinley	1900	"A full dinner pail"
Warren Harding	1920	"Return to normalcy"
Calvin Coolidge	1924	"Keep cool with Coolidge"
Herbert Hoover	1928	"A chicken in every pot and a car in every garage"

Dwight Eisenhower	1952	"I like Ike"
Barry Goldwater	1964	"In your heart you know he's right"
Bill Clinton	1996	"Building a bridge to the 21st century"
George W. Bush	2000	"Compassionate conservatism"

Lapel buttons were first used in the 1896 presidential campaign between William McKinley and William Jennings Bryan. By the 1920s, improvements in lithograph technology made buttons easier (and cheaper) to produce. Buttons helped candidates achieve name recognition and made it easier for them to identify their supporters (Trent & Friedenberg, 1995). Once candidates could convince people to wear their pin, they could more likely count on winning their vote. Candidates also hoped these supporters would convince friends and neighbors to support them. Crowded rooms with voters all wearing the same campaign button may also have had the effect of demonstrating a bandwagon of support for the candidate. Yard signs and posters were useful, too, because they communicated that all the residents in the neighborhood or all the merchants on the block favored the candidate. These signs might even prompt people to begin discussing the candidate with their friends and neighbors, capitalizing on the benefits of interpersonal influence as a campaign strategy.

Pins, yard signs, bumper stickers, posters, and billboards are still found in many campaigns but perhaps not relied on as much as they used to be. The primary factor seems to be cost. Although the cost varies dramatically according to the material used, the number of colors being duplicated, and even the region of the country, the costs can be substantial. Yard signs that are 24 by 28 inches, for example, may cost about $1.50 each when purchased by the thousand. Buttons and bumper stickers may cost from 25 to 75 cents each, also when purchased by the thousand. Many campaigns choose to make the buttons available only to supporters who are willing to purchase them, so in some cases they may prove to be a source for campaign revenue.

Yard signs are especially common and useful in local elections because it may be more cost efficient for a candidate (say, for city council, the state legislature, or the school board) to blanket the district with yard signs than it would be to purchase print or broadcast ads that reach many voters outside of the district. In major cities such as Los Angeles, the cost of purchasing television or radio ads is prohibitive for all but the best-capitalized candidates, so lawn signs continue to be a very popular form of campaign advertising. Driving through Los Angeles during mayoral campaigns can yield a surprisingly accurate picture of how different ethnic communities will likely be voting, as the number of yard signs for the competing candidates varies from neighborhood to neighborhood. In many areas, yard signs have sparked problems. Signs of rival candidates are sometimes stolen or defaced. In addition, campaign posters and signs are so widely used in some cities that they have created a litter problem. After the election, the signs may remain up for weeks or months because, win or lose, few campaigns devote much energy to removing their signs from telephone posts or from public property.

NEWSPAPER DISPLAY ADVERTISEMENTS

Many candidates for public office purchase display advertisements in newspapers and magazines. Often these advertisements list the names of important or prominent citizens in the community who support the candidate. Newspaper ads enable the candidates to briefly highlight some of their positions on key issues and to announce public events and speaking engagements. Newspaper ads tend to reach better-informed voters who are more likely to turn to the print media for their political information. Major urban newspapers such as the *New York Times*, *Washington Post*, and *Los Angeles Times*, or important national newspapers directed to specialized audiences, such as the *Wall Street Journal*, are considered "prestige buys" and are often selected for the publication of lobbying or issue-focused ads. These full-page ads frequently urge policy makers or elected officials to support certain legislation. For example, lobbying groups might run such ads to urge support for or express opposition to a particular bill pending in Congress. Sometimes the administration or the State Department is the intended target of such messages. Pro-Israeli and pro-Arab ads, for instance, often compete with each other, urging support for alternative positions that the United States might take in Middle East peace negotiations. Such ads frequently encourage supporters to write to their elected officials and are aimed at keeping the issue in the public's mind and convincing those who have the power to act that the public is watching them.

A recent trend that has developed is the purchase by activist groups of full-page newspaper ads that are created to urge readers to turn to the Internet for additional information. These ads use traditional print media to arouse citizen attention and then direct people to the Web site where elaboration of the group's message is almost free of cost. Among the many groups that have used such ads are the National Rifle Association, the World Wildlife Fund, the National Right to Life Association, and the People for the American Way. Such ads are often intended to benefit or undermine one candidate or another in the race. For example, in the 2004 presidential campaign the liberal activist group MoveOn.org used this strategy to attempt to increase support for Kerry, while a group known as the Swift Boat Veterans for Truth employed the same technique to win votes for Bush.

Newspaper advertising has not always been an option for political advertisers. In earlier years most newspapers were fiercely partisan and unwilling to accept advertisements from candidates whom they did not support. Because newspapers are not "common carriers," they were not legally obliged to print advertisements or publish stories that they did not wish to carry.* In the 1850s, for example, only 5 percent of newspapers in the United States were self-identified as politically neutral or independent, and many of those that were not neutral would not accept paid advertisements for candidates whom they did not support.

THE ADVENT OF RADIO

The invention of radio marked a new era in political advertising. In 1924 there were three million radios in America; by 1935 there were ten times more (Jamieson, 1992). In 1924, both presidential candidates, Democrat John W. Davis and Republican Calvin Coolidge, purchased radio time for speeches. The Republicans spent $120,000 on radio and

---

* Acting on the assumption that the airwaves are public property and that broadcasters use them under license as long as they advance the public interest, the Federal Communications Commission (FCC) enacted a series of rules governing the provision of "equal time." These rules have been challenged but upheld in a series of Supreme Court cases (the most important of which was *Red Lion Broadcasting Co. v. Federal Communications Commission*, 1969). The equal time provision ensures public access to broadcast media in three areas. First, broadcasters who permit a candidate for political office to campaign on their stations must give equal opportunities to all other candidates for the same office. Second, broadcasters must meet the requirements of the fairness doctrine. Broadcasters who air stories about public issues or controversies must allow for a right of rebuttal. If an attack is made on the character, honesty, or integrity of any person or group, then that group must be notified, provided with a transcript of the comments, and given an opportunity to respond (Graber, 1993, p. 67).

The Supreme Court, however, has made an important distinction between print and broadcast media with regard to the provision of equal time. Because newspapers do not operate on a public license (i.e., anyone who wishes to do so is permitted to purchase a printing press and publish his or her own newspaper), the Supreme Court ruled in *Miami Herald Publishing Company v. Tornillo*, 1974) that as long as newspapers do not libel or slander people or publish top secret information, they are free to publish whatever they choose, unhampered by legal restraints. Citizens may request the right to respond to a story or attack, or they may request the right to purchase an advertisement, but they have no right to demand publication of a retraction or of their defense (Graber, 1993, p. 66).

the Democrats $40,000, and the Republican Coolidge won the election (Diamond & Bates, 1992). Encouraged by those results, the Republicans in 1928 earmarked the majority of their publicity money for the purchase of radio time (Jamieson, 1992).

The advent of radio transformed campaigning. As Jamieson (1992) noted:

> Over the course of 100 days in the campaign of 1896, William Jennings Bryan, by his own account, had made 600 speeches in twenty-seven states and had traveled over 18,000 miles to reach 5 million people. In a single fireside chat delivered while seated in his parlor, Franklin Delano Roosevelt reached twelve times that number. (pp. 19–20)

With the invention of radio, audiences no longer had to leave their homes and join an assembled crowd to be a part of a political campaign. Voters could listen to campaign rhetoric from the comfort of their own living rooms. This also, of course, led to an increasingly passive role for the electorate and perhaps diminished some of the festivities and frivolity that had marked earlier electoral campaigns in America.

The use of radio demanded a new set of skills from the nation's politicians. The fiery orators of the earlier age gave way to candidates who were more capable of generating intimate conversations with the inanimate microphone. Franklin Roosevelt's mastery of radio during his "fireside chats" marked the transition of the U.S. presidency into the electronic age. Roosevelt reached almost 60 million listeners with his broadcasts and helped calm and give hope to a country traumatized by the Great Depression and World War II (Jamieson, 1992).

President Ronald Reagan turned to radio during his first term in office when he discovered that it was an effective medium for communicating with voters in a format in which he could control the content of his message and did not have to confront hostile questioners. Even today the current president delivers a weekly Saturday morning radio address and often uses this broadcast to announce new policy initiatives. Although the actual live audience for these programs is tiny, the White House Press Office releases the transcripts so that other media can report on what was said. The broadcasts thus receive significant news media attention and are carefully plumbed by national political reporters for information about the administration's political agenda and upcoming initiatives. The party that is not in power at the moment is given the opportunity to select a spokesperson to reply to these weekly messages. The people selected to give those responses are often those whom party leaders consider to be "rising stars" who might have bright political futures. Recently, the Democrats (as the party not in control of the White House) moved to have a weekly address given in Spanish, recognizing the increasing influence of Latino voters in the United States.

Even though radio advertising is far less important today, now that it has been replaced by the extensive use of television advertising, it is still important to many candidates. Radio continues to have some distinct advantages as a medium for political advertising. The costs, both to produce the advertisements and to purchase airtime, are far lower than they are for television. The costs of purchasing radio advertisements differ widely, however, depending on the size of the radio market, the number of competing stations, the health of the economy, and the number of listeners likely to be tuned in at any particular time (as determined by audience share ratings). Most political advertisers purchase time during the hours when radio listening audiences are the largest: when people are commuting to or from work. It is not surprising that radio advertising is especially important in those areas where people spend a lot of time in their cars, either because they must drive long distances or because they are stuck in traffic (Paletz, 1999).

A unique benefit of radio advertising is the ability to target specific groups of voters on the basis of the station's format. Thus, for example, a candidate who wishes to reach younger voters might purchase time on stations emphasizing a Top 40 format, older voters by purchasing time on a classic rock or easy-listening format, or perhaps more blue-collar voters by purchasing time on a country-western format. Likewise, there are radio stations that appeal to ethnic minorities (a Spanish language radio station has the largest audience share in the Los Angeles market) or to ideologically committed listeners (on both the political left and the right, although as was discussed in Chapter 5, there are many more conservatively oriented commercial radio stations, perhaps because the liberals are listening to National Public Radio). Unlike most television stations, newspapers, or yard signs, which are seen by a wide cross section of voters, radio draws listeners who tend to select stations that reflect their interests and self-identity (O'Keefe, 1989).

Radio is not without its disadvantages as an advertising medium, however, since few listeners give their full attention to the broadcasts. Most people today listen to their radios while giving their primary attention to some other task, making it far less certain that they will concentrate on or recall what they hear. Furthermore, anyone who has been in a car with young radio listeners knows how frequently they will hit the button to change the station the moment the music stops and the ads begin. A recent innovation that has expanded the reach of radio, however, is that stations are increasingly streamed live and often archived on the Web. We will examine the impact of Web radio in Chapter 8 on new technologies.

THE TELEVISION CAMPAIGN

In most campaigns for statewide or national office, television spots are now the dominant mode of campaign advertising. The first political spots on television were broadcast during the 1952 election by the Eisenhower campaign. One of these first ads featured a dancing cartoon figure of Uncle Sam leading a circus elephant wearing a banner bearing a likeness of Eisenhower. Parading behind the elephant was a diverse array of American men and women drawn from a variety of different occupations and all singing the jingle "You like Ike, I like Ike, everybody likes Ike for president. . . ."*

Clearly, the purpose was to win name recognition, communicate that Eisenhower enjoyed the support of people of different socioeconomic means, and simulate the old-fashioned campaign parades of earlier days in this new visual medium. Eisenhower also introduced a series of advertisements called "Eisenhower Answers America." In these spots the candidate is seen answering the questions posed to him by ordinary citizens. The ads are especially visually interesting because the questioners and the candidates do not appear in the same frame. The questioners are always captured in a pose in which they appear to be looking up, directing their questions to the candidate who might be standing above them on a platform. The former general, on the other hand, is captured in a commanding pose, looking down at the unseen audience, and sternly scolding the Democrats for the mess they have made of the country. These ads, which seem positively primitive by contemporary standards, nonetheless captured the attention of voters and the imagination of campaign consultants. The Democratic candidate who opposed Eisenhower in 1952, Governor Adlai Stevenson of Illinois, was unwilling to appear in his own spots. He did, however, permit others to speak, and even sing, on his behalf. One of his most

---

* This ad, the Stevenson ads, and hundreds of other ads from presidential campaigns over the past five decades, can be seen at the Web site "The Living Room Candidate," hosted by the American Museum of the Moving Image. See http://livingroomcandidate .movingimage.us/election/index.php?ad_id=. Retrieved on February 13, 2007.

memorable spots featured a lounge singer crooning, "I love the gov., the gov. of Illinois. . . ."

After Stevenson lost the 1952 election to Eisenhower, he reconsidered his refusal to appear in his own ads. In a 1956 rematch between the two men, Stevenson did appear in his own ads, albeit in a manner that revealed how completely uncomfortable he was in selling himself to the American people that way. For example, in a remarkable ad entitled "The Man from Libertyville [Illinois]," the governor invites viewers into his library for a heart-to-heart chat. Before going further, however, he warns his audience that the library is different today than it normally would be because of the presence of all the TV cameras and cables. He also explains that although he marvels at the wonderful benefits of campaigning on TV, he will not permit it to dominate his campaign because he feels he must travel so that he can meet and listen to the people.* Stevenson's appearance in his own ads, perhaps because he seemed so unsuited to this new medium, was not enough to change the outcome of the race, as he lost to Eisenhower for the second time.

In the 1960 race both John Kennedy and Richard Nixon made extensive use of television ads, and both were eager to appear in their own ads. The Nixon ads emphasized a sober and statesmanlike Nixon posed in an austere office setting. The Kennedy ads featured very tight camera close-ups obviously intended to emphasize the candidate's handsome looks and youth. Kennedy also made heavy use of clips from the televised Kennedy-Nixon debates to demonstrate his command of the issues and his ability to think on his feet and forcefully communicate his ideas. Finally, in a ground-breaking ad, Jacqueline Kennedy appeared and spoke in Spanish in an attempt to reach Latino voters. This ad proved especially controversial both because it, for the first time, made the candidate's spouse an active participant in the campaign and because many argued that anyone who could vote should be able to understand and follow the campaign in English.†

The appeal of advertising on television greatly increased with each election cycle as the number of American homes that possessed television sets increased. In 1952, 34.2 percent of American homes had a TV; 1956, 71.8 percent; 1960, 87.1 percent; 1964, 92.3 percent; 1968,

* This ad can also be seen at "The Living Room Candidate" Web site: http://livingroomcandidate.movingimage.us/election/index.php?nav_action=election&nav_subaction=overview&campaign_id=166. Retrieved on February 13, 2007.
† These ads are available at http://livingroomcandidate.movingimage.us/election/index.php?nav_action=election&nav_subaction=overview&campaign_id=167. Retrieved on February 13, 2007.

94.6 percent; 1972, 95.8 percent, and 1976, 97 percent (Television history, 2006). As we noted in Chapter 5, today in the United States there are more television sets than there are people. As television viewing became more and more central to how American families lived their lives, and as exposure to all forms of television ads increased, it is not surprising that political candidates became increasingly interested in using this form of communication to attempt to sway potential voters.

Until 1964, most political advertisements consisted primarily of cartoons or "talking head" spots with the candidates speaking directly to voters. In 1964, the style and content of TV ads markedly changed. In that year the first sharply negative or "attack" advertisements surfaced on television. The style of ads changed again in 1968, as more visual images and "gimmicks" were used to communicate with voters (Devlin, 1986). As technology has improved and public tastes and expectations have become more sophisticated, the nature of political advertisements on television also became more sophisticated. Ronald Reagan's campaign for reelection in 1984 truly broke new ground. Many of President Reagan's ads did not feature the candidate but instead used a montage of film clips. One such ad showed a boat sailing into a harbor, a bride kissing her grandmother, a family carrying a new rolled carpet from their station wagon into their home, and an American flag waving. As these images were shown, a narrator declared, "It is morning again in America." Another Reagan ad showed a picture of a large grizzly bear (clearly suggesting the animal representation of the Soviet Union), with a voice intoning "There is a bear in the woods." As the bear comes face to face with the silhouette of a lone hunter (the visual image of the independent-minded cowboy president perhaps?), the voice asks, "Isn't it smart to be as strong as the bear?"* Only the soundtrack informs the viewer that this is a political message and not a product advertisement or entertainment programming. Although few candidates since have been able to match the production values or creativity of these 1984 ads, they have borrowed heavily from their style.

As the use of television political spot advertising has increased, the amount of money spent on these campaigns has likewise increased. Bennett (1996, p. 137) reported that in 1988 the presidential candidates spent $500 million on their campaigns. Most analysts predict that in the 2008 campaign the candidates will spend more than $1 billion on

---

* See http://livingroomcandidate.movingimage.us/election/index.php?nav_action=election&nav_subaction=overview&campaign_id=173. Retrieved on February 13, 2007.

their campaigns (Lightman, 2007; Mosk, 2007). It is not just presidential candidates who are raising and spending vast sums of money to buy expensive television ads; so also are congressional and senate candidates. In the 2006 midterm congressional elections, for example, House winners raised a record average of $1.1 million, and in races where challengers beat incumbents, those challengers raised an average of $1.4 million. This represented a 10 percent increase since the 2004 election (House winners raised a record, 2006). Senate races, which are conducted statewide and thus are even more expensive to wage, also require candidates to raise vast sums of money for advertising to be competitive. Causin, Howard, and Miller (2005, p. 2) wrote, "It is no longer possible to run for Senate with less than $3 million in the campaign coffers, in any state in the union. And in other states (California, Wisconsin, Minnesota, Missouri, Florida, Washington, Michigan, Pennsylvania, and New York), a candidate won't be competitive with less than $10 million in the coffers in 2006." In past campaigns, more than 50 percent of the money raised for congressional and senate campaigns has been spent on paid media (Taylor, 2001).

The increased amount of money devoted to television spot advertisements has, as might be expected, had a profound impact on the numbers of ads to which voters are exposed. In the weeks before the Iowa caucuses, for example, the television stations in Des Moines, the state's largest city, are often literally sold out of time slots and in some cases have to preempt regular advertisers to make room for the political spots. Because there is so much competition for ad space in the days before an election, TV stations are permitted to sell time at their highest published "book rate." Thus, owning a local TV station can be a lucrative investment. Even though the audience for broadcast TV has been shrinking in an era when people have access to cable television channels and the Internet, local TV stations can earn enormous profits. In 2000, for example, the average Fortune 500 company had a profit margin of 6.8 percent, the average network TV affiliate station a profit of 30.2 percent, and the average independent local TV station a whopping 42.3 percent. Local TV stations in "swing states" where the presidential race was especially close or where there were closely contested U.S. Senate races did especially well (How broadcasters' ad revenues rise, 2001). Given that the flow of money into and out of campaigns has increased in every election cycle and can be expected to continue to increase, local TV stations can be expected to continue to prosper.

Many political analysts noted that the massive infusion of cash fundamentally changed the early election contests (both the caucuses and primaries). These changes will, of course, be magnified in the 2008 presidential race because so many states—including heavily populated states such as California, New York, and Illinois—have moved up the dates of their primaries to have a greater impact on the selection of the candidates. With the crush of early contests and the crowded field of candidates, these early races can no longer provide as much opportunity for "retail" politics—where candidates meet voters face to face in small, intimate, informal gatherings. Instead, the dominance of polished and very expensive ad campaigns means that door-to-door campaigning in small towns in Iowa and New Hampshire will be replaced by television campaigning, and candidates will devote more of their time trying to raise the vast sums of money necessary to succeed. The lengthening of the presidential campaign and the compression of the primary calendar mean that the nominees for both parties are now selected so early that by the time many voters get to cast their ballots in their state's primary election, the race for the nomination is all but finished. It is thus ironic that the changes in party nominating procedures that were created to give ordinary voters more input into the selection of their party's candidates—moves designed to get politics out of smoke-filled rooms and into the open air that we discussed in Chapter 2—may have contributed to this situation of diminished voter input.

DIRECT MAIL ADVERTISING

In addition to the dramatic increase in television spot advertising, recently candidates have increasingly used direct mail advertisements to promote their candidacies. Direct mail is especially useful in campaigns where the voting districts and television media markets do not match up very well. In most large cities, for example, candidates for Congress or for mayor who wish to purchase media time are forced to pay advertising rates based on a market that includes many voters outside their districts or the boundaries of their cities. These rates are often prohibitively expensive. The Los Angeles media market—also called the ADI, or area of dominant influence—for example, is the second largest in the nation. Los Angeles has nineteen commercial and four noncommercial TV stations serving approximately 5 million households in Los Angeles, Ventura, Orange, San Bernardino, and Inyo counties (Nielsen Media Research, 2002). The average cost of a thirty-second television ad in Los Angeles is eighteen times higher than the average cost in a small media market (Ansolabehere, Gerber, & Snyder, 2001).

As a result, as TV advertising rates soar, it is much more likely that candidates for local races will turn to direct mail instead of TV ads to reach voters (Ansolabehere, Gerber, & Snyder, 2001).

In many primary campaigns, candidates mail to all registered members of their party. In general elections, candidates may tailor their mailings. Some strongly partisan mailings will go only to the members of their party, while other mailings may also go to those who registered as independents or who declined to state a party preference. Candidates can also address their messages to "occupant" and mail to every mailing address in their district, but this is not a very efficient way to reach voters or spend campaign revenues. Research suggests that people are much more likely to open and attend to mail that is addressed to them personally than they are to solicitations that are not so addressed (Armstrong, 1988). In closely contested elections, voters can face a barrage of mail so overwhelming that it is sometimes difficult to make particular pieces stand out and be remembered. To achieve this, many advertisers have turned to increasingly negative attack-style mailings that question the competence, integrity, and motives of the opposing candidates. In recent city council races in Los Angeles, for example, mailings have alleged that the opposing candidate(s) is a drug addict, a convicted felon, philanderer, high school dropout, captive of special interests, or refused to pay child support or misrepresented his resume. Because mailings can be targeted based on party registration, demographic analysis, organizational memberships, zip codes, and other criteria, these messages can be adjusted to fit the perceived prejudices of intended recipients.

Direct mail adverting has been shown to be a very effective means for candidates and political action committees to mobilize voters to go to the polls. Direct mail solicitations are also an effective way to secure campaign donations. Finally, direct mail has been linked to advances in public opinion polling as an important means of identifying potential supporters. We will discuss this use for direct mail in greater detail in Chapter 7.

One other form of direct mail advertising merits discussion. In many areas individual candidates, political parties, or special interest lobbying groups have developed "sample ballots" that list the preferred candidates for various offices and state positions on ballot propositions, bond issues, and the like. These "samples" are designed in such a way that a voter can simply carry them into the booth and thus vote in accordance with this slate of candidates and issues. In some cases these sample ballots are genuine, and the people and issues on them are indeed endorsed by the sponsors. In other cases, however, somewhat unscrupulous consultants have simply sold space on the sample ballots to candidates who would not be so endorsed. For example, in my heavily Democratic and also heavily minority-dominated city council district in Los Angeles, in almost every election cycle flyers claiming to be "Your Official Democratic Voting Guide" are mailed out. Often these sample ballots identify the Democratic nominees for the top-of-the-ticket races for president, governor, U.S. senator, and U.S. representative. But then they begin slipping in the names of Republican candidates for lesser offices such as state treasurer, secretary of state, insurance commissioner, and so forth. They also frequently list judicial or school board candidates and take positions on state propositions that would not be supported by the Democratic Party. This form of deceptive advertising seeks to exploit voters' lack of knowledge about most of these candidates and political issues. I strongly suspect that this same technique is used in other cities in the nation and have no reason to believe that it is only Republican candidates who are willing to engage in such efforts to mislead voters.

TELEPHONE ADVERTISING

Another form of political advertising that has become increasingly common as a result of new developments in communication technologies is the computer-assisted telephone call. The development of new computer-dialing programs enables advertisers simultaneously to call thousands of households at relatively low cost. Sometimes this strategy is used to make blanket calls to reach everyone in a neighborhood or voting district, but more often the calls are targeted in an attempt to reach specific voter demographics or interest groups identified through polling or microtargeting techniques (we will discuss the use of these polling techniques and the use of phone calls that misrepresent advertising messages as public opinion polls in Chapter 7). Gerald Sussman (2005) wrote:

> The system of predictive dialing software (also called computer-assisted telephone interviewing) enables telemarketers to automatically dial a list of people appearing on a computer screen, filtering out busy signals, telephone messages that a line is not in service, and answering machines—to respond only to a live "hello." A computer automatically connects a contact with an available telemarketer, who can then begin reading the standardized pitch or questionnaire, or it can leave a prerecorded message. (p. 92)

Sussman (2005) noted that some telemarketing firms boast that they can make more than 100,000 calls an hour. This advertising strategy is often used in efforts to remind voters to go to the polls on Election Day.

It is now common to use prerecorded messages that offer endorsements by other elected officials or by celebrities. For example, in 2004 I received phone calls urging me to vote for Senator Kerry with recorded messages by former president Bill Clinton, Senator Dianne Feinstein, Senator Barbara Boxer, and actor Ed Asner. What is not clear is precisely how effective such phone calls are in motivating voters. It is well understood that most people do not like to be interrupted during the dinner hour (the preferred time for making such calls because that is when most people are likely to be at home) by telemarketers. The use of the prerecorded messages may be especially unpopular. At least one study found that campaigns might be better off avoiding the recorded messages and having live volunteers make the calls. This same study argued that the use of recordings rather than live volunteers might be one factor in the decreased voter turnout in recent elections (Reed, 2007).

The cost of the telemarketing is so low, however, that in the absence of clear evidence that the calls create a backlash of angry citizens toward the candidate or the political party, the use of such calls will likely continue. In 2003, the federal government created the "Do Not Call" registry wherein people could notify the telemarketers that they no longer wished to receive unsolicited phone calls. Approximately 95 million Americans have registered on this list. Due to First Amendment concerns, however, being identified on that list does not limit the ability of political candidates, parties, or interest groups to telephone you to spread political messages. Nonetheless, the very creation of the list and the public's frustration with the commercial use of such calls has diminished the effectiveness of telephone advertising (Abelson, 2005).

ADVERTISING STRATEGIES

Research suggests that people actively seek information that they can use to help them fill in the gaps in their understanding of their world (Dervin, 1981). Because people's needs differ at various points in time, the strategic goals of political campaigns also differ. Pfau and

Parrott (1993) identified three stages in campaigns. In the first stage, the goal is to generate awareness of the candidate, voter recognition of what the candidate stands for, and an understanding of how the candidate's election might serve their interests. At this stage most voters lack information, although there tend to be huge gaps in knowledge between the most politically active and less active voters. There is also substantial evidence that at this stage voters are very susceptible to new information and are heavily influenced by it (Kennamer & Chaffee, 1982; Pfau & Parrott, 1993). During the awareness stage, voters also seek information on the candidate's character. Often this stage coincides with the primary campaigns, during which the candidates pursue their party's nomination for office.

The second stage is the discrimination phase of the campaign. At this point the voters begin to compare the candidates. Now the challenge for the campaigns is to present information that highlights the strength of one candidate and the weaknesses of the competing candidates. Attack messages are frequently used at this stage to draw attention to the differences among candidates (Pfau & Parrott, 1993). In this stage of a campaign, candidates are also seeking to establish themselves as legitimate contenders—that not only are they sufficiently qualified to serve, but also that they stand a realistic chance of winning office. Voters are often reluctant to support with either their checkbooks or their ballots candidates who do not seem to have at least reasonable prospects for success.

The final stage is the postdecision stage. At this point voters have decided which candidate they are going to vote for, but they continue to seek information that reinforces their judgment. They need messages that bolster their opinion and refute other messages that might cause them to doubt their choice (Pfau & Parrott, 1993). There is also evidence that advertisements at this stage in the campaign are very helpful because they reinforce supporters, boost staff morale, help raise campaign funds, and preserve the sense that the campaign has genuine momentum. This helps to explain why even those candidates who are very far ahead in a race—often, for example, congressional candidates who do not face serious opposition—will continue to purchase advertising to send a message to their supporters and keep them motivated to ensure that they will turn out to vote on Election Day. Messages at this stage of the campaign are also designed to win active participation from supporters to enlist their efforts in getting their friends, neighbors, and family members on board the campaign as well.

WHAT POLITICAL ADVERTISING CAN ACHIEVE

Most studies suggest that political campaign advertising has some impact on the outcome of elections and on voter learning about candidates and issues, but the research findings have been neither consistent nor definitive. Patterson and McClure (1976) argued that political commercials offered more information to shape voter knowledge about the candidates than did televised political campaign news. Some scholars supported these findings (for example, Brians & Wattenberg, 1996; Drew & Weaver, 1998; Just, Crigler, & Wallach, 1990), whereas others argued that TV campaign news coverage contributed more to political knowledge than did advertisements (Hofstetter, Zukin, & Buss, 1978; Zhao & Chaffee, 1995). Almost all scholars would concede, however, that there are limits on how much advertising can be expected to achieve. It is not likely, for example, that even the wisest political advertising strategist could have succeeded in crafting an image of George W. Bush as a scintillating and charismatic speaker. Most scholars argue that although advertising can influence levels of knowledge, shape opinions, and influence voter choices, at some point the ads must come face to face with political reality (Popkin, 1994). Precisely what a candidate may accomplish with campaign advertising depends in part on the voters' beliefs about the candidates and the issues identified prior to the start of the campaign. Thus, the most effective campaigns do not fundamentally alter the political landscape but instead ride the wave of public opinion by linking the message of the ads to the news stories surfacing in the media (Ansolabehere & Iyengar, 1994).

It is important to note that most studies that have examined the effectiveness of political advertisements have focused on television ads because this form of advertising so thoroughly dominates today. As new forms of advertising—for example, on the Internet—become more common, we can expect that scholars will begin to devote more attention to assessing the impact of these messages.

Research has suggested that political commercials may help set the agenda for campaign news and for those issues that voters will see as important (Boyle, 2001; Ghorpade, 1986; Holbert, Benoit, Hansen, & Wen, 2002). The notion that the ads set agendas has not been confirmed by all researchers, however; Benoit, Leshner, and Chattopadhayay (2005) found that although political ad viewing seemed to predict political knowledge, perceptions of candidate character, attitudes toward candidates, and interest in the campaign, it did not significantly predict the perceived importance of certain issues or the likelihood of voting.

Research has strongly suggested that political advertising may play a significant role in how voters perceive candidate images and that this impact may be greatest in the earliest stages of a campaign rather than in the closing days of a campaign as the election draws near (Cundy, 1986). Although we have grown accustomed to seeing a flurry of TV ads in the final days of a campaign, Chaffee (1981) suggested that this is actually a time of relative stability, with probably no more than 1 percent of the eventual voters actually making up their minds in September or October. Of course, given how close the 2000 and 2004 presidential elections were, this 1 percent could certainly have made a difference in the outcome.

Political spots have been shown to be more effective than other forms of media in conveying information to less-interested and less-informed individuals (Goldstein & Ridout, 2004). Political advertisements achieved the highest level of impact with voters who have some prior interest in the candidate or the subject addressed in the spot (Grunig, 1989; Mendelsohn, 1973). Atkin and Heald (1976) found that respondents who were actively seeking information were likely to recall more about the political advertisements that they observed than were those not actively seeking information. Ansolabehere and Iyengar (1995) found that nearly half of all people who were exposed to a thirty-second advertisement could not recall that they had seen a political advertisement just a half-hour earlier. Furthermore, the researchers found that 20 percent of those who had not been exposed to any advertisements claimed to have seen one. Other research suggests, however, that political advertisements are more likely to be recalled by viewers than are product advertisements. The study speculated that this is because political advertisements are newer and often shorter than other advertisements (cited by Yeric, 2001, p. 136). Issues of ad timing and frequency of exposures to ads greatly complicate any attempts to assess the impact of political ads. As Goldstein and Ridout (2004, p. 223) declared:

> Existing research, for instance, tends to ignore the possibility that an ad aired three months before Election Day may have a different impact than an ad aired the day before the election. One possibility is that people have little incentive to pay attention to the campaign so many months before they must vote, and even if they do pay enough attention to receive an early message, they are likely to have forgotten it three months later. On the other hand, an ad aired early may have a greater impact because partisan attachments are not yet activated. Despite these possibilities, almost all empirical research treats all ads, regardless of when they are aired, equally.

It is also clear that exposures to political ads are by no means uniform. In presidential races, for example, voters in contested or "swing" states will be far more likely to see many political ads, whereas voters in safely "blue" or "red" states will likely see few ads. In addition, ad buys are often clustered in particular media markets and on specific types of programming, factors that certainly affect how likely it may be that any individual viewer will see the ads. Finally, some campaigns raise and spend huge amounts of money on ads and thus can produce and display many different ads in multiple buys across a wide array of channels. Cash-strapped campaigns, on the other hand, may have the resources to produce only one or two ads (often with lower production values) and may be able to purchase only one or two limited exposures. During the 2008 primary campaign, viewers saw far fewer ads for Representative Dennis Kucinich (D—Ohio) than they saw for Senator Hillary Clinton.

Spots are somewhat effective, however, even in cases where there is unwillingness to consider the message. Joslyn (1981) reported that spots can help overcome voters' predispositions and opinions because exposure to television spots is essentially involuntary. The impact of spots is also great because the spots may be ubiquitous. In a closely contested race between well-funded contenders, there may be so many spots that viewers cannot avoid being exposed to them (Louden, 1990).

Walker and Dubitsky (1994) suggested that spots are far more likely to be effective if viewers like them. Consequently, they suggested that humor, vibrant colors, engaging music, clever plot lines, and dramatic scenes would enhance the appeal of advertisements. Perloff and Kinsey (1992) surveyed campaign consultants regarding what kinds of spots were most effective. They discovered that most consultants believed it was vitally important to reach voters with emotional appeals and that appearance and images mattered substantially more than did extensive amounts of information.

Ansolabehere and Iyengar (1995) reported that even small doses of campaign advertising might be sufficient to influence voters' preferences. In their study, exposure to a single thirty-second spot advertisement boosted the sponsoring candidate's share of the vote by nearly 5 percent. The researchers' explanation for this effect was that the very brevity of the ads might increase their value because audience attention spans are so short. They also noted that ad makers like to use instantly recognizable cultural symbols and scripts (for example, Social Security cards, construction workers in hard hats, flags, attentive children in classroom settings, and so on). These symbols and icons reinforce long-standing cultural values (Pollay, 1989).

The emphasis on values does not increase voters' understanding of complex policy alternatives very much, but it may give them confidence that they can decide between competing candidates on the basis of their character and suitability for elected office. Media-dominated campaigns have thus transformed elections into contests between candidates rather than contests among competing parties, competing value systems, or competing ideologies (Joslyn, 1986). Joslyn (p. 178) went so far as to argue that this kind of campaigning ends up "impoverishing the electorate" as it fosters a "throw the rascals out" mentality (p. 181).

NEGATIVE ATTACK-STYLE ADVERTISEMENTS

Negative political advertising, although not new, has become increasingly common in the United States. In fact, it must now be considered a standard practice (Lau & Pomper, 2002; Schenck-Hamlin, Procter, & Rumsey, 2000). Patterson (2002, p. 50) declared that "negative advertising has become a defining feature of presidential politics." Negative ads can be direct and explicit in their attack, or they can be indirect and can operate primarily through innuendo. In the past, few negative ads offered intensely personal attacks because there is such a great risk of incurring voter backlash (Gronbeck, 1992). It seems now, however, that the use of such personal attacks may be increasing (Yeric, 2001). Negative ads are believed to be more attention grabbing and more likely to stick in voters' minds than are positive ads (Devlin, 1995; Perloff & Kinsey, 1992).

Although attack politics have long been a part of American elections—Patterson (2002, p. 50) cited the Thomas Jefferson versus John Adams campaign of 1800 as an example—most communication scholars think that the first truly negative television advertisement was the "Daisy Spot" produced for President Lyndon Johnson's campaign in 1964. In this spot, which ran on television only once, a camera focuses on a little girl standing in the middle of a field picking petals off a daisy. She is counting each petal as she picks it: "One, two, three, four, five, seven, six, six, eight, nine, nine." Suddenly the girl is startled and looks up. Then a man's voice, booming as if heard over a loudspeaker at a missile launch site, is heard: "Ten, nine, eight, seven, six, five, four, three, two, one." The visual switches to a close-up of a nuclear explosion, and the blast is heard. Then the visual cuts to white letters on a black background: "Vote for President Johnson on November 3." Meanwhile, the announcer says, "The stakes are too high for you to stay home" (Diamond & Bates, 1992, p. 124).

The spot played on the public's anxieties about Republican presidential nominee, Arizona senator Barry Goldwater. Earlier in the campaign Goldwater had mused that it might be appropriate to "lob nuclear bombs into the men's room of the Kremlin" (Diamond & Bates, 1992, p. 125). Goldwater had also opined that tactical nuclear weapons might be of use in securing an end to the conflict in Vietnam, and he had opposed the Comprehensive Nuclear Test Ban Treaty with the Soviet Union (Sabato, 1981). The Daisy Spot advertisement sought to communicate that the U.S. presidency is too important and powerful an office to fall into the hands of someone who might recklessly use the most deadly weapon known to humankind.

Goldwater and his Republican partisans were appalled by the Daisy Spot and protested so loudly and forcefully that the ad was withdrawn. The damage was done, however, as the ad was replayed in TV news broadcasts and discussed in newspaper stories. The Johnson campaign produced other negative ads as well, including one very powerful ad that showed a little girl eating an ice cream cone while the narrator warned that Goldwater's willingness to test additional nuclear weapons would put more radioactive poisons into the atmosphere and that those poisons might get into the food chain (Diamond & Bates, 1992, p. 129). Soon the Goldwater campaign began to produce its own attack-style ads, accusing Johnson of political corruption and of being responsible for the moral decline in America that had caused the increasing rates of violent crime (Diamond & Bates, 1992, p. 140).

Johnson's landslide victory over Goldwater convinced many candidates and campaign consultants that the negative ads were effective, especially if they resonated with public perceptions already held and if they seemed to be supported by other news stories, such as the seemingly reckless statements by Senator Goldwater. As might be expected, the use of negative ads dramatically increased in ensuing campaigns (Hart, 2000; Yeric, 2001). In 1968, Richard Nixon's campaign produced ads focusing on civil disturbances and crime in U.S. cities, suggesting that Vice President Hubert Humphrey and the Democrats were responsible for this violence and chaos (Diamond & Bates, 1992). The Humphrey campaign responded with ads ridiculing Nixon's vice presidential running mate, Spiro T. Agnew. In one such ad the visual display shows a TV set with the words "Agnew for Vice President?" on the screen. Meanwhile, the audio track consists only of uproarious laughter. Finally, the visual display changes to "This would be funny if it weren't so serious" (Diamond & Bates, 1992, p. 173).

By the time of the 1972 campaign, negative ads had become so common that few political candidates were willing to forgo their use.

In the 2006 California Democratic gubernatorial primary campaign, for example, both candidates Phil Angelides and Steve Westly pledged that they would not run negative ads. As the race tightened, however, Westly broke the pledge and began running ads attacking Angelides (Finnegan, 2006). Soon Angelides responded in kind, and the race turned very nasty. Angelides won the Democratic primary election and ran against the incumbent governor, Arnold Schwarzenegger, in the general election. As might have been predicted, Republican Governor Schwarzenegger made use of the Westly attacks on Angelides with ads that said, "Here is what fellow Democrat Steve Westly had to say about Phil Angelides."

Unlike product commercials that appear on television, political commercials are not regulated either to ensure their truthfulness or to prohibit distortions or deceptions. This is not to suggest that there are no consequences to the use of negative ads, however, for some research suggests that the use of negative ads can boomerang and undermine public support for the candidate who chooses to run them (Garramone, 1984; King & McConnell, 2003). This was certainly the case for Westly in the 2006 gubernatorial California primary race (Finnegan, 2006).

Many voters dislike negative advertising and may hold the sponsor of the ads accountable for their displeasure (Garramone, 1985). Even if such ads are shown to work in one election, they can leave a bitter memory in the people's minds. In 1988, for example, Vice President George H. W. Bush ran a brutal negative campaign against Democratic challenger Massachusetts governor Michael Dukakis. Bush blamed Dukakis for allowing convicted murderer "Willie" Horton, an African American, out on a weekend furlough from the penitentiary.* While he was out of prison, Horton was convicted of kidnapping a couple, stabbing the young man, and raping the woman. Many charged that this ad had racist implications (for example, see *U.S. News'* Barone accused, 2004). Another Bush ad showed a prison gate that was a turnstile with inmates freely leaving, thus suggesting that Dukakis's approach to convicted criminals was to create a "revolving door" policy that quickly released them to offend again. Bush was elected in 1988, coming from far behind in the race after planting doubts about Dukakis. Some experts claimed that when President Bush tried to make character attacks against Democratic challenger Bill Clinton in 1992, however, the strategy

---

* The convict's actual name was William Horton. He never personally used or was known by the nickname "Willie." Jamieson (1993, pp. 50–51) suggests that he was called Willie, a name that stuck in the ad because an African American named Willie would be more frightening to Caucasian voters (calling up sinister images from the days when slave masters gave nicknames to their property) than he would be if he were called by his given name, William.

backfired and actually drove up Bush's negative numbers (Shogan, 1996). One such ad, for example, featured a half-dozen ordinary Americans who expressed their anxiety about Clinton's lack of integrity, speculated about how he "dodged the draft," declared that he was "not honorable," and concluded that he was "scary."* The public reaction to this ad may suggest that candidates lose credibility when they resort to negative ads too frequently or make attacks that seem unfair (Shogan, 1996).

A similar scenario unfolded in the 2001 and 2005 elections for mayor of Los Angeles. In 2001, city attorney Jim Hahn defeated former Speaker of the State Assembly Antonio Villaraigosa in a campaign dominated by negative TV ads that not so subtly sought to increase public anxieties about a Hispanic mayor (York, 2001). These ads, which seemed to allege that Villaraigosa might be sympathetic to gangs and to illegal drug users, were described and discussed in Chapter 4. Villaraigosa, who had pledged to run a positive campaign, was reluctant to strike back. In politics, though, good deeds seldom go unpunished. Villaraigosa suffered badly for his unwillingness to travel the low road. Although he had won the primary vote by 5 percent, he lost the run-off by 7 percent in an election that clearly split along racial lines. Villaraigosa won more than 80 percent of Latino voters, while Hahn won 85 percent of African American voters and also won the majority of Caucasian voters from the Valley. The ad campaign left a very bitter taste in the mouths of many Los Angelinos, however, which was made evident in the 2005 rematch between the two candidates. When in 2005 Hahn again sought to raise the claim that Villaraigosa was tolerant of drug users and neighborhood gangs, loud howls of protest arose from both the Villaraigosa campaign and from the city's best-known reporters and pundits. Indeed, discussions of Hahn's nasty tactics in the previous election were used to frame media discussions of his strategy in the 2005 campaign, thus blunting the effect of his message and damaging his public image (Hollihan, 2005). Villaraigosa won by a wide margin in 2005 to become the first Hispanic mayor of Los Angeles since the 1870s.

One strategy that permits candidates to attack their opponents while lessening the potential that the attacks will damage their own reputations is to have independent groups or individuals run the attack ads (this strategy also has implications under the laws governing campaign finances, which we will discuss in Chapter 10). The use of attack

* This ad can be viewed at http://livingroomcandidate.movingimage.us/election/index.php?nav_action=election&nav_subaction=overview&campaign_id=175. Retrieved on September 7, 2007.

ads by these supposedly independent entities allows candidates to distance themselves from the harshest attacks. Maintaining a distinct separation between the campaign and the independent committees is a requirement of federal law, but it is sometimes difficult to achieve in practice. Senior campaign staffers and candidates certainly want to avoid direct contact with the committees so that they can at the very least establish "plausible deniability" if the public or the media pundits who shape the public's agenda consider the attacks inaccurate or unduly harsh.

Senator John Kerry certainly felt the sting of such attack ads in the 2004 campaign, when an independent group known as the "Swift Boat Veterans for Truth" ran an aggressive national advertising campaign claiming that Kerry had misrepresented his war service in Vietnam and that he had not in fact earned the Silver Star medal for heroism under fire that he had been awarded. The ads aimed at Kerry's military service were clearly designed to undercut a central story told by the Kerry campaign that the senator was uniquely qualified to lead the nation because of his heroic service to his country during wartime. The ads not only reached a large national audience, but they also received extensive media attention and thus became an important issue in the campaign. Although it is not clear that the ads directly influenced the outcome of the election, at the very least they proved distracting in that they pulled the Kerry campaign away from the messages it wished to emphasize (Dobbs, 2004).

One of the more interesting research findings with regard to negative advertisements is the suggestion that these types of ads are more likely to appeal to Republican and independent voters than to Democratic voters. Ansolabehere and Iyengar (1995) suggested that Democrats tend to be more readily persuaded by positive than by negative appeals. The researchers also suggested, however, that Republicans and independents are less likely than Democrats to trust government or to have faith in politicians. As a result, they are more likely to find negative ads believable and compelling.

In fact, Ansolabehere and Iyengar (1995) suggested that the only kind of political advertising that independents find effective is negative advertising. In their study, independent voters registered no response at all when they saw a positive ad for either a Democrat or a Republican, but when they saw a negative ad, they registered a 6 percent shift in preference toward the sponsor of the ad. This finding almost ensures that the use of negative ads will continue, if not increase, for today one out of every three voters considers himself or herself to be an independent. In only a handful of states do those claiming to identify with one of the parties constitute a clear majority of the voting-eligible population. In statewide and national elections, candidates must capture their own base of support and the support of some political independents to gain office. Ansolabehere and Iyengar (1995, p. 95) argued, "Candidates can solidify their base with all sorts of advertising, but they must also sway the independent vote, and doing so *requires* negative advertising. As independents become more numerous in the American electorate, attack advertising will become more common in American campaigns." Ansolabehere and Iyengar (1995) further suggested that this situation constitutes a dilemma for Democrats. If they attack, they risk alienating their partisan supporters. If they do not attack, they are unlikely to win the votes of the independents. Republican candidates, on the other hand, have every incentive to use negative ads, for doing so appeals to their base of supporters and to the independents that they seek to win over to their side.

THE CONSEQUENCES OF NEGATIVE ADVERTISING

Researchers have been very consistent on one issue: People claim they do not like negative ads. Public opinion polls and focus group interviews consistently report that the public objects to this form of advertising. And yet the use of negative ads persists because campaign consultants and candidates have become convinced that these ads work. Research on the consequences of negative ads on voter participation, support for the political system, and confidence in government and elected officials has been far less clear. Two different and competing theories have emerged.

The first theory suggests that negative ads demobilize voters and discourage political participation (Ansolabehere & Iyengar, 1994, 1995). According to this theory, negative ads are especially important in discouraging the participation of independent voters because they tend to intensify the partisan character of the political campaigns while also contributing to distrust of the electoral process and pessimism about the value of one's own vote (Ansolabehere & Iyengar, 1995). Ansolabehere and Iyengar (1994, 1995) conducted large-scale controlled randomized experiments across time to prove their demobilization hypotheses. Other researchers, using alternative research methods including field studies, have had difficulty replicating their findings. Instead, their research has lent support for a second and competing theory that negative ads actually serve to stimulate voter interest in the campaign. Goldstein and Freedman (2002) argued:

It has been suggested, for example, that rather than turning voters away from politics, campaign criticism may actually increase citizens' political engagement by raising issues that are important to voters and sending the message that something significant is at stake in a given election. Negative charges imply that one's vote choice—and one's vote—matters and that citizens should care about the outcome of a race. Moreover, prior works suggest that negative ads may help stimulate voter turnout because they provide a significant amount of information relevant to the voting decision; because such negative information may be given greater weight in political judgment than positive messages; and because negative appeals may produce stronger affective responses, leading to heightened enthusiasm for candidates, greater engagement with the election, and possibly increased motivation to learn more about the candidates. (p. 723)

The antithetical research findings are at least in part a product of the methodological challenges inherent in undertaking these types of studies. Laboratory experiments create an unnatural viewing environment in which respondents observe the ads and then are questioned about them. On the other hand, many field studies are challenged by the inherent difficulty in estimating if and how many times viewers were exposed to the negative ads. Often these studies ask respondents to recall and "self-report" whether they saw an ad and then to describe how it affected them. Such studies are closely related to voter turnout. Those who recall the content of specific ads are more likely to be more politically engaged and thus are more likely to vote.*

Another challenge in undertaking this kind of research is that citizens may not see negativity in precisely the same way that social scientists might classify it. For one thing, those who intend to vote for a candidate tend to perceive that candidate as the more positive of the two in a race and the opponent as the more negative (Brooks, cited by Sigelman & Kugler, 2003, p. 146). Viewers' level of knowledge about politics and their awareness of the issues under discussion in the campaign also seem to affect their evaluation of the tone of the ads. As Sigelman and Kugler (2003, p. 151) observed, "A sophisticated understanding of politics can help onlookers differentiate tactics they see as hard-hitting but legitimate from those they consider unfair. People who are well informed may see dramatic attacks as oversimplified and gratuitous, whereas others appreciate the clues that such attacks provide about the candidates." This finding may help explain why negative ads have

---

* For a discussion of this controversy, see Ansolabehere, Iyengar, and Simon (1999) and Wattenberg and Brians (1999).

the most impact on independents. Because many independents are less partisan, they may be less interested in closely following politics and less likely to be actively seeking information. When confronted by negative messages, they may be more inclined to pay attention to them, become turned off, and decide to stay home on Election Day. Both Ansolabehere and Iyengar (1995) and Lau and Pomper (2001) reported that independent voters were especially turned off by negative advertising. As the number of registered independents increases, their impact on the outcome of elections will grow.

There also seems to be a point at which negative ads begin to be seen as so patently unfair that they provoke much stronger public reactions than they would otherwise. As Lau, Sigelman, Heldman, and Babbit (1999, p. 736) argued, citizens may be able to make subtle distinctions in viewing the ads that cause them to judge some of the charges exchanged between the candidates as fair game and others as foul play. The kind of subtle distinctions that viewers likely make in evaluating ads suggests that different ads will affect different people in different ways. As Clinton and Lapinski (2004, p. 69) summarized their study, "We find no evidence that exposure to negative advertisements decreased turnout and little that suggests it increases turnout. Any effect appears to depend upon the message of the advertisement and the characteristics of the viewer."

Even in the absence of clear empirical evidence regarding the impact of negative advertising on the electorate, it is useful to return to the first and virtually uncontested premise discussed in this section: Voters consistently report that they do not like negative ads. It also seems convincing that these ads coarsen and cheapen electoral campaigns. Candidates today are increasingly likely to call each other names, question each other's integrity, and accuse each other of being irresponsible, mean spirited, unqualified, unethical, and immoral. Then, once the election is over, the loser concedes, wishes the winner well, and pledges support for the political process. Meanwhile, the winner gratefully acknowledges his or her worthy challenger and claims a mandate to govern. These attempts at postelection civility sometimes seem woefully phony and inadequate after the spiteful campaigns that have just been waged. Is it any wonder that Americans come to see politics as a game or that they, as the respected journalist E. J. Dionne (1991) asserted, start to hate politics?

It is one thing to be asked after an election to support the newly elected candidate that you did not support because your differences were pragmatic or ideological. It is quite another matter to be asked to support a newly elected official when you have been told throughout the campaign that the differences between you and that candidate are moral and that he or she cannot be trusted. We have witnessed in the United States an increasingly polarized, distrustful, and often angry electorate. Opponents of President Clinton not only disliked his politics, but they accused him of drug smuggling, ordering the murders of political opponents, and covering up the murders of others (Weiss, 1997). In the 2004 presidential campaign, attack ads may have been even worse. As Dennis Jones (2004) wrote on the Web site Counterbias, if you believe the political ads that you saw, then you believe the following:

> John Kerry is a cynical liar who embellished his war record, unfairly rewarded himself with undeserved medals, and returned home to heap scorn upon his fellow veterans while gathering glory unto himself for political purposes; in his political life he has positioned himself on every side of every issue in a craven attempt to curry favor with every possible constituency; as a candidate for president he tries to deceive the voters about his desire to gut intelligence, hamstring the military, and undercut the troops in the field as they attempt to valiantly free the enslaved people of the world in the war on terror; he is a moral coward who is for killing babies, deviant lifestyles, and declining morals; he looks French, if elected will turn the keys to the government over to the French; most importantly, he has never met a tax increase that he doesn't like and can be counted on to immediately flush the economy down the drain after he assumes office. To his followers he is a saint.
>
> Likewise, George W. Bush is a craven coward who has repeatedly lied about his un-American stint in the National Guard; the president is a hopeless idiot who serves the wishes of a group of devious advisors against the welfare of the "little" people; he has single-handedly shipped hundreds of thousands of manufacturing jobs overseas and lied about how good it is for the economy; he hates school kids, veterans, the poor, the middle class—practically everybody except the wealthiest among us; he likes dirty water, fouled air, and he wants to cut down every tree in sight; most importantly, he knowingly lied about the WMD [weapons of mass destruction] in Iraq in a successful attempt to lead our country into a war in Iraq to reward his cronies in the oil business. To his followers he is a saint.

Such persistent polarization in campaign rhetoric makes it increasingly difficult for leaders to govern and makes problem solving and creating compromises, the essential day-to-day business of democratic governance, almost impossible to achieve.

Over the years, many campaign communication scholars have expressed concern that Americans have come to rely so heavily on television spot advertising to elect leaders. For example, Xinshu and Chaffee (1995) argued:

> Some candidates may use commercials purposively to inform voters about issue positions. But that is not a stable, predictable pattern; a campaign manager for a winning candidate is as likely to be admired professionally for deft use of image enhancing or personal attack ads, or of direct mail and partisan appeals, say, as for ads that might enhance voters' learning. Televised political advertising is not a channel to which the enlightenment of the electorate can—or need be entrusted. (p. 54)

Critics of political advertising have argued that the dependence by many voters on television spots for political information has created a "rich-poor gap" for political information. Moore (1987, pp. 186–187) has claimed that this knowledge gap between people who get their information from newspaper articles and those who get their information from spot ads further enhances the power advantages in our society that high-status voters already enjoy. Certainly, this is a self-inflicted harm, however, as the best way for voters to achieve increased political power and influence is to inform themselves about political issues by reading newspapers, magazines, and online news sources, watching TV news broadcasts, and then turning up to cast their votes on Election Day.

As we have already noted, however, some research has suggested that exposure to political ads contributes at least somewhat to knowledge about the issues and candidates in the campaign (Shyles, 1986). Almost all scholars would agree, however, that improving the content of political ads in an attempt to prevent them from actively misleading voters or misrepresenting issues would serve the public interest. The problem is that no one seems to know precisely how to meet this goal. Some have gone so far as to suggest that it may be necessary to ban the short thirty- and sixty-second ads or regulate their content by limiting a candidate's message to discussions of his or her own qualifications for office (Kellner, 1990, p. 192). Such an extreme solution, however, would almost certainly fail to survive court scrutiny because it seems so patently inconsistent with the First Amendment protection of free speech, especially political speech.

One strategy that has been implemented is the media's increased scrutiny of the content of political ads. This attention to advertising is sometimes referred to as "ad watch" programs. These are columns in newspapers or segments on television news programs in which the political ads themselves become the subject for investigative journalism. A variety of different Web sites also comment on the truthfulness of the claims offered in political ads.* Reporters or even public bloggers examine the ads to assess their accuracy and determine whether they seem fair or misleading. Kathleen Hall Jamieson (Campaigns for sale, 1999, pp. 11–14), the former dean of the Annenberg School for Communication at the University of Pennsylvania, created a "newsroom guide" primarily directed to television and radio reporters who may wish to develop recurrent story lines that examine political ads. The document encouraged reporters to think about questions like the following:

- Who is paying for the ads?
- How do the campaigns pick the times and shows to advertise on?
- Who is being targeted?
- Are the ads truthful?
- Who are the ad makers and consultants who create these ads?
- What is their reputation?
- What is their skill?
- Are the groups buying airtime those we know, and are they from our community?
- Is there a connection between candidates and some of the groups buying ads?

The document also discussed the criteria by which a station might decline to run certain ads and counseled reporters on possible wording to use in framing their news stories about ads that they find objectionable.

Some researchers who studied ad watch programs, however, questioned their effectiveness (Gobetz & Chanslor, 1999; McKinnon & Kaid, 1999). Some research suggested that the focus on the ad watch coverage might actually increase the public's attention to the ads. The fear is that discussing the ads in newspaper articles or on TV broadcasts merely serves to confirm that the issues mentioned in the ads are worthy of continuing public attention (Ansolabehere & Iyengar, 1995).

One might also question whether ad watch stories will make a difference for those voters most likely to have been influenced by the original exposure to the ads. Those voters likely to be persuaded by deceptive or misleading ads probably do not read the newspaper, tune into the broadcast news shows, or read political information on the Internet. They are, after all, the citizens targeted in those ad campaigns

* For example, Factcheck.org, Adcritic.com, or Campaignadwatch.com.

precisely because they get most of their political information from spot advertisements.

Many critics of American electoral politics have suggested that the only way to improve electronic political campaigning is to make available to all candidates some free television time. One suggestion is that candidates have time available each night to explain themselves to voters, answer questions phoned in by voters, and respond to charges or attacks leveled by their opponents. Another proposal would provide government-funded "vouchers" that candidates could exchange in return for broadcast time (Citizens, meeting in community forums, 2001; Taylor & Ornstein, 2002). Despite the persistent interest in the idea of free airtime, however, it seems unlikely that we will see a legislative proposal to achieve this policy change in our lifetime. Simply put, those already elected to public office understand that they benefit from the rules of the game as they currently exist. Therefore, attempts to level the playing field may increase the likelihood that political challengers will become better known and be able to successfully challenge these incumbents. It thus seems likely that the current situation in which every election is more expensive than the one that came before—and the ads are more mean spirited than those that came before—will continue into the foreseeable future.

CHAPTER 7

Telling the People What They Want to Hear: The Importance of Public Opinion Polls

When it was time for President Clinton and his family to make plans for their summer vacation in 1996, they discussed returning to one of their favorite vacation spots: Martha's Vineyard in Massachusetts. Before they could finalize their plans, however, they were enmeshed in a conversation with Dick Morris, their controversial political advisor, and Mark Penn, their public opinion pollster.* After consulting a complex polling grid, Morris and Penn determined that people whose votes were up for grabs in the 1996 election tended to like baseball, hiking, camping, and new technologies. Morris urged the first family to rethink their vacation plans. Rather than go to Martha's Vineyard, he suggested that they go to Jackson Hole, Wyoming. They could hike in the mountains, ride horses, sleep in a tent, fish, and publicize their new high-tech camping gear. Despite his notable lack of enthusiasm for the idea, the president was ultimately persuaded and the first family spent their holiday in Wyoming. The strategy seemed to work. The vacation netted coverage on the nightly network news programs every evening. The Clinton family seemed to enjoy the same things that many middle-class suburban families enjoyed. His polling numbers continued to improve. It is noteworthy that when Hillary Clinton began to seriously contemplate a candidacy for the U.S. Senate seat from New York, the first family openly discussed whether they should spend their 1999

* Dick Morris's embarrassing episode with the Washington, D.C., prostitute who shared her story with a tabloid newspaper was discussed in Chapter 5. It is noteworthy, however, that Morris was a controversial figure even before that story broke because he seemed to be willing to work for any candidate who was willing to pay his fees. In addition to working with the Democrats, and especially President Bill Clinton, he worked for the Republicans, including one of the most conservative members of the Republican Party, the late Senator Jesse Helms (North Carolina). For a discussion, see Pooley (1996).

holiday in the Adirondack Mountains or on Shelter Island near New York City (Seelye, Clintons, 1999).

Political campaigns have become increasingly complex in recent years. Candidates for major political offices now conduct media-focused campaigns that require them to spend more and more money to win elections. The development of campaign strategies, the creation of persuasive messages, and the production and placement of advertisements — all reflect both the art and the science of modern campaigning. To justify the huge expenditures required to conduct a campaign in the media age, candidates must convince themselves and their donors that they are spending money wisely, discussing issues that will benefit them, and targeting voters who are most likely to go to the polls and vote for them. The result has been a dramatic increase in the use of public opinion polling to guide campaign strategies and the decisions that candidates, elected officials, and their advisors must make. Different people interpret poll data in different ways and end up making very different strategic choices. Typically, however, these choices are made with an eye toward making choices that will work. Schell (1996) made this observation:

> The candidates have long since learned that the path to power is far smoother if one gives the people what they already believe they want than if one undertakes the arduous business of persuading them to want something else. Instruments of the utmost refinement have been designed to detect the faintest ripple in the public mood. (p. 72)

As discussed in Chapter 5, public opinion polls have also become increasingly important to the reporters assigned to cover political campaigns. Members of the news media seem to believe that their audiences are more interested in stories reporting who is ahead in the race, who has momentum, and who may be losing ground than in stories discussing substantive political issues. As a result, in recent years there has been a dramatic proliferation both in the number of public opinion polls and in the degree to which they dominate electoral news coverage. Some observers suggest that public opinion polls have a significant impact on voter expectations for how well a candidate will do in an election and thus may also affect voter behavior (Irwin & van Holsteyn, 2002). A repeated barrage of polling may have the effect of essentially declaring a contest decided before any votes are cast or before the public has gleaned enough political information to make an informed choice. For example, former Iowa governor Tom Vilsack announced that he was dropping out of the race for the 2008 Democratic presidential nomination on February 23, 2007, almost a full year before the voters in his home state of Iowa would go to their caucuses to register their opinions in the first meaningful contest during the primary season. Upon leaving the field, Governor Vilsack expressed his frustration that he was so far behind in the polls, and because the media focused so strongly on the poll numbers, he was unable to attract financial contributors or to focus attention on the message of his campaign (Leavey, 2007). In contrast, those candidates who were deemed to be leading the pack and who thus were presumed to have the best prospects for securing their party's nomination, Democrats Hillary Clinton and Barack Obama and Republicans Rudy Giuliani and Mitt Romney, were finding it much easier to raise money and to attract media attention to their campaigns.

Most Americans are familiar with the large independent firms that poll potential voters and publish results in newspapers and magazines. For example, the Gallup, Harris, and Roper polls have been conducted for decades. In addition, several new polling firms or independent research foundations have appeared on the scene relatively recently, including the Zogby, Rasmussen, and Pew polls. Also, many large media companies now conduct their own polls (e.g., the New York Times/CBS News Poll, the Washington Post/ABC News Poll, the Time/CNN Poll, and the Los Angeles Times/Bloomberg Poll). Political opinion polling has become a multimillion-dollar business. Traugott (2001) noted that eighteen organizations produced a final estimate of the outcome of the 2000 presidential election, compared to nine who did so in 1996, and only six in 1992. The number of polls undertaken and of polling organizations increased again in 2004. One study reported that 273 national polls were conducted in the immediate run-up to the 2004 presidential election (Wlezien & Erikson, 2005).

Hundreds of small private polling and marketing firms provide services directly to political candidates, political action committees, and political parties. Even after candidates win elections, they depend on pollsters as they attempt to shape public policies and pursue legislative agendas. President Clinton was especially sensitive to polling data, and his pollster is reported to have met personally with the president on a regular basis after Clinton took office (Bauman & Herbst, 1994). President George W. Bush campaigned on the promise that he would give polls and focus groups no role in his administration, and as a result he deliberately sought to keep the White House polling operations low profile, even going so far as to keep the identity of his pollsters, Jan van Lohuizen and Fred Steeper, out of the press. Nonetheless, the Bush administration spent millions of dollars on polling. Bush's closest political advisor, Karl Rove, was keenly attentive to poll results and personally ordered that specific polls be conducted to help shape the administration's legislative and rhetorical strategies (Tenpas, 2003).

The 2008 presidential candidates were retaining the services of pollsters and conducting voter surveys more than a year in advance of the first primary votes (Corley, 2006). Candidates need accurate polling information to develop their message strategy, allocate their campaign resources, and convince possible donors of their viability, especially in a crowded field such as the 2008 presidential race.

The use of political polling has also increased because the production of polls often serves the interests of the organization publishing poll results. Frankovic (2005) observed:

But in the new world of media, polls also provide attention for the organization doing them. A news organization (or a college or university) can promote its "brand" by conducting a poll, especially one that will be reported by other media. News partnerships (CBS News/New York Times, ABC News/Washington Post, NBC News/ Wall Street Journal) receive automatic publicity for one partner in the other's media. Although conducting branded polls may create risks for an organization (by fostering potential attacks by partisans who dislike a poll's results), the news media have accepted these risks. (pp. 694–695)

THE HISTORY OF POLITICAL POLLING

The first public opinion polls in the United States were probably the preelection informal straw polls conducted by the *Harrisburg Pennsylvanian* during the 1824 presidential campaign (Denton & Woodward, 1990). Voters were asked if they intended to vote for Andrew Jackson, Henry Clay, John Quincy Adams, or William H. Crawford (Smith, 1990). These were certainly not scientific polls like those we encounter today; instead, they were often surveys conducted by partisans eager to express their own opinions and, perhaps, to shape the electoral results.

The best known of the early national straw polls was conducted by the *Literary Digest* beginning in 1924. Gathering names from voter registration rolls, tax lists, telephone directories, and automobile registration files, the *Digest* sent out ballots by mail (approximately 10 million in 1936). Based on data from the returned ballots, the *Digest* correctly predicted the outcomes for the 1924, 1928, and 1932 elections, even though the informal polls relied on unscientific sampling methods and had an average state error rate of approximately 10 percent (Rosenstone, 1983). In 1936, however, the *Literary Digest's* forecast of a landslide win for Republican Alfred M. Landon over Franklin Delano Roosevelt sounded the death knell to large national straw polls. It now is apparent that Americans who owned automobiles and telephones, especially during the Great Depression, were predominantly upper class and Republican, for Roosevelt was reelected by a wide margin. In addition, even though the poll used a very large sample, the return rate was poor, perhaps because even the cost of a stamp for something as frivolous as returning a poll was too expensive for some Americans. The editors of the *Literary Digest* were humiliated, and the publication folded soon thereafter (Herbst, 1995).

Scientific polling began during the 1930s when George Gallup conducted surveys on behalf of his mother-in-law, Mrs. Alex Miller, the first woman secretary of state in Iowa. Gallup also conducted studies to forecast the 1936 presidential election outcome, and although his error rate was a substantial 6.8 percentage points (compared to the *Literary Digest's* whopping 22-percentage-point error rate), he at least correctly forecast a Roosevelt victory (Rosenstone, 1983). Gallup's efforts increased the visibility of this new scientific field of polling and attracted the attention of political candidates.

Dwight D. Eisenhower consulted Gallup in 1952 to select the themes for the first television advertisements in which the candidate appeared. In 1960, John F. Kennedy took advantage of his father's personal wealth and spent heavily on polling during the primary campaign. He used the polling results to hire his campaign advisors and consultants and to target potential issues, locate sympathetic voters, and plot an Electoral College strategy that helped him focus his investments of time and advertising (Denton & Woodward, 1990). His opponents, who did not have access to personal fortunes and who had to raise money from supporters, lacked the money to conduct their own polls and hire a full team of professional consultants, and thus they quickly fell behind.

The use of political pollsters became even more common during the 1970s, as new computer technologies made possible the rapid analysis of poll results. In 1976 the Carter and Ford campaigns each devoted about $500,000 to polling, and in 1980 Carter and Reagan spent approximately twice that much in the general election (Rosenstone, 1983).

Patrick Caddell was the first political pollster to become a member of a president's inner circle of advisors after an election when he tracked the mood of the electorate for Jimmy Carter throughout his presidency (Denton & Woodward, 1990). Since that time, every administration has made sure that its pollster was close at hand, continually monitoring public sentiment and advising the president on policy positions and message strategies. The extent to which a sitting president made use of his pollster, however, has differed significantly. For example, Murray and Howard (2002) reported that Presidents Reagan and Clinton were far more interested in using poll results to shape policy choices and message strategies than were Presidents Carter and George H. W. Bush. Whereas Reagan and Clinton polled often and consistently throughout their terms in office, Carter and Bush polled less frequently in noncampaign years.

THE POLLS AND CAMPAIGN STRATEGY

Political candidates use data from public opinion polls to evaluate whether they should run for a particular office and to determine how to steer the course of their campaigns. Public opinion polls identify the issues that seem to be of most concern to the voters and provide suggestions on how those issues might best be addressed. Poll data inform both the creation and the execution of candidates' public statements and positions on the issues. Polls help candidates identify possible supporters, as well as voters who are almost certain to support their opponents. Polls are useful in assessing how much knowledge voters have about the candidates and the issues and in determining how the candidates are perceived with regard to their personal image. This knowledge enables candidates to address voter apprehensions and permits them to emphasize their strengths.

Opinion polls also provide candidates with information about how the resources of the campaign might best be allocated. By identifying their likely supporters, candidates determine which voters they wish to encourage to cast ballots. Polls also help candidates identify those voters that they would just as soon see stay home on Election Day. Once candidates learn from the polls where they are hopelessly behind or very far ahead, they can bypass additional campaigning in those areas or decrease the number of advertising buys in those areas in favor of devoting their time, energy, and money to more closely contested precincts, districts, states, or regions. During the 2000 and

2004 presidential campaigns, for example, voters in some states had very few opportunities to see or hear the candidates in person or even to see their ads on television, whereas voters in so-called "swing" states— that is, those states that could go for either candidate (in these campaigns the swing states included Florida, Pennsylvania, Ohio, Nevada, and New Mexico, to name just a few)—were barraged with both ads and candidate appearances. Polling is useful to the candidates because states that will be considered in-play vary from election to election, depending on the candidates nominated, the health of the local economy, or the particular issues that may emerge during the course of the campaign.

Candidates also use polls to monitor the effectiveness of their campaigns and to spot trends that develop as an election nears. They use favorable poll results to attract donations and to attempt to demonstrate the momentum of their candidacies. Candidates depend on accurate and reliable political information from their polls but virtually never benefit from the public release of unfavorable poll results. Consequently, there may be times when the design of a poll and the public release of results are subjected to manipulation that may lead to a deceptive interpretation of these results.

LET THE CONSUMER BEWARE

Not all polls are equally scientific or accurate. Pollsters must carefully design their studies and construct a suitable sample. In addition, they must write and test the questions; interview respondents; carefully enter, tabulate, and "clean" the data; and then analyze and report the results. Although this chapter does not provide a comprehensive introduction to the design and implementation of a public opinion poll, it does briefly summarize some of the central issues related to polling.

Sampling

Perhaps the most important aspect in the creation of any research study is the design of the sample and the careful control over its implementation. The theoretical objective of sampling is to ensure that every individual in the population under study has a known chance of falling into the sample. Using probability theory, the pollster can compute the likelihood that a respondent will be included. Through *stratification*, the sample can be divided into characteristics that measure elements of the population.* For example, the sample might be stratified to ensure an appropriate distribution by region (such as East, Midwest, South, and West); by urbanization (such as rural, urban, suburban); or by race, ethnicity, religion, party affiliation, and so on.†

The size of the sample required is determined by statistical and probability theory. In many national polls, a sample of between 1,200 to 1,500 respondents is used to represent the views of all American voters (Asher, 1992). Researchers seek to reduce as much as possible the amount of sampling error—that is, the difference between the estimates obtained from the sample and the true population. Investigators often seek national samples of sufficient size to generate a sampling error of about 4 percent or less. This means that if the sample indicates, for example, that 52 percent of the respondents approve of the president's performance, the actual value is likely to be in the range of 48 to 56 percent (52 percent plus or minus 4 percent). Then the researchers compute a confidence level. A 95 percent confidence level means that in 95 out of 100 samples selected, the sample would generate an estimate of approval within the range of 48 to 56 percent (for a discussion, see Asher, 1992, p. 60).

Obviously, the researcher wants the smallest sample size that is statistically possible because the major costs incurred in conducting a poll are likely to be the interviewing and data-gathering expenses. The higher the rate of return (or the more interviews yielded as a percentage of the total sample), the smaller a sample size needs to be. As just mentioned, the 1936 *Literary Digest* poll failed in predicting the outcome of the Roosevelt-Landon election not only because the initial sample was skewed but also because the response rates were very poor and those who did respond were more likely to favor Landon than Roosevelt (Squire, 1988).

Careful weighting of a poll's results can also enable researchers to adjust for the variations in their sample. Statistical weighting can account for the differences, for example, in the number of persons living in a particular household, homes with two phone lines (which have a higher probability of being surveyed), and bias caused by nonresponse rates or refusals (Cantril, 1991).

---

* Stratified sampling is a statistical method for measuring a population when it is assumed that subpopulations will vary. Stratified sampling measures each of these known subpopulations or strata individually and then measures them after attaching an appropriate statistical weight.
† For a complete discussion of sampling, see Asher, 1992, pp. 53–66; Cantril, 1991, pp. 92–108.

Constructing the Survey

Selecting a suitable sample is only a part of the survey researcher's task. He or she must also carefully construct the survey instrument. The wording and order of the research questions can have a significant impact on the results. Critics of survey instruments have complained that many polls oversimplify issues; contain slanted, loaded, opaque, or technically incompetent questions; and then proclaim results to support a position that was never queried (Mauser & Kopel, 1992).

Even relatively minor nuances in a poll's construction can alter the accuracy of its results. For example, Cantril (1991, p. 133) reported evidence that political candidates fare better in polls when their names are mentioned first; he illustrated this point by citing a 1988 Roper Organization poll wherein Democratic candidate Michael Dukakis held a twelve-point lead over Republican George H. W. Bush when Dukakis's name was mentioned first and only a three-point lead when his name was placed second. Conscientious researchers, aware of order effects, can minimize this impact by alternating the order of the candidates' names in the survey. Question order can also have an effect on questions seeking to determine respondents' opinions on political issues. As McDermott and Frankovic (2003) observed:

> Experimental research demonstrates two different question order effects. The first effect is that of "opinionation"—political questions that are asked later in a survey are more likely to generate substantive responses than those asked early in a survey. The second is one of "direction"—answers to early questions may influence the direction of answers to subsequent questions under some circumstances. (p. 246)

To illustrate the potential significance of this finding, they observed that "'don't know' responses to a presidential job approval question were 8 percentage points lower when respondents were given other political attitude questions to answer first" (McDermott & Frankovic, 2003, p. 246).

Studies have suggested that measuring public opinion is particularly difficult when highly complex subjects are at stake. The wording of the question can be especially important when the public might be uninformed about the subject matter. As an illustration, Cantril (1991, p. 212) discussed an October 1973 survey in which respondents were asked, "Do you think President Nixon should be impeached or not?" Twenty-five percent said "yes," 56 percent said "no," and the remaining

19 percent had no opinion. The next question asked about the concept of impeachment but did not use the term: "Do you think the entire Congress should begin to look into the innocence or guilt of President Nixon in the Watergate matter or not?" Sixty-three percent favored an initiative by Congress, 30 percent opposed it, and only 7 percent were not sure. Admittedly a congressional investigation is not the same as an impeachment resolution, but the degree of difference in the two results suggests that respondents may have been unclear about the meaning of the term *impeachment*.

The concept of impeachment is indeed confusing. A president can be impeached by a majority vote in the House of Representatives, but the case against the president is then tried in the Senate, where a two-thirds majority vote is required to sustain a conviction and to force him or her from office. Because public opinion polls were understood to be important to the final outcome of the process, reporters covering the Clinton impeachment proceedings in 1998–1999 took great pains to explain the process of impeachment to clarify the rare legal process for concerned voters.* Despite the possibility that the public was confused in responding to pollsters' questions regarding Clinton's impeachment, the results of the public opinion polls certainly prevented Democrats from breaking ranks and siding with the Republicans to vote to impeach the president. Without the support from Democrats, there was no way that the Republicans could win the number of votes in the Senate required to force President Clinton from office (Fineman, The survivor, 1999; Thomas, 1999).

Public opinion on moral or religious issues is especially difficult to measure. The blunt wording of many survey questions does not seem to tap into the nuances and subtle distinctions that characterize many moral controversies (Adamek, 1994). Abramowitz (1995) has argued, for example, that public opinion polls on the issue of access to abortion have shown markedly inconsistent results according to the way in which the circumstances permitting abortion are named. Many polls indicate that only a small number of Americans, perhaps as few as 10 percent, oppose abortion under all circumstances, whereas approximately

---

* Sensing that impeachment was unpopular with the public, many Republicans in the House of Representatives argued that their votes to impeach were their moral and ethical responsibility but not really the same as saying that the president should be forced to leave office. That decision, they argued, would be reached only if the Senate convicted the president. Democrats, on the other hand, argued that it was irresponsible for House Republicans to vote to impeach the president if they did not believe he should be forced to leave office. It is not surprising that the public was confused about the meaning of *impeachment* (Apple, 1998).

47 percent oppose any restrictions on the right to terminate a pregnancy. These findings suggest that a substantial majority of the American public favors the right to terminate a pregnancy under some circumstances. There seems to be, however, little agreement as to what the acceptable circumstances might be or how to express and measure them consistently in a public opinion poll (e.g., to assure the birth of a baby of a desired gender, in cases of rape or incest, in the event of danger to the mother's life, to terminate a fetus likely to be born with severe birth defects, or in the presence of some other "clear need"). Almost certainly, survey questions can skew public opinion on the issue of abortion by emphasizing very powerful language. For example, the phrase "partial birth abortion"—which refers to a specific abortion technique that linguistically calls to mind that it is a human life being "partially born"—likely will elicit a different response than the more neutral "late-term abortion."

"Push Polling"

Sometimes campaign operatives, under the guise that they are conducting a research poll, are actually up to something quite different than a genuine attempt to learn more about public opinion on a candidate or an issue. Some unscrupulous pollsters use surveys in an attempt to solicit donations or sell products. Thus, a newspaper may conduct a survey of newspaper readers as a ruse to sell subscriptions. Push polling occurs when someone attempts to influence someone while using the deception that they are merely conducting a poll. Such attempts may seem harmless, but these blatant manipulations of public willingness to respond to surveys may have the effect of decreasing the credibility of all polls and discouraging people from participating in future surveys (Brehm, 1993).

Push polling can also serve as a deliberate attempt to misrepresent public opinion on an issue. In 1996, for example, Texas attorney general Dan Morales proposed to undertake a lawsuit that would require tobacco companies to reimburse his state for the money spent treating smoking-related illnesses. He was soon visited by tobacco industry lobbyists who claimed that the results of a private poll undertaken by a political consulting firm named Public Opinion Strategies reported the people of Texas wouldn't support Morales's plan. As Morales examined the survey results, however, he recognized that it was actually a push poll, designed not to gauge public opinion but to sway it. As Kaplan (1996) observed:

The poll's script began with basic, unobtrusive political questions—then quickly zeroed in on Morales. "Elected officials are held to high standards in public life," the script read. "Here are some reasons people are giving to vote against Dan Morales." Among the reasons: Morales was "pro–affirmative action"; he "supports gun control"; and his 1994 campaign contributed money to Louis Farrakhan's Nation of Islam. (Morales's staffers had purchased two tickets to a dinner thrown by a local chapter of the Nation of Islam.) Those polled were also told that Morales's proposed lawsuit could cost thousands of jobs, prevent the attorney general from fighting crime, and reward only a few wealthy personal injury lawyers. Finally—the spin complete—those polled were asked what they thought of the suit. It's hardly surprising that they overwhelmingly opposed it.

A much more damaging and misleading form of push polling occurred during the 2000 Republican primary campaign in South Carolina. The issue first surfaced when a woman in the audience informed Senator John McCain that during a telephone push poll the night before, her 13-year-old-son had been told that the Arizona senator is a "liar and a cheat." When asked about push polling later that day, McCain's primary rival in South Carolina, Governor George W. Bush, replied that he would fire anyone in his campaign who engaged in such practices. Despite this denial, the Bush campaign admitted that it was calling voters in South Carolina, ostensibly to survey their opinions but also to tell them that Senator McCain was using "negative campaign tactics" (Push polling, 2000).

The actual story of what the Bush campaign was doing in South Carolina is a bit more sordid than the candidate admitted. A company known as Voter/Consumer Research, hired by the Bush campaign, was calling South Carolina voters. The company did not identify itself as working for the campaign but instead asked voters to respond to a poll. After a few perfunctory questions asking voters whether they were registered Republicans, had been following the campaign, and intended to vote in the primary, the questions quickly turned to Senator McCain. The questions included the following, as reported by the *New York Times* (Pointed questions, 2000):

Q: Here are three points people have made about John McCain's position on taxes. Please tell me for each of these whether you strongly approve, somewhat approve, somewhat disapprove, or strongly disapprove.

(a) John McCain's plan does not cut tax rates for 71 percent of all taxpayers.

(b) John McCain's plan will increase taxes on charitable contributions to churches, colleges, and charities by $20 billion.

(c) John McCain says he never voted for a tax increase, but he wrote legislation that proposed the largest tax increase in United State history.

Q: John McCain calls the campaign finance system corrupt, but as chairman of the Senate Commerce Committee, he raises money and travels on the private jets of corporations with legislative proposals before his committee. In view of this, are you much more likely to vote for him, somewhat more likely to vote for him, somewhat more likely to vote against him, or much more likely to vote against him?

Q: John McCain's campaign finance proposals would give labor unions and the media a bigger influence on the outcome of elections. Again, in view of this, are you much more likely to vote for him, somewhat more likely to vote for him, somewhat more likely to vote against him, or much more likely to vote against him? (p. A16)

An even more odious example of push polling in this same South Carolina primary campaign occurred when someone, perhaps again people working for Bush, raised the issue of race. As Davis (2004) wrote:

The McCains, John and his wife, Cindy, have an adopted daughter named Bridget. Cindy found Bridget at Mother Teresa's orphanage in Bangladesh, brought her to the United States for medical treatment, and the family ultimately adopted her. Bridget has dark skin. Anonymous opponents used "push polling" to suggest that McCain's Bangladeshi born daughter was his own, illegitimate black child. In push polling, a voter gets a call, ostensibly from a polling company, asking which candidate the voter supports. In this case, if the "pollster" determined that the person was a McCain supporter, he made statements designed to create doubt about the senator.

Thus, the "pollsters" asked McCain supporters if they would be more or less likely to vote for McCain if they knew he had fathered an illegitimate child who was black. In the conservative, race-conscious South, that's not a minor charge. (p. 1)

Kathleen Frankovic, the director of surveys for CBS News, told the *New York Times* that the use of push polling was now "fairly common." She further observed that campaigns used such partisan polling to test attack lines for future negative advertisements (cited in Yardley, 2000, p. A16). Michael W. Traugott, the president of the American Association for Public Opinion Research, indicated that such polling constituted a "negative experience" for most citizens and that it had "deleterious effects" because it "increases their cynicism about politics and politicians" (cited in Yardley, 2000, p. A16). Although such surveys may provide the pollsters with an effective strategy to gain voters or to discourage voters from voting for the opposing candidate and might also help them test the effectiveness of negative campaign themes (in much the same way that product advertisers test their messages), they are not reliable assessments of public opinion and thus do not constitute polls in a traditional sense.

CONDUCTING THE POLLS

Polling and survey data can be collected in many ways. The determination of which method is most appropriate varies, depending on the nature of the data being sought and the types of questions the researcher wants to ask respondents. Each data collection method has distinct advantages and disadvantages.

Mail Surveys

Polling firms frequently mail questionnaires to respondents to learn about their opinions. One advantage of mailed questionnaires is their relatively low cost. Because they are self-administered, there are no interviewers to train or support, and interviewer bias does not contaminate the results. Also, because of the privacy afforded by this method of questioning, people may feel that their anonymity is better ensured and thus they may be more candid and truthful in their replies (Asher, 1992).

Mail questionnaires can be sent to specific people, permitting the researcher to target specific subjects. Because these questionnaires are self-administered, however, there is no way of knowing who actually completes them. Because mailed questionnaires give respondents an opportunity to think about their answers, they may also reveal more carefully reflected opinions. As a result, some advocates of mail surveys claim that pollsters get fewer "off the top of their heads" answers that are not carefully considered. There are also serious problems with mail surveys, however; one is the belief that people with relatively little education are likely to be underrepresented in mail surveys because they have difficulty reading the questions and following directions (Ayidya & McClendon, 1990).

It is also more difficult to get respondents to return mail survey questionnaires than when other technologies are employed. Studies suggest that respondents are more likely to return questionnaires that are addressed to them individually than surveys addressed to "Occupant," but even individually addressed questionnaires are often not returned. Pollsters may also choose to send a preletter notifying respondents that a survey is coming and explaining the projected use for the data, then send the actual questionnaire, and finally send a postcard reminder to encourage responses (Dillman, Sinclair, & Clark, 1993). Some polling or issue analysis marketing firms will even attach a token gift (a $1 or $5 bill, a gift card, etc.) in the belief that such a gift may make a respondent feel morally responsible to complete and return the mailed survey.

The construction and clarity of the questionnaire, the length of time required to complete it, and even the color of the paper that it is printed on have all been shown to affect the expected response rate (Asher, 1992). Mailed questionnaires are a poor choice if the researcher needs quick turnaround on the data because it often takes several weeks for the questionnaires to be returned (Asher, 1992).

Telephone Interviews

Most political polling today is conducted through telephone interviews. Unlike mailed questionnaires, telephone interviews can be completed quickly, sometimes in a day or two, and they provide an almost instantaneous reaction to a political speech or a breaking news event. By using random-dialing computer programs, researchers can also quickly assemble a random sample (Asher, 1992). Typically, pollsters purchase lists of working phone numbers and then stratify the samples by state and county. Then they decide what percentage of U.S. homes would likely be found in such an area to determine how many calls to place in that area (Voss, Gelman, & King, 1995).

Although telephone interviews have many advantages, they can still pose challenges for researchers. Despite the fact that most Americans own telephones, there are nonetheless economic class biases against low-income voters who may not have phone service, have to share a phone with other family members, or may be difficult to reach by phone because of their work schedule. Research has also suggested that African Americans and Hispanic Americans are often underrepresented in phone polls, that elderly citizens may be less likely to respond to pollsters, and that as a result poststratification statistical manipulations must be used to weight the data to ensure proper samples (Kaldenberg, Koenig, & Becker, 1994; Voss, Gelman, & King, 1995).

Researchers have also reported that the time of day at which pollsters call can profoundly skew their results. Weekday-only calls, for example, produce a Republican bias, presumably because middle-class voters (who are the staple of the Republican Party) do not have to work evenings as often as do working-class Democrats (Lau, 1994).

Another challenge facing telephone pollsters is the fact that many respondents are either not home or are home but refuse to participate in the survey. These nonrespondents skew the sample and call into question the accuracy and meaning of the poll results (Brehm, 1993). Pollsters are also aware that many Americans use answering machines to screen their calls. The use of answering machines potentially makes it more difficult to achieve a representative sample. Answering machines are more often used by families with higher incomes, younger people, and better-educated people. They are also more frequently used by urban and suburban citizens than by those living in rural areas. All these characteristics mean that pollsters must calculate the number of calls not completed because of the differential use of answering machines (Oldendick & Link, 1994; Piazza, 1993).

Over the past decade, the number of telephone sales calls to people's homes has increased dramatically, a fact that also serves to make it more difficult for pollsters to get respondents to answer their surveys. In response to public demands for more privacy and an uninterrupted dinner hour, the federal government in 2003 created a "Do Not Call Registry" on which people may list their phone numbers to avoid unsolicited phone calls. Calls to encourage people to vote or in support of particular candidates or issue positions and calls by political pollsters are not limited by this legislation. Nonetheless, confusion abounds, and sometimes people who are called by pollsters decline to participate in the polls, citing as their reason the fact that they are listed on the "Do Not Call Registry" (Traugott & Lavrakas, 2006). The rate of refusal among potential poll respondents has dramatically increased, from about 25 percent to more than 50 percent today (Curtin, Presser, & Singer, 2005, p. 90).

Most pollsters have established procedures for calling back those subjects who were not home or whose phone was answered by a machine; some attempt to call back twice more, others as often as six times (Cantril, 1991; Voss, Gelman, & King, 1995). Most pollsters do not call back when the subject answers the phone but refuses to participate in the study, yet some do attempt one return call (Voss, Gelman, & King, 1995).

Recently, a new challenge has arisen with regard to telephone surveys: the difficulty of producing a representative sample due to the fact that many people no longer have land lines but instead rely solely on their mobile phones. Most polling organizations do not include cell phone numbers in their telephone sampling frames for political polls, and it is currently illegal for auto-dialers, which most polling firms use, to call cell phones (Rosenstiel, 2005). There may also be challenges because many calling plans charge for incoming calls, and these charges may also serve to discourage respondents from participating in a survey even if they are called. Keeter (2006) wrote:

> Given that younger citizens are more likely than older ones to live in CPO [cell phone only] households, considerable speculation arose that their omission would create a bias in preelection polls. Many believed that the polls might understate John Kerry's support, given his greater popularity among younger voters. The potential danger of CPO households for the polls was discussed in at least 150 separate news stories in major newspapers, news magazines, or the broadcast media during the four weeks prior to the [2004] election. (pp. 88–89)

Keeter's (2006) study, however, suggested that the absence of CPO households in the surveys did not prove to be a significant factor in the 2004 campaign and that the national polls were accurate. Still, he concluded that the problem could become far more significant in the future. Keeter argued that most households still see a benefit in having a landline, including better audio quality, spotty cell phone service, and the use of a single number where multiple family members can be reached. If these advantages are diminished either by changes in the telephone business environment (new calling plans that provide free incoming calls and a more reliable 911 emergency service, for example) or by new developments in technology that improve cell phone signals, then the number of people giving up their landlines will increase, and the impact on poll results could become far greater.

Another issue with regard to telephone surveys concerns whom pollsters choose to survey within a household. Different pollsters use different criteria in making this selection. Gallup typically requests the youngest male age 18 or older, and if there are no adult males at home, then the oldest female. Harris usually requests the youngest male, and if there is no male available, then the youngest female. Some pollsters simply ask for the adult whose current birthday occurred most recently (Voss, Gelman, & King, 1995). Pollsters' policies also differ in terms of counting respondents who are not registered to vote, but the probability of voting and determining likely voters is almost always a weighted characteristic in the poststratification manipulations (Voss, Gelman, &

King, 1995). All political pollsters recognize that a large percentage of respondents will be unlikely to vote and that the opinions expressed by nonvoters in interviews may be substantially different from those of voters. In the United States, nonvoters are more likely to select the Democrat when asked to choose their preferred candidate. Thus, some sort of screening process to help identify likely voters is essential. Most pollsters ask respondents if they voted in past elections and if they are registered to vote. They then ask registered voters a series of additional questions designed to help predict the likelihood that they will vote in the upcoming election. Respondents are assigned a statistical "score" that can be tallied and weighted to help determine how to evaluate their responses (Erikson, Panagopoulos, & Wlezien, 2004). For the most part, modern polling techniques have made these predictions of likely voters highly accurate.* Now, however, it may be more difficult to make such predictions, given that campaigns go on so long that people are more likely to be influenced by news events or other factors that can motivate or discourage voting (Erikson, Panagopoulos, & Wlezien, 2004).

Internet Polls

In the years to come, more and more polling will likely be conducted via the Internet. Online polling is certainly less expensive than polling conducted via the phone. For survey houses that conduct many polls each year, the savings can be significant. Although there continue to be challenges that the population of Internet users differs from the general population—Internet users are more often younger, more likely urban, and better educated—these differences are shrinking as access to the Internet is increasing (we will discuss the use of the Internet in political campaigning in greater detail in Chapter 8).

Internet polling readily permits comparison studies of groups of voters who may already be Internet users but who differ by age, gender, geographic region, religion, or some other meaningful characteristics. Internet polls can be conducted very quickly, and summary poll results can also be produced rapidly, often in just a few hours. Another potential benefit of Internet polls is that they are more interactive. Respondents can be shown pictures, film clips, segments of speeches, or actual ads prepared for the campaign and then queried about what they have just seen.

* It is arguable that Senator Clinton's surprising victory in the New Hampshire primary in 2008 resulted because the pollsters were not successful in their predictions of likely voters.

Advances in Internet technology suggest that in the future respondents might be more candid and willing to respond to an Internet poll than they would be to a telephone survey because they might believe that the polling Web site is secure and that their privacy is protected. Online respondents also might give more truthful responses to questions that they find uncomfortable or embarrassing when they are asked by a live interviewer on the phone.

Personal Interviews

Personal interviews typically offer the richest and most complete information, as respondents are more likely to answer questions in a face-to-face setting. Trained interviewers are also able to directly record such nonverbal behaviors as fidgeting, nervousness, or other signs of uneasiness or lack of interest in the survey. It is difficult to train interviewers to be consistent in such evaluations, however, and an obvious expense is involved in supporting interviewers in the field. In addition to their salary, interviewers must also be provided with transportation, lodging, and meals. Personal interviewing is much less efficient, as it takes a great deal of time to collect the data. Because the interview is a social situation, poorly trained interviewers may unknowingly alter the dynamics of the interview and contaminate the data (Asher, 1992).

All interviews, whether conducted face-to-face or over the telephone, run the risk of introducing interviewer effects in the data collection. The interviewer's demeanor, competence, and performance can have a profound impact on the success of the interview (Asher, 1992). In addition, a guiding assumption of survey methodology is that similarity between interviewers and respondents on important social characteristics increases the validity of the information obtained in the interview (Hurtado, 1994).

There is also evidence that the race of the interviewer might have a significant effect on the results of a poll. Although race can influence the results of all interview polling, it is most significantly a factor in face-to-face personal interviews. Finkel, Guterbock, and Berg (1991) reported that in an election contest in Virginia between an African American and a Caucasian candidate, Caucasian respondents were 8 to 11 percent more likely to express support for the African American candidate when interviewed by an African American pollster than when interviewed by a Caucasian pollster. This research suggests that the inclination to feel social pressure to demonstrate one's egalitarian views may account for the fact that all published preelection surveys of the Virginia contest overestimated the vote share of the African American candidate and eventual winner, Douglas Wilder. The polls predicted a 10-percentage-point margin for Wilder, but he won with only a .4 percent lead over his opponent (Finkel, Guterbock, & Berg, 1991).*

Kuran (1995) provided further evidence of such racial "preference falsification." In 1990, David Duke, a former Grand Wizard of the Ku Klux Klan, ran for a U.S. Senate seat from Louisiana. Polls suggested that Duke would garner no more than 25 percent of the vote, but he wound up with 44 percent, including 60 percent of the white vote. Kuran (1995) argued that preference falsification is so problematic that most public opinion polls on issues related to race relations and affirmative action are untrustworthy. He claimed that few Americans are willing to express their true feelings about affirmative action for fear of being labeled racist and that, consequently, public policy mandating affirmative action has actually served to increase racial hostility toward minorities. Kuran made the following argument:

> Preference falsification promotes, fortifies, and preserves myths. Myths arise because the preconceptions that control our interpretations are based partly on social proof. Preference falsification distorts social proof by removing from public discourse facts and arguments that powerful groups deem unmentionable. As such, it has a profound effect on the evolution of private knowledge. It imparts credibility to myths by shielding them from corrective disclosures. (p. 241)

It will be very interesting to observe how closely the preelection polls are to the actual ballot counts in the 2008 presidential election, where we have a female candidate, an African American candidate, and a Mormon candidate. In each case we may discover a gap between what people tell pollsters before the election and their actual behavior on Election Day.[†]

---

* If Caucasian voters are likely to be subtly (or not so subtly) racist against African American candidates or elected officials, then it may also be the case that minority voters might more likely be sympathetic to a minority candidate and to support minority elected officials. Howell and McLean (2001) did discover that black respondents were more likely to support black mayors because of their racial identification, whereas white respondents were more likely to focus on independent measures of job performance.

[†] Pre-election polls in the 2008 New Hampshire primary predicted that the African American candidate, Senator Obama, would win, yet Senator Clinton won an upset victory. Racial preference falsification may have been a factor in this surprising outcome.

Tracking Polls

Tracking polls are surveys conducted on a series of days with the goal of monitoring small shifts in public opinion. Often used to detect changes in the relative standing of candidates, tracking polls are widely used both by campaign pollsters and by the media (Cantril, 1991). The reason these polls are believed useful is the notion that they will capture the dynamic relationship between public news stories and/or campaign events and candidate evaluations (Moore, 1999). Campaign staffs like them because they provide assessments of the impact of candidate speeches, shifts in message strategy, political debates, and so on. Reporters like them because they provide a dynamic daily news story to help frame the horse race press coverage they believe the public craves (Traugott, 2001).

Some tracking polls ask the same questions of different respondents day after day. Then a "rolling average" is reported. The challenge in this approach is that sample sizes tend to be relatively small, and as a result, it is possible to get dramatically different results from one day to the next (Cantril, 1991; Wlezien & Erikson, 2002). In a rarer practice, some tracking polls follow a "panel" of respondents and interview them over the course of several days or weeks to monitor changes in opinion (Cantril, 1991).

Tracking polls do achieve at least one of their purposes: They demonstrate the degree to which voter opinions are susceptible to breaking news stories or to public events (Shelley & Hwang-Du, 1991). Political candidates spend large sums of money to conduct tracking polls because they are the most effective means of determining how the candidates' advertising, issue positions, and speeches are influencing the voters (Denton & Woodward, 1990).

The value and accuracy of tracking polls are, of course, somewhat difficult to judge. These polls are designed to provide a snapshot of a campaign at a given moment in time. Thus, comparing the results of a poll on any given day to the results of the final election is a largely meaningless exercise. In addition, multiple firms conduct tracking polls, and the data often suggest that the polls do not always move in a simultaneous or predictable fashion (Wlezien & Erikson, 2002). Indeed, sometimes significant variations occur in the same poll from day to day. Because tracking polls typically use much smaller sample sizes than other polls, some of this volatility and variability may simply be due to sampling error or to differing organizational notions of who are "likely voters" (Traugott, 2001). Given that these tracking polls have become increasingly common and given also that the results of tracking polls dominate media coverage and candidate strategies, it is important that those making use of the data from such polls pay especially close attention to how the data has been collected, weighted, and analyzed (Traugott, 2001).

Focus Groups

Focus groups are not polls per se, but they are a related enterprise. Focus groups bring together a small number of individuals with known demographic characteristics for an informal and open discussion of issues framed by a pollster and raised by a moderator. By analyzing the conversation, researchers determine how people come to view issues, how they respond to the views of others, and what language people use to express their political sentiments. Focus groups give pollsters the nuances of public expression that sometimes enable campaigns to express the issues in language that is well understood by and resonates with voters.

Compared to public opinion polls, focus groups are less expensive and provide data very quickly. Participants can view a campaign commercial or listen to a speech and then respond to it (Cantril, 1991). Focus groups can also allow campaigns to test messages on unique segments of potential voter populations—for example, on younger or elderly citizens, minority citizens, military veterans, and so forth.

Both George H. W. Bush and Michael Dukakis made heavy use of focus groups in the 1988 presidential campaign. Cantril (1991) claimed that in 1988 the Bush campaign gathered groups of Democrats in focus group discussions to probe for weaknesses and vulnerabilities in Dukakis's record. From these discussions they learned that voters might become concerned about the prison furlough of William ("Willie") Horton, Dukakis's veto of a bill mandating the Pledge of Allegiance in schools, and the pollution of Boston Harbor (Cantril, 1991, p. 139).

Because of the small samples used in focus group research, they cannot be expected to supplant conventional polling techniques, but more and more campaigns will likely use focus groups to construct and evaluate their campaign rhetoric. A primary goal in the use of focus group research is to produce the daily "talking point" that shapes the candidate's message and also makes its way into the news frame the media use to report the day's events. From these daily "talking points" can also emerge labels that persist in the campaign discourse, perhaps because they have linguistic appeal and become memorable. Thus, in the 2004 campaign, Senator John Kerry was a "flip-flopper," whereas George W. Bush cast himself as a "steadfast leader" (Bodenner, 2004). The campaigns may also use focus groups to test things as simple as what necktie a candidate should wear in an important public appearance (Bodenner, 2004). Finally, the media may sometimes convene their own focus groups merely for the purpose of attempting to shape a campaign news story. In 2004, for example, the national daily *USA Today* convened its own focus groups in Ohio to ask possible voters to evaluate the appeal and effectiveness of the television ads being run by the Bush and Kerry campaigns. Their study reported that participants did not much care for any of the ads, did not consider them persuasive, and especially disliked the negative spots (Memmott, 2004). The results of this focus group study illustrate the limits of focus group polling, of course, because research studies consistently show that that negative ads are effective and influence the outcome of elections, even if they might do so by angering possible voters so much that they decline to go out and cast their ballots.

Exit Polls

Exit polls are interviews conducted with voters as they leave the polls on Election Day. Typically, pollsters ask respondents not only whom they voted for but why, and what issues motivated their vote. These polls provide the media with the ability to project the outcome of an election before the actual votes are tabulated.

Sometimes the reporting of the results of the exit polls has been very controversial. In 1980, for example, the media projected that Ronald Reagan had defeated Jimmy Carter in the Electoral College before the polls had even closed in the West, a move that many critics claimed suppressed voter turnout in the West, costing several incumbent Democratic senators, representatives, and governors their seats (Delli Carpini, 1984; Sudman, 1986).

An even more dramatic controversy developed in the razor-thin 2000 presidential contest between Vice President Al Gore and Texas governor George W. Bush. Gore's hopes were raised early in the evening on Election Day when the broadcast networks, looking at exit poll results, declared that he would win the closely contested states of Michigan, Pennsylvania, and Florida. The projection was offered even though the polls in the panhandle region of Florida, which is in the central time zone, were still open. With these wins under his belt, it appeared that Gore would coast to victory. Then, only a couple of hours later, the network pollsters reconsidered the Florida results and declared the state "too close to call." In the predawn hours of the next day, the networks announced that Florida had gone to Bush, and he was proclaimed the president-elect. Gore called Bush to congratulate him on his victory. Public press conferences were scheduled for Gore in Tennessee and for Bush in Texas. However, just moments before he was to speak to his crestfallen supporters, Gore learned that Bush's lead in the actual tabulated vote count in Florida was minuscule and shrinking. The vice president once again phoned Bush and, in a testy conversation that revealed the fatigue and frayed nerves of both men, withdrew his concession. Instead of knowing who was the president-elect, the American public now faced uncertainty as the Florida votes were subjected to a recount.

Many improprieties in the Florida vote totals were discovered in the days and weeks that followed, and the vote totals shifted back and forth as the battle moved into the state and ultimately the federal courts. On November 26, 2000, Florida's Secretary of State Katherine Harris (who had been appointed to office by George W. Bush's brother, Florida Governor Jeb Bush, and who had cochaired the Bush presidential campaign fund-raising committee in Florida) certified the state's election results, declaring Bush the winner by 537 votes, out of the more than 6 million cast in the election. Harris also indicated that she would not permit any county to further amend its vote totals. Gore appealed this decision. On December 8, the Florida Supreme Court ordered that the manual recounts be resumed and that the certified vote totals be amended to include the revised Palm Beach County votes. George Bush then appealed to the U.S. Supreme Court, which suspended the manual recounts on December 9, pending a hearing. On December 12, the U.S. Supreme Court, in a five-to-four decision, ruled that the manual recounts in Florida be halted under the equal protection clause of the U.S. Constitution, because the Florida Supreme Court had not provided a uniform standard for counting the ballots. The U.S. Supreme Court also held that although such a uniform standard might be constructed, there was simply not enough time to do so, as Florida law mandated that the state's electors must be determined by December 12. The effect of this ruling was that no further counting of disputed votes could take place, and thus the outcome of the election was decided. The Supreme Court's ruling was itself highly controversial, with many critics arguing that the decision was ill considered and poorly reasoned and that the Court had permitted itself to become viewed as highly partisan.* It might well be that the public would have been more inclined to patiently await the counting and recounting of the votes cast in the state had the media not reported the exit poll claim that Governor Bush had won.

The exit polling again proved controversial in the 2004 presidential campaign. Before noon on Election Day, news stories began to appear on the Internet that the exit polls showed Senator John Kerry leading incumbent President George W. Bush in several closely contested states. Many reporters and commentators began to hint that a Kerry victory was underway. When the actual votes were counted after the polls closed, however, it became evident that although the election was very close, Bush had won. Conspiracy theories abounded, and some went so far as to claim that the exit poll results indicated that there had been a theft of the election and a massive electoral fraud, especially in Ohio, the last of the big states to be decided and the one that produced Bush's victory in the Electoral College (Lindeman & Brady, 2006).

Despite the controversies, however, exit polls are useful because they explain and help candidates, reporters, and historians alike understand the meaning of the outcome of the vote. Citizens do not write on their ballots what issues are most important to them, what policy actions they prefer, or which candidates they find most objectionable. But when they are interviewed in an exit poll, voters are often asked about their position on issues, about specific policy alternatives, about candidate personality traits, and even about what events, advertisements, or speeches they remember as meaningful from the campaign. Were the outcomes of the 2006 midterm congressional elections a mandate for change, as the new Speaker of the House of Representatives, Nancy Pelosi, claimed? Exit polls might help to answer this question.

Exit polls following primary races help candidates refine their strategies as they move on to other states and plan for the general election campaign. Exit polls after the general election campaign provide elected officials important information about what policies the public might support. Once elected to office, political leaders use this polling information in claiming their mandate to govern and in crafting new legislation. Exit polls are especially useful because the questions asked are answered by actual voters. Pollsters conducting surveys before an election have to predict the likelihood that a respondent will actually cast a vote. With exit polls they know they are questioning people who have voted.

---

* For an excellent discussion of the Florida election, media coverage, and the controversy in the courts, see Toobin (2001).

INTERPRETING AND REPORTING THE RESULTS

The value of any public opinion poll, regardless of how it is conducted, is also dependent on how carefully the results are interpreted and reported. There are many challenges to interpreting poll results. An important one is figuring out what the answers to the questions really mean. By their very nature, most public opinion polls structure the expression of opinion. By focusing on a particular set of issues and taking them as "political givens," polls ask people to react to the issues as they are framed by political and media elites. The answers to these questions are then formed into Yes, No, and No Opinion categories. Sometimes, unknown candidates emerge in a political contest because pollsters include their names in "trial heat" surveys that pit them against other political candidates. From the very fact that they are mentioned in the public opinion polls, these candidates may gain visibility and credibility (Miller, 1995). In the 2008 presidential campaign polls, for example, former vice president Al Gore and former Speaker of the House Newt Gingrich were frequently included in sample polls even though neither had declared himself to be a candidate.

Structuring the expression of opinion means that public opinion polls end up reinforcing status quo assumptions and policy choices and, by implication, discouraging politically extreme opinions that challenge the established political hierarchy (Miller, 1995). In much political polling, the act of asking plants the answer; people seem not to form their political opinions until they are asked to express them. Moreover, what respondents invent at the moment gets subsequently reported and influences others' opinions, as if the poll numbers themselves were the essence of the news story (Anderson, Dardenne, & Killenberg, 1994).

By reducing the range of acceptable political choices, and especially by pressing pollsters to seek very rapid public responses to meet publication deadlines, public opinion polls also serve to manufacture political consensus into centrist or moderate political positions. Respondents are discouraged from giving "I don't know" or "no opinion" answers, and thus they are pressured to commit themselves to opinions that are probably not very well thought out or that they could not comfortably articulate if called upon to do so in their own words (Rucinski, 1993).

Opinion polls also have difficulty measuring the intensity of support, both for a particular candidate and for a policy position. *Weak support*, *leans toward*, *favors*, and *strongly favors* responses are often jumbled together in the tabulation of results. The less crystallized an opinion is, the more difficult it is to measure and the less valuable are the poll results (Lau, 1994). This lack of information can be especially troublesome during the primary season, when voters do not know much about many of the candidates and are actively seeking information to help them make up their minds. It may also explain why public opinion often seems to be highly volatile (Jennings, 1992).

Polls can have a dramatic influence on shaping public opinion, however, particularly during the primary phase of the campaign when relatively unknown candidates are striving to gain name recognition. As has already been argued, most voters are loath to "waste" their votes. They want to vote for someone they believe has a legitimate chance to win. Research has suggested that political opinion polls can have a significant bandwagon effect and thus can influence the behavior of the media, of other candidates, and ultimately of the voters themselves (Bartels, 1985; Irwin & van Holsteyn, 2002; McAllister & Studlar, 1991).

In addition to influencing the public's identification of suitable candidates, the emphasis on reporting political opinion polls as news increases the likelihood that politicians will be tempted to formulate their policies based on polling data rather than on the merits of alternative positions. Thus, Anderson, Dardenne, and Killenberg (1994) argued:

> The media ability to help a politician constantly monitor fluctuating personal popularity might irrevocably deflect governmental policy debate from issue-based and ethical questions of "What should we do?" to the image-based question "How are we doing in the polls?" Insider leaks and trial balloons become ploys in such a gaming strategy: "We'll test the waters with an unnamed source leak—then if the public reaction isn't positive, we'll disavow it." (pp. 180–181)

Too often, the way in which poll data are reported "stops conversations" by seeming to settle issues. Instead, news media reporting should seek to "start conversations" that lead to genuine and enhanced understanding of complex issues (Anderson, Dardenne, & Killenberg, 1994, p. 178).

The way that the media choose to talk about the polls also has consequences. As Frankovic (2005, p. 684) commented, "Over time, almost without notice, the numbers and percentages that the media use to represent what Americans think have morphed into something less tangible, the more general phrase 'polls say.'" Frankovic conducted a Lexis-Nexis search and discovered that the use of the phrase "polls say" in the press jumped from 4,500 references in 1992 to more than 11,000 in 2004. The phrase is significant because it suggests that reporters might not be focusing on a close evaluation of the results of a particular poll, including an evaluation of the measures of statistical difference, the margin of error, or the confidence level that the researchers report for their data but are instead reporting on the state of American opinion as if it were a more settled dimension of the American psyche, at least at that moment in time. Frankovic (2005, p. 685) further noted that "invoking 'the polls' quantifies information and gives apparent precision to news coverage and the appearance of expertise to reporters. The poll numbers substitute for political experts and let the reporter, who invokes the authority of 'the polls,' assume that role."

In an attempt to encourage better media coverage of poll results and to ensure that carefully conducted scientific polls are sorted out from the rest, nonprofit organizations have provided suggestions to reporters on how to better frame their news stories. For example, the group Public Agenda offered a series of questions journalists should ask about poll results. The questions included: Who did the poll? Who paid for the poll? How many people were interviewed? How were they chosen? What area—nation, state, region—or what group—teachers, lawyers, Democrats, Republicans—were these people from? Are the results based on all the people interviewed? Who should have been interviewed and was not? When was the poll done? How were the interviews conducted? What is the sampling error? What questions were asked? In what order were the questions asked? What other polls have been done on this topic, and how do their results compare? Is this poll newsworthy? (Public agenda, 2007).

THE COSTS OF ANONYMITY

Advocates of public opinion polls claim their primary benefit is that they permit people to express themselves privately and make known their innermost thoughts. These advocates claim that polls encourage government to be more responsive to the public's needs and interests because politicians feel the constant pressure of approval ratings (Crespi, 1980; Margolis & Mauser, 1989). The ability to respond anonymously to public opinion pollsters has even been compared to the anonymous act of voting (Lasswell, 1941).

Others believe, however, that the anonymous expressions of opinion given to pollsters are very different from the act of voting. Pollock (1976, p. 229) argued that anonymous public opinions are often poorly thought out and reflect "crude and unsupported stereotypes" for which individual respondents are seldom held accountable. Peters (1995, p. 20) agreed: "The querying of people in private contexts where anonymity is guaranteed, the typical practice in survey research, completely fails to capture a public element. Much is at stake in a public utterance; little where the speaker has no identity or voice."

Peters (1995) further argued that what has been lost in public opinion research is the notion of "public" in the sense in which German philosopher Jurgen Habermas used the term. Habermas (1962/1989) stressed that to create meaningful public participation and deliberation in democratic societies, we must create the possibility for people to communicate in an open sphere in which knowledge claims are asserted, arguments advanced, refutations offered, and opinions openly evaluated. Habermas cited the current dominance of public opinion polls as an illustration of the "degeneration" of the public sphere because such surveys give the illusion of citizen participation yet serve to structure public opinions into arguments framed by elites to meet status quo assumptions.

Public opinion polls create an aggregate model of public opinion, a declaration of public views that may be without an essential center. Polls measure opinions along a continuum of choices but may not reflect the views of ordinary citizens. Peters (1995) argued that this sense of public opinion actually represents a "visible fiction" in which the citizens do not create public opinions through their conversations but instead have their opinions represented to them through the machinery of modern polling and the participation of an eager and willing press.

THE MANDATE OF PUBLIC OPINION

Even though public opinion as constituted through polling might be regarded as a fiction, it is an important fiction because political candidates and elected officials are always claiming to act in response to the "will of the people." As McGee (1975) argued, "The people" is a troublesome concept because the people cannot appear "in person." The scale of modern social order prevents the assembly of the entire populace. Thus, symbolic representations of the social whole must be circulated before dispersed people. If persuasive, these representations invite the public to act as a unified body. Rhetoric is the means by which to articulate such common beliefs and identities, and the fictions, if persuasive, become the material political reality as the facts and fictions intermingle.

Public opinion thus becomes an important symbol whether or not it is a fact, because it can so readily be claimed as a mandate. The mass media and politicians are jointly involved in the creation of this sense of the "public will" (Bennett, 1993). Public opinion so constituted, however, can be very evanescent. For example, the strong support that seemed to exist for the invasion of Iraq and the toppling of the Saddam Hussein regime evaporated, but the war still dragged on.

In modern political campaigns, candidates do not merely identify their audiences; they constitute them. In other words, they bring them into existence through their campaign discourse. As Barkin (1984, p. 252) observed, "Confronted with a diffuse and heterogeneous public, the candidate must create a sense of affiliation and identification—in the issues he [*sic*] chooses to raise, in his treatment of the opposition, in the image of himself that is projected." These audiences are created by telling voters what they want to hear—based on the results of public opinion polls, which in essence shape and create public opinion as much as they reflect it.

Candidates and political lobbies alike emphasize the results of political opinion polls that show their positions are popular. Anytime an elected official declares that he or she is disregarding the polls, it is a safe bet that the official is currently stuck with poor poll numbers. Faced with poor poll numbers, officials will often attempt to discredit those results. Machinations may include manipulating surveys through the selection and wording of questions and will almost always include attempts to "spin" the results so that they can create a story that advances their own interests. The strategic interpretation of polls is an essential element of modern electoral politics. Polls legitimate candidates and are used to justify policy changes. They often create a self-fulfilling prophecy of public support for candidates and their ideas.

As noted earlier, the results of public opinion polls dominate much political reporting today. Reporters cover the campaign as a "horse race" in which momentum and the game of meeting or failing to meet expectations become the substance of the story (McDermott & Frankovic, 2003; Patterson, 2005). There may be some self-deception on the part of reporters here, as it may be that the incessant focus on the dynamics of the campaign and the "game" of politics interests re-porters more than it does the consumers of news. People often grumble about politicians who seem willing to pander to the voters and to say whatever might seem to help them win an election (Schell, 1996). In addition, pollsters and the reporters who present their results as news are themselves increasingly under public attack as somehow misleading and unfair. Critics have proclaimed, often on Internet blogs, that even the most respected polling houses are conducting "rigged polls." In 2002, the Independence Party of Minnesota formally complained to the Minnesota News Council that the Minnesota poll conducted by the *Minneapolis Star Tribune* was biased because of the newspaper's long-standing editorial support for Democratic Party candidates. In 2004, an advocacy group took out a full-page ad in the *New York Times* claiming that the Gallup Poll's preelection estimates were slanted toward George Bush, suggesting that the slant might be the result of deliberate bias as evidenced by the fact that the retired co-chairman of the organization, George H. Gallup Jr., was personally very religious and favored the Republican candidate (Daves & Newport, 2005).

Noted political reporter E. J. Dionne (1991) suggested that the increasing level of political cynicism and disengagement in the United States might be due to the emphasis on polling and on the marketing of political candidates and their policy proposals:

> After two centuries in which the United States stood proudly as an example of what an engaged citizenry could accomplish through public life, Americans view politics with boredom and detachment. For most of us, politics is increasingly abstract, a spectator sport barely worth watching. Election campaigns generate less excitement than ever and are dominated by television commercials, direct mail, polling, and other approaches that treat individual voters not as citizens deciding their nation's fate, but as mere collections of impulses to be stroked and soothed. (p. 9)

It is popular in America to complain that politicians are out of touch with the voters. An alternative explanation, however, is that most politicians spend too much time trying to be faithful to what their polls tell them the voters want and not enough time seeking to lead the public, spark meaningful public conversations on the issues, and solve complex problems.

CHAPTER 8

The Impact of New Communication Technologies on Political Campaigns

Candidates who are seeking political office in the United States have readily adapted their campaign strategies to take advantage of newly emerging technologies. Following development of the railroads, candidates embarked on "whistle-stop campaigns" to speak to audiences. The invention of the airplane and eventually the commercial jetliner permitted candidates to travel quickly from one campaign event to the next and thus made possible the national campaign tour. The telegraph permitted the rapid transmission of campaign news. Reporters could travel to hear candidates speak and then wire their stories, even texts of the speeches, back to their home newspapers for publication, thereby enabling readers to follow the campaigns. The invention of the radio and television allowed candidates to speak directly to voters who chose not to leave their homes to participate in political campaigns. Many of the new technological developments have given advantages to those candidates who are most proficient in the new forms of campaigning.

Recently, campaigns have begun to rely heavily on personal computers, which enable candidates to keep detailed records on every person who contributes money, volunteers time, endorses the candidate, and so on. In addition, computer databases enable campaigns to maintain extensive amounts of information about voters. For example, campaign staff can research and rapidly access data regarding voters based on demographic characteristics (e.g., gender, average age, income, number of persons residing in the household, number of bathrooms in the home), neighborhoods (e.g., levels of crime, quality of schools, access to health care or transportation services), political interests (party registrations, donations to past campaigns or causes, church, or other group memberships), consumption habits (newspaper and magazine subscriptions, Web site visits), and so on. As Howard (2006, p. 131) noted, "As citizens, we increasingly live in a political subculture that has been conceived with us in mind." Although the level of access to all these sources of information differs from campaign to campaign, with only well-funded campaign operations making use of some of these data, more efficient computers, combined with user-friendly software programs, have enabled even low-budget local campaigns to undertake sophisticated studies of their target voters that go well beyond what well-funded campaigns might have been able to accomplish only a few years ago, and the information is now available much more quickly (Witte & Howard, 2002).

Candidates use the computerized databases to cross-reference polling and census data, shape messages, and communicate messages to possible voters. In addition to traditional message channels, today messages can be circulated through cable television, DVDs mailed to homes, direct mail, faxes, or electronic mail (e-mail). As Howard (2006, p. 3) noted, "Political communication technologies have become so advanced that it is possible for campaign managers to send significantly different messages to potential supporters."

The fax machine and e-mail have already markedly changed campaign communications. Howard (2006, p. 7) noted that the fax machine first played a major role in the 1988 presidential election when both the Democratic and Republican National Committees used a technique they called "blastfaxing." By faxing the important messages, or "talking points," of the campaign directly to supporters, the campaigns not only stayed connected with their followers but also sought to influence the conversations that these followers could have with others. Armed with these talking points, supporters could seek to persuade others and could respond to attacks made on their favored candidates. These early attempts at communicating specific messages to specific targeted voters were positively primitive when compared to the use of e-mails and the development of the Internet.

THE INTERNET

The Internet is a global computer network that enables users to send e-mail, other forms of text messages, graphics, and video. Since its development, the Internet has fundamentally reshaped communication. People now use the Internet to communicate with friends, swap photographs, download music, access news and information, and sell products. It should not be surprising, given this multitude of uses, that the Internet has had a significant impact on political campaigns, citizens' political activism, and communication with elected officials.

The number of Americans using the Internet has increased dramatically — indeed, exponentially—over the past decade. A 1999 study reported that approximately 80 million Americans were online (The dawn of e-life, 1999). By 2007, studies claimed that 211 million Americans, or almost 70 percent of the U.S. population, was online. The number of users in the United States represents almost half the number of people online worldwide (Top 20 countries, 2007). The rate of Internet usage has increased as more and more American homes acquired personal computers. In 2006, 64 percent of American homes subscribed to the Internet, with many others going online either at work or in Internet cafes (LeClaire, 2006).

Despite the expansion in access to and use of the Internet, however, there continue to be substantial differences in usage attributable to age, income, and area of residence. These differences are often referred to in academic and policy discussions as the digital divide. For example, a 2006 study reported that 88 percent of 18- to 29-year-olds, 84 percent of 30- to 49-year-olds, 71 percent of 50- to 64-year olds, and 32 percent of those aged 65 and over used the Internet. Those in the lowest-income households were much less likely to use the Internet. Approximately 53 percent of adults living in households earning less than $30,000 in annual income go online versus 80 percent of those whose income is between $30,000 and $50,000; 86 percent of adults in households with annual income between $50,000 and $75,000; and 91 percent of adults living in households earning more than $75,000. Education also has a significant role to play in Internet access. While 40 percent of adults who have less than a high school education use the Internet, 64 percent of adults with a high school diploma, 84 percent of adults with some college education, and 91 percent of adults with a college degree go online (Madden, 2006). Recent immigrants and those who have limited English language proficiency are also far less likely to use the Internet. For example, only about one-third of those who speak only Spanish are connected online (Fox, 2007).

The gap between Internet access in rural versus urban communities seems to be shrinking but is not yet closed. In a 2006 study, 62 percent of rural households reported owning a home computer versus 73.1 percent of households in metropolitan areas. Similarly, 54 percent of rural households reported having Internet connectivity versus 64.3 percent of metropolitan households. The most significant remaining difference, however, was in the type of connection; 27.4 percent of rural households report connecting to the Internet with a broadband connection, compared to 43.9 percent of metropolitan area households (Koprowski, 2006). The type of connectivity is significant because a broadband or high-speed connection permits a Web user to have a much more satisfying Internet experience. Trying to download video clips, for example, with a simple modem connection and a phone line can be extraordinarily slow and frustrating.

THE INTERNET AND POLITICAL CAMPAIGNS

E-mails were a commonly used means to communicate campaign messages to voters in the 1990 campaign season (Chadwick, 2006; Ganly, 1991). Perhaps the first campaign where the Internet arguably affected the outcome of an election occurred in the 1998 gubernatorial contest in Minnesota. Phil Madsen, executive director of the upstart Reform Party in Minnesota, declared that the Internet served as the "central nervous system" of Jesse Ventura's successful campaign for governor. The campaign, which engineered the election of the former professional wrestler and radio talk show celebrity to Minnesota's highest office, mobilized voters through the use of e-mail. For months, the Ventura campaign had no physical headquarters—just a growing e-mail list. Two-thirds of Ventura's fund-raising pledges arrived via the Internet (Fineman, 1999). The campaign's biggest single event, a seventy-two-hour final drive through the state, was coordinated entirely by e-mail through its Web site. Ventura won the election with 37 percent of the vote against two very well-known and prominent candidates representing the two major parties (Raney, 1998). Although some technology experts dispute the claim that the "Jesse-Net" Web site actually made the difference in the outcome of the election, virtually all concede that coordinated e-mail efforts are invaluable tools for campaigns seeking to mobilize volunteers. Most political consultants would now agree that the Internet is best understood not as a stand-alone strategy but as an integral part of a modern campaign message circulation strategy. When effective, the online messages reinforce the messages developed offline (More comments on the Internet, 2006).

The Internet permits candidates and their campaigns to respond very quickly to events and to the messages circulated by their opponents. This practice was already well established by the time of the 1996 presidential campaign, when both the Clinton and Dole campaigns created "rapid response" e-mails, the successor to the "blastfaxing" mentioned earlier. The campaigns sent out daily messages addressed to thousands of reporters, political action committees, party members, labor union officers, and other opinion leaders. The messages not only articulated the goals of the candidate's own campaign but also raised questions and concerns about the arguments raised by the other side. During the presidential and vice presidential debates in 1996, for example, both campaigns put out point-by-point rebuttals to claims made by the other side (Dole-Kemp truth watch, 1996; Setting the record straight, 1996). These messages sought to control the flow of news about the debates and to influence the way in which reporters told the story of the debates. The messages were almost instantaneous. In fact, the first draft of the Clinton campaign's responses to the arguments that Senator Dole offered in the first presidential debate was sent out to reporters before the debate had even concluded. The use of rapid response e-mails has now become commonplace in virtually all campaigns. This development prompted Dyson (2004) to comment, "Perhaps the most important thing technology has done—for this election and for politics and life in general—is shorten our timescale. Stories that used to unfold over days now unfold in hours or even minutes. Politicians and pundits give instant rather than considered reactions."

By the 1998 midterm elections, approximately 64 percent of major party challengers for Senate, House, and gubernatorial office maintained a Web site, while only 28 percent of incumbents saw a need to campaign on the Web. The best predictor of whether a candidate would have established a Web site was how close the election was: In 81 percent of the closest races, both candidates had Web sites, and in all but six races considered by preelection polling to be a toss-up, both candidates had Web sites as of mid-October (The Web and the Net, 1998). Although the presence of political campaigns on the Web was much more common in 1998 than in previous elections, it is not clear that these Web campaigns received much attention from voters. According to one exit poll, 88 percent of people who used the Internet in 1998 claimed that they received no political information from it (cited in The Web and the Net, 1998). Neither were the 1998 Web campaigns especially effective as a source for raising campaign funds. For example, the Web site of the Barbara Boxer for U.S. Senate campaign, which was considered by experts to be among the best campaigns conducted up to that time on the Internet and that was directed to Web-savvy California voters in the Silicon Valley, raised only $25,000 online (The Web and the Net, 1998).

All the leading candidates for the presidency in 2000 maintained a strong Web presence. The most noteworthy difference between the Internet campaigns of 1996 and those of 2000 was the increased sophistication of the candidates' Web sites. There was a dramatic increase in the use of color, the number of pictures, the variety of textual content, and the use of video clips. Many of these changes were a result of the fact that more and more Web users had access to high-speed connections and thus could download the larger files required to transmit these new forms of information. Web users who visited candidate Web sites in 2000 could volunteer their time, contribute funds, purchase campaign buttons or stickers, engage in discussions with other citizens, learn where the candidate was appearing next, and respond to polling questions. Vice President Gore's site featured an area marked "just for kids" and provided detailed voter registration requirements and information state-by-state. Gore broke new ground in the 2000 presidential primary campaign by offering a Spanish-language version of his Web pages (Fineman, 1999).

The 2000 campaign also saw a significant increase in the use of the Internet by those seeking political information. As more and more Americans acquired personal computers and began to use e-mail (by 2000 approximately 50 percent of the U.S. public had Internet access), more also turned to the Web to learn about the campaign (Bimber & Davis, 2003). Exit polls suggested that almost a third of those who voted reported that they went online for political information (cited by Howard, 2006, p. 1). Also in 2000, Senator Bill Bradley (D—New Jersey) became the first candidate to raise $1 million online in his challenge to Vice President Gore for the Democratic presidential nomination (Howard, 2006).

In perhaps one of the more sophisticated, and controversial, applications of the new technology in the 2000 campaign, the Green Party used the Web to orchestrate a system of coordinated vote swapping (Worley, 2001). As Howard (2006, p. 13) noted, the Green Party sought to win 4 percent of the vote in the general election so that they could qualify their candidate, consumer advocate Ralph Nader, for federal matching funds in subsequent elections. At the same time, the party realized that many liberals would be loath to vote "Green" when Vice President Gore was locked in such a tight race against Governor George W. Bush for fear of tipping the Electoral College results to the Republican candidate. As a result, Gore supporters were asked to vote for Nader in states where Gore was certain to win, and Nader supporters agreed to vote for Gore in states where Gore's victory was uncertain.

Approximately 30,000 people agreed to the swap, including some 1,400 Nader supporters in Florida who agreed to vote for Gore.* Of course, we do not know how many of these voters may have actually honored their agreement to swap votes. We do know, however, that although this vote swapping clearly did not tip the election results, it did introduce the notion of "tactical voting" as a strategic use of the new communication technology that would inspire other political activists to explore similar alternatives in other elections (Chadwick, 2006).

Another noteworthy development in the 2000 campaign was that much more information about campaign donors and the campaigns to which they contributed became available to reporters covering the campaigns and to the voters themselves. Web sites such as OpenSecrets .org and Followthemoney.org provided extensive information easily accessible to Web users. Contributors were identified by name, zip code, industry in which they worked, candidates to whom they contributed, and so on. Lists also provided people with information about how candidates might be beholden to specific interests, political action committees, and regions of the country (Engle, 2001).

Chadwick (2006, p. 162) declared that "the presidential campaign of 2003–2004 was the first real Internet election in the United States." The most noteworthy aspect of this campaign was the tremendous early success of the Howard Dean campaign. Dean began the campaign as an almost unknown former governor of tiny Vermont. His early polling numbers placed him at or near the bottom of the list of potential Democratic candidates. He had almost no money on which to run. What Dean did have, however, was a message and a means to get that message out to his supporters. Dean was the most vocal presidential candidate in expressing opposition to the Iraq war, a position that was proven to be especially appealing to younger voters and left-leaning political activists who were also far more likely to be active online. Recognizing the potential to make maximum use of the Internet to expand his base of supporters, Dean hired political consultant Joe Trippi. Dean, Trippi, and other members of his staff began to meet with Scott Heiferman, the owner of an obscure Web site called Meetup.com. Chadwick reported (2006) the following:

> The purpose of Meetup was very simple. Rather than using the Web to bring people together in virtual communities, the plan was to get

---

* As it turned out, Gore lost the popular vote to Bush in Florida by a mere 537 votes, while Nader captured approximately 97,000 votes in the state. Had the vote swapping been more successful, Gore instead of Bush would have been elected president.

them to meet in physical places, like bars, coffee shops, and restaurants. Individuals could register their names and locations on the site and establish local Meetup groups based on their interests. Heiferman . . . saw Meetup as a way of using the Internet to create real-world social networks. (p. 162)

The Meetups quickly became very popular. In February 2003, there were five Meetups, attended by only a few hundred people; a month later, there were seventy-nine Meetups, and in December that same year, there were 800 Meetups, and the virtual Dean group had 140,000 members (Chadwick, 2006). The 2003 experience suggested, however, that the new social networking technologies alone were insufficient to build excitement for a campaign. The John Kerry presidential campaign, for example, tried to copy the Dean strategy and organize its own Meetups. Those events never really caught on with people, however, as Kerry's Meetup supporters numbered less than 19,000 people at the close of the primary campaign (Chadwick, 2006). The most likely explanation was that to fully benefit from this tactic, the candidate had to have a message that would appeal to Internet users and that would motivate them to turn out for these types of events. It helped, in Dean's case, that the candidate enjoyed strong support among younger voters who were also more likely to be heavy Internet users and, frankly, also more likely to be single and eager to use these kinds of events to meet other people their age who shared their political passions.

The use of the new technology-inspired gatherings as a way to bring like-minded people together was tremendously helpful in bringing volunteers into the Dean campaign, and these volunteers gave the campaign more the character of a spontaneous social movement than the highly structured and controlled consultant-driven campaigns that most candidates now conduct (Cornfield, 2004). Dean's campaign slogan was "You have the power." The slogan seemed to genuinely reflect the style of decision making in the campaign, and local organizers were given wide latitude to create messages and plan events as they saw fit. As Cornfield (2004, p. 3) noted, "Balancing the positive energy flow of a movement with the precise coordination of an organization presents the next generation of campaigners with perhaps their greatest challenge."

The Dean campaign's other great achievement in 2004, however, was that it clearly proved for the first time that the Internet could be an effective means to raise campaign funds. One strategy that the campaign used was to send out specific appeals based on news stories that were breaking that day. By e-mailing messages discussing specific news issues directly to supporters and likely supporters, the campaign sought to take advantage of liberals' anger about the Bush administration and especially about the war in Iraq. These techniques also took advantage of the viral nature of Internet communications because supporters were encouraged to forward these messages to their friends, family members, and colleagues at work (Trippi, 2004).* Cornfield (2004) gave a particularly good example of this strategy:

> In July 2003 the Dean campaign took advantage of news reports about an upcoming $2,000-a-plate Republican luncheon featuring Vice President Dick Cheney. Up, out, and around the Dean network went word of "The Cheney Challenge"—could Dean supporters raise more money than the luncheon by the time it took place?—accompanied by a Web video of the candidate munching on a "three-dollar" turkey sandwich. Cheney's lunch raised $250,000 from 125 guests. The on-line fund-raising gimmick netted the Dean campaign $500,000 from 9,700 people and great publicity about its grassroots enthusiasm and prowess. (p. 2)

The Dean campaign's successful effort to raise money via the Internet was, without doubt, the most significant new technology story about the 2004 campaign. It has been estimated that approximately 280,000 individual donors contributed about $40 million, for an average contribution of $143 (Singel, 2004).

If the Dean campaign illustrated the positive possibilities of the new communication technologies, however, it also starkly revealed the problems that these technologies could pose to candidates. When Dean failed to achieve the level of support that he anticipated and that the media had predicted for him in the 2004 Iowa caucuses, he spoke to an assembled crowd of his supporters and attempted to rally them to continue the campaign in New Hampshire. Seeking to inspire his young supporters, Dean permitted himself a scream of defiance that his campaign would not be denied victory and that he intended to fight on. The "scream" seemed incredibly inappropriate to his image as a serious candidate for the nation's highest office. A video clip file of the scream was repeatedly played on television news programs, made its way onto the entertainment programs (such as *The Tonight Show*), and was sent as an e-mail attachment to Internet users around the country. The expo-

---

* The term *viral* in this sense refers to viral marketing. People are encouraged to pass on a message, and soon it spreads from person to person in much the same way that a pathogen from a disease spreads. Social networking sites such as MySpace, Friendster, and YouTube are, for example, important Internet sites for such marketing.

sure badly damaged Dean's campaign, and he fared worse in the New Hampshire primary than he had in Iowa. The Dean campaign ended soon after (Chadwick, 2006; Singel, 2004). The importance of the Internet for sharing video clips and the potentially devastating effect such clips could have on a campaign also played a role in the 2006 midterm elections.

Another noteworthy aspect of Dean's 2004 campaign was its extensive use of unauthorized and unofficial blogs. Blogs, short for Weblogs, are Web sites controlled by the primary contributor. Comments are usually made in a breezy journalistic style, often involving the telling of personal narratives, and are posted to the site in reverse chronological order so readers see the most recent posts first. Most blogs invite interactions between the original author and readers, who are encouraged to offer their own opinions. The use of blogs first became popular between 1998 and 2000, when several reporters and political commentators developed their own blogs. The Iraq war especially energized both the number of blogs and the audience for these sites. Until the Dean campaign, however, organized presidential campaigns had not been inclined to engage in blogging (Singel, 2004).

What the Dean campaign learned was that these online journals permit candidates, campaign staff members, activists, reporters, and ordinary citizen commentators to contribute their observations about daily events, news stories, and campaign messages and strategies. The benefit of blogs is that they can create a feeling of genuine interactivity, thereby giving participants a sense of personal empowerment. The dangers in these forms of messaging include the fact that the campaign must surrender most of its control over the formation of messages (campaign aides who are expressing their own opinions can seem to be speaking on behalf of the candidate), and reporters can use them to post observations that might never have survived close scrutiny by their editors. Many people also worry that the result is a surplus of messages of questionable veracity (conspiracy theories, for example, abound in blogs) and a public audience that may not be well equipped to evaluate the quality of the claims that they are reading because they lack familiarity with the new media.*

* Scholars across a wide range of academic disciplines have become interested in how people come to understand, depend on, and evaluate different forms of media. This is often referred to as media literacy. A recent subject of concern is how the new media environment has changed the mediascape and what consequences these changes may have for media literacy and for civic education. For example, see the Center for Media Literacy Web site: http://www.medialit.org/. Retrieved on September 10, 2007.

The Dean campaign's successes prompted the other candidates in the 2004 campaign to also make more significant efforts to communicate with potential voters online. John Kerry and John Edwards also created blogs, attempted to arrange their own Meetups, and solicited online donations. Although the Kerry campaign's early efforts had little success, once Dean dropped out of the race, many of his online supporters switched their support to the Kerry-Edwards ticket. As a result, the intensity of their online campaigning increased as did the contributions they received online (Chadwick, 2006).

The campaign for George W. Bush also expanded its online efforts. The campaign claimed that 6 million people were receiving its e-mails and therefore getting regular updates of news from the campaign. Chadwick (2006, pp. 166–167) argues that the Bush site was less interactive than the Democrats' sites. Perhaps this was because the Dean campaign in particular had been a kind of insurgency movement that was most appealing to committed liberal activists united by their opposition to the war in Iraq. On the other hand, Chadwick (2006) also acknowledged that the Bush site offered very diverse content and was innovative in its use of Internet design features. Chadwick (2006, p. 167) noted that whereas Kerry raised about a third of his total contributions, or about $5.7 million online, Bush earned $9 million online.

All of the 2008 presidential candidates maintained active Web sites, but the Democratic candidates' sites, at least during the primary campaign, seemed to get the most traffic. Two possible explanations may account for this result. First, there was consistent evidence throughout most of the 2008 campaign that the Democrats were politically engaged to a more significant extent than in past elections and were following the campaign more closely than were Republicans, perhaps due to the unpopular Iraq war and the very low approval ratings held by President Bush (Nagourney, 2007). Second, there was evidence that younger voters—who also tend to be the most likely voters to seek information online—were more likely to favor the Democratic candidates (Campaign '08: Analysis of key voter groups, 2007).

Among Democrats, Senator Barack Obama, the candidate who had strong appeal with young voters, saw the most traffic to his Web site (Campaign '08, 2007). For example, a Nielsen/Net rating survey for July 2007 found that Obama's campaign site racked up 717,000 unique visitors who stayed around for an average of eight minutes each—a long visit in cyberspace. Senator Clinton's had 437,000 visitors who stayed for eight minutes and seventeen seconds, fewer visitors but more curious. Former senator Edwards drew 348,000 visitors, but they did not spend much time there, averaging only three minutes and forty-three seconds. Among the Republican candidates, former senator Fred Thompson had 381,000 unique visitors, but they stayed only an average of one minute and thirty-five seconds. Former New York City mayor Rudy Giuliani drew 124,000 visitors for an average of seven minutes and thirty-three seconds, and former Massachusetts governor Mitt Romney drew 116,000 visitors for an average of forty-nine seconds (Frederick & Malcolm, 2007).

ACCESSING NEWS ONLINE

As discussed in Chapter 5, the number of people who claim to read a daily newspaper has been dropping for years, as has the audience for nightly network news programs. At the same time, more and more people are turning to the Internet for their news. As Howard (2006) observed:

> The proportion of people who had ever gone online rose from 23 percent in 1996 to 59 percent in 2004. By 2004, some 31 percent of the population reported going online on a daily basis for news, approaching the proportion of the population that read a daily newspaper. The proportion of people who especially went online for political or campaign news grew from 4 percent in the 1996 elections to 57 percent in the 2004 elections. The proportion of adults who look for news or information about politics on a *daily* basis during campaign periods was 17 percent in the 2004 elections. However, respondents were also asked whether they had ever gone online to look for news or information about that specific election period, and the population who responded positively grew from 6 percent in 1996 to 30 percent in 2004. (pp. 19–24)

Because the Internet is primarily a "pull" rather than a "push" technology (television or radio audiences are exposed to specific news stories without intentionally seeking them out when they watch or listen to news programs, whereas Internet users typically must go to Web sites and then click on specific stories to download political news onto their computers), we can assume that those who turn to the Internet to seek political news will be those actively interested in politics. Approximately 25 percent of the adult population reported that they learned something online in 2004 that helped them decide how they would cast their votes (Howard, 2006).

Some researchers have argued that the Internet compares favorably with traditional print sources in enhancing political knowledge (Pfau, Houston, & Semmler, 2007). Others, however, have argued that the quality of the Internet news experience depends on what sites users go to for news, how much time they spend on those sites, and whether they permit themselves to confront information that does not tend to confirm what they already believe to be true (for example, see Sunstein, 2001).

Which Web sites attract the most attention from those seeking political information? It seems that the most election news seekers turn to well-known news organizations for information. In the 2002 midterm elections, for example, nearly two-thirds (64 percent) of online election news consumers visited the sites of major media organizations like CNN and the New York Times, or local news organizations such as the newspaper in their own city. This percentage was up from the 2000 campaign, when 55 percent turned to such sites. This study also suggested that more explicitly and narrowly focused political sites also showed increased traffic. Approximately a third of online election news consumers (32 percent) said they went most often to government and candidate Web sites or sites that specialize in politics, up from 19 percent in 2000 (Political sites gain, 2003).

A 2006 study reported that 46 percent of Internet users said that they turned to Web sites of national TV organizations (such as CNN or MSNBC); 39 percent to portal Web sites (such as Yahoo! or Google), 32 percent to the Web sites of local daily newspapers, 31 percent to the Web sites of local TV news stations, and 20 percent to Web sites of a national daily newspaper. International news sources (such as BBC or al Jazeera) received attention from 12 percent of Internet users, and 9 percent consulted blogs (Horrigan, 2006). Studies also suggest that online newspapers have extended the reach of national newspapers, such as the *New York Times*, the *Washington Post*, and *USA Today*. Although more than nine out of ten readers of print newspapers read their local newspapers, only about half of readers of online newspapers do so, with many of the rest instead choosing to spend their time reading the national newspapers (Online papers modestly, 2006).

There also seem to be significant differences in usage patterns between those who relied on a "dial-up" connection and those who had high-speed broadband Internet access. High-speed Web surfers were far more likely to rely on the Web as a source for news, more likely to visit a greater number of sites, and more likely to set their browsers to give them regular headline updates or information on topics that uniquely interested them. Those with access to high-speed Internet connections are also more likely to have higher incomes and be better educated. Finally, perhaps as a result of their generally higher social and economic status, and perhaps because of their exposure to a wide range of online news sources, these users tended to be more likely to serve as opinion leaders as they shared information that they learned with others (Horrigan, 2006). Often online news users achieve their status as opinion leaders as they e-mail to their friends and colleagues stories that they find interesting or provocative. Approximately 60 percent of Internet users reported that they have had news stories mailed to them (25 percent indicated that this had happened within the past week), and 40 percent reported that they had mailed stories on to others (Online papers modestly, 2006). As Horrigan (2006, p. 9) commented, "For the heavily engaged broadband user, it is clear that online news occupies a central place in his or her daily newsgathering habits in a way that distinctly differs from other broadband users."

Access to Internet sources seems not to have increased the amount of time or attention that average citizens devote to seeking news, and average online news consumers continue to spend far more time each day getting news on television or radio or in the newspaper than they do getting it online (Online papers modestly, 2006). Readers' usability studies have suggested that those consuming information online differ from those seeking it through other sources. It seems that online news consumers are even more likely than ordinary newspaper readers to attend primarily to headlines, to skim stories, and to not read stories in their entirety. For example, Web readers tend to skim over sites rather than read them intently (often they will not click to move on to a second or third page). They also tend to be more proactive than print readers or TV viewers, hunting for the information that they are interested in learning rather than passively taking in what the source presents to them (Dube, 2006). The different habits in news consumption clearly suggest that writers will be most effective when they adapt their reporting style to suit the new medium and tailor their content in a way that best enables them to tell their story (Dube, 2006).

New technological innovations, ever increasing download speeds, and new strategies in Web design and in adapting reporting strategies to the online environment have all affected online news users' habits. One can far more easily now, for example, access video feeds. The very popular YouTube Web site contains an extensive collection of politically focused materials, including television excerpts from news broadcasts, interview shows, candidate speeches, and past debates. YouTube also features a fascinating mix of professionally produced news content, campaign-controlled messages such as sample advertisements, and videos shot by amateur filmmakers, sometimes using their cell phones to capture candidates in unguarded moments. In the 2006 midterm elections, George Allen, the incumbent Republican senator of Virginia, learned about this new technology and its power the hard way when he was caught on film referring to an audience member of Indian descent, who supported his opponent, with the racially derogatory term "Macaque" (sometimes spelled "Macaca" in press accounts; Allen's listening tour, 2006). The video was not only played over and over on the Web, but it quickly leaped onto television screens as well and soon became the defining story in a very close campaign. Allen, who had frequently been touted as a GOP presidential contender, ended up losing a very close election to his Democratic opponent (Fiske, 2006).

Many find this new and innovative use of video technology exciting because it turns even ordinary citizens into news producers and helps reveal the "genuine" candidate as he or she exists beneath the surface image typically revealed in a very heavily managed and scripted campaign. Others, however, worry that such moments may in fact be distractions that will mislead voters by getting them to focus on insignificant image issues instead of on more substantive issues of policy. These critics also worry that following candidates around with cell phone video cameras will further blur the line between the public and personal dimensions of candidates' lives and in the process discourage talented people from subjecting themselves to the rigors of running for public office. As one commentator observed:

> They face the threat of diminishment by comparison with virtual personalities, on the one hand, and, on the other, incessant pressure from journalists angling for a gotcha moment because that's the only interesting thing they can do. So politicians package themselves for protection—and end up looking phony as well as flawed. . . . By allowing videos of gaffes to be isolated, posted, and repeated, YouTube has intensified and hastened the cycle of building up and tearing down. (Clark, 2006)

In the new media environment:

> Politicians are no longer able to tailor their messages to finite audiences: state fair attendees, senior citizens, the party faithful. Each appearance now holds the possibility of being captured and rebroadcast to the larger public. This means that politicians and their handlers

need to develop new forms of communicating with a cynical and empowered audience. (Clark, 2006)

One of the more amusing "YouTube moments" in campaign 2008 was the release of the "Obama Girl" video. In this MTV-style video, a very attractive young woman—who is depicted in various scenes in a bikini or in very short shorts—sings about her "crush" on Obama and her devotion to his cause. The video was viewed almost 4 million times on YouTube in the first three months following its release, and it was frequently replayed on TV news programs.* Although the video was both humorous and fun and may have helped the candidate appeal to youthful voters, it certainly did not help Obama spread his message that he was a candidate of substance.

Recognizing the power of YouTube to facilitate the rapid transmission of political video clips, candidates in the 2008 race decided to embrace rather than resist the technology. YouTube offered the 2008 candidates the opportunity to post whatever materials they wished in an easily accessed and convenient portal that readily permitted voters to compare the candidates. Candidates took advantage of this site to post new ads, excerpts of campaign speeches, scenes of them questioning witnesses in legislative hearings, and glimpses of them spending time with family members.

Another new communication technology that has now begun to influence politics is the mobile phone. The new generation of mobile phones has become important in politics because these are multimedia instruments capable of taking and transmitting photographs and video clips. The phones are also useful, of course, for their ability to rapidly transmit text messages, and these messages have already been demonstrated to have a significant impact on politics. Castells, Fernandez-Ardevol, Qiu, and Sey (2007) noted the following:

> Control of information and communication has been a major source of power throughout history. The advent of the Internet and of wireless communication allows the development of many-to-many and one-to-one horizontal communication channels that bypass political or business control of communication. Therefore, new avenues are open for autonomous processes of social and political mobilization that do not rely on formal politics and do not depend on their framing in the mass media. (p. 209)

---

* The "I Got a Crush on Obama" video can be seen at http://www.youtube.com/watch?v=wKsoXHYICqU. Retrieved on September 12, 2007.

Castells and his colleagues went on to cite examples of the power of text messaging and wireless technology in influencing the election outcomes in the Philippines, South Korea, and Spain. Activists, especially younger citizens, used the technologies to exchange political messages, set up demonstrations and protests (sometimes referred to as "flash-mobs"), challenge conventional media reporting of political events, and mobilize citizens to go to the polls. The influence of this technology has already been felt in the United States as well, although perhaps not yet as dramatically as in these international examples. Castells et al. argued that protesters used wireless technologies to organize their activities to maximize their effectiveness and thwart police efforts to control them during the Republican National Convention in New York in 2004 (see pp. 185–213). Although the long-term implications of this technology are not yet clear, the conclusion offered by Castells et al. (p. 213) seems, if anything, understated: "When the dominant institutions of society no longer have the monopoly of mass-communication networks, the dialectics between power and counterpower is, for better or for worse, altered forever."

A 2006 study reported that 6 percent of Americans were receiving news headlines or reading news reports on their mobile phones, and about half that number did so at least a few times a week. Many others access such information with their handheld computers (PDAs, or personal digital assistants), and still others download news stories onto their iPods. Although only a small number of people—perhaps about 7 percent of the general public—access news via these devices, the numbers heavily skew toward younger people. As access to these new technologies expands and as the numbers of those who have grown up with these technologies increase, we can expect that these new technologies will be an ever more important source of political news (Online papers modestly, 2006). Young people are also linking social networking sites such as MySpace to their mobile phones so that they can more quickly and readily connect to others. In 2007, MySpace was also emerging as an important site for the sharing of political information and political activism (Kharif, 2006). While former North Carolina senator John Edwards was promoting his candidacy for the Democratic presidential nomination on twenty-three different social networking sites, Senator Barack Obama (D—Illinois) had the most "friends" on MySpace and the largest numbers of viewers of his YouTube videos (Vargas, 2007).

Most experts who have studied the effectiveness of different online political campaign strategies insist that there are no clear templates that suggest what works best (Graff, 2005). Instead, highly creative people are encouraged to develop their online strategies as integral components of their overall campaign strategies so that one seamlessly reinforces the other (More comments on the Internet, 2006).

The Internet has proven especially useful as a tool that enables citizens to contact elected officials and to access government services online. Just as some studies worry, however, that access to virtual communication in social networking sites may decrease the likelihood that people will go out and make contacts in real space, others fear that use of the Internet may discourage other forms of political participation. One study suggested that this was precisely the case. It reported that "46 percent of occasional Internet users contacted a public official in the past year versus 34 percent of frequent users. Only 31 percent of those never using the Internet made contact. Thirty-one percent of occasional Internet users attended a political event versus 22 percent of frequent users. Only 12 percent of those never using the Internet attended an event" (Reeher, 2006). These findings suggest that those who are sufficiently interested in politics to go online either to access information, discuss politics, or contact an elected official are more likely to attend a live political event. Yet, at the same time, there is a tipping point at which those who are most actively involved in online political activity begin to see it as a substitute for other forms of political activity.

CYBERSPACE AND THE PUBLIC SPHERE

The dominant metaphor shaping American concepts of arguments in the public political arena has, for many years, been the notion of a marketplace of free ideas. The marketplace supposedly revealed relative strengths and possible flaws in arguments and in policy positions through the deliberations of an enlightened and capable public. The public evaluated arguments to select an appropriate course of action. This philosophy—of citizens actively involved in public life, informed about issues, and motivated by shared social concerns—represents the essence of the values of pluralism that are often cited as the greatest source of stability for American democracy (Dahl, 1972).

Alexis de Tocqueville, a French statesman and author who visited the United States in the 1830s, wrote that the great challenge for the young American democracy would be the artful balancing of individual versus communal interests. He declared, "Citizens who are bound to take part in public affairs must turn from their private interests and occasionally take a look at something other than themselves" (cited in Bellah et al., 1985, p. 38). The American educational philosopher John Dewey asserted the importance of determining the balance between private concerns and public interests when he wrote that "humans are, by nature associative and that all social activities have consequences. Some affect only the person causing them and so may be designated 'private.' But in modern, democratic life, the majority of acts produce consequences that affect others. By doing so, they not only *are* public: they *create* a public" (cited by Martin, 2002, pp. 387–388). Balancing what is "private" and what is "public" becomes one of the great challenges in a democracy. Citing Dewey's theories, Martin (2002) explained:

> The rise of democracy and industrialization has made the problem of the democratic public immensely more complicated than it was in earlier periods of history. Democracy is the consequence of a "large and varied number of particular [democratic] happenings." But a democracy in an industrial age makes the regulation of its public interest more complicated than do most other forms of government, for democracy creates a weak, unruly public, uncertain of what "the public interest" might be and why or how to regulate it. Democracy and industry have combined to make the relations of multiple publics so subtle, so far-reaching, so infinitely extended and interconnected that the varied publics of modern democracy can no longer easily identify themselves and coordinate their interests. (p. 388)

While Dewey, writing at the dawn of the twentieth century, could not have imagined—let alone anticipated—developments such as the Internet, his thoughts on the creation of an engaged public could not be more timely. Yet, even his remarks leave us with as many questions as answers. Although the Internet has certainly altered power structures and made the public more unruly—while also helping individuals and groups find each other, organize, mobilize, and coordinate their interests—has it helped or hindered people's ability to think about the public interest?

The image of society as a marketplace of fair competition among roughly equally empowered competitors each hawking their ideas is appealing, yet the notion has always been badly flawed. Most people, experts and ordinary citizens alike, understand that the marketplace has in some meaningful ways always been rigged to favor some and to disadvantage others. In the economic sphere of commercial trade the marketplace was replaced first by the department store and then the mega-mall. Large corporations control the production, distribution, and sale of products and influence consumer choices through massive advertising campaigns. Entire sections of the economy (e.g., agriculture) and defense industries evade reliable cost accounting (Bellah et al., 1985).

Many similar inequalities have emerged in the political marketplace, and ordinary citizens have lost their voice (Balthrop, 1989; Goodnight, 1982, 1991). Political participation is not expressed through immediate contact with political figures or even through party activities; for most of us, participation means watching candidates present their messages through short mass-mediated commercials, viewing snippets of campaign hoopla on the evening news, and subconsciously responding to the bumper stickers or yard signs that we encounter. The final political act for most citizens is the trip to the polls to cast their ballots, an act that is so anonymous and for which there is so little social accountability that many never even bother to register to vote let alone go to the polls. Thus, what passes for our system of representative democracy often grinds on without the participation of many citizens and serves only to entrench the power of the existing elites (Hollihan, Riley, & Klumpp, 1993).

The great casualty of the decline of the political marketplace has been the lost opportunity for meaningful public debates and dialogues on complex questions of public morality. Thirty-second spot television advertisements that encourage voters to ask themselves "Are you better off today than you were four years ago?" are poor substitutes for attending political rallies where citizens hear speeches, interact with neighbors, and express their own political opinions, thereby subjecting them to public scrutiny and rebuttal. Some critics worry that the new technologies such as the Internet, which encourage individual citizens to write directly to their elected representatives to protest, for example, the release of a convicted felon into their neighborhood, may increase the tendency to individualize politics. Such political activity intensifies an already prevalent "not in my backyard" political attitude while diminishing the ability of all citizens and elected officials to consider the necessities of the common good (Shapiro, 1999).

To encourage citizens to think communally, we need to reinvigorate the public sphere and create opportunities for meaningful public debate on complex social issues (Habermas, 1962/1989). A healthy public sphere in which arguments are formed, tested, and evaluated helps an emergent democratic community shape its policy choices through the broad participation of an active and involved citizenry (Klumpp, Riley, & Hollihan, 1995).

Although it seems unwise to put too much confidence in the Internet or cyberspace as the next great hope for a reinvigorated democratic public sphere, many researchers and analysts have optimistically asserted that this most recent information revolution can strengthen democracy because it enables smaller, weaker actors to compete on a more equal playing field with bigger, stronger actors (Ronfeldt, 1991). The writer A. J. Liebling once commented, "In America, freedom of the press is largely reserved for those who own one" (cited in Katz, 1996, p. 2). Katz (1996) argued that this is being reversed now because individuals with computers can communicate their messages to large audiences:

> The Internet has, in fact, redefined citizenship as well as communications. It is the first worldwide medium in which people can communicate so directly, so quickly, so personally, and so reliably. In which they can form distant but diverse and cohesive communities, send, receive, and store vast amounts of textual and graphic information, skip without paperwork or permission across borders. Where computers are plentiful, digital communications are nearly uncensorable. This reality gives our moral and media guardians fits; they still tend to portray the computer culture as an out-of-control menace harboring perverts, hackers, pornographers, and thieves. But [Thomas] Paine would have known better. The political, economic, and social implications of an interconnected global medium are enormous, making plausible Paine's belief in the "universal citizen." (p. 6)

Wilhelm (2000, p. 15) would have described such views as those of *neo-futurists*—people who, he declared, have "an uncritical faith in progress, an acceptance of novel, fast-paced technologies as juggernauts (laying the groundwork for a hopeful future), and a distrust of obsolescing technologies and institutions as enervated and inimical to creative impulses." Wilhelm contrasted these utopians with *dystopians*, who see only the dangers in cyberspace because they are "wary of emerging and telecommunications technologies' potential to disrupt social and political life. Their point of departure is recovering essential qualities waning in contemporary society, such as a dependence on face-to-face political interactions, thought to be more authentic than mediated exchanges." Perhaps not surprisingly, given how he characterized the extreme positions just outlined, Wilhelm (2000, p. 15) also talked about the emergence of *technorealists* and placed himself in this category. According to Wilhelm, *technorealists* are technology professionals, journalists, and academics who "suggest that people need to think critically about the role that tools and interfaces play in everyday life. This movement recommends a new form of criticism in which technology is assessed from the standpoint of its impact on human values."

Wilhelm (2000, p. 33) went on to argue that assessing the impact of new communication technologies on public and political life requires a consideration of *inclusiveness*, the importance of assuring that the development of these new computer-mediated forms of political participation are genuinely open to all citizens; and *deliberation*, the degree to which they facilitate interactions in which the arguments put forth by participants can be validated intersubjectively in a public space. In short, cyberspace will not be helpful to the goals of genuine democracy if some people are denied access to the Web (perhaps because of cost or because they lack access to high-speed connectivity) or if people find themselves talking only to others who already share their opinions or exposing themselves to sources of information (blogs, self-controlling news browsers, etc.) that give them only one-sided viewpoints.

Another consequence of the Internet as a site for political deliberation is the lack of privacy in cyberspace. It is possible for governmental agencies, companies, political campaigns, and marketing firms to learn about our Web usage habits. By putting "cookies" on our machines, they know how often we have accessed their sites, what time we spend there, what stories we read, and what sites we visited just before and just after visiting their sites. Anyone who has used the Internet to purchase products—for example, books on Amazon.com—probably already understands this power. (Whenever I go to Amazon.com, for example, I am not only greeted by name, but I am also shown a dozen new books to consider addressing topics that I have expressed an interest in during previous visits.) Certainly, political campaigns and political interest groups are capable of the same message tailoring. Can citizens really acquire the information they need to develop informed opinions if they rely on a technology that works so effectively to give them only one side of a story? Howard (2006, p. 185) argued that this technology was likely to result in the production of "thin citizens," people who "can respond quickly to political urges and need not spend significant amounts of time contemplating political matters." The Internet is a rich source of information, but the ease with which that information can be tailored to individual needs, interests, and appetites has consequences. As Howard (2006) noted:

> Thin citizens do not need to expend much interpretive labor in their political lives, because they use information technologies to demark political content they want in their diet. They choose which editors and which issues take priority and minimize their exposure to random or challenging information. . . . The thin citizen participates in five-minute protests through the computer by signing electronic petitions forwarded by friends and family, for example. Political hypermedia have been designed to permit, and promote, thinned citizenship roles. (p. 185)

Howard (2006) further clarified his point:

> Traditionally, a large portion of the political information we had digested each day was through random encounters with newspaper headlines and other opinions, but political hypermedia are designed to remove the risk of random exposure to political content from our lives. Hypermedia provide political content in sequence, in context, in patterns determined either by the set criterion of users or by campaign managers. Hypermedia campaigns are designed to present information in a largely unmediated form or in a form that is mediated by the citizen's own filtering preferences. These privatized public spheres are self-selected, nonrandom groups of people deliberately producing and consuming political content. (p. 197)

The creation of a healthy public sphere demands that people be exposed to enough common sources of information that they have shared experiences upon which to shape their political conversations. The Internet, even as it enhances the construction of communication networks that connect individuals to each other to achieve political goals, may undermine the formation of an engaged public with the capacity to act collectively to address shared social problems.

The Internet then has emerged as a place where citizens who are interested in political news can go and get more and better information than has ever before been accessible. They can have instant daily access to newspapers not just in their hometown but from around their nation or the world. They can find out who is donating to political campaigns; learn candidate positions on issues; watch videos of news clips, speeches, or campaign advertisements not available in their area; read blogs; and contribute their own content and become producers of political discourse. At the same time, the Internet also threatens to undermine opportunities for other forms of social and political interaction. There has long been a rich-poor information gap in the United States. Those who read their daily newspapers, listen to candidate debates, watch TV news programs, and perhaps attend live political events have long had more information on which to base their opinions and decide their votes than those who do not become so engaged. In the Internet era, however, the rich-poor information gap threatens to become a chasm. Political elites seem to be gaining far more information and exercising their voices with more authority and with a greater impact on the political process. If our political system becomes ever more responsive to the interests of elites—a direction in which it arguably already has been moving—then we must consider how effectively such a system will be able to meet the needs of the less empowered or to achieve a sense of the common good. The Internet has already proven to be a most effective means of surveying public opinion, maintaining and making available extensive amounts of data, and tailoring messages to individual needs and interests. As a result, it has contributed to the use of wedge issues as activists on the right and the left are drawn together in conversations with others who already share their opinions. The next encouraging step would be for new developments in communications technology to provide insights into how to find a balance in these competing interests.

One very interesting new development seeks to capitalize on Internet technology as a form of civic education, especially targeted toward youth. For example, some developers have begun to design interactive political games in which competitors are encouraged to think strategically not just about how they can win the game by achieving their stated political or policy objectives but also do so in a way that reduces social conflict, builds social capital (the advantages that people accrue from living and working in communities), and encourages a search for the common good (Kaye, 2005). Perhaps it should not surprise us that technology-crazed citizens are looking to new forms of technology to address problems of the political sphere that have been aggravated by new developments in technology.

CHAPTER 9

Televised Campaign Debates

The political campaign season in America is essentially without end. Candidates for statewide or national office typically begin planning their campaigns and refining their electoral strategies years before the election is to take place. Often these early activities include embarking on the "rubber chicken" circuit to raise money, increase name recognition, and test the waters for their candidacies well before formally announcing their intention to seek office. If elected, most politicians immediately begin to plan their reelection campaigns. Furthermore, many elected officials view the challenge of getting their legislative or policy initiatives passed as merely additional campaign objectives. We thus live in a time of the permanent campaign.

Given the inevitability of these campaigns and the fact that voters are continually barraged by campaign messages, it is not surprising that voter interest and attention are difficult to sustain. This is especially the case now, given that states have moved their primaries earlier and earlier so they can maximize the potential impact that their residents have on the selection of the presidential candidates. There are key moments in campaigns, however, when voters do give some attention to evaluating their political choices. Voters may pay attention to the presidential campaign during the Iowa caucuses or the New Hampshire primary, for example, because these elections represent the first face-to-face test of the candidates. Voters probably pay attention to a few of the ads and perhaps even read about the candidates to decide how they will cast their vote in their own state primary elections. Really dedicated and interested voters may tune in for some television coverage of the party nominating conventions, although the number of persons watching the Democratic and Republican National Conventions has declined deeply in recent years as the networks have significantly reduced the amount of time given over to the conventions (Network TV, 2005).

The moments in the general election campaign, however, that are most likely to engender voter interest are the nights when the candidates compete in televised debates. These debates attract attention because they come as close to "good television" as political discussions ever can. They have a sense of confrontation and clash, there is a media buildup of anticipation, and then, of course, there is a follow-up discussion of who won the debate. Most important for many viewers, there is a real sense of drama and the very real possibility that one candidate or the other will commit a major gaffe that might derail his or her candidacy.

Televised presidential debates were first held in 1960, when Vice President Richard Nixon debated Senator John Kennedy in four sixty-minute confrontations. No debates were held for the 1964, 1968, and 1972 elections because one of the two candidates was so far ahead in the polls that he deemed the debates unnecessary (meaning that he believed a debate was not likely to further his interests and potentially capable of causing damage to his candidacy).* The decision to debate or not to debate, as well as the decision regarding the number of debates, timing, and format, has routinely been made by the candidates and their campaign staffs through a process of negotiation. It should not come as a surprise, therefore, that the desire to further the interests of the candidate guides these choices, rather than concern for greater public knowledge about the issues (Friedenberg, 1979).

Debates have taken place in every presidential election since 1976 and now seem to have been institutionalized, not by law or formal agreement but because the American public has deemed them an important and useful election ritual. Presidential candidates who declare themselves unwilling to participate in televised debates would likely face the wrath of the media and the voters. During the 2000, 2004, and 2008 presidential primary campaigns, there were so many debates between the Democratic and Republican candidates that the contests had difficulty attracting a significant television audience or print media coverage. During the 2004 campaign, the Democratic candidates participated in fifteen separate debates in the run up to the general election. The first debates in the 2008 presidential campaign were held in

---

* It is worth noting that even though Republican candidate Richard Nixon was significantly ahead of his Democratic opponent Hubert Humphrey in most preelection polls, the final outcome of the 1968 election, at least in terms of the popular vote, was actually quite close. Nixon won 43.4 percent of the popular vote and Humphrey won 42.7 percent. Third-party candidate Governor George Wallace won a surprising 13.5 percent. The electoral vote tallies were far more one-sided, with Nixon winning 301 electoral votes versus Humphrey's 191 and Wallace's 46.

April (the Democratic candidates) and May (the Republican candidates) of 2007, and more than two dozen debates were tentatively planned for the 2008 primary campaign (West, 2007). The television audiences for many of these primary debates are minuscule. In the 2000 campaign many of these primary debates attracted approximately 1.5 million viewers. This was about 300,000 fewer viewers than the least-popular television show reported in the weekly Nielsen ratings (Berke, Debates seen, 2000). Interest seemed to be somewhat higher in the 2008 campaign, especially among Democrats, who may have been especially interested in seeing an end to the Republican occupation of the White House. The cable network MSNBC, the only network to air a live broadcast of the first primary debates in the campaign, reported that approximately 2.2 million people tuned in to see eight Democratic contenders debate in the first confrontation hosted in South Carolina (Shear, 2007).

Despite the fact that few viewers may tune in for these primary campaign debates, pundits, academic researchers, and campaign advisors alike argue that these contests do make a difference. They help set the tone for television news coverage, which can later help create substantially larger audiences; they highlight many substantive issues and differences in the candidates' views; and they can help either enhance or diminish a candidate's momentum and credibility in the presidential sweepstakes.

In the earliest years of televised presidential debating, the contests were sponsored, planned, and organized by the League of Women Voters. The League left most of the actual discussion about formats and schedules to the candidates and their advisors. To lend some order and structure to the general election debates, the Commission on Presidential Debates (CPD) was created in 1987. The CPD, composed of members from both the Republican and Democratic parties, encourages and facilitates the scheduling of presidential debates and supports research and scholarship into alternative debate formats that might best serve the interests of the voting public (Carlin & McKinney, 1994). The CPD has also been charged with deciding whether third-party or other minor party candidates would be invited to participate, a decision that has been and continues to be a source of great controversy.

The Federal Election Commission (FEC) demands that the debate sponsors have a plan for determining who is invited to participate. In 1996 the CPD ruled that only candidates who stood a realistic chance of being elected could debate. This decision kept Reform Party candidate Ross Perot and other minor party candidates from participating in the contests (Apple, 1996). The decision to limit participation to the two leading candidates rather than extending it to three or more candidates has become one of the most controversial aspects of planning and scheduling debates. Some have argued, for example, that any candidate who qualifies for federal campaign funds should be entitled to participate in the debates (Gailey, 1996). There is no doubt, however, that increasing the number of candidates in the debate changes the dynamics of the encounter. Having two candidates slug it out in a face-to-face encounter permits them to respond to each other's arguments and clarifies the differences between the candidates representing the major parties. When a third candidate or additional candidates are allowed to join the debate, the likelihood increases that the trailing candidates will gang up on the front-runner. This essentially happened in the 1992 presidential debates when both Clinton and Perot turned their attacks on the incumbent, President George H. W. Bush. The other alternative that may affect the debate outcome occurs when the two leading candidates confront each other but allow the minor party candidate to escape unscathed. Many claim that this happened in the three-way race for governor of Minnesota in 1998, when Republican candidate Norm Coleman and Democratic candidate Hubert Humphrey III ignored the upstart challenger (and former professional wrestler) Jesse Ventura in their televised debates. Meanwhile, Ventura established himself as a legitimate contender by being allowed to share the stage with the front-runners, scored big points by charming the television audience, and ended up winning the election (Smith & Whereatt, 1998). A similar situation occurred in the South Carolina primary debate between Senator John McCain and Governor George W. Bush in February 2000. The supporters of Green Party candidate Ralph Nader argued strongly during the 2000 and 2004 presidential campaigns that their candidate should be included in the presidential debates. Nonetheless, the CPD stuck to its position and limited participation to the nominees of the Republican and Democratic parties.

Televised political debates have historically been of significant interest to voters. In 1960, 55 percent of the electorate watched or listened to at least part of all four debates between Richard Nixon and John F. Kennedy. Approximately 80 percent of the electorate saw or heard at least part of one of the four debates (Kraus, 1988). In 1976, 89 percent of American households tuned in to at least one debate between Gerald Ford and Jimmy Carter. In 1980, 83 percent of Americans viewed at least one debate between Carter and Ronald Reagan. The number of viewers of the presidential debates began to decline in 1984. Approximately 66 percent of Americans watched the first debate between Walter Mondale and Ronald Reagan, and only 57 percent tuned in for the second debate (Kraus, 1988). Although the downward trend continued in 1988 and 1992, the presidential debates continued to be by far the most viewed campaign events in the election seasons (Carlin & McKinney, 1994).

The campaign debates between President Clinton and Senator Bob Dole for the 1996 election attracted a smaller viewing audience than any of the previous presidential debates had drawn. The Nielsen ratings suggested that about 43 percent of the nation's television sets were tuned in to the first of the 1996 presidential debates. This represented a significant drop from the 1992 debates, but nonetheless, the debates attracted many more viewers than did any other moment in the 1996 campaign (TV viewers, 1996).

Although the audience size increased in 2000 compared to 1996, there was significantly less interest than in earlier years. Approximately 25 million fewer Americans watched the 2000 presidential debates than watched the 1992 debates. Sixty percent of American households watched in 1980, while only 30 percent watched in 2000, even though it was the closest election in the twentieth century (Kelley, 2004). The 2004 debates, which occurred in the midst of one of the most polarizing election campaigns in history, saw a modest increase in public interest, as 33 percent of Americans tuned in to see incumbent president George W. Bush debate Senator John Kerry (Wattenberg, 2005).

Media pundits and candidates themselves often see debates as the defining moments in the campaign. As communication scholars Kathleen Hall Jamieson and David Birdsell (1988, p. 37) argued, "In politics, debating reveals problem-solving abilities, habits of mind, and electoral appeal. . . . Besides revealing the power of a set of ideas, the information gained from the debates allowed voters to judge the worth of those who would one day seek elective office. Public access to debate extended the sense of citizen engagement in the affairs of the democracy." Another benefit of campaign debates is that they are a constant reminder, both to the participants and to the observers, that no matter how heated and bitter the campaigns become, the debates are "lawful" contests governed by rules. Jamieson and Birdsell (pp. 39–40) also noted, "This lawfulness makes each debate a demonstration of controlled disagreement, at once exciting because it generates passion, and reassuring because it buttresses social and political conventions. By showcasing differences in a context that highlighted the orderly resolution of disputes, debates helped to conserve the political system and educate the electorate."

ARE TELEVISED DEBATES "REAL" DEBATES?

Perhaps the most common complaint about televised presidential debates is that they bear little resemblance to formal academic debates. Critics claim that the presidential debates lack clash, are characterized by vague and diffuse arguments, and contain little evidence and analysis. They further contend that the press panelists who ask the questions often play an intrusive role that poorly serves the public's interest (see Auer, 1962; Carlin, Howard, Stanfield, & Reynolds, 1991; Dauber, 1989; Hogan, 1989b; McCall, 1984; McClain, 1989; Weiler, 1989). Some critics have lamented that the presidential debates better resemble "joint press conferences" than substantive debates on complex policy issues (Kraus, 1988; Pfau, 1983).

As a result of these complaints, much discussion has centered on the format of the debates. The formats have varied from contest to contest but have typically been worked out by the candidates (or their advisors) themselves, often in consultation with media leaders, the sponsoring organizations (e.g., the League of Women Voters), and since 1987, the nonpartisan Commission on Presidential Debates. Much experimentation in formats has occurred. For example, the 1992 debates followed four different formats, including a town hall format in which undecided voters could pose questions to the candidates. This format proved popular with viewers and has been used several times since.

A new twist on the town hall format occurred during the 2008 primary campaign. A virtual town hall was created when viewers at home were able to ask questions of the candidates by uploading them on video clips to the Web site YouTube. Michael Bassik, who specializes in online political advertising, noted that YouTube offered an "exponentially greater opportunity to reach a young, active, passionate audience, one that is far bigger than the combined audiences of the nightly newscasts and the five debates that have been shown on television so far this season. For those five debates, the majority of viewers were older than 55" (cited by Seelye, 2007). The content of the debate was certainly unique. The candidates were asked about their views on global warming by a melting snowman, a lesbian couple asked if the candidates would allow them to be married to each other, a man caring for someone with Alzheimer's disease asked a healthcare question while sitting next to that person, and someone asked the candidates how they talked to their own children about sex. The broadcast was described as "revolutionary," and it did succeed in drawing a larger audience of younger viewers (Garofoli, 2007).

Most presidential debates now, however, use a single moderator rather than a panel of questioners (for a discussion, see Carlin & McKinney, 1994). Although no format that has been tried has been deemed perfect by participants, reporters, or the public, Carlin and McKinney (1994) have asserted that participants in their focus group studies of the 1992 debates preferred the use of a variety of formats and liked the single moderator better than a panel. The selection of the moderator for the debates has often been fiercely contested by the candidates and their campaign advisors. In 2000, Jim Lehrer, a news anchor for PBS, moderated all three presidential contests. In 2004, Lehrer moderated the first debate, Charles Gibson of ABC the second, and Bob Schieffer of CBS the third. Benoit, Hansen, and Hansen (2001) argued that the questions asked by professional journalists often failed to match up especially well with the topics that seemed of most interest to potential voters. Other critics of current debate practices have observed that candidates seem to spend more energy debating the journalists asking the questions than they do their opponent (Lamoureux, Entrekin, & McKinney, 1994). As McKinney (2005, p. 214) reported, "Journalist's questions were also found to be more argumentative, accusatory, and leading than those from undecided citizens." Academic debate coaches have argued that the best format would be one in which the candidates directly questioned, confronted, and refuted each other without the benefit of a moderator (for example, see Frana, 1989). This format, which was used during the Lincoln-Douglas debates, has not been used for televised presidential debates, however, perhaps because the candidates are not confident of their debating abilities. The participation of a moderator and a panel of questioners reduces the likelihood that one candidate could begin to dominate the conversation by drilling more and more deeply into a topic area that most benefited his or her campaign.

Many critics have also complained that candidates in these debates are given little opportunity to develop sustained and well-reasoned arguments because their speaking times are so short and there are so few opportunities to ask or answer follow-up questions (for example, see Carlin, 1989; McKinney, 2005). Hinck (1988) argued, however, that it would be a mistake to make televised political debates more like formal academic debates. He regarded televised political debates as "rhetorical events" that call for deliberation about candidates' potential leadership abilities, and he argued (p. 4), "The purpose of a presidential campaign is to select a leader to govern the nation, not to generate argumentation worthy of a philosopher's assent."

Still other studies have suggested that substantial argumentative clash does occur in these presidential debates and that participants use both evidence and analysis to support their arguments. Ellsworth (1965), for example, studied the Nixon-Kennedy debates of 1960 and concluded that both candidates used more evidence and analysis in developing their arguments in those debates than they did in other campaign situations. Riley, Hollihan, and Cooley (1980) used the primary elements of Ellsworth's category system to examine the Carter-Ford contests of 1976 and found that Ford used substantially more evidence and analysis to support his arguments than did Carter but that Carter was a much more aggressive debater who sought to put the incumbent President Ford on the defensive by relying primarily on declarative critical statements about Ford's achievements in office. Riley and Hollihan (1981) undertook a similar content analysis of the Carter-Reagan debate of 1980. They found that Carter was much less critical of his opponent in 1980 than he had been four years earlier because he was the incumbent who was forced to defend his own record. This study also demonstrated that Carter used significantly more evidence and analysis in 1980 than he had in 1976 and that his choice of topics differed as well. In 1976 Carter had focused primarily on the economy, criticizing President Ford for the poor rate of economic growth and the high level of inflation and unemployment during his tenure in office. In 1980, however, when the poor economy was more likely to be blamed on the policies of Carter's own administration, he preferred to talk about energy supplies and the impact of the Arab oil embargo on the growth of the American economy.

In a follow-up study, Hollihan and Riley (1981) sought to determine whether subjects who viewed a videotape of the Carter-Reagan debate could identify when a candidate used evidence or analysis to support his position and whether the use of either evidence or analysis actually enhanced the appeal of the better-supported argument. The study found that viewers could correctly identify evidentiary and analytical statements but that they were just as likely to find a declarative statement—an argument offered without evidentiary or analytical support—compelling, if that statement conformed to their previously held opinions. This finding suggests that those who view televised debates are seeking to confirm their own political opinions and trying to establish that the political stories or narratives they believe to be true can be interpreted as both coherent and sensible, a view substantiated by Conrad (1993).

THE EFFECTS OF DEBATES ON VOTER KNOWLEDGE AND VOTING BEHAVIOR

Even though televised debates are important symbolic moments in the campaign, social scientists who have systematically studied these contests have sometimes disagreed about the extent to which they actually determine the outcome of elections. Most research conducted around the 1960, 1976, and 1980 debates, for example, suggested that the major effect of those debates was to reinforce existing party and candidate loyalties and to provide voters with greater information about the issue positions held by the candidates (Pfau & Kang, 1991; Zhu, Milavsky, & Biswas, 1994). Evidence also supports the notion that the information contained in political debates is more likely to be recalled and that the more debates someone watched, the greater the accumulated political knowledge (Benoit, Webber, & Berman, 1998; Jamieson & Adasiewicz, 2000). The debates are also useful in helping voters develop "perceptions of candidates' competence and persona" (Pfau & Eveland, 1994, p. 161).

Evidence shows that the debates also have an agenda-setting effect. As Benoit, McKinney, and Holbert (2001) reported:

> Watching a presidential debate can influence the perceived importance of decision factors (policy, leadership) as well as the importance of specific issues. Watching a debate can alter impressions of which candidate is most desirable on the issues and how the candidates rate on character traits. Furthermore, watching a debate can increase voters' confidence in their vote choice. (p. 270)

In another study Benoit, Webber, and Berman (1998) found that respondents who watched the first 1996 presidential debate were able more accurately to link candidates with their issue positions, to offer assessments about candidate character, and perhaps most significantly, more likely to offer policy reasons than character reasons to explain their voting decisions than were respondents who did not see the debate.

Clearly, voters seem to find televised debates useful in discriminating between candidates. The debates, perhaps not surprisingly, may be far more useful in offering important new information about challengers than they are about incumbents who are already well known to viewers (Benoit & Hansen, 2004). Zhu, Milavsky, and Biswas (1994) reported that the 1992 debates proved especially useful to voters who were seeking information about the least known of the candidates, Ross Perot, and that viewers seemed to learn less new information about the better-known candidates, Bush and Clinton. Overall, however, Zhu and colleagues asserted that the 1992 debates made positive contributions to rational decision making by helping the audience learn about the substantive issue stances that separated the three candidates.

Sears and Chaffee (1978), in their study of the 1976 presidential debates between Ford and Carter, reported that the debates did not set any new issue agenda for the campaign but that they did summarize the main issues in the election in a way that helped voters gain a clearer picture of the differences between the candidates. Miller and MacKuen (1978) agreed that the 1976 debates made a distinctive and measurable contribution toward increasing the electorate's information level, but they also agreed that the effects of the debates were distorted by viewers' predispositions about the candidates. Dennis, Chaffee, and Choe (1978, p. 328) argued that candidate debates may function as a "catalyst." Although debates may not directly affect how voters will cast their ballots, they may add information to the environment in which the bonding of other elements—especially partisan predispositions and perceptions of the candidates' personalities—takes place.

The degree to which viewers' partisan beliefs influence their perception of the candidates' performance in the debate goes beyond the way in which the candidates lay out their issue positions. Shields and MacDowell (1987) reported that partisanship was the most important factor influencing how viewers judged the appropriateness of the candidates' emotional responses. In their study of the 1984 debates, Shields and MacDowell (p. 85) marveled at the following: Right-leaning observers commented on then Vice President Bush's firm and decisive emotional stance and used terms such as *relaxed, firm, enthusiastic*, and *comfortable* to describe him; left-leaning observers, without exception, interpreted Bush's emotionality unfavorably with terms such as *whiny, defensive, giggly*, and *shrill*.

Researchers have suggested that the debates are useful sources of information about the candidates' character and personality because they allow viewers to observe how the candidates respond under pressure and how they might shape our society and culture if elected (Leon, 1993; McKinnon, Tedesco, & Kaid, 1993). According to Pfau and Kang (1991), what viewers most sought from the debates was information about the candidates' similarity to themselves as well as their credibility, competence, sociability, and character. Similar results were reported by Winkler and Black (1993), who noted that in their study the most frequently mentioned reasons for determining winners and losers in the October 11, 1992, Bush-Clinton debates were the candidates' confidence/presence, specificity of response to posed questions, honesty/trustworthiness, use of an attack strategy, and connection to issues that viewers deemed important. Winkler and Black also noted that the underlying reasons people cited were consistent and did not seem to be significantly related to the respondents' age, gender, education, or party affiliation.

A relatively unknown or underdog candidate's performance in a televised debate can often help him or her appear to be a credible alternative. Rowland (1986) argued that Ronald Reagan's performance in the 1980 debate against President Carter made the Republican challenger seem an acceptable alternative to the incumbent and helped rebut public perceptions of Reagan as unintelligent and unsuited for national office. The opposite can also occur, of course. In the 1992 vice presidential debate, Ross Perot's nominee for vice president, retired admiral James Stockdale, performed so badly that he appeared woefully unsuited for national office and may have damaged public perceptions of Perot and the Reform Party (see Carlin & McKinney, 1994, p. 191).

The debates do seem to stimulate voter interest in the election, attention to the campaign, and awareness of the candidates' positions on the issues (Kraus, 1988). Televised debates are also useful to voters because they provide a fairly rich source of information about the candidates and their favorite issues while requiring a minimal expenditure of time and effort on the part of the voters (Miller & MacKuen, 1978). Miller and MacKuen's research (p. 277) also suggested that the more the 1976 debates were watched, the more information viewers gained about the candidates, even when political cognition, education, partisanship, and political attentiveness were all controlled for in the regression analysis. Furthermore, the debates had the greatest impact on those viewers who were least politically attentive. As a result, the debates become very useful tools for voters who may lack a deep and sustaining interest in politics but nonetheless want to make comparative evaluations of the competing candidates. Reid, Stohl, and Stauffer (2006) found that exposure to televised political debates not only increased political knowledge, but it also seemed to contribute to higher levels of political participation among younger voters. This finding is significant because 18- to 24-year-olds tend to be the least politically engaged of all American citizens. This is not to suggest that politically apathetic voters actively seek out the debates as a source of information, however, for those who are interested in politics and who hold highly partisan views are more likely to tune in to the debates than are those who lack interest. It does suggest, however, that relative to other sources of political information, debates capture the attention of many apathetic citizens and thus expose them to political discussions that make a substantial contribution to their political information (Miller & MacKuen, 1978).

Although campaign debates may not be ideal exercises in rational decision making, compared to thirty-second spot advertisements and glimpses of candidates getting on and off airplanes, they are truly information rich. As Carlin (1989, p. 211) argued, "Candidates do present policy positions, compare their philosophies and positions to those of their opponent, take issue with an opponent's statements, present evidence and analysis." Furthermore, Carlin and McKinney (1994, p. 3) observed, "Of all the campaign information sources available for voter education, only debates provide voters with an opportunity to view the candidates side by side for an extended period of time. Debates are the closest thing to a job interview that candidates and the voters will ever experience."

Despite the fact that research consistently demonstrates the importance of televised presidential debates in increasing voter knowledge and interest in the campaign, the data are mixed in terms of explaining how a candidate's debate performance will affect voter choices. One difficulty in measuring debate effects and sorting them out from other political effects is that those who view debates may themselves be different from those who do not. Kenski and Stroud (2005) reported, for example, that debate audiences were more likely to hold partisan views, had higher levels of political interest, and were more likely to discuss politics with their friends and family members than those who did not watch the debates. Because these debate viewers are also more likely to attend to political news and information, it may be difficult to assess very precisely the effects of exposure to the debates.

Lanoue (1991) reported that these debates are seldom cited as the key factor influencing voters' decisions. This is consistent with the findings by Miller and MacKuen (1978) and Sears and Chaffee (1978) that a candidate's debate performance may have only minimal long-term effects on the evaluations of the candidate or on voter preferences. It is worth noting, for example, that in the 2004 campaign, viewer interest in the debates increased somewhat from recent years and that Senator John Kerry was seen as the winner in all three of the presidential debates over incumbent president George W. Bush. Yet, Kerry lost the election. Kerry's success in the debates, however, did help keep his hope alive and dramatically affected the momentum of his campaign (Newport,

2004). These results should remind us that these debates, important as they may be, are only brief moments in a long campaign process. As McKinney and Carlin (2004, p. 214) argued, "As debates are but one component in a very large complex campaign message environment, a full understanding of their influence will not be found by continuing our usual direct-effect investigations of the isolated debate exchange; rather analysis should examine how debates interact with many other campaign events and messages."

Substantial anecdotal evidence testifies to the role that debates can play in influencing the outcome of a campaign. For example, in 1996, when voters were asked where they "learned a lot" about the presidential candidates, they cited the presidential debates as the most useful source of information. Fully 45 percent of respondents claimed the debates were the most important source of information, 32 percent cited newspaper stories, 30 percent television stories, 23 percent newspaper editorials, 21 percent news magazines, 18 percent television analysis following a debate or speech, and only 5 percent political ads (Where voters get information, 1996, p. 1).

THE "SPIN"

One of the most frequent sources of complaints about televised debates is the "spinning" that goes on immediately before and after them. Before a debate begins, the "spinners" play the expectations game. They inevitably sing the praises of their opponent's debating skills while simultaneously minimizing their own candidate's abilities and downplaying the importance of the debate. Prior to the 1996 presidential debates, for example, the Dole camp sought to dampen the expectations for their candidate's performance by emphasizing how adept President Clinton was on his feet. Meanwhile, the Clinton camp told reporters that Dole had garnered years of experience in debating during his time in the Senate and that consequently they had great respect for his skills (Berke, Dole camp, 1996). Both campaigns tried to lower the expectations for their candidate and to raise the expectations for their opponent in the hope that doing so would help their candidate seem more effective when reporters and the public made their assessments following the debate.

Similarly, in 2004 the Kerry campaign emphasized President Bush's extensive experience in nationally televised debates because he had participated in debates against Vice President Gore. For example, Joe Lockhart, a senior advisor to Kerry, said Bush had won every debate in which he had participated. "Debates, in the modern political system, are not won by the person who knows the most information; they're won by the person who is most persuasive for their position," Lockhart said. "And George Bush has proven time and time again that he is a very persuasive debater. It does, of course, seem at times like he doesn't have all the facts straight, but he seems to do it in a way that gives you a sense of commitment and a sense of what direction he wants to go." Meanwhile, Dan Bartlett, White House communications director, emphasized that Kerry was a skilled debater, pointing to the seven "epic debates" he had in 1996 with then governor Bill Weld in the U.S. Senate race in Massachusetts. The Democrat, according to Bartlett, was an all-star debater in college and had honed his skills during twenty years in the Senate (cited in Campaigns spin debate advantage, 2004).

The most intense spinning takes place after the debate. The campaigns routinely place a dozen or more spokespersons in the auditorium so they can be interviewed by reporters immediately after the debate. The goal, of course, is to influence how the reporters write their stories summarizing the debate so that they favor the candidate in question. Consequently, campaign spokespersons never admit that their candidate was anything less than brilliant and insightful or that the opposing candidate succeeded in accomplishing anything. It is almost comical to watch desperate campaign aides scramble around the auditorium following a debate seeking reporters to interview them.

The media also construct a spin on the debate. Not content to allow the public to make its own judgment regarding the key moments, media pundits often interview one another, seeking to offer explanations and accounts of who won the debate, who profited most by the debate, and who committed a major blunder or gaffe. This type of media coverage of debates has produced significant criticism; for example, Hogan (1989b, p. 224) complained, "The media's trivialization of presidential debates reaches full flower, of course, in the 'instant analysis' which follows each debate. Mixing their sports metaphors with reckless abandon, the media 'experts' speak of 'knockout blows,' 'hitting it out of the park' and 'prevent defenses' concerned only with 'who won' and 'the big gaffe.'"

Research studies have suggested that postdebate press commentary can have a profound effect on public perceptions of who won a debate, particularly when the media emphasize how one candidate made a major gaffe. In the 1976 debate between Carter and Ford, for example, Ford argued that Poland was "free from Communist domination." The remark dominated subsequent press discussion of the debate.

Patterson (1980) pointed out that a preponderance of voters questioned within twelve hours of the debate thought that Ford had won the contest, but those who were interviewed twelve to forty-eight hours later, after press coverage of the Ford gaffe gained wide exposure and shaped interpersonal discussions, thought that Carter had won the debate. Patterson (p. 123) declared, "The passing of time required for the news to reach the public brought with it a virtual reversal of opinion." This is consistent with Elliott and Sothirajah's (1993) conclusion that postdebate analysis influenced viewers in the direction of postdebate commentary.

Bennett (1981, p. 310) explained the interest in candidates' gaffes by noting, "The attention of press and public seems to shift from the monotony of the campaign to any activity that represents a departure from the routine. The most newsworthy (and, perhaps the most noteworthy) departures from electoral routine are those occasions when candidates blunder, lose control, or otherwise create embarrassing flaws in their carefully staged performances." Many people no doubt recall the tumble that Bob Dole took from a platform in Chico, California, as the defining moment in his failed 1996 campaign; certainly the television networks replayed the film often enough to imprint it on the public's memory (LaGanga & Broder, 1996). Dole, mindful of the power of the televised image of his fall, got quickly to his feet and made a joke about it. Vice President Dan Quayle, however, was never able to overcome his image as an intellectual lightweight because of his failure to spell the word *potato* correctly. Images can stick, particularly if they confirm already held public impressions of a candidate (LaGanga & Broder, 1996). Howard Dean's campaign for the Democratic presidential nomination in 2004 was undone when he was caught and soundly ridiculed for his "scream" of encouragement to supporters following his loss in the Iowa caucuses (Chadwick, 2006). The first serious debate gaffe of the 2008 presidential campaign arguably occurred in the first contest between Republican contenders held in May 2007 at the Ronald Reagan Library in Simi Valley, California. Former Wisconsin governor and former secretary of health and human services Tommy Thompson, in response to a question, said a private employer morally opposed to homosexuality should have the right to fire a gay employee. Minutes later in the Spin Room, Thompson's spokespeople were actively seeking out reporters to reverse his position, saying he misspoke because he had misheard the question (Bock, 2007).

Madsen (1991) argued that it is a mistake to view the televised debates and the spinning both by the campaigns and by the media as distinct events that should be separated from each other. He argued that the debate itself is but one "fragment" of discourse, the postdebate spin is another related fragment, and the media response is a third. Madsen claimed that the public must weave these fragments together to form the overall text of a campaign and that no one fragment should be privileged over any other. Instead, he argued, the partisan commentary is tied to other campaign texts. Combining these fragments permits the public to engage in a type of meta-debate about their pre- and postdebate expectations and the fulfillment of those expectations by the candidates.

Although viewers now seem quite aware that they are being "spun" in the moments just before and just after a presidential candidate debate—Fox News even went so far as to refer to one of its political discussion shows as the *No Spin Zone*, a title that seemed to drive liberal candidates and media voices crazy—some research suggests that social context and social influence can have a significant effect on audience reactions. In short, when audiences see that others seem to have been persuaded by a candidate or, conversely, have found a candidate's arguments to be unpersuasive, that observation tends to have a significant impact on their own thinking. The researchers claim that presidential debates are sufficiently ambiguous contests that they are "fertile ground for informational social influence" (Fein, Goethals, & Kugler, 2007, p. 165).

THE "APPEARANCE OF RATIONALITY"

Even though televised campaign debates may be far from ideal, they attract more viewers than any other form of campaign discourse, and they seem to offer important and useful information. They also preserve an appearance of deliberative rationality in the American electoral process. When the candidates engage in face-to-face discussion, they provoke a media conversation about those issues. The media's focus on the debates helps spark a broader public conversation about the issues in the campaign. Because the debates attract large numbers of viewers from across the political and ideological spectrum, they get large numbers of Americans talking about the same issues and concerns.

Carlin (2005) conducted a series of studies in which she organized groups of citizens to watch presidential debates together and then questioned them about their experiences:

Participants indicated that debates are the single most valuable voter education tool that they have as citizens. For those who have not had time to follow the campaign closely, debates serve as a means of summarizing the major issues and positions that evolved throughout the campaign. Regardless of level of knowledge prior to the debates, participants believed that the debates provided one of the few opportunities to limit media influence in the telling of the campaign story and the only opportunity to view the candidates side-by-side. Participants indicated that they could learn about the way the candidates would perform as president based on how the pressures of the debates were handled. (p. 228)

The experience of bringing people together to watch the debates and to share some significant common political moments is itself useful to the promotion of democracy. Shared political experiences help spark shared conversations, and the real work of participatory democracy is conducted through the conversations that shape our personal identity and help us relate to one another. Thus, the debates, by helping preserve a lively public sphere, nurture and sustain our democratic system. We should therefore seek opportunities to engage people in talking about issues of common concern, and one important way to achieve this is to create common "texts" of political arguments that most if not all Americans are exposed to and can discuss with relatives, friends, and coworkers. Independent of outcomes, the act of participating in public life should be rewarding and satisfying, and political conversations should interest and engage us as citizens. As Ackoff (1994, p. 78) asserted, "Participation, which is a form of self-determination, is itself a major source of satisfaction and therefore of improved quality of life."

Observing televised debates and then talking about the issues that emerge in those debates informs voters about the issues, mobilizes them toward political action, and helps citizens develop the skills necessary for self-governance. As Greenberg (1986) observed:

The emergence of democratic and fully developed human beings is possible only in a fully democratic participative society. . . . Participation is the principal social process by which human beings, practicing the arts of self-direction, cooperation, and responsibility, liberate their capacities and thereby become whole, healthy, and integrated persons. As a consequence of participation, the individual develops the attitudes and skills essential to the participation in other social spheres including the political. (p. 19)

Participatory democracies require these conversations. We need to seek and nurture more opportunities for large segments of the American public to converse about the issues and problems that both link us together and divide us from each other. As Tarde (1898) observed, political conversation can be a brake on the power of government and can help preserve the "unassailable fortress of liberty."

CHAPTER 10

Financing Campaigns:
The Relationship between Money and Politics

The Republican Party lost control of both the House of Representatives and the Senate in the 2006 midterm elections. The most significant issue that dominated public discussion and that led to this outcome was the lack of progress—or some might even say the worsening situation—U.S. forces faced in Iraq. The second most important issue, however, was probably the myriad of ethical and corruption charges leveled at members of Congress. The most flagrant case involved Representative Randy "Duke" Cunningham (R—California), who was forced to resign his seat, convicted, and eventually sent to federal prison on corruption charges. Cunningham pled guilty to taking $2.4 million in bribes. Prosecutors claimed that Cunningham "demanded, sought, and received" illicit payments in the form of cash, home payments, free use of a yacht, a Rolls-Royce, and rooms full of French antique furniture from four coconspirators, including two defense contractors who were seeking favors in government contracts (Babcock & Weisman, 2005). As part of his plea agreement, Cunningham agreed to "wear a wire" in an attempt to help the FBI gather information about other corrupt political insiders (Burger, 2006).

The Cunningham investigation and conviction was only the first of many news stories during this election cycle about the corrupting influence of money on congressional politics. Representative Robert W. Ney (R—Ohio) chose not to seek reelection to a seventh term after he was linked to lobbyist Jack Abramoff, who had been convicted of fraud, tax evasion, and conspiracy to bribe public officials. Court documents claimed that Ney helped Abramoff's clients win government contracts, supported legislation helpful to Native American tribal gaming, and helped prevent the passage of minimum-wage legislation for a garment maker in the Northern Mariana Islands. In exchange, Ney received campaign contributions, expensive vacations, sports tickets, restaurant meals, and concert tickets (Weisman, 2006).

Perhaps the most damaging of the ethics investigations to the Republican Party, however, was the indictment by a Texas grand jury of House Majority Leader Tom DeLay (R—Texas) on a charge of criminally conspiring with two political allies to funnel illegal corporate campaign contributions into the 2002 Texas state elections that helped the GOP redraw the map of Texas congressional districts. The redistricting enabled the Republicans to gain seats and thus cement their control in the 2004 congressional elections. The indictment forced DeLay to step down from his leadership post and ultimately to surrender his seat. It also effectively silenced one of the Republicans' most vocal, effective, and highly partisan leaders (Smith, 2005). DeLay was nicknamed "the Hammer" because he was so successful in the practice of hardball politics. DeLay understood how to enforce discipline on the Republican members of the House so that his party could advance its legislative agenda. His indictment became a hot-button issue for the Democrats. The House Democratic leader, and later Speaker of the House, Representative Nancy Pelosi of California, said, "The criminal indictment of Majority Leader Tom DeLay is the latest example that Republicans in Congress are plagued by a culture of corruption at the expense of the American people" (cited in Smith, 2005, p. A01).

The Republicans were not the only party to face serious ethical challenges in the 2006 elections. The Democrats faced a congressional corruption scandal of their own. Representative William Jefferson (D—Louisiana) was the subject of a fourteen-month bribery investigation. Court documents suggested that Jefferson was caught on videotape accepting $100,000 in $100 bills from a Virginia investor who was wearing a wire. A few days later, the FBI searched Jefferson's home and found $90,000 of the cash (identified by serial numbers) wrapped in aluminum foil and stuffed into frozen food containers in the freezer (Lengel & Barakat, 2006). Jefferson not only refused to resign his seat in Congress, but he ran and was elected to a ninth term, besting his rival by a margin of 20 percentage points. Jefferson's reelection certainly diminished the credibility of Speaker Pelosi's claim that the Democrats would return integrity to the Congress (Kuhnhenn, 2006). Jefferson was eventually indicted on sixteen counts of bribery when a grand jury found that he had used his office to solicit almost a half million dollars in cash and approximately 34,000 shares of stock. If convicted and sentenced to the maximum penalty on all counts, he could serve 235 years in prison (Walsh & Alpert, 2007).

These examples do not by any means constitute "politics as usual." The cases described here are extreme as reflected by the legal sanctions threatened or imposed. Although the number of political officeholders who are actually enriching themselves by diverting campaign funds for personal use is probably small, public skepticism about political leaders and the corrupting influence of money in politics is an understandable result. As Sabato (1989, p. 4) declared, "The appearance of corruption can be as damaging to the political system as the reality because it may have the same tainting effect on the body politic by increasing public cynicism and alienation."

The late Jesse Unruh, a leading California politician, once declared that "money is the mother's milk of politics" (cited in Paletz, 1999, p. 197). Applying Unruh's metaphor, it is clear that the mother's milk flows more freely today than ever before, and there is no end in sight. Every national election is more expensive than the one that came before, with the 2008 presidential campaign expected to be the first $1 billion election in U.S. history. To be considered a serious contender, a candidate must raise at least $100 million (Edsall & Cillizza, 2006).

On April 1, 2007, almost a year before the first primary in the 2008 election, candidates' campaign chests were already overflowing. In their required filings reported to the Federal Election Commission (FEC) the candidates shattered all previous records for money donated and spent in support of a presidential campaign. Senator Hillary Clinton (D—New York) raised $26 million in the first quarter of 2007, three times more money than any presidential contender had ever received by this point in a presidential election. Clinton's money came primarily from organized labor interests, the entertainment community, and the network of supporters developed by her husband, former president Bill Clinton. On the same day, former senator John Edwards (D—North Carolina) reported that he had raised $14 million, much of it coming from fellow trial lawyers. Also on the same day, advisors to Governor Bill Richardson (D—New Mexico) said they expected to report $6 million; Senator Christopher Dodd (D—Connecticut) reported raising $4 million; and Senator Joseph Biden Jr. (D—Delaware) reported about $3 million (Kornblutt, 2007). A couple of days later, Senator Barack Obama (D—Illinois) reported that he had raised $25 million. Altogether in this reporting period the Democratic candidates, including minor candidates, reported a total of $78 million in contributions to wage their campaigns for the 2008 presidential nomination (Nagourney, 2007).

The second quarter reports filed by the Democratic candidates on July 1, 2007, again shattered all previous records. Obama raised $32.5 million, which was more money than all Democratic candidates combined raised for the same period four years previously. What was even more impressive was that Obama's campaign claimed to have received contributions from 154,000 individual donors, a signal of a grass roots effort that is almost unparalleled in contemporary political campaigns. Clinton reported that she raised $27 million, a total that would have set a record in any previous campaign but for Obama's success. Edwards reported that he raised $9 million, Richardson raised $7.2 million, and Dodd raised $3.25 million (Morain, Raising, 2007).

Although the Democrats were winning the early race for cash—a race that some have called "the money primary" because candidates must prove their ability to raise funds to even be considered "legitimate" contenders for office—the Republican candidates were also raking in substantial donations. In the first quarter, Republican contenders reported a total of $51 million in contributions (Nagourney, 2007). Indeed, the money given to Republican contenders would have been sufficient to beat the achievements of prior candidates and would have dominated the news coverage had the Democrats not been so highly energized and motivated by their intense dislike of the Bush administration and their fervent desire to end the war in Iraq. Even leading Republican spokespersons acknowledged that the Democrats were achieving early fund-raising successes because their most partisan followers were more "hungry" and eager to achieve power than were Republicans (Nagourney, 2007).

Among the Republican contenders, the leading fund-raiser in the first quarter was former Massachusetts governor Mitt Romney, who raised $20 million, primarily from Wall Street interests and his fellow members of the Mormon Church. Former New York City mayor Rudy Giuliani reported raising $15 million, primarily from Wall Street, and Senator John McCain (R—Arizona) came in third with $12.5 million in contributions from a wide range of donors from across the nation (Kirkpatrick, 2007). In a clear demonstration of the power of media framing to set expectations, McCain's total was depicted as a colossal disaster for his campaign hopes. Because many considered the senator to be a front-runner for his party's nomination, he was expected also to be a front-runner in the "money primary." Instead, by coming in third, he sparked speculation that he was being punished by party stalwarts for his strong support for the recently passed campaign finance reform law known as the McCain-Feingold bill, which McCain had jointly

sponsored with Senator Russell Feingold (D—Wisconsin). (This legislation will be discussed in greater detail in the next section of the chapter.) McCain's poor fund-raising performance prompted him to refocus
his efforts and seek more contributions from big donors with deep
pockets. The challenge here, of course, is that this move seemed to
contradict his long-held and highly visible opposition to the unhealthy
influence of these types of contributors on the political and legislative
process. The result was a shift to a campaign strategy that seemed fundamentally to undermine his reputation as a fierce independent that
had made him such a popular figure among nonpartisan voters in the
2000 presidential campaign (Shear & Kane, 2007). Even in the 2000
campaign, however, McCain faced a significant challenge in trying to
advocate campaign finance reform while still raising sufficient funds
to gain election. In short, McCain has long been forced to try to take
advantage of the very system that he railed against. As Charles Lewis
of the Center for Public Integrity declared, "The portrait McCain likes
is the one of the plain-talking crusader who's bucking the system. The
one many others see is that of a politician who rarely breaks ranks with
the special interests that finance his campaign" (cited in Pooley, 2000,
p. 42).

The second-quarter 2007 fund-raising reports revealed that the Republican presidential candidates had slipped further behind the Democrats. The top Republican in the money race was Rudy Giuliani, who
raised $17 million. In second place was Romney, who reported a take
of $14 million, but this figure was deceptive because it included $6.5
million from his own personal funds that he gave to his campaign.
Trailing still further was McCain, who raised only $11.2 million in this
quarter and as a result was forced to rethink his campaign strategy once
again and lay off more than half of his paid staff. Altogether the top
three Republican candidates raised $92 million in the first half of 2007
compared to the $133 million raised by the top three Democrats
(Morain, Romney loans, 2007).

Today's politicians, whether Democrats or Republicans, are essentially caught in a vise. They need massive amounts of money to gain election and reelection. To get this money, they must petition those who
have it. Those who have it and are willing to donate it typically have
an interest in pursuing certain policy positions. They are understandably
reluctant to donate to politicians who will not support their interests
once in office. This in turn makes most politicians highly responsive to
the interests of their most significant donors.

Critics of our political campaign system have long argued that it is imperative that we try to wean our politicians from their dependence on the "mother's milk" of political contributions. Almost a decade ago, for example, Drew (1999) declared:

> The culture of money dominates Washington as never before; money now rivals or even exceeds power as the preeminent goal. It affects the issues raised and their outcome; it has changed employment patterns in Washington; it has transformed politics; and it has subverted values. It has led good people to do things that are morally questionable, if not reprehensible. It has cut a deep gash, if not inflicted a mortal wound, in the concept of public service. (p. 2)

The argument that Drew offered then seems even more convincing today. The debate over political campaign financing reforms has been going on for decades. A brief historical summary will help provide some context for the situation that currently exists.

CAMPAIGN CONTRIBUTION CONTROVERSIES IN RECENT CAMPAIGNS

In today's campaign environment, political candidates, and even an incumbent president, may become almost entirely consumed by the pursuit of campaign contributions. Arguably the most significant and memorable modern controversy regarding the flow of money into the hands of politicians was the Watergate scandal, which brought down a president. In 1972, the media reported that President Richard Nixon had received large cash contributions to support his bid for reelection. Follow-up stories revealed that some of these funds (including a check from Dwayne O. Andreas, an agricultural industrialist) found their way into the hands of the Watergate burglars who were arrested attempting to plant illegal listening devices in the Democratic Party headquarters. The news accounts of rampant political corruption and of a White House awash in secret campaign donations and thus able to finance such sordid and illegal activities eventually provoked so much public outcry that Congress enacted legislation establishing strict legal reporting requirements detailing the source of all contributions to federal campaigns (Smith, 2006). The reporting requirements, helpful as they were to the political process, did not solve all the problems of money in politics. Although there have been too many such controversies since

Watergate to detail them all, a few examples from recent elections testify to the persistence of the problem.

During the 1996 presidential race, reporters discovered that wealthy donors had unique access to the Clinton White House. Hundreds of contributors to the Clinton campaign (or the Democratic National Committee) were invited to spend the night in the Lincoln bedroom of the White House (Krauthammer, 1997). A night in the Lincoln bedroom was not the only perk that the Clinton campaign and the Democratic National Committee offered to potential donors. Indeed, there was a virtual menu of alternatives. A gift of $12,500 would get a donor dinner and a photograph taken with the president at a fancy Washington hotel. A gift of $50,000 would buy coffee with Clinton and top administration officials at the White House. A generous $250,000 gift would purchase a full day at the White House. Guests could swim in the pool, play on the tennis court, bowl in the president's private bowling alley, enjoy a barbecue on the lawn, tour the Oval Office, and perhaps even catch a film in the presidential theater (Fineman & Isikoff, 1997).

Even at these extravagant prices, there was no shortage of well-heeled donors eager to get the blue ribbon treatment. The administration acknowledged that the White House hosted 103 fund-raising coffees in 1995 and 1996 and that 938 guests had accepted invitations to sleep in the White House since 1993 (Frammolino & Fritz, 1997, pp. 1, 12). Although about half the overnight guests were relatives, long-time friends, or public officials, the guest list still reads like a who's who of money and power. Clearly the Clinton campaign and the Democratic National Committee profited from the use of the Lincoln bedroom. No wonder the Clintons were so pleased when daughter Chelsea went off to Stanford University; her departure made another bedroom available! The White House overnights and coffee klatches at "Motel 1600" may have been tacky, but they were arguably not illegal. Although there is a legal prohibition against soliciting campaign donations on government property, White House press secretary Mike McCurry emphasized that donors were not solicited inside the White House; they were not asked for money until a later date (cited in Frammolino & Fritz, 1997, p. 12).

There are different accounts regarding who came up with the idea of raising campaign funds through White House sleepovers, but documents released by the administration revealed that President Bill Clinton, in his own handwriting, approved the plan. Although this was certainly not the first time that a U.S. president made time in his schedule to meet with large contributors, the systematic pursuit of large donors in

1996 and the willingness to use the prestige of the White House as an inducement to secure such contributions had never before been so blatant.

The cast of characters invited to meet with President Clinton in exchange for substantial donations posed a problem for the Democrats. The Clinton visitors included a Chinese arms company official, a convicted stock swindler, a multimillionaire who had been forced to pay a huge fine for illegally wiretapping his employees, and an Indonesian banking family eager to influence U.S. trade and investment policies toward its homeland (Bunting & Frammolino, Cash-for-coffee, 1997; Gibbs, 1997).

These stories not only headlined the evening news, but they also provided substantial new material for Jay Leno and David Letterman, as well as hundreds of lesser-known comedians. Although the shabby accounts of White House pajama parties for wealthy corporate donors may have been humorous, these investigations led to other inquiries into fund raising that was taking place in Asian American communities, including claims that foreign nationals were contributing to the Clinton-Gore reelection campaign in an attempt to gain access to the administration in the hope that they might influence U.S. policies. In the firestorm of political charges and countercharges that followed the news reports of the Democrats' "Asia Connections," there were many claims that the Democrats broke the law by accepting donations from nonresident foreign nationals. Allegations even surfaced that the government of the People's Republic of China intentionally and deliberately violated U.S. law by channeling campaign contributions to the Democrats in an attempt to influence U.S. foreign policy. The Chinese government vociferously denied this claim (Kempster, 1997).

The flap over contributions by nonqualified donors persisted throughout the latter months of the 1996 campaign, and in response, the Democratic Party announced the return of millions of dollars in donations. So many contributions ultimately had to be returned that the Democratic National Committee ran up a $10 to $12 million dollar debt (Bunting & Frammolino, Democratic Party, 1997). As might be expected, the Republicans howled about the Democrats' fund-raising schemes. They demanded an FBI investigation, saw to it that a federal grand jury was convened, and called for the appointment of an independent special prosecutor (Weiner, 1997). Four independent special prosecutors had already been appointed to investigate the administration, however, so this was hardly newsworthy. Despite intense demands for the appointment of a special prosecutor, Attorney General Janet Reno, who ultimately decided the issue, declined to make such an appointment (Suro, 1997).

Throughout the 1996 campaign, Republican candidate Senator Bob Dole hammered away about the fund-raising issue, lambasting the Clinton administration for its fund-raising tactics. Yet, despite his persistent attacks, the issue never seemed to catch the attention or interest of the voters (LaGanga & Shogren, 1996). One reason that the allegations against the Clinton campaign may have failed to spark much outrage is that the Democrats forcefully argued that the Republicans had long been raising funds in a similar fashion. At the same time that the Republicans proclaimed themselves shocked by the revelations about aggressive fund raising by Clinton, Gore, and their staffers, veteran lobbyists and congressional aides acknowledged that Capitol Hill was riddled with remarkably similar practices. Campaign checks were frequently reported to have changed hands on Capitol Hill, and congressional aides reported further that it was routine for checks to be accepted in congressional offices. The *Los Angeles Times* reported, for example, that even as he led a very public protest against Clinton and Gore, House GOP Conference chairman John A. Boehner (R—Ohio) distributed campaign checks from tobacco lobbyists while he strolled around the House floor during a roll call. The Democratic House leadership pointed this out to the press but later had to admit that they had done the same (Hook & Chen, 1997, p. 22).

The Democrats also alleged that since 1980 Senator Dole had solicited $103.4 million to bankroll his various political pursuits as well as a charitable foundation and his own conservative think tank. In addition, special interests contributed corporate jets for Dole's use 538 times during a span of six years. One of Dole's largest campaign donors was the Gallo family, the largest winemaker in the United States. In return for its very substantial contributions—$274,000 to Dole's political campaigns and $705,000 to his charitable foundation—the Gallo family persuaded the senator to cosponsor legislation amending the estate tax law to guarantee that any inheritance taxes due on its large estate could be paid out in installments. In addition, Dole interceded on the family's behalf in some trade disputes over labeling on U.S. sparkling wines, and he sponsored legislation to help Gallo purchase advertising for its wines in Europe to increase the market share for U.S.-made wines overseas (Bunting, 1996).

In addition to the news accounts of the cozy relationship between Dole and the Gallo family, there were reports about his willingness to accept hefty donations from Dwayne O. Andreas (the same donor whose contribution had helped fund the Watergate break-in) and his large agri-business, Archer-Daniels-Midland. Andreas had long been a supporter of and contributor not just to Nixon and Dole but to politicians of all stripes, including Bill Clinton. After Dole received a large contribution from Andreas, one of his last acts as Senate majority leader was to block a bill that would have paid to clean up Florida's Everglades by taxing sugar producers. Dole proposed instead that the government pay the entire bill for the cleanup directly from the U.S. Treasury, thereby eliminating the need to tax growers. Archer-Daniels-Midland saved millions in the deal because one of its most profitable commodities is high-fructose corn syrup, a sweetener for soft drinks and other products whose price is tied to the cost of sugar (Bunting, 1996).

Democrats also pointed out that over the years Dole had often come to the aid of tobacco firms, which in turn have been very generous to him. Since 1986, large tobacco firms had contributed $239,150 to Dole's political campaigns and more than $6 million in soft money (contributions given to a political party rather than to any individual candidate and thus under the laws in effect at the time not subject to legal limits) to the Republican Party. An internal memorandum from the Philip Morris Company, the largest tobacco company in the United States, was leaked to the media. The memorandum described Dole as "too valuable a friend to alienate over issues unrelated to tobacco" (cited in Bunting, 1996, p. 8).

President Clinton's campaign kept repeating that the Republicans were linked to the tobacco industry, even though over the years the Democrats as well as the Republicans had greatly profited from tobacco dollars. In the 2005–2006 campaign cycle, for example, 78 percent of tobacco company political contributions went to Republicans and 22 percent to Democrats (Campaign contributions by tobacco interests, 2006). In the decade before 1994, however, when the Democrats lost control of Congress, Democratic candidates received as much tobacco money for their individual campaigns as did Republicans (Fritsch, 1996).

Campaign funding was also an issue in the 2000 presidential election campaign, although the issue was not quite as prominent in the media or in candidate speeches as it had been in 1996. This may have been because both candidates were too busy scooping up the campaign cash to spend too much energy worrying about the consequences or the impact on our political system. The amount of money contributed to and spent by the presidential candidates greatly increased in 2000. George W. Bush, who at the time was governor of Texas, raised more than $193 million, and Vice President Al Gore raised more than $132 million.

Both candidates in this race also accepted federal matching funds (for Bush they represented 35 percent of his total and for Gore 62.5 percent), so the total amount spent on the 2000 campaign was far greater than the funds raised from donors would suggest. In both campaigns most individual contributions came from individuals contributing more than $200 (42 percent for Bush and 24 percent for Gore), and only about 10 percent of contributions to both Bush and Gore came from individuals contributing $200 or less (Opensecrets.org, 2000). These figures suggest that the candidates in 2000 were not encouraged to spend much time or effort trying to raise funds from small donors because the amount of time required may not be worth the effort.

One major party candidate who was eager to talk about the corrupting influence of money in politics in the 2000 campaign was Senator John McCain, who was challenging Bush for the Republican Party nomination. McCain had long railed against the special access that large donors could have to elected officials and the way in which these contributions distorted public policy. He was especially concerned about money that could be donated in the form of "soft" contributions. As Bennett (1996, p. 136) argued, the term *soft money* referred to a loophole in campaign finance laws that permitted unlimited donations to political party organizations as long as those funds were not placed in the budget of any particular candidate's campaign. These contributions were often used to fund get-out-the-vote (GOTV) efforts, polling, and state campaign coordinating operations. Certainly such expenditures, even if not controlled by individual candidates, could be used strategically to benefit particular presidential or congressional campaigns.

So much soft money was contributed that the total donated came to rival the amount raised by the campaigns themselves. Bennett (1996, p. 140) argued that these soft money contributions were often little more than "quasi–money laundering operations" for individual candidates. Most party ideological positions were shaped around a particular candidate's positions. The party leadership was controlled by the candidate's staff, the key soft money fund-raisers were often campaign insiders, and the national campaign strategy was often calculated around how the hard and soft money expenses were to be divided. In addition, if the soft money was not available to fund registration and GOTV drives, then candidates would be forced to expend funds from their own campaigns for these efforts. Not having to spend campaign funds, on the other hand, left more money available to purchase advertising.

The huge soft money contributions purchased a lot of political influence. In the 1996 election alone, the Center for Responsive Politics identified four $2 million-plus contributors: Philip Morris (the tobacco giant), American Telephone & Telegraph, the Association of Trial Lawyers of America, and the Teamsters Union. The financial services industry gave more money—nearly $60 million—than any other sector. Organized labor spent about $35 million (1.6 billion reasons, 1996). What did soft money contributors hope to achieve with their donations? In 1995, thirty-two defense contractors who were building B2 stealth bombers gave $8 million to help reelect incumbent members of Congress. Congress in turn voted to spend $493 million to buy the planes, despite the fact that the Pentagon said it did not want or need them (The greening, 1996). This is not a bad return on an investment. Alexander and Corrado (1995, p. 276) cited another example: They noted that Dwayne O. Andreas of Archer-Daniels-Midland (notice how this name keeps reappearing) was a big GOP supporter, but after Clinton was elected, Andreas gave $400,000 to the Democratic National Committee. About two weeks after Andreas gave the Democrats a check for $100,000 and cochaired a presidential dinner, the Environmental Protection Agency (EPA) issued a ruling that would give ethanol an estimated 10 percent of the auto fuel market by 1996—a big gain for Archer-Daniels-Midland, which controlled 70 percent of America's ethanol.

Stories of members of Congress who change their votes on particular pieces of legislation after receiving substantial contributions are common. The greater problem, however, is probably not the vote switching that occurs on the "big" issues but instead the influence these close and cozy relationships with big donors may have on the "small" issues that do not attract much publicity or on issues about which the public is indifferent, divided, or ignorant (Grenzke, 1990). For example, in 1999 the House and Senate passed the District of Columbia Appropriations Act. Hidden in the act was Section 6001, which was devoted to ensuring "Superfund Recycling Equity." The section was inserted by Senator Trent Lott (R—Mississippi), who was then Senate majority leader, to absolve the nation's scrap metal dealers from having to pay millions of dollars in cleanup costs at toxic waste sites. Senators from both parties accepted Lott's insertion. As Barlett and Steele (2000, p. 38) wrote, "This early Christmas present to the scrap-metal dealers—who contributed more than $300,000 to political candidates and committees during the 1990s—made them very happy. Others in the recycling chain were not so happy. All of a sudden they were potentially responsible for millions of dollars in damages the junkmen might otherwise have had to pay." Barlett and Steele argued that this example is all too typical of how one set of citizens—those who have the ability to make substantial political contributions and know how to "play the game"—have an advantage over other citizens and businesses that do not.

Another business executive who clearly mastered this game was Carl Lindner, the head of Chiquita Bananas. Lindner, his family members, his companies, and senior executives in these companies donated approximately $5.5 million in campaign contributions during the 1990s. Although Lindner gave generously to both parties, most of his contributions went to Republicans. What did he get in return? The U.S. government essentially launched a trade war with the European Union to attempt to secure access for Chiquita Bananas to European markets. To pressure the Europeans, the Clinton administration imposed punitive 100 percent tariffs on a wide range of European products imported to the United States. Most big businesses in the United States, which themselves contribute to political candidates, were successful in getting their products (which they marketed, distributed, or used in the manufacture of finished goods) struck from the list. Small businesses that lacked political clout, however, were affected by the newly imposed tariffs (How to become a top banana, 2000).

Still another example of the friendly relationship between donors and politicians in the collection of soft money is the contributions given to help host the national political conventions. In 1996, taxpayers paid each party $12 million to hold national conventions so the parties would not be motivated to seek money elsewhere. Nonetheless, each party set up host committees in the convention cities to solicit additional funds. In 1996, each host committee raised another $12 million from corporations and individuals. Thus, both Chicago (the Democratic site) and San Diego (the Republican site) were the scenes of countless private receptions for delegates in hotel suites, yachts, and restaurants, paid for by businesses, trade associations, lobbyists, labor unions, and others. Many of the parties hosted for state delegations were paid for by these special interest contributors, and "the party meetings became orgies of special interests' wining and dining those who make public policy" (Big money, 1996). These huge soft money donations continued in the 2000 campaign as well. As the public advocacy group Common Cause (Common Cause and Democracy 21 file comments, 2003) reported:

> In 2000, the Philadelphia host committee for the Republican Convention had twelve "platinum benefactors"—or donors of $1 million or more—including AT&T, General Motors, Microsoft, and Motorola.

There were an additional eight "gold benefactors" who gave $500,000 or more, fifteen "silver benefactors" at the level of $250,000 or more (including both Enron and Global Crossing [companies that would soon fail in a most spectacular fashion]), and twenty-seven "bronze benefactors" of $100,000 or more. The Los Angeles host committee for the 2000 Democratic convention had ten "primary partners" who gave $1 million or more—again including AT&T, General Motors, and Microsoft—three at the $500,000 level, ten at the $250,000 level, and twenty-five "trustees" who gave $100,000 or more.

What did these large corporate contributors hope to gain from these donations? Common Cause asserts that they "get access to political decision makers, from whom they hope to extract favors: tax breaks, subsidies, a sweetheart program to sell more of their products, or special regulatory breaks" (Common Cause and Democracy 21 file comments, 2003).

At least one fund-raising controversy has already emerged in the 2008 presidential primary campaign. Senator Hillary Clinton's campaign chose to give to charity $23,000 that it had received from Norman Hsu, and to review thousands of dollars more that he had raised from his friends and colleagues, after learning that he was under criminal investigation for allegedly defrauding investors (McIntire & Wayne, 2007). The accusations against Hsu were especially embarrassing for the Clinton campaign because the story rekindled memories of the 1996 fund-raising scandals in which Asian moneymen were accused of funneling suspect donations to President Bill Clinton and Vice President Al Gore (McIntire & Wayne, 2007). Despite Hsu's possibly shady business dealings, however, there was no clear evidence that he broke any laws in raising or donating money to this campaign. The Hsu story received more extensive press coverage than it might have otherwise, however, when Hsu skipped out on a scheduled court appearance in California. He was later discovered in Colorado, where he was reported to be despondent and possibly suicidal. Hsu eventually surrendered to authorities and was indicted on charges that he had defrauded investors of more than $60 million (Oliphant, 2007).

THE BIPARTISAN CAMPAIGN REFORM ACT OF 2002

As already noted, Senator John McCain has long been a vocal supporter of campaign finance reform. In 1998, McCain joined forces with Senator Russell Feingold to propose a bill that would ultimately be called the Bipartisan Campaign Reform Act (BCRA) of 2002. The orgy of special interest contributions during the 1996 and 2000 campaigns and the recurrent news stories about the influence that big donors sought and often received in return for their soft money donations kept the issue alive in the press and in Congress. Nonetheless, the forces of resistance in Congress had been able to prevent legal reform. The cynical view might suggest that they did so because they benefited so handsomely from the system already in place. The more frequently expressed reason for their opposition, however, was the belief that the proposed reform represented nothing less than a wholesale assault on the First Amendment right to free speech and political association. Opponents of the reform legislation also claimed that the new law would discourage individuals and groups from participating in campaigns and thus reduce the flow of information available to influence the electorate (Corrado, Mann, & Potter, 2003).

The battle over campaign finance reform went on for seven years, and the proposed reforms were debated in three successive Congresses. As Corrado, Mann, and Potter (2003) observed:

> By 1999 it became clear that a majority in both houses favored reform, but proponents lacked the sixty votes needed to defeat a filibuster. A breakthrough was finally achieved in 2002. The Senate initially passed S. 27, known as the McCain-Feingold legislation for its principal sponsors . . . in March 2001 on a 59 to 41 vote. Following a long delay and extensive parliamentary maneuvering, the House responded by passing H.R. 2356, the companion bill known as Shays-Meehan, for its principal sponsors, Republican Christopher Shays of Connecticut and Democrat Martin Meehan of Massachusetts, on February 14, 2002, by a vote of 240 to 189. On March 20, 2002, the Senate approved the House-passed measure by a 60 to 40 vote, thereby avoiding a conference to reconcile differences between the two bills. Despite expressing "reservations" about the legislation, President George W. Bush signed the reform act into law on March 27, 2002. (p. 3)

The most significant change wrought by the new legislation was a ban on soft money contributions. With the passage of this law, the political parties and campaign committees of individual candidates were permitted to raise and spend only hard money contributions received from individuals and political action committees (PACs); no labor or corporate contributions were permitted. In addition, state party organizations were now required to use hard money contributions to fund GOTV or voter registration drives in the 120 days preceding an election or any other activities designed to influence a federal election during an election year (Section-by-section summary of McCain-Feingold, 2007).

Another provision of the act was a compromise designed to help offset the funds that were lost with the ban on soft money contributions by raising the limits on hard money individual contributions, which had not changed since 1974. Individual contribution limits were raised from $1,000 to $2,000 per election (primary and general elections are considered separate elections), and the individual aggregate limit was increased from $25,000 to $37,500 per year. Individuals were also permitted to contribute $25,000 (up from $20,000) of this annual aggregate limit to the national political party committees and $10,000 (up from $5,000) to state party committees. These limits were indexed for inflation every odd-numbered year and thus will increase with each ensuing election (Section-by-section summary of McCain-Feingold, 2007).

Finally, the McCain-Feingold bill created new limits on the expenditures by PACs. The new law required that a disclosure report be filed with the Federal Election Commission within twenty-four hours of an expenditure being made. These disclosures had to identify the name of the person buying broadcast time and the name of the committee treasurer, provide contact information, and supply the names and addresses of all donors contributing over $1,000. In an attempt to define the boundary between hard and soft money donations and thus clarify when the individual contribution limits could be imposed, the McCain-Feingold bill defined *electioneering communications* as expenditures for advertisements or other communications that were coordinated with a candidate or party committee. The bill also prohibited corporations and labor unions from running or indirectly financing electioneering communications identifying or targeting a federal candidate within thirty days of a primary or sixty days of a general election (Section-by-section summary of McCain-Feingold, 2007).

The McCain-Feingold bill was almost immediately appealed to the courts based on the First Amendment claims just mentioned. This case would not be the first time that the courts had considered attempts to regulate money in politics. Previous attempts to limit political spending had been blocked by the U.S. Supreme Court, which ruled in *Buckley v. Valeo* (1976) that limiting expenditures by individuals and committees was tantamount to limiting both the quantity and diversity of political speech (Matasar, 1986, p. 13). The Court also ruled in *First National Bank v. Bellotti* (1978) that corporations have the same free speech rights as do individuals, and thus corporations cannot be restricted in the amount of money they are permitted to spend to influence public sentiment in

a referendum (p. 16). The assumption in both Court decisions is that
people should be exposed to a wide array of arguments on an issue, and
thus all sources should be heard.

Senator Mitch McConnell (R—Kentucky) filed the principal lawsuit seeking to overturn the ban on soft money contributions. Acting on
his behalf and drawing heavily upon the earlier decision in *Buckley v.
Valeo*, lawyers asked the courts to overturn the law because of its ban
on unregulated soft money, its provisions regulating issue advertisements, and its limitations on the coordination of expenditures. Former
independent special prosecutor Kenneth Starr,* who filed a brief on
McConnell's behalf, claimed that the McCain-Feingold reform bill
"constitutes a frontal assault on First Amendment values, the likes of
which have not been seen since the Republic's infancy. . . . Rarely has
Congress acted with such utter disregard for so many constitutional
limits on its power" (cited by Urofsky, 2005, p. 194).

The case ultimately made its way to the U.S. Supreme Court, which
announced its 5 to 4 decision in 2003. Justices John Paul Stevens and
Sandra Day O'Connor coauthored the majority opinion and were joined
by Justices David Souter, Ruth Bader Ginsburg, and Stephen Breyer;
Justices Clarence Thomas, William Rehnquist, Antonin Scalia, and
Anthony Kennedy dissented. The Court upheld most of the provisions
of the Bipartisan Campaign Reform Act related to soft money limitations and individual contribution limits. A majority of the Court found
that the law had met the constitutional requirements that it be "closely
drawn" and also that the government had an important interest in preventing "both the actual corruption threatened by large financial contributions and the eroding of public confidence in the electoral process
through the appearance of corruption" (cited by Urofsky, 2005, p. 207).

The 2003 decision upholding the constitutionality of the BCRA
was, however, short-lived. In June 2007, a new Court, now under the
leadership of Chief Justice John Roberts (who replaced Rehnquist) and
joined by Samuel Alito (who replaced O'Connor), forged a new 5–4
majority that struck down those provisions of the law that placed restrictions on television advertisements paid for by corporate or union
treasuries within the final thirty days before a primary election or the
final sixty days before a general election (Greenhouse & Kirkpatrick,

---

* Kenneth Starr led the investigation into whether President Bill Clinton committed
  perjury when denying that he had a sexually intimate relationship with White House
  intern Monica Lewinsky. The investigation led to the impeachment action against
  Clinton by the House of Representatives. Clinton was eventually acquitted of the
  charges following a hearing in the U.S. Senate.

2007). The Court now ruled that these restrictions unduly limited speech. The majority opinion, written by Chief Justice Roberts, declared, "Discussion of issues cannot be suppressed simply because the issues may also be pertinent to an election. Where the First Amendment is implicated, the tie goes to the speaker, not the censor" (cited by Greenhouse & Kirkpatrick, 2007, p. A18).

Although this new decision did not completely overturn the BCRA of 2002—it left in place the soft money ban that is contained in a separate section of the law—most experts conceded that the effect would be to undercut the ban on soft money by permitting a largely unlimited flow of money from corporate treasuries to pay for broadcast advertisements in the closing days before elections (Savage, 2007). The Court's 2007 decision also suggested that it might only be a matter of time before the entire law would be declared unconstitutional. Justices Scalia, Kennedy, and Thomas voted with the majority but refused to sign onto the majority opinion because it did not take this step. The four dissenting justices (Stevens, Souter, Ginsburg, and Breyer) declared that this new ruling would invite "easy circumvention" of the soft money ban and in essence gut the enforcement of the law (Greenhouse & Kirkpatrick, 2007).

For those who had long pressed for significant campaign finance reform legislation and had been encouraged by the passage of the BCRA, the 2007 Court decision was a significant disappointment. Those who had worried about the law's detrimental effect on the First Amendment, on the other hand, were delighted. It is also noteworthy that the opposition to the McCain-Feingold Act came from a diverse coalition. The 2007 court case was brought by the Wisconsin Right to Life Committee (a conservative anti-abortion rights group), which was joined in briefs filed by the American Civil Liberties Union, the AFL-CIO, the U.S. Chamber of Commerce, and the National Rifle Association (Greenhouse & Kirkpatrick, 2007; Savage, 2007).

Although many, including the dissenting justices, argued that the 2007 Court decision undermined the impact of the BCRA, there is significant evidence that so many flaws in the new law had been revealed during the 2004 presidential election campaign that the law had already been shown to be ineffective. The 2004 election also illustrated how difficult it would be to regulate campaign finance given how truly shrewd and creative political candidates, consultants, lobbyists, and ideological activists can be in taking advantage of such flaws.

When the McCain-Feingold Act eliminated direct soft money contributions, donors in the 2004 campaign sought a new mechanism for funneling money toward achieving their political goals. The primary means to achieve this were 527 political organizations (tax-exempt organizations named for a section of the federal tax code). These organizations are permitted to engage in voter mobilization efforts, issue advocacy, and other political activities short of expressly advocating the election or defeat of a federal candidate.

In the spring of 2004 liberal activist groups began their efforts to form 527s to mobilize voters to prevent the election of President George W. Bush to a second term. Groups such as America Coming Together, The Media Fund, and MoveOn.org began attracting significant support from both large and small donors. Republicans protested these efforts to the Federal Election Commission, but on May 13, 2004, the FEC voted to delay a decision on regulating 527 committees. Republicans were thus given every motivation to begin pursuing their own 527 efforts. In a joint statement Marc Raciot, chairman of the Bush-Cheney reelection campaign, and Ed Gillespie, chairman of the Republican National Committee, declared that the FEC's refusal to set clear rules on 527s "sets the stage for a total meltdown of federal campaign finance regulation in 2004" (cited by Edsall, 2004, p. A09). Senators McCain and Feingold also saw the danger that the FEC's decision would undermine their legislation. In a joint statement they said: "As a result, a flood of soft money will enter the system which will violate the letter and the spirit of the law" (cited by Edsall, 2004, p. A09). These warnings proved more than apt. Fifty-three committees that focused "largely or exclusively on the presidential election" raised $246 million for the 2004 election (Presidential campaign finance, 2004). The Center for Public Integrity reported that altogether, 527 committees raised and spent just over a half-billion dollars during the 2003–2004 elections, which was twice the amount spent during the 2002 cycle. Although 527s had been operating for years, the 2004 campaigns marked the "first time they played a major role, perhaps a decisive role, in determining the outcome of a national election" (527s in 2004 shatter previous records, 2004). Drawing data from the required filings with the federal government, the Center for Public Integrity reported that the liberal group America Coming Together, which raised more than $78 million, collected the most money. Six separate committees that focused primarily on the presidential election raised more than $10 million each, and three raised $40 million or more (527s in 2004 shatter previous records, 2004).

The 527 groups attracted huge contributions from very large and wealthy contributors. The largest donors to liberal 527s included George

Soros ($23,700,000), Peter Lewis ($23,347,220), and Stephen Bing ($13,700,465). The largest donors to conservative 527s included Bob Perry ($9,640,000), T. Boone Pickens ($5,122,000), Roland Arnall ($5,000,000), and Alexander Spanos ($5,000,000). Altogether, the fifteen individuals who gave the largest contributions during the 2004 campaign donated a whopping $125,810,744 to 527s, with the vast majority of these contributions devoted to affecting the outcome of the presidential contest between Bush and Kerry (527s in 2004 shatter previous records, 2004).

Much of this money went directly into broadcast and direct mail advertising — 30 percent for the liberal groups and 78 percent for the conservative groups. Not surprisingly, most of the advertising dollars were devoted to the most closely contested battleground states. Residents of Ohio, Florida, Colorado, Maryland, Wisconsin, and Pennsylvania were, as a result, the most likely to be exposed to the 527 messages (527s in 2004 shatter previous records, 2004). It is not just the volume of such messages in closely contested states that may have affected the outcome of the 2004 presidential election; it is also the nature of the messages constructed. The 527 groups were typically funded by individuals who were strongly partisan (either for liberal or conservative causes) and thus highly motivated to create very strident and often negative attack-style campaign messages. In addition, because the 527 groups were by law independent from the candidate's official campaigns, they were not to "coordinate" their message strategies with those developed by the campaigns. This permitted the 527s to develop their attacks while also allowing the candidates to publicly disavow these messages and thus somewhat minimize the impact of any possible public backlash. Media investigations into various 527 groups on both the left and the right, however, reported that several of these groups shared professional staff and advisors with the Bush and Kerry campaigns, thus discrediting the claim that these operations were really as separate and independent as claimed (Rutenberg & Zernike, 2004).

Although liberal groups such as America Coming Together and MoveOn.org helped mobilize Democratic voters and had a significant impact in the election, the group Swift Boat Veterans for Truth (which spent only $17 million) probably made the biggest splash in the media. Senator Kerry had built much of his image campaign around his heroic military service in Vietnam. The Swift Boat Veterans 527 claimed in a series of very controversial ads that Kerry had exaggerated his service record, that he did not deserve the medals he was awarded for combat, and that as a result he was somewhat of a fraud who could not be counted on to lead the nation in a time of conflict. The media picked up these accusations and succeeded in blunting Senator Kerry's campaign message (Westen, 2007). Magleby (2004) argued, "The Swift Boat Veterans attack was masterful. This group delivered a message that the Bush campaign and the RNC [Republican National Committee] could not, and Bush got the best of both worlds because he could decry 527s and benefit from their activities at the same time."

Magleby (2004) cited a survey undertaken in September 2004 that asked voters what they knew about Kerry's military record. He reported that 76 percent of respondents mentioned issues or concerns advanced in the Swift Boat Veterans' ads, 33 percent mentioned the controversy over his medals, and 19 percent referred to his having participated in the anti–Vietnam War protests. Those who mentioned the themes developed in these ads were also more likely to express a critical view of Kerry and less likely to come to his defense. The suggestion then is that the ads had an impact on the attitudes of the electorate, especially because they were cited and discussed by many other news reports. An independent research group called Public Opinion Strategies reported that voters in six battleground states were most deeply affected by three different commercials, all of which were either pro-Bush or anti-Kerry: the Swift Boat ads, the "Ashley" ad (that featured President Bush consoling a 16-year-old girl who lost her mother in the September 11, 2001, terrorist attacks), and an ad that used images of a wolf pack to symbolize the dangers caused by terrorists. Each of these ads suggested that the United States faced a threatening and hostile world filled with adversaries seeking to destroy the nation and that Senator Kerry could not be depended on to provide leadership in such dangerous times (cited by Birnbaum & Edsall, 2004; Westen, 2007).

Although the Democrats were responsible for first pumping new life and energy into the 527s in the 2004 campaign, they may have ended up doing more harm to their candidate and their own interests than any benefits reaped. The conservative anti-Kerry messages seem to have had a greater impact on the outcome of the election than the anti-Bush messages, and before the election was finished, Republican 527 groups outspent the Democrats on television and radio ads by almost three to one (Birnbaum & Edsall, 2004). Westen (2007) claimed that the Kerry campaign, convinced that people did not like negative attack ads, made a conscious decision not to respond to the Swift Boat ads in the first few days that they were on the air. Yet, Westen (2007, pp. 343–344) argued that "Kerry's silence was confirming exactly what

Bush was saying about him: that he was weak and indecisive in the face of aggression (an attack on his honor)."

The Democrats chose to spend a greater share of their 527 money on voter turnout efforts, and as a result they had less money to invest in spot advertising. Magleby (2004) found that the expenditures by the Democratic-leaning 527s may have had a significant impact on voter turnout as a result of their well-organized voter outreach efforts. As an example he cited the efforts of the Sierra Club pro-environment 527, which targeted more than 400,000 voters in nine key states with eight to twelve contacts via phone, mail, and door-to-door communications. Likewise, MoveOn.org used 70,000 volunteer staff members in 10,000 precincts in contested states to turn out likely Democratic voters.

The FEC did eventually attempt to regulate the 527 expenditures but waited until after the 2004 elections to act. Weissman and Ryan (2007) reported the following:

> In November 2004, the FEC rejected reform groups' recommendations that 527s involved in federal elections be treated as "political committees" subject to "hard money" contribution limits. Instead the Commission adopted two broad regulatory changes that affected only some of these groups in 2006. . . . Most significantly, it decided that any solicitation indicating that even a portion of the receipts would "be used to support or oppose the election of a clearly identified candidate" would generate "contributions" within the meaning of the Federal Election Campaign Act. An organization (whether a 527 entity or not) with at least $1,000 in contributions can be required to register as a political committee and observe federal contribution limits *if* the Commission also determines that the organization's "major purpose is federal campaign activity." The first public application of the new FEC approach was the Commission's September 2005 suit against the Republican-oriented Club for Growth. In its complaint, the FEC asserted that the Club's 527 operated as a political committee during the 2004 election. . . . Recently citing in part FEC regulations, the Club decided to abandon its 527 structure for a new 501(c)(4) entity focused on "pro-growth advocacy." (p. 3)

The inadequacy of the FEC's 2004 regulations was immediately apparent if these groups could avoid regulation merely by reconstituting themselves under a different section of the U.S. tax code.

The new 501(c)(4) organizations took advantage of a loophole in the federal tax code that allowed them to continue funneling money into their favored political causes in an attempt to influence the outcome of candidate elections and to shape public policy. In a very short time, many other 527 groups (on both the left and the right) created their own 501(c)(4) spin-off groups (Weissman & Ryan, 2007). The outcome thus seems clear: When soft money contributions could no longer be sent directly to candidates or parties, the use of 527 groups increased. Attempts to regulate the 527 groups led to expanded use of 501(c)(4) groups. One can imagine that future attempts to regulate these groups will be met by still other clever strategies. The 501 groups may pose even greater danger than have the 527s, for as long as the 501(c) groups can claim that "political campaign intervention" or "federal campaign activity" is not their primary purpose, their contributions and expenditures may remain largely undisclosed. Many unions or trade associations have taken advantage of this loophole and have declined to disclose their efforts, arguing that their political activities are secondary to their social welfare or trade development roles (Weissman & Ryan, 2007, p. 7).

Most of the discussion thus far has focused on presidential campaigns, but 527 and 501(c) groups can also have an impact on congressional and state and local races. For example, 527 groups have played an important role in federal congressional elections. In 2005–2006 these groups spent approximately $143 million (up from $125 million in the 2002 midterm elections) to try to influence the outcome of House and Senate races. Democratic-leaning 527s outspent Republicans by more than 2 to 1, perhaps an indication of the degree of polarization in the country and the level of antipathy Democrats have toward Republicans because of the Iraq war. Once again large donors were the most significant factor in the flow of money. Nearly half of the total contributions came from a mere 104 individual donors who gave between $600,000 and $9.75 million (Weissman & Ryan, 2007, p. 2).

The most significant activities by 501(c) groups in 2006 were by labor unions and business development groups, such as the U.S. Chamber of Commerce, but there were many other such groups, including Americans for Job Security, Defenders of Wildlife Action Fund, League of Conservation Voters, National Right to Life Committee, NARAL Pro-Choice America, National Right to Life Association, and Focus on the Family, to name just a few (Weissman & Ryan, 2007). Because 501(c) groups, unlike 527s, do not have to disclose their donations and expenditures, use of these groups "has the potential to leave an increasing amount of federal campaign activity outside the reach of disclosure" (Weissman & Ryan, 2007, p. 10).

Most experts surveying this regulatory landscape, from both the left and the right, seem convinced that the essential goal of the McCain-Feingold legislation—reducing the flow of soft money into politics—remains unmet (for example, see Smith, 2006). Indeed, Weissman and Ryan (2007, pp. 15–16) declared, "It is very likely that there will be a substantially larger sum of soft money present in the 2008 presidential as well as congressional elections. These funds will be provided and wielded by individuals and groups using broad, multi-entity strategies to influence elections."

This discussion thus illustrates the many challenges faced in attempts to regulate campaign funding. The increasing flow of money into campaigns has dramatically changed the way candidates seek election in the United States and sparks chicken-or-egg questions. Did the demands of the new media environment create the need for the huge volume of political contributions that many believe threatens to undermine American democracy? Or did the tremendous volume of cash coming into campaigns—motivated by donors' needs for political favors—enable candidates to abandon old-fashioned "retail" politics and switch to expensive new "high-tech" campaigns? No matter which came first, both have occurred. Today's candidates are very dependent on paid political advertising, pollsters, and expensive consultants, and because they can raise huge amounts of money from donors currying political favors, they have become increasingly independent of their political parties and of the constituents whom they supposedly represent. The influx of cash threatens to further increase public cynicism about politics and decrease the public's confidence in their leaders and their government.

POLITICS AS USUAL

Both Democrats and Republicans are quick to criticize each other as beholden to special interests. Democrats claim that the Republicans are in the pocket of corporate elites, and Republicans claim that the Democrats are owned by organized labor and trial lawyers. It is clear that both parties are raising huge amounts of money and that most of this money comes from those who can afford to give. Political participation in the United States, including voting, direct participation (such as volunteering), and donating money to candidates or political causes, is increasingly skewed to those with higher incomes. As Mankinson (2002) asked, "Why do the candidates descend with such regularity into places like Manhattan, Los Angeles, Silicon Valley, and Houston? As Willie Sutton said so famously when asked why he robbed banks, 'That's where the money is.'"

Mankinson (2002) argued that "just a tiny fraction of Americans— one-tenth of 1 percent—contributed $1,000 or more to a federal candidate, PAC, or party . . . and people with that kind of disposable income are not randomly distributed in every neighborhood." Three cities— New York, Washington, and Los Angeles—are the biggest sources of political donations by individuals to presidential and congressional campaigns. Individual contributors in New York City alone gave more money than did individuals from nineteen states combined. Thus, no matter where candidates are running for office, they are likely to visit Washington, New York, and Los Angeles with an open hand. In fact, many candidates get more money from these areas than from their own home districts. A zip code listing of the twenty neighborhoods with the largest amount of individual political contributions in 2004 included seven neighborhoods in New York City; two in greater Los Angeles; six in or around Washington, DC; two in Chicago; and one each in Palm Beach, Florida; Dallas, Texas; and Greenwich, Connecticut (Top zip codes, 2006).

It should not surprise us that people with higher incomes have more disposable income, a greater vested interest in protecting their wealth, and as a result are more likely to donate money to political causes and candidates. Those who are financially better off are more likely to be politically active in every capacity. As Plumer (2007) wrote:

> People in the $75,000 bracket are much more likely than those in the $15,000 bracket to join a political advocacy group like the National Rifle Association or the NAACP (73 percent versus 29 percent) and much more likely to make campaign contributions (56 percent versus 6 percent). Indeed, in the 2000 election, 95 percent of those donors making substantial campaign contributions came from households earning over $100,000. While high-income donors don't usually *bribe* politicians to do their bidding, they do get more face time with their representatives, during which they can frame issues and concerns in ways amenable to their interests. (Over half of donors in a 2000 poll reported speaking directly with a major elected official, as opposed to 9 percent of regular voters.)

Plumer (2007) also argued that this skewed political participation has negative consequences and that the "massive disparities in wealth and income really do distort the democratic process—by allowing a tiny seg-

ment of the population to wield outsized influence in the political realm."
He also observed:

> Between 1979 and 2004, the richest 1 percent of Americans saw their
> after-tax incomes triple, while those of the middle fifth grew by only
> 21 percent and those of the poorest fifth barely budged, according to
> Congressional Budget Office data. By the late '90s, the richest 1 per-
> cent of American households held one-third of all wealth in the U.S.
> economy, and took in 14 percent of the national income—a greater
> share than at just about any point since the Great Depression.

Bartels (2005) argued that this income disparity did not just happen
but that it has been a product of the evolving nature of our political system:

> The political process has evolved in ways that may be detrimental to
> the interests of citizens of modest means. Political campaigns have
> become dramatically more expensive since the 1950s, increasing the
> reliance of elected officials on people who can afford to finance their
> bids for reelection. Lobbying activities by corporations and busi-
> nesses and professional organizations have accelerated greatly, out-
> pacing the growth of public interest groups. And membership in
> labor unions has declined substantially, eroding the primary mecha-
> nism for organized representation of blue collar workers in the gov-
> ernmental process. (p. 2)

Bartels (2005, p. 2) then cited a report of a Task Force on Inequality
and Democracy that concluded that "rising economic inequality will
solidify longstanding disparities in political voice and influence, and
perhaps exacerbate such disparities."

In an attempt to provide empirical evidence that the flow of money
does influence policy outcomes, Bartels (2005) undertook a study of
senators' voting patterns in the 1980s and 1990s on specific roll call votes
on the minimum wage, civil rights, government spending, and abortion,
reporting the following:

> Senators in this period were vastly more responsive to the views of
> affluent constituents than to constituents of modest means. Indeed,
> my analyses suggest that the views of constituents in the upper third
> of the income distribution received about 50 percent more weight
> than those in the middle third (with even larger disparities on spe-
> cific salient roll call votes), while the views of constituents in the bot-
> tom third received no weight at all in the voting decisions of their
> senators.

Jacobs and Page (2003) studied U.S. foreign policy and came to some very similar conclusions. They discovered that political leaders in the executive branch and Congress gave significant attention to the opinions of business leaders, political elites, and experts in the shaping of foreign policy. Yet, the opinions of ordinary citizens "seemed to exert little or no significant influence on government officials, except on very high-salience issues and perhaps in certain limited issue areas." As Mankinson argued, the gap in political donations between the wealthy elites and ordinary citizens has created a two-tiered political system: "In politics there's a first class section and a second class section. People in first class get the perks. They get treated well and there is no question they will be extremely well represented" (cited in Wayne, 1996, p. E5).

The perks available to the donors in first class, and the implications of their influence in the formation of U.S. foreign policy, are not insignificant. At the time that this chapter is being written, the United States has doled out more than $30 billion for the reconstruction of Iraq following the toppling of Saddam Hussein. In constant dollars this amount is more than any single European nation received under the Marshall Plan for economic reconstruction following World War II. In fact, it is three times more money, again in constant dollars, than was given to Germany, where all of the major cities and the national infrastructure were destroyed (Miller, 2006). The amount of money seems like an extraordinary act of generosity from American taxpayers to the people of Iraq. Miller (2006), however, believed otherwise:

> Much of the money didn't go to Iraq. Billion by billion, politicians in Washington could not resist such an enormous pot of money. They constantly intervened in Iraq's reconstruction to benefit friends, constituents, and occasionally business partners. Usually the intervention did more to aid American corporations than impoverished Iraqis. The favors were passed in typical Washington style—behind closed doors, between lobbyists and politicians, at committee meetings that left no trace of fingerprints. What appeared to be a remarkably generous foreign aid package was in fact a remarkable program of domestic handouts and corporate welfare. For a predominantly Muslim country, Iraq became an especially rich source of pork. (pp. 42–43)

Miller (2006, pp. 43–44) offered several examples of such pork flowing to U.S. corporations with close ties to the White House. These included a $7 billion contract to KBR, a subsidiary of Halliburton Company, that was negotiated in secret and to which no other companies were invited to submit bids. Vice President Dick Cheney is the former CEO of Halliburton. Miller also cited the example of a $680 million contract awarded to the Bechtel Corporation; again, the bids were conducted in a highly secretive fashion, even though the company would become responsible for coordinating the reconstruction of "every bridge, road, power plant, and school that the federal government deemed necessary." The board of directors of Bechtel includes many leading Washington politicians and former high-ranking officials, among them George Shultz, who was secretary of state in the Reagan administration.

Why is so much more money being spent on campaigns today? The costs of advertising time, polling, and campaign travel have increased in recent years, to be sure, but not nearly enough to account for the increased expenditures. Why, then, do candidates have such an acute need for more money? The most likely answer is simply that the money is available to them. The District of Columbia and most state capitals seem to be awash in special interest money, this money is readily available to candidates, and they have eagerly taken it.

Recent public opinion polls suggested that the approval rating for Congress is about 25 percent. Furthermore, only 14 to 15 percent of Americans give Congress high marks for honesty and integrity (Koch, 2006). Yet, despite these dreadfully low approval ratings, typically more than 90 percent of congressional candidates who run for reelection win, and most win handily. As Greene and Hernson (2002) declared:

> Incumbents possess a number of advantages over their opponents. They enjoy greater name recognition among voters and better access to the media. They possess tremendous fund-raising advantages with political action committees, wealthy donors, and even individuals who make small contributions. In addition, incumbents typically assemble more professional campaign organizations and almost always have more political skill than do their opponents. Given these advantages, it comes as little surprise that barring illness, scandal, or sheer incompetence, most incumbents are virtual shoo-ins for reelection.

Some of the public frustration over the performance of Congress may be due to the fact that the vast amounts of money available to members of Congress have served to diminish the degree to which they are accountable to their constituents. The access to almost unlimited sums of money enables incumbents in Congress to set up permanent political campaigns, operations that free them from some of the parochial interests of their political parties, districts, or states. Incumbent candidates are also able to raise much of their money from out-of-state contributors.

Because they are already members of Congress, they are more likely to be well known. Challengers, on the other hand, are often unknown outside their state, so they have less ability to raise money. There are exceptions to this, of course, and these tend to occur in very high-profile races that become "nationalized" because of the perceived significance of the targeted incumbent. Thus, for example, the challengers who ran against leading national figures such as former senator Tom Daschle (D—South Dakota) or former representative Tom DeLay (R—Texas) managed to secure significant funds from out-of-state contributors. Incumbents have significant advantages in almost every race, however, because they are already connected to important donor networks, and donors naturally prefer to give their money to candidates with a proven track record of victory (Greene & Hernson, 2002).

Although some may argue that voters should have the chance to unseat legislators whose positions they disagree with whether they are their own elected officials or those from other states, it is not clear that the flow of so much special interest money into politics is desirable. Access to such money does not further the election of legislators who are responsive to broader public interests. As Sabato (1989, p. 1) observed, "The rise of special interest politics at times threatens to create a selfish, atomized society where the generalized and superior national good is subordinated to the particularized needs of narrow, greedy, but prominent and loud groups—a recipe for disaster, with the whole becoming less than the sum of the parts." We have already discussed this problem of "super-individuated" politics occurring in response to the increased reliance on public opinion polls (Chapter 7) and as a result of new developments in communication technologies (Chapter 8).

Another loophole that has allowed big donors to circumvent campaign finance laws to influence the political process is a technique known as *bundling*. This term refers to the practice of an individual or organization not only soliciting contributions but also collecting the checks and then giving them to the candidate in each donor's name. The gift is attributed to the donor on campaign reports, but it is the fundraiser who is allowed to claim the political credit for the bundled gifts. There is no limit on the amount of money that an individual or an organization can accumulate and donate through bundling. The Bush campaign in 2000 and 2004 demonstrated how effective bundling can be in raising vast amounts of money and in providing connections between donors and the candidate. Individuals who raised at least $100,000 in bundled contributions were declared "Pioneers." In 2004, there were 940 who qualified for membership in this group. Those who raised

$200,000 in bundled contributions were declared to be "Rangers." In 2004, 323 qualified for this distinction (Payola pioneering, 2004).

How does this cozy relationship with wealthy and powerful donors influence politicians? The late Senator Paul Simon (D—Illinois) offered the following explanation:

> If I get into a hotel, say, at midnight, and there are twenty phone calls waiting for me—nineteen from people whose name I don't recognize and the twentieth from someone who gave me a $1,000 campaign contribution, at midnight, I'm not going to make twenty phone calls. I might make one. Which one do you think I make? (Cited in Kubiak, 1994, p. 14)

West (2000) characterized the current system of campaign financing as "checkbook democracy" and made this comment:

> It is a system characterized by large contributions, secret influence, citizen cynicism, weak public representation, and increasingly unaccountable elected officials. Big money tied to private interest groups has disrupted democratic elections, raised the volume of negative ads, and turned off the general public. . . . The need to raise large sums of money leads public officials to pay more attention to donors than voters. (p. 7)

Representative Barney Frank (D—Massachusetts), a long-time advocate of campaign finance reform, noted, "We're the only people in the world who are expected to accept thousands and thousands of dollars and not be influenced by them" (cited in Kubiak, 1994, p. 20).

ONLY THE WEALTHY NEED APPLY

As already noted, the current campaign finance system gives incumbents a strong advantage. They can raise huge war chests, operate somewhat independently from party leadership, and communicate directly to voters through paid advertising. This situation makes it especially difficult for challengers to battle incumbents. Challengers either must have the ability to quickly gain the support of wealthy donors or invest their own personal fortune in seeking election. The courts have ruled that there is no limit on how much of their own money candidates can spend, as long as they do not accept the public funds that are available to presidential candidates. If they choose to accept the public financing, then they are limited to $50,000 in personal or family contributions to their own campaign (Alexander & Corrado, 1995).

In recent elections a number of very wealthy candidates have stepped forward to seek office. In the 1994 California Senate race, for example, Republican candidate Michael Huffington spent almost $30 million of his own money, only to narrowly lose the race to incumbent Democratic senator Dianne Feinstein (Bennett, 1996). Ross Perot spent some $60 million in personal funds in his unsuccessful attempt to capture the presidency in 1992, but he did manage to secure almost 20 percent of the popular vote (Berke, 1996). In 1996, magazine publisher Steve Forbes spent between $25 and $30 million of his personal funds in his quest for the Republican presidential nomination. After blasting front-runner Robert Dole with negative ads in Iowa and New Hampshire (and perhaps doing incalculable damage to Dole's prospects), Forbes dropped out of the race. He ended up winning only 71 delegates to the Republican convention, less than 10 percent of the number needed for nomination, and he spent between $352,112 and $422,535 for each delegate that he gained (Tollerson, 1996). Forbes's children apparently failed to persuade him not to spend their inheritance, for Forbes was back in the race for the Republican nomination in 2000.

In the 2008 presidential race Republican candidate and former Massachusetts governor Mitt Romney, whose net worth was said to be between $190 and $250 million, donated $2 million of his own funds to his campaign and indicated that he was ready to dig deeper and contribute more if that was necessary (Kuhnhenn, 2007). More proved necessary, because four months later he loaned his campaign another $6.5 million (Morain, Romney loans, 2007). Romney seems almost like a pauper, however, compared to New York City mayor Michael Bloomberg. Bloomberg, who headed a worldwide media empire, was a lifelong Democrat who became a Republican in order to run for mayor. A billionaire, Bloomberg set a new record when he spent $74 million to get elected in 2001. He broke his own record and spent $77 million on his 2004 reelection campaign (Ketupa.net, 2007). When he announced in June 2007 that he was leaving the Republican Party and declared himself an independent, there was immediate speculation that he intended to run for president. Although Bloomberg insisted that he had no intention of running for any office in 2008, stories began to circulate almost immediately that he was indeed planning to enter the presidential race and that he was willing to spend as much as $500 million of his personal fortune to gain the White House (Grunwald, 2007).

Certainly Bloomberg, or any other independent candidate, would face long odds on gaining election to the presidency. Research has suggested that most candidates who invest large sums of their personal fortunes in their campaigns fail to gain office. But this occurs because they are usually running against incumbents who have the advantage of name recognition and their own huge campaign war chests. Another strong argument suggests that the very process of asking people to give money to support your campaign is helpful in that it provides contact with possible voters and visibly demonstrates political skills (Steen, 2006). Asking for contributions also helps donors feel that the candidate is more likely to understand their concerns and thus may give them a greater sense of urgency to work to secure the candidate's election. Nonetheless, many wealthy candidates do win elections. They may also succeed in frightening off other candidates, thus narrowing the field and limiting the choices available to voters (Steen, 2006).

Personal wealth and standing in the community have always been helpful to those seeking election in the United States, but the importance of personal wealth has probably never been greater. The weakened influence of political parties means that candidates must be able to put their case for election directly before the voters through the media—which requires money, and more than all but the very wealthy are able to muster. Again, one wonders how long a government can preserve the support and backing of all its citizens when it is made up only of the country club and polo set.

CAMPAIGN FINANCE REFORM

The occupants of the White House and the elected members of Congress are people who have demonstrated their ability to succeed in the game of fund raising to gain political office. Having benefited from the system as currently practiced, they are understandably reluctant to tamper with it. Furthermore, the current Supreme Court has expressed its reluctance to allow any new campaign finance regulations that might in any way diminish the rights to free speech. Thus, crafting new regulations that might reform how campaigns are financed will be extremely difficult. It is unlikely that dramatic changes will be made in regulations in the near term. It is also likely that each new election will be more costly than the one before.

The enforcement of current campaign laws has been left largely to the Federal Election Commission, which seems to have been intentionally designed to be a toothless tiger. As Brooks Johnson (cited in Reiche, 1990, p. 238) argued, "Congress designed the [Federal Election] Commission to fail, building in the propensity for partisan deadlocks, insisting on the appointment of pliant Commissioners, and creating a morass of procedural defenses for suspected wrong-doers." The FEC is composed of six members, three selected by each party. In 2000 the Republicans asked President Clinton to appoint Bradley Smith to the FEC, even though Smith openly called for the repeal of the entire Federal Election Campaign Act and expressed his strong opposition to any form of campaign finance regulation. Despite the fact that Clinton strongly disagreed with Smith's position on the issues, he felt he had no choice but to nominate him out of fear that the Republicans would block any alternative nominee (Hansen, 2001).

The one development in recent years that might help address some of the problems posed by the ever-increasing flow of money into political campaigns is the new transparency that is available as a result of the Internet. Web sites such as Opensecrets.org, Fundrace.org, Publicintegrity .org, Maplight.org, and Followthemoney.org, to name just a few, provide accurate and current information about political candidates, donors, and PACs. These Web sites help reporters and individual citizens learn who is supporting the various candidates and how their positions on important issues and key votes might have been influenced by these donations. Such information helps shape public dialogue and debate and may help ensure that citizens hold their elected officials to high ethical standards. For these sites to be effective, however, citizens will have to be attentive and engaged in the political process.

Another strategy that has long been proposed as an alternative to campaigns dominated by paid political advertising and the huge budgets that such campaigns demand is to require broadcasters to provide free airtime to candidates. Given the hundreds of millions of dollars spent on political advertising, broadcasters have been the greatest beneficiaries of all the cash spent on contemporary campaigns. Thus, some argue that broadcasters should be required to provide free airtime if they wish to keep their licenses to operate. Given the current attitudes in Washington, however, it is unlikely that free airtime will be mandated. Even without such a requirement, however, citizen activists should strongly encourage their local television stations (since local TV is the primary source of news to more people than any other media source) to present a nightly mix of candidate minidebates, interviews, and issue statements during the last few days of campaigns.

Media leaders and candidates alike frequently respond to demands for campaign reform by asserting that the public simply does not care about these issues. No doubt there is some evidence to support this claim of public apathy. As has repeatedly been my argument, the apathy is itself a result of the forces that have conspired against citizen participation and that leave people feeling powerless to make a difference. But people must, somehow and in some way, be made to care. The salvation of our political system demands that citizens again be "plugged in" to their political system.

CHAPTER 11

Campaigning and Governing

Many citizens pay almost no attention to politics. They do not read a daily newspaper, avoid watching news on television, and seldom seek out news-oriented Internet sites. Such people notice political messages only when the paid political advertisements intrude on the television programs they are watching and thus become impossible to ignore or when one of their friends or relatives brings up the subject of politics in conversation. Given such a limited exposure to political news and information, it is not surprising that the political attitudes of many Americans are shaped almost exclusively by television spot advertisements or by their friends' or relatives' comments and complaints about politics or politicians.

Even those citizens who make a concerted effort to stay informed about political issues—those who read newspaper stories on political events or watch the nightly news—learn more than is told in the supposedly objective stories constructed by the reporters. They are also directly exposed to the messages generated by candidates during their campaigns. The advertising campaigns, messages tested with focus groups, and constructed images of the candidates thus contribute substantially to the dramas that give life to politics in the United States.

Campaign rituals and rhetoric do more than merely shape the public's perception of political issues and candidates; they also shape voters' attitudes about the political system, their own situation in the world, and their fellow citizens. In addition, the strategies that political candidates adopt to achieve success in their political campaigns now often serve as the model for how they should govern as elected officials. As I have already stated, we are in the era of the permanent campaign. The inner circle of advisors of the president of the United States includes pollsters, and the president consults with political strategists in charting the administration's policy course. Thus, Karl Rove, whose expertise was in planning campaign strategy and winning elections, served as one of President George W. Bush's closest White House confidants. Rove was said to have been deeply involved in such important strategic policy choices as the decision to wage war in Iraq and the conduct of that war (Froomkin, 2007). Rove also advised Bush that it would be wise to fire U.S. attorneys who did not seem sufficiently committed to the Republican political agenda in their decisions about which cases to pursue.

The firings of eight such attorneys, many of whom had recently been praised for their outstanding job performance, roiled the political scene in 2007. Hearings were conducted on Capitol Hill, and leading Democrats, many legal experts, academics, and op-ed writers argued that the Bush administration had wrongly politicized the U.S. Justice Department (Coleman, 2007). The controversy lingered in the news for months, and it led to the claim that Alberto Gonzales, the Attorney General of the United States, perjured himself when he testified before Congress that he had not discussed the decision to fire the eight attorneys with anyone in the White House. Although President Bush strenuously defended Gonzales, who was his close friend from Texas, Gonzales ultimately chose to resign his post (Myers & Shenon, 2007).

It is understandable, and perhaps even desirable (although this view would likely be contested by many), that elected officials would carefully consider the political ramifications before espousing their positions on issues. Today, however, matters substantive, trivial, and even mundane are viewed through a political prism. As already noted, President Clinton consulted his pollsters and political strategists before choosing the site for his family's summer vacation. Focus groups are asked to evaluate what color neckties they prefer. President Reagan's advisors convinced him that he should be seen in cowboy boots and western-style work shirts on his visits to his Santa Barbara ranch. President Carter's advisors persuaded him to wear cardigan sweaters to create a more casual and informal tone when giving speeches from the White House.

The inclusion of such political strategists and image makers in day-to-day governance has reinforced a public perception that there is something somehow insincere and contrived about contemporary governance. President George W. Bush's communications staff proved especially adept at staging events. For example, when Bush delivered a speech at Mount Rushmore, the White House positioned the platform for television crews off to one side, not head on as other White House event planners had done. As a result, the cameras caught Bush in profile, his face perfectly aligned with those of the four presidents carved in stone on the mountain (Bumiller, 2003). The staged public events can backfire, of course. The most noteworthy example occurred in 2003 when the

White House came up with the idea of dressing President Bush in a flight suit and having him land on the aircraft carrier *Abraham Lincoln* in an Air Force plane to give a speech announcing the end of major conflict in Iraq. Media strategists noted that Bush advisors "had choreographed every aspect of the event, even down to the members of the *Lincoln* crew arrayed in coordinated shirt colors over Mr. Bush's right shoulder and the 'Mission Accomplished' banner placed so as to perfectly capture the president and the celebratory two words in a single shot. The speech was specifically timed for what image makers call 'magic hour light,' which cast a golden glow on Mr. Bush" (cited by Bumiller, 2003). At the time, Democrats ridiculed the trip as an expensive political stunt. In the months and years to follow, however, the memory of the event became even more tarnished by the focus on the contrast between the message displayed on the banner and the daily news accounts of continued violence in Iraq.

Given that contemporary political candidates are continually challenged to develop strategies to reach "persuadable voters," is it surprising that so much energy is focused on staking out policy positions that are achievable rather than on focusing on more comprehensive or possibly even superior solutions? The very conditions that give shape to contemporary politics emphasize a pragmatic rather than idealistic mindset. Whereas in the past elected officials surrounded themselves with advisors who had significant experience in serving their political party or actually holding elected office, in recent years presidential staffs, for both Republican and Democratic administrations, have been heavily populated with young and ambitious campaign strategists whose primary experience has been in running campaigns. While the elected officials, cabinet officers, advisors, and party figures of the past may have been shaped by a coherent political philosophy and a lifelong commitment to a particular political ideology, today's officeholders and their staffs are just as likely to be motivated by the political pragmatism learned through experience in the campaign industry. One of President Bill Clinton's closest advisors during his first term, for example, was George Stephanopoulos, who joined the Clinton campaign when he was not yet 30 years of age. Stephanopoulos was given a wide range of assignments, including political advisor, public relations manager, policy expert, and crisis manager. He helped prepare the Clinton budget proposals, counseled on the choice of Supreme Court nominees, and advised on the desirability of military actions (see Stephanopoulos, 1999, p. 5). Although some claimed that President George W. Bush's staff was older and contained more appointees with extensive Washington experience than had Clinton's, a study by Tenpas and Hess (2002) reported that Bush's appointees were in fact about the same age and possessed about the same level of experience as had Clinton's.

In contemporary politics there is an almost complete melding of the responsibilities between those whose expertise is in the game of politics and those charged with formulating the polices or administering the executive branch of government. Gould (2005, p. B01) argued that "continuous campaigning" has evolved into the governing style of choice for recent administrations, including "stage-managed events, orchestrated by masters of spin [that] provide the appearance of a chief executive in charge of the nation's destiny." Gould went on to argue that the creation of an "illusion of an executive in perpetual motion" is easier to sustain than one of a government consisting of experts crafting policies to respond to the nation's problems.

CAMPAIGNS BREED CYNICISM

Americans today seem to be increasingly inclined to see politics as a game in which candidates on both sides are insincere and will do whatever it takes to win. As we have already argued, people are becoming cynical about their elected officials and their government. A recent poll, for example, reported that just 16 percent of voters believe that the federal government today reflects the will of the American people. These figures reflect a sharp decline from the 1990s, when more than 30 percent of voters routinely thought that government reflected the will of the people (16% say government, 2006). Sometimes such cynicism is deliberately created. Candidates can win elections either by encouraging voters to vote for them or discouraging them from voting for their opponents. Sometimes the latter is much easier to achieve. Thus, candidates do what they can to convince the other side's supporters that they shouldn't bother voting. Shanto Iyengar, whose work on negative campaigning was discussed in Chapter 6, has called such voter suppression "a dirty little secret" (cited by Harwood, 2004). In addition to negative attack ads, direct mail, and phone calls attacking the opponent in a campaign, some campaigns have also called voters to suggest that background checks will be conducted at the polls in the hope of finding people with outstanding warrants (e.g., for traffic offenses or other criminal violations). Such efforts to discourage voting are sometimes very explicit. For example, the former executive director of the New Hampshire Republican Party pled guilty to hiring a telemarketing company to jam Democrats' get-out-the-vote telephone lines on Election Day 2002 (cited by Harwood, 2004).

Other efforts to discourage voters may be less extreme. Candidates, for example, often seek to schedule events in such a way that the voters will not pay attention to them. In the 1996 presidential race, for example, Stephanopoulos explained, the Democrats wanted to schedule the debates as early as possible before people were really paying attention to the election, "because we didn't want them to pay attention. . . . The debates were a metaphor for the campaign. We wanted the debates to be a nonevent" (cited in Broder, 1997, p. B9). When Governor Arnold Schwarzenegger of California was running for reelection, he agreed to participate in only one debate. He also limited the scheduling of that debate. It was broadcast on a Saturday evening, in a traditionally low-viewer time slot. The hour-long forum also competed for public attention against a Los Angeles Dodgers versus New York Mets baseball playoff game and Pac-10 football (Sparks fly, 2006).

The increasing use of negative campaign ads has also led to a tendency to view political campaigns as battles in an ongoing war. Contemporary political campaigns devote significant resources to conducting research into issues that can be used against the opposition. Green (2004) noted that, in years past, this opposition research was left to volunteers and college kids. Now, however, it is a profession run by experienced investigators. They scour court records, divorce proceedings, and school newspapers; interview childhood acquaintances; and even follow candidates around with video cameras hoping to turn up material that can become the subject of political advertising, turned over to YouTube, or even more effectively given over to mainstream media. Tim Griffin, one of the leaders of George W. Bush's opposition research team in the 2000 campaign against Al Gore, declared, "We think of ourselves as the creators of the ammunition in a war. We make the bullets" (Green, 2004). Conducting political campaigns as warfare, however effective it may be in winning elections, may also turn off voters and increase their cynicism.

We discussed the increasing use of negative ads and the debate in the scholarly community about their impact on voter turnout and cynicism in Chapter 6. Although the data on the consequences of such negative ads do not unequivocally prove that such ads directly discourage voter participation, many studies have suggested that the public responds to negative campaigning by becoming more cynical about politicians and political institutions. There is clear evidence that voters do not like such negative ads and that they see them as one of the most distasteful aspects of contemporary campaigns (Freedman & Lawton, 1999). A study conducted by researchers at Harvard found the following:

> Although turnout was up sharply in 2004, tens of millions of vote-eligible Americans did not vote on Election Day. A fourth of these nonvoters said that they have virtually no interest in voting. Some of those who expressed interest in voting but did not vote this time gave reasons that indicate they would be hard to lure to the polls in almost any case. Eighteen percent of the interested nonvoters said they are disgusted with politics. (The vanishing voter, 2004)

Some studies have suggested that the increased level of cynicism caused by negative campaigns has caused some voters virtually to withdraw from the political process. They become less likely to attend to political news or conversations; they do not vote; and because they so thoroughly despise the negative messages, they come to dislike all politicians and regard them either as corrupt and self-serving or as serving only special interest lobbies. Thus, many citizens, because they believe they are personally powerless, profess not to care who wins elections (Ansolabehere & Iyengar, 1995).

Such feelings of powerlessness may eventually lead to feelings of alienation from government, and alienation may lead to decreased respect for law, the courts, and the political ideals of equality, justice, and liberty that define our national sense of purpose. As Bennett (1996) argued:

> People are adrift psychologically in a system that offers few guideposts or orientations. Washington, the national symbolic center, has become a negative. Politicians, the hope for government action, have also become negatives. Parties, the great guideposts for people seeking direction, are strange amalgams of independent-minded representatives proclaiming themselves new and different from the old models. In such an environment it is not surprising that people change their minds or lash out in frustration at the most commonly available symbols and targets for emotion: government, Washington, Congress, politicians, the press, and passing presidents. (p. 56)

The nature of contemporary electoral politics may have contributed to the creation of an angry, volatile, discouraged, and cynical electorate. A recent CBS News poll (Poll: Americans say, 2007), for example, found that 48 percent of those polled believed that the future for the next generation would be worse than for the current generation (up 10 percent since 2000); 72 percent of respondents said that they believed that if the Founders came back today, they would be disappointed in the nation; and only 19 percent of respondents believed that the country was moving in the right direction—the lowest number recorded in the CBS poll since the question was first asked in 1983.

The consequence of negative campaigning and increased cynicism may be corrosive of civic trust. As Bennett (1996, p. 57) concluded, "People may vote for the politician with the most emotionally appealing promise, or the one whose ads most effectively demonize the opposition, but what kind of bond is built between the citizen and the representative in the process? What kinds of expectations are created that government could possibly fill?"

Some scholars have defended negative advertising. For example, Geer (2006, p. 136) claimed that negativity can "enrich the information environment available to citizens. If we want voters to have access to more discussion about important issues presented with specificity and evidence to support candidates' appeals, then negative information has clear advantages over positive information." Geer's claim that a message must be negative in tone and content to clarify distinctions between the messages of competing candidates is not persuasive, however, especially when he cites as support for his argument research studies conducted in 1960 and 1970, an era in which voters were exposed to far fewer negative messages.*

Even Geer (2006, p. 137), who devoted his entire book to defending the use of negative attack ads, acknowledged that the public does not like them, as he admits, "The battling, fights, and disagreements between candidates during campaigns could lead voters to lose faith in elections and have less trust in government overall." He asserts, however, that "there is not a causal connection between the rise of negativity and the decline in trust and turnout we have witnessed over the last forty-five years" (p. 137). His conclusion, taken on its own terms, is suspect. Perhaps proof of single causality is lacking, but to claim "no connection" seems to willfully ignore the data that suggest a correla-

---

* Geer (2006, p. 136) claims, "Scholars have long argued that campaigns would be better able to perform their democratic functions if voters had access to such [comparative negative] information." To support his claim, he cites Kelly (1960) and Thompson (1970). It is not clear that either of these studies could have inferred either the number of negative messages to which voters today are exposed or the intensity of such messages. As discussed in Chapter 6, the first intensely negative TV ads broadcast in a national presidential campaign did not occur until 1964, and the notorious "Daisy" ad run by the Lyndon Johnson campaign in that election was pulled after it was aired only once.

tion, including the Harvard University poll just cited. Indeed, the research he cites in this same paragraph offers a very strong suggestion of
a causal correlation between negativity and increased cynicism, if not
direct causation.*

The increased level of cynicism may also be a result of a decreasing
level of respect and civility in public political discourse. As British his-
torian Andrew St. George (cited in Carter, 1998, p. 23) argued, "Democracy itself can be seen not only as a type of government but as a system
of manners, a form of social life." Carter (1998) goes on:

> Civility . . . is the set of sacrifices we make for the sake of our com-
> mon journey with others, and out of love and respect for the very idea
> that there *are* others. When we are civil, we are not pretending to like
> those we actually despise; we are not pretending to hold any attitude
> toward them, except that we accept and value them as every bit our
> equals before God. (p. 23)

Increasingly, politics has moved in a direction in which political opponents are cast as "enemies." They are not seen as entitled to their own
opinion, or even as mistaken, but instead are described as wrong and
sometimes even as immoral. Perhaps the most dramatic example of
this was the Nixon White House, which actually kept an "enemies list."
Unfortunately, the exposure and public condemnation of this list did

---

* Geer (2006, p. 137) cites two books by Hibbing and Theiss-Morse (1995, 2002). In
addition, the works by Ansolabehere and Iyengar (1995); Ansolabehere, Iyengar,
Simon, and Valentino (1994), and Ansolabehere, Iyengar, and Simon (1999) provide strong evidence for a causal correlation, if not single causality, between exposure to negative advertising and increased levels of cynicism. Geer (2006, p. 137)
also argues that negativity has long been a part of U.S. electoral politics, arguing
that his "small sample of newspaper ads from 1916 to 1956 suggests that negativity
has remained about the same—attacks constitute one-third of the appeals presidential candidates make to the public." There are multiple problems with this argument.
First, it assumes that all that matters is the percentage of negative messages and not
the content of those messages or the manner of exposure. Geer seems to assume that
those newspaper ads had the same or similar effect on persons exposed to them as
do the television ads that predominate today. This is an argument with little merit
because the TV ads are ubiquitous and cannot be easily avoided. As a result, they
reach people who are not actively seeking information by consulting newspapers
(these claims are all considered in greater detail in Chapter 6 of this text). Second,
it assumes that the content of the advertisements is equally negative, an argument
that Geer makes no attempt to prove. Third, it assumes that a text-based message
has the same impact on an audience as a message containing text and visual content, such as a TV spot. Scholars have argued that visual arguments may gain greater
influence over audiences because they activate a pattern of thinking that may only
be expressed visually (Shelley, 1996).

not reduce the level of incivility; indeed, it has been increasing (Carter, 1998; Geer, 2006; Hart, 1999; Sinopoli, 1995).

Incivility is reflected in negative advertising, push polling (discussed in Chapter 7), and increasingly in some of the media conversations about campaigns (Kamber, 1997; Patterson, 2002). In short, the tenor of the conversations that shape and report contemporary campaigns is now sometimes startlingly mean-spirited. Political exchanges often include comments that would never be considered acceptable in ordinary conversations in schools or workplaces. One of the most dramatic moments in the 2008 presidential campaign, for example, occurred when Elizabeth Edwards, the wife of Democratic candidate Senator John Edwards, called into the television program *Hardball*, on which the conservative columnist and political commentator Ann Coulter was appearing. Mrs. Edwards challenged Ms. Coulter for her personal attacks on her husband. In January 2008, Coulter had called Edwards a "faggot" at a conference attended by conservatives. Edwards called in and asked Coulter to "stop the personal attacks." She also accused Coulter of "defacing the country's political dialogue." Coulter not only refused to apologize, but she escalated her attacks, telling the interviewer on ABC's *Good Morning America* a few days later, "I've learned my lesson. If I'm gonna say anything about John Edwards in the future, I'll just wish he had been killed in a terrorist assassination plot" (Memmott & Lawrence, 2007). Coulter was not the only media personality ready to wish death upon a political enemy. Bill Maher, the host of HBO's controversial political discussion program *Real Time with Bill Maher*, offered similar comments. In a discussion of a suicide bombing outside Bagram Air Base in Afghanistan when Vice President Dick Cheney was inside meeting with base commanders, Maher declared that "more people in the world would live if Vice President Dick Cheney died" (cited in TV host Bill Maher suggests, 2007).

Not all scholars are concerned with the increased level of incivility in politics. Brooks and Geer (2007) argued that it is not negative messages or even incivility in a general sense that seems to upset voters; rather, voters become upset when the incivility is reflected in personal attacks. Even in the case of such personal attacks, however, these authors claimed that their study shows the following:

> [There is] no evidence that even the most despised of candidate messages—negative, uncivil, trait-based messages—are harmful to the democratic engagement of the polity. We see no relationship between message type and political trust or political efficacy. We see no relationship between campaign tone and message recall. And, in fact, we

see some suggestive evidence that those least-liked, least valued kinds of messages may modestly stimulate two things that we tend to care a great deal about improving as a society: political interest and likelihood to vote. (p. 12)

Brooks and Geer (2007, p. 12) further argued that their findings are especially noteworthy because "America is polarizing. Whether we talk about 'red' or 'blue' states or the partisan battles that seem to define the halls of Congress, polarization is part and parcel of contemporary American politics." These scholars optimistically conclude that their research suggests that "the American electorate is quite resilient to the nasty exchanges now prevalent in U.S. political discourse" (p. 12). Of course, one can also very reasonably surmise that the intense polarization and the partisan battles that Brooks and Geer said define contemporary politics in the United States are themselves a product of the negativity and lack of civility in political discourse.

Brooks and Geer (2007) are no doubt correct in their claim that intensely personal and uncivil attacks do drive up interest in campaigns and in political issues for those who may already hold strongly partisan convictions. For example, the Edwards campaign was quick to make use of the Coulter comments on their Web site as a reason for Edwards's supporters to become engaged in the campaign and to give money to help elect their candidate (Memmott & Lawrence, 2007). Perhaps it is just my personal preference (although if so, it seems that the vast majority of Americans would agree with me) or perhaps it is a product of my education as a scholar of human communication—a discipline that has developed around the pursuit of reasoned but respectful discourse— but I remain convinced that such incivility in our political conversations is unacceptable. It demeans us as individuals, diminishes the values of democratic pluralism that have been a source of our national identity, provides terrible lessons for our children about how to conduct themselves when confronted with others who may disagree with them, and is a cancer that will continue to worsen as it comes to be seen as an accepted practice.

CONTEMPORARY POLITICAL PRACTICES MAY RESULT IN FLAWED POLICY MAKING

Another reason that we should be concerned about the ways political campaigns and political discussions are conducted today is that many of these current practices may result in poor public policies. The conduct of contemporary campaigns makes it more difficult for elected officials to govern. One specific example of this is the increased use of public opinion polling. Such polling has made it much easier for campaign strategists to identify clusters of voters with similar opinions and then to design messages that are tailored precisely to the opinions and interests of these clusters. The result is that messages are designed to create voter factions that can be addressed with highly personalized message strategies that are carefully selected after being rigorously tested in focus groups. Such campaign strategies increase the likelihood that voters will see and understand their own needs and those of persons like themselves very clearly, but voters will not be encouraged to think more broadly about the needs or interests of others. The tendency is to appeal to all voters as clusters of special interests, not as citizens united by a set of shared values, mutual interests, or common problems. Appealing to voters as representatives of special interests has resulted in campaign messages that divide voters on ethnic, social, and economic class fault lines.

Candidates today are increasingly encouraged to identify "wedge" issues that separate voters into interest groups and mobilize them to action. Examples of wedge issues that developed during the 2004 campaign and that persisted into the 2006 congressional campaigns include the debate over whether individual states should be permitted to sanction gay marriages, the use of federal funds for embryonic stem cell research, and the so-called right to die or assisted suicide legislation. Historically, abortion rights, gun control, and affirmative action have also proven to be wedge issues that sharply divide voters.

One wedge issue that persistently divided American voters into competing political camps during the 1980s and 1990s was access to public assistance programs, or what we commonly refer to as welfare programs. President Reagan was one of the first national political leaders to discover that welfare reform was a hot-button issue for many voters. As the *Washington Monthly* (The mendacity index, 2003) reported:

> Over a period of about five years, Reagan told the story of the "Chicago welfare queen" who had eighty names, thirty addresses, twelve Social Security cards, and collected benefits for "four non-existing deceased husbands," bilking the government out of "over $150,000." The real welfare recipient to whom Reagan referred was actually convicted for using two different aliases to collect $8,000. Reagan continued to use his version of the story even after the press pointed out the actual facts of the case to him.

Such discourse was highly effective, suggesting as it did that such "welfare queens" were scamming the system and gaining access to benefits that they did not deserve. Reagan further insisted that welfare should be limited to the "truly needy" and that it should not be expected to sustain people over a long period of time but should instead be understood as a social safety net to help people get back on their feet (Rosenbaum, 1981). Republican strategists determined that a significant majority of Americans were extremely frustrated by the current welfare system and eager to see substantial reforms.

Westen (2007) argued that these arguments proved to be effective in activating political beliefs about race differences, with Republicans far more likely to believe that blacks stay on welfare as a matter of choice because they lack the will to work. Democrats, on the other hand, were more likely to believe that people "are poor through no fault of their own" and that "this is a rich country, which could afford to do more to help the poor" (Westen, 2007, p. 230). Democratic candidates and their consultants recognized that a significant percentage of their supporters were inner-city residents, minorities, and the rural poor, groups that were far more likely to be dependent on government assistance. As a result, most Democrats defended the welfare system as it currently existed. The issue drove a sharp wedge into the voting public as candidates and elected officials from both parties sought to appeal to moderates and independents.

The issue dominated political conversations for several years. In 1996, Republican legislators succeeded in passing reform legislation that placed new restrictions on welfare and removed significant numbers of people from the welfare rolls. The bill that they ultimately passed and presented to President Bill Clinton for his signature created a lifetime welfare limit of five years and required that the head of every family receiving welfare find work within two years or risk having the family lose benefits. The bill also required unmarried teenage mothers to live at home and stay in school to receive benefits, and it denied legal immigrants most welfare benefits, food stamps, and access to Medicaid during their first five years in the country (Church, 1996).

Republican strategists sought either to force President Clinton to veto the bill and face the wrath of moderates or sign the bill and anger elements of his core Democratic Party constituency (Broder, 1996). Heeding the advice of his controversial political advisor Dick Morris, Clinton ultimately agreed to sign the reform bill, having been convinced that a veto might severely damage his reelection prospects even though he believed that the bill was badly flawed and would cause genuine harm to many innocent children (Reich, 1997).

Even many of the bill's Republican sponsors acknowledged that there were troublesome provisions of the new welfare law. First, they admitted that it was not fair to deny benefits to legal immigrants. Because these immigrants are not citizens, however, they cannot vote and thus have no significant political power or influence. Second, although the goal of moving welfare recipients into jobs was a worthy one, virtually all studies acknowledged that the number of welfare clients denied benefits within the next two to three years would far outnumber the number of new jobs that might be created. In New York City, for example, 13.1 percent of the population (or 470,000 adults) received welfare benefits. At the current rate of job growth, if every job gained by the local economy were given to a New Yorker currently on welfare, it would take twenty-one years for all 470,000 adults to be absorbed into the economy (Finder, 1996). The problem was worse in other cities where both the percentage of welfare recipients was higher and the rate of job growth was dramatically lower. In Detroit, for example, 26.1 percent of the population was on welfare when the new bill was signed; in Cleveland the figure was 22 percent, in Milwaukee 15.3 percent, in Chicago 14.4 percent, and in Philadelphia 14 percent (Finder, 1996). Former senator Alfonse D'Amato (R—New York) acknowledged that "there will be some hardships and some dislocation; no doubt there will be some who fall through the cracks. We will watch out for the problems, but we should not allow that to prevent us from moving forward" (cited in Finder, p. 10).

An assessment of the impact of the 1996 welfare reform bill undertaken by the Center on Budget Priorities unfortunately confirms that the bill has had a strongly negative impact. The study reports that families forced off the welfare roles have difficulty finding employment, that poverty rates are very high and remain so over time, that these families experience significant hardships, that many such people are disabled or have serious health problems that have limited their employment prospects, and that the number of women and children living in poverty has increased. Even though poverty rates declined during the economic boom years of the late 1990s, the rates today are significantly higher than they were in 1996. The rates of homelessness, hunger, and severe material hardships are all significantly higher for women and children than they were in 1996 (Fremstad, 2004).

Although it is arguable that the welfare system in the United States was in dire need of repair, it is also possible to offer a compelling argument that wedge politics, tracking polls, and hasty election eve decision making did not represent the shrewdest form of policy making. President

Clinton, by signing the bill, kept his campaign pledge from the 1992 election that he would "end welfare as we know it" and sent a clear message that he really was the "new Democrat" that he claimed to be, but he created a wealth of uncertainty for many poor children (Berke, Clinton to sign, 1996; Scheer, 1996). Since the passage of this bill in 1996, the income gap between the wealthiest and poorest of Americans has become larger than ever in our nation's history and has doubled since 1980, when President Reagan assumed office (Johnston, 2007).

Another contemporary issue that demonstrates the difficulty of governing in the current political environment is immigration policy. Immigration has been a controversial political issue in the United States for many years. It is estimated that there may be as many as 12 million illegal immigrants in the United States (Klein, 2007). Public opinion polls suggest that a very large majority of the American people see illegal immigration as a serious problem. For example, a Los Angeles Times/Bloomberg poll taken in June 2007 (Immigration, 2007) posed this question:

"Compared to other problems facing the country, how big a problem is illegal immigration? Would you say it is one of the most important problems facing the country, or is it an important problem but not one of the most important, or is it not all that important, or is it not important at all?"

	One of Most Important %	Important %	Not All That Important %	Not Important at All %	Unsure %
6/7–10/07	31	55	10	3	1
6/24–27/06	32	55	8	5	—

That most Americans viewed illegal immigration as an important issue, however, did not necessarily equate with a willingness to take a hard-line position on immigrants who were already in the United States illegally. A USA Today/Gallup poll conducted April 13–15, 2007, reported support for the idea that illegal immigrants should be provided a path to citizenship. For 42 percent of Americans the preferred approach to dealing with illegal immigrants is to require them to leave the United States but then allow them to return and become U.S. citizens if they meet certain requirements. Another 36 percent would prefer an even more liberal system that allows illegal immigrants to remain in the United

States while they work toward meeting requirements needed to gain citizenship. Only 14 percent of the public would take the position that illegal immigrants should be forced to leave the country with no opportunity to return (Saad, 2007).

A long-running public conversation about illegal immigration and control over U.S. borders emerged in Congress, on the campaign trail, over talk radio, on the Internet, and in coffee shops and living rooms. Citizen activists formed groups such as the Minuteman Project. This group lobbied on behalf of immigration reform and sent volunteers to watch over the borders to try to prevent immigrants from entering the country illegally. In opposition to the proposals to further tighten border security, pro-immigration marches, composed largely of Hispanics but also including many others, took place in major cities across the United States, in some cases drawing huge crowds of peaceful protesters.

Many Americans seemed convinced that the flow of illegal aliens into the United States had taken jobs from American citizens, depressed wages, imposed a burden on schools and hospitals, and even sparked an increase in crime. Others argued that these workers labored in jobs that citizens were no longer willing to do, that they enriched the diversity of our communities, and that they were merely a living testimonial to the American dream, to the vitality of our economy, and to the principles represented by the Statue of Liberty. Organized labor, which most often sided with Democrats on political issues, split on this issue. Some unions, most notably those in the service industries, supported the immigrants; others supported the calls for stricter regulations to improve wages for their members. Many industrial leaders, particularly in high-technology fields, sought an immigration reform bill that would put greater emphasis on individual merit in processing immigration applications so that it would be easier for them to recruit foreign-born engineers and scientists. At the same time, many naturalized American immigrants wanted changes in immigration laws that would make it easier for them to bring their relatives from their home countries to the United States. Clearly, this was an issue wherein people found sources of both agreement and sharp disagreement.

Senators Edward Kennedy (D—Massachusetts) and John McCain (R—Arizona) consulted with the Bush White House in crafting compromise legislation that might respond to the concerns of voters across the political spectrum. The senators proposed a new immigration reform bill that President Bush agreed to support. The bill would continue building a 700-mile fence along the border with Mexico, double the size of the U.S. Border Patrol, and increase enforcement efforts to prevent employers from hiring undocumented workers. The bill also contained provisions to allow undocumented immigrants already in this country to earn legalized status. The proposed bill would allow them to become citizens after about twelve years if they learned English, passed a criminal background check, paid any back taxes they might owe, and paid a $2,000 fine. The bill also contained a provision for a "guest worker" program for immigrants to work in the United States under temporary visas (Klein, 2007).

The Kennedy-McCain bill seemed to be precisely the kind of compromise legislation with the potential to gain support. It responded to the perception that the American people seemed to want meaningful immigration reform to solve a strongly perceived problem, and it did so in a manner that seemed to give advocates on both sides of the immigration debate a bit of something that they could claim as victory. Indeed, public opinion polls suggested that the bill did indeed have strong public support. For example, the Los Angeles Times/Bloomberg poll asked the following questions and reported these results (Immigration, 2007):

"One proposal would allow undocumented immigrants who have been living and working in the United States for a number of years, and who do not have a criminal record, to start on a path to citizenship by registering that they are in the country, paying a fine, getting fingerprinted, and learning English, among other requirements. Do you support or oppose this, or haven't you heard enough about it to say?"

	Support %	Oppose %	Haven't Heard %	Unsure %
6/7–10/07	63	23	12	2
6/24–27/06	67	18	12	3

"One proposal is to create a 'guest worker' program that would give a temporary visa to noncitizens who want to work legally in the United States. Do you support or oppose this, or haven't you heard enough about it to say?"

	Support %	Oppose %	Haven't Heard %	Unsure %
6/7–10/07	49	26	22	3

"One proposal is to establish a point system for new immigrants that gives more weight to professional qualifications and command of English than to those having family already in the United States. Do you support or oppose this, or haven't you heard enough about it to say?"

	Support	Oppose	Haven't Heard	Unsure
	%	%	%	%
6/7–10/07	34	23	38	5

The U.S. Chamber of Commerce, the high-tech industry, Roman Catholic bishops, many Hispanic organizations, farming and agriculture lobbyists, restaurants, hotels, and the construction industry all supported the proposed bill (Pear, 2007). It seemed, from the results of these polls, that the public supported the bill as well. Leading senators from both the Republican and Democratic parties endorsed it, and President Bush lobbied for its passage. Yet the bill failed on the Senate floor. How could this have happened? What prospects do we have for future immigration bills if a bill that enjoyed this level of support could not gain approval? Some analysts argue that the bill was killed due to the efforts of relatively small numbers of citizen activists who were stimulated into action by talk radio, organized through communications on the Internet, and who communicated with legislators via telephone calls, e-mails, and faxes (Pear, 2007). Whether one believes that the passage of this particular immigration reform legislation would have been a wise choice is really not the point. The point is rather that in the current political environment, and using currently available communication technologies, it is very difficult to achieve bipartisan political compromise. Contemporary political conversations are often so polarized that well-organized and vocal political activists may be able to thwart the will of the majority.

DIVISIVE POLITICAL DISCOURSE UNDERMINES ATTEMPTS TO ACHIEVE NATIONAL UNITY

The stability of the American political system depends on the fact that after an election is completed, the people need to have some sense of confidence that the party in power will strive to serve the collective needs of the entire electorate, not just the needs or interests of their partisans. The use of wedge political strategies and negative advertising has the potential to undermine public confidence that their interests will be considered if the party that they did not support is elected. It seems today that ethnic, economic, and social class divisions increasingly determine the political fault lines in the United States. These distinctions are deepened by campaign practices and often by political media. Political advertising may be the worst offender. Diana Mutz argued that television advertising "inflames viewers' emotions and decreases their ability to remember or accept opposing arguments as legitimate" (cited by Broder, 2004).

A review of the outcomes of recent elections reveals evidence of an increasingly polarized electorate. In the 2000 election, exit polls suggested that Vice President Gore captured 90 percent of African American votes, 63 percent of Latino votes, and 55 percent of Asian American votes. No exit poll data on the Native American vote is available, but most have historically voted Democratic. Combined, people of color accounted for almost 30 percent of Gore's total vote, although they were only 19 percent of voters. On the other hand, whites constituted almost 95 percent of Bush's total vote (Wing, 2003). Results in the 2004 presidential elections were similar. Senator Kerry won 88 percent of African American votes, 56 percent of Asian votes, and 53 percent of Latino votes. The Bush campaign made a significant effort to deepen support among Latino voters and did achieve some success (Election results, 2004). In 2000, 62 percent of Hispanic voters chose Gore, and 35 percent chose Bush (Sailer, 2000). In 2004, however, 53 percent of Hispanic voters chose Kerry, and 44 percent voted to reelect President Bush (Murray, 2006).

Income is also a significant predictor of voter choice. In 2004, for example, voting patterns by level of income were as follows (Election results, 2004):

Vote by Income	Bush	Kerry	Nader
Under $15,000 (8%)	36%	63%	0%
$15–30,000 (15%)	42%	57%	0%
$30–50,000 (22%)	49%	50%	0%
$50–75,000 (23%)	56%	43%	0%
$75–100,000 (14%)	55%	45%	0%
$100–150,000 (11%)	57%	42%	1%
$150–200,000 (4%)	58%	42%	*
$200,000 or more (3%)	63%	35%	1%

* Represents a statistically insignificant number of respondents.

In the 2000 and 2004 elections, much was made of the partisan "red" versus "blue" divide. There is increasing evidence that this divide is deepening as more and more Americans find themselves "living in separate enclaves, with distinctive lifestyles, attitudes and partisan leanings shared among neighbors" (Broder, 2004). These divisions are intensified as congressional districts are gerrymandered in a way that creates districts where like-minded voters find their voices either intensified or nullified. Redistricting has produced far fewer competitive congressional districts, which has resulted in increased polarization in the conduct of the House. This congressional polarization has intensified in recent elections. In 1996, there were more than 100 congressional districts that went in different directions (splitting between the parties) in presidential and House elections. In 2000, there were 86 such districts. In 2004, only 59 of 435 congressional districts went in different directions (Balz, 2005).

Many experts argue that a historic strength of the U.S. political system has been the relatively little ideological difference between the major parties, thus encouraging a politics of moderation and incremental policy making (Downs, 1957; Hinich & Munger, 1994). Today, however, as Layman, Carsey, and Horowitz (2006, p. 84) argued, there is evidence that "the two major parties are growing increasingly polarized, with the Republican Party moving in a conservative direction on nearly all major issues of public policy while the Democratic Party stakes out consistently liberal ground." Although these researchers suggest that there might be many reasons for this increased polarization within the parties, they conclude that the emergence of networks of hard-core and highly committed policy activists within the two parties are the most likely explanation for this new extremism (Layman, Carsey, & Horowitz, 2006). Such potential activists are identified with modern polling techniques, appealed to with messages tested in focus groups, and communicated with via TV and direct-mail advertising, as well as new technology Web sites. As the number of such activists has increased, Layman, Carsey, and Horowitz (2006, p. 104) noted, it has "probably increased the incentives for party candidates and elected officials to take ideologically extreme positions on multiple policy agendas, which in turn has pushed the parties' coalitions toward more polarized positions on various issues."

The kind of polarization that we now see in our politics may make it almost impossible for government to act on difficult and fiercely contested issues. In 1996, candidates Bill Clinton and Robert Dole argued about the need to create a bipartisan solution to solve the impending shortfall in revenues to support Social Security and Medicare to meet the growing demands on the system as baby boomers aged and became eligible for these programs. Such revisions have still not happened, and the problem looms larger with each passing year. As already discussed, a majority of the American people wants to see immigration reform, but that, too, has proven too vexing a problem for political compromise to be achieved.

LOBBYISTS AND SPECIAL INTEREST GOVERNANCE

Lobbyists, those who advocate for the interests they represent in the halls of Congress, in state legislatures, and in city halls, have long played an important role in American politics. We discussed the possibly corrupting influence of lobbyists in some detail in Chapter 10. My arguments against the proliferation of special interest politics may make it sound as if I believe lobbying should be eliminated. Even if I did seek such an outcome, which I do not, I am not so naive as to believe it could ever be achieved. It is understandable that farmers, schoolteachers, physicians, computer chip manufacturers, attorneys, food processors, labor unions, gun owners, environmentalists, and a myriad of other individuals and groups have come together to pursue their own political objectives. As an individual citizen, I find myself agreeing with the political goals of some of these lobbying interests and opposing the positions taken by others. The challenge for our democracy, however, is to attempt as much as possible to keep these lobbyists' activities out in the open so that deals are not cut in secret. Doing so means being vigilant to maintain requirements that lobbyists be registered and that their political donations and gifts (including free meals, vacations, invitations to speaking events, sports and concert tickets, use of company airplanes, etc.) be carefully logged and monitored and reasonable ceilings imposed.

One issue that we have not yet discussed, however, but that is also of obvious concern is the "revolving door" between government service and lobbying. Former members of Congress now routinely return to Washington to serve as highly paid lobbyists, prowling the halls of the Capitol, buttonholing their former colleagues, and appealing for the passage of legislation that advances the interests of their clients. Likewise, state legislators who retire their seats or are turned out of office often wind up lobbying in the state capitol buildings. Members of the executive branch of government who used to regulate key industries are actively sought out to serve as lobbyists promoting the interests of firms doing business in the same sectors of the economy. Although there is no reason to believe that in any single case the promise of future employment resulted in favorable votes in the legislative chamber or a willingness to look the other way when serving in the executive branch, there have certainly been cases in which such corruption was proven to have occurred. There have also been many cases reported recently regarding the family members of elected officials who are engaged as lobbyists. A study by Public Citizen's Congress Watch, which advocates for consumer rights in Congress, found at least thirty-two examples of congressional family members who lobby Congress (cited by Kranish, 2006). One can easily imagine that the spouses or sons and daughters of congressional colleagues can enjoy unique and special attention in the corridors of Congress.

Members of Congress have a natural interest in bringing home "pork" to their districts. It is understandable that the voters in a district will judge their senator or representative on how effective he or she may have been in winning federal funds for transportation projects, hospitals, research programs, military bases, and other projects that will benefit the folks back home. Today, however, there is an increasing tendency for members of Congress to hide the pork in the form of "earmarks"—pet projects that legislators sneak into spending bills in closed-door sessions. The number of such earmarks has increased dramatically in recent years. The 2006 transportation bill included more than 6,300 projects valued at more than $24 billion. As Kirkpatrick (2007, p. 1) observed, "Earmarks have proven ripe for cronyism, corruption, and abuse." Indeed, in today's environment, legislators will pursue pork even when it does not benefit their home district. The most flagrant recent example was that of Alaska Republican representative Don Young, who introduced a $10 million earmark to build a road to link a Florida country club to Interstate 75 via a new freeway entrance. This earmark resulted after a Florida real estate developer who owned more than one thousand acres adjacent to the country club—acres that were certain to increase in value with the construction of the new road—helped raise $40,000 for Young at an event held in a Florida hotel. The lobbyist who helped coordinate the event declared, "We evidently made a very good impression on Congressman Young; we got $81 million to expand Interstate 75 and $10 million for the Coconut Road interchange" (cited by Kirkpatrick, 2007, p. 1). It is worth noting that the Republican congressman whose district would receive the funds for the new road did not seek the funds, and the local planning commission twice voted not to use the money. The commission reversed itself only after Representative Young wrote a letter warning that the refusal to expend the money might threaten the county's access to future federal dollars (Kirkpatrick, 2007). Later, when a reporter sought to question Young about the inclusion of the earmark in the transportation bill, "Mr. Young responded with an obscene gesture" (Kirkpatrick, 2007, p. 29).

In refusing to explain or offer a defense for the earmark, Representative Young was also "flipping off" the American people and essentially suggesting that the $40,000 to enrich his campaign fund entitled him to $10 million of their taxes. Although this is only one case, and a pretty flagrant and extreme case at that, it does illustrate how the legislative process can be corrupted by such cozy relationships between lobbyists and elected officials and how the confidence of citizens in the integrity of their political process can be destroyed.

THE POLITICS OF CHARACTER AND THE SEARCH FOR SCANDAL

Despite my previous arguments about the importance of maintaining vigilance regarding the potential for corruption and scandal, it might surprise readers to learn that I believe our political campaigns have become *too* focused on the politics of personal character. Political advertisements today increasingly raise questions regarding the character of the opposing candidate. Likewise, the media seem especially concerned about the need to uncover scandals and unlawful behavior by political candidates and elected officials. The persistent focus on scandal and misconduct has served to increase public cynicism about politics and politicians. This is, of course, not an entirely new phenomenon. Throughout U.S. history, when elected officials have disappointed the public or failed to live up to their high expectations, there have been charges of corruption. Certainly, there have been cases in which the charges were very well founded. The presidencies of Ulysses S. Grant, Warren G. Harding, and Richard M. Nixon are probably best remembered for the taint of corruption that surrounded them. Both Grant and Nixon had impeachment proceedings initiated against them, and Harding might have been similarly charged had he not died in office before the process was formally under way. In addition to these most notorious cases, there have been charges of corruption leveled at many other presidents. John Adams and John Quincy Adams, who may have been among the most incorruptible men in U.S. political history, were both harried throughout their administrations by claims that they abused the power of their office. Rutherford B. Hayes, himself a paragon of propriety, was called "His Fraudulency" for having allegedly "stolen" the 1876 election from Samuel J. Tilden. Harry S Truman, who is today something of a folk hero owing to his plain-speaking candor and character, was buffeted by charges of cronyism and labeled "the Senator from Pendergast" because of his connections to Kansas City's political boss, Thomas J. Pendergast (Brinkley, 1997). Lyndon B. Johnson was sullied by claims that he had accepted money in return for political favors, and investigations into the financial dealings of several of his key advisors made frequent headlines in the press. Jimmy Carter endured Bert Lance's banking woes and the investigations into his brother Billy's lobbying on behalf of Libya. Both the Reagan administration and the George H. W. Bush administration were the subjects of extensive investigations into whether they approved illegal arms sales to Iran and then diverted the proceeds to the Nicaraguan Contras to support their attempt to overthrow the left-wing Sandinista regime, a scheme that also violated the law.

The politics of personal attack and the search for scandal seemed to reach their full fervor during the Clinton years. Clinton became only the second president in U.S. history to face an impeachment proceeding in the U.S. Senate. Four independent counsel investigations were undertaken during Clinton's first term, not to mention a myriad of congressional and FBI probes into alleged wrongdoing by the president, First Lady, vice president, cabinet officials, Democratic Party fund-raisers, and Clinton friends and cronies. The sheer number and variety of ethical imbroglios surrounding the Clintons was mind-boggling. Even though Clinton was not convicted by the Senate and forced from office for his web of lies regarding his inappropriate relationship with White House intern Monica Lewinsky, the episode left a strongly bitter residue in the minds of the president's supporters and enemies alike.

The politics of character and character assassination have come to dominate the U.S. political scene. The search for scandal has almost become institutionalized as a political weapon. There seems to be a preoccupation with uncovering corruption today that is far more intense than at any period in our nation's past. In earlier eras charges were made, investigations were conducted, and for the most part the work of government went on with the candidates or elected officials allowed after a time to clear their names and continue to serve in office. Today, however, the search for scandal, the investigations into alleged scandals, and the self-righteous declarations of moral outrage have become regular features of public life. Congressional investigations into administration misdeeds, once considered a rarity, are now the norm. During the Clinton years, the use of special investigators and prosecutors became so commonplace that it seemed a misnomer to call them "special." Although the number of special prosecutors appointed to investigate wrongdoing during the Bush administration was smaller, one was appointed to investigate White House leaks to the media during what became known as the "Valerie Plame" affair. U.S. Attorney Patrick Fitzgerald investigated whether members of the administration violated the law and leaked the name of Ms. Plame, an undercover CIA officer, in an attempt to undermine the credibility of her husband, who had written a report critical of the Bush administration's policies in Iraq. That investigation eventually resulted in the conviction of Lewis "Scooter" Libby, the chief aide to Vice President Dick Cheney, on four counts of perjury for lying to the FBI and to a grand jury (Lewis, 2007). In addition, both Democrats and Republicans in Congress supported calls for the appointment of a special prosecutor to investigate whether Bush's attorney general, Alberto Gonzales, had perjured himself in testimony before Congress (Schmitt, 2007). As mentioned earlier, Gonzales eventually resigned his office under a cloud.

Toobin (1999, p. 7) argued that the increasing use of special prosecutors has become a political rather than a legal tactic. He further observed, "The legal system's takeover of the political system steered a great deal of partisan conflict from legislatures to courtrooms." In the process, the legal system has become infused with the intense partisanship of electoral politics. Brinkley (1997) said the following:

> It makes no difference any longer whether times are bad or good, whether the public is aroused or uninterested, whether the evidence of corruption is strong or weak. The political scandal machine grinds on inexorably, impervious to the world around it. Accusations of scandal, once raised, seem never to go away. Instead, they make their circuitous way through an endless series of hearings in investigations that seldom bring anything to resolution. (p. M1)

In the post-Watergate era the media seem especially preoccupied with ferreting out scandals great and small, and no doubt media interest in candidates' character and ethics has inspired politicians to make charges and countercharges of ethical wrongdoing. The lessons of Watergate apparently suggested to reporters that politicians were willing to lie to the American people to cover up their mistakes or ethical lapses. Unfortunately, there have been a sufficient number of presidential lies—

about everything from sexual indiscretions to weapons of mass destruction—seemingly to justify such skeptical media coverage. There seems to be a perception that today's candidates are less honest than those who came before. For example, Carl Cannon (2007) argued that presidents from Washington onward have always lied, although he says George W. Bush's lies were more flagrant and more dangerous, because they took the nation to war, and thus merit closer media scrutiny.

Once the smell of scandal is in the air, it is difficult for the media not to become almost completely absorbed by it, especially when the scandal involves gossipy tales of sleazy "sexcapades" in the Oval Office, as it did during the Clinton administration. Despite the fact that the public claimed to be disgusted with the media fixation on the Clinton-Lewinsky scandal, media moguls have long known that sex sells. The astounding Nielsen ratings for Barbara Walters's interview of Monica Lewinsky in March 1999 provided strong evidence of the public's fascination with the characters in this sordid drama. More than 70 million Americans tuned in for at least part of the two-hour interview, making it the most watched news program ever broadcast by a single network. In fact, that 20/20 episode was the second most watched program of the year, after the Super Bowl (Monica makes history, 1999).

The confluence of forces in the Clinton-Lewinsky scandal was staggering. The scandal featured a capable president with many admirable talents who was supported by a solid majority of the American people. Yet he also possessed a seemingly obsessive desire to pursue women—a libido so out of control that he would risk his presidency, his reputation, and his marriage on a foolish dalliance with a young intern, even when he was already being sued by another woman for sexual harassment.* Added into this mix of character flaws were a knee-jerk impulse to deny and deceive when cornered and a willingness to discredit all those around him, including his wife and closest advisors, by also deceiving them and forcing them unwittingly to tell lies on his behalf (Pathway to peril, 1999).

The events in the drama were related to the public by the media's storytellers, who have become increasingly motivated by the need to gain the attention of an audience that is not interested in substantive political issues but accustomed to being titillated by stories about sex. Mainstream newspapers, network news programs, print tabloids, and

---

* Clinton was being sued by Paula Jones, a low-level administrative staff employee of the State of Arkansas, who alleged that Clinton had exposed himself to her in a Little Rock hotel room while he was serving as that state's governor in 1991 (Baker, 1998).

gossipy entertainment programs such as *Inside Edition* all compete for audiences, and sex attracts audiences in every medium. These scribes and broadcasters have come to distrust all politicians and to presume that they all tell lies. They have also discovered that scandal stories, especially sex scandals, gain public attention. Thus, they have taken a strong interest in uncovering sensational news stories—ideally stories about sex, marital difficulties, drug use, and the like—about the private lives of all celebrities, including politicians.

Also playing a very active role in this drama were the many political partisans who despised and distrusted President Clinton and also intensely disliked his wife, now Senator Hillary Clinton (D—New York) because of her strongly feminist views. To these enemies, the Clintons were the products of the permissive counterculture era of the 1960s. The personal attacks and distrust of President Clinton had been fueled by decades of negative political advertising, the ranting of conservative media gurus such as Rush Limbaugh, and Web sites that have alleged conspiracies even more insidious than previously thought imaginable. Some Clinton haters went so far as to claim that Clinton had murdered his political enemies. The fixation, for example, on the suicide of former Clinton aide Vince Foster, and the claim that the Clintons either had Foster murdered or at the very least actively sought to cover up the reasons for his death, persisted for months even though the Park Service police, the Washington, DC, police, the Federal Bureau of Investigation, and the U.S. Justice Department all dismissed these claims as preposterous (Weiss, 1997). So persistent were the rumors of conspiracy, however, that even Republican members of Congress continued to make such charges. For example, Representative Dan Burton (R—Indiana) claimed that Hillary Clinton's attempts to cover up the billing records of the Rose law firm, where she and Foster had been partners, may have been in some way responsible for either Foster's death or a cover-up of the real story behind that death. Eventually, special prosecutor Kenneth Starr was persuaded to investigate the claims of White House involvement in Foster's death. Starr ultimately ruled the death a suicide and admitted that he could find no reason to allege a White House cover-up (Starr says, 1998).

Late-night comedians went wild working the Clinton-Lewinsky relationship into their nightly TV routines. Internet joke lists related in unambiguous terms the public's fascination with the White House tryst. Conservatives—both in Congress and on talk radio—called for Clinton's impeachment. His character became a fundamental issue of contention in much of the conservative rhetoric that Republicans used to whip up enthusiasm for their party in the 1998 midterm elections. In August 1998, President Clinton, after appearing before the grand jury, acknowledged his "inappropriate intimate contact" with Lewinsky but continued to deny that he had committed perjury. On September 9, 1998, Starr delivered to the House Judiciary Committee thirty-six boxes of evidence supporting a report in which he laid out eleven possible grounds for impeachment. The evidence described in graphic detail the president's encounters with Lewinsky, including their use of props. Starr's disclosure increased the clamor among congressional Republicans, both in chambers and in public statements, for the initiation of an impeachment inquiry. Despite the public's obvious appetite for news stories, interviews, and jokes about the sex scandal, it seemed to have no enthusiasm for impeachment. This was demonstrated when the Democrats actually gained five House seats in the 1998 elections, and exit polls showed that nearly two-thirds of voters did not want Clinton impeached (Pathway to peril, 1999).

Public opposition to impeachment notwithstanding, conservatives in the House decided to press on. Several factors likely accounted for their persistence. First, many ideological conservatives, especially those who represent the religious right, were indeed morally outraged by the president's behavior, and they strongly and genuinely believed that he was unfit for office. They also discussed how he had avoided the draft, experimented with drugs, and now been proven to have cheated on his wife. Certainly, such a man did not have the moral authority to serve as president. They also believed that the American people would ultimately share this view once they learned all the sordid details of the affair and of the clumsy attempts to cover it up. Many conservatives did not sense any ambiguity in this episode. They felt that what the president had done was a "mortal sin" and there could be no redemption without the acceptance of his penalty. He could not merely expect forgiveness; he had to admit his guilt and leave office. The Congress, many Republicans argued, had a responsibility to act morally and to press this case, even if the public did not support their efforts (Alvarez, 1999).

Moral outrage was without question a factor in the conservatives' decision to pursue the case. A second explanation, however, might be found in the "game" of politics. With all due respect to the strong sense of moral principle that no doubt shapes the actions of most members of the U.S. Congress, political considerations do influence many of their decisions. So why did these conservative members of the House of Representatives pursue Clinton's impeachment when a majority of the public, at least according to the polls, opposed it? The answer has to do with the nature and structure of the House of Representatives. Most members of Congress are elected in "safe" seats. When congressional districts are created or adjusted every decade following the national census, much gerrymandering occurs. It is in the interest of both parties to ensure that most districts are created in such a way as to be securely Democratic or securely Republican. Doing so guarantees a certain orderliness and stability to political life. Thus, most congressional representatives need only be concerned with the political sentiments of voters in their own districts and not with public sentiments at large, but they must please the voters in their districts, particularly those within their own party. A large plurality of Republicans favored the impeachment and removal of the president, but an equal number of independents, and an even larger plurality of Democrats, opposed it (Brownstein, 1998). Overall, in September 1998 only 18 percent of Americans questioned in one poll wanted the president impeached, 7 percent reported that they did not know, 41 percent wanted the matter dropped, and 34 percent wanted a motion of censure. Yet, the key factor for the incumbent Republican congressional representatives was that in this poll nearly 60 percent of Republicans who declared themselves likely to vote in the midterm elections favored impeachment (Brownstein, 1998). Because it is Republican partisans who keep these members of Congress in their safe seats in power, because the Republicans controlled the House Judiciary Committee and the floor of the House of Representatives, and because it takes only a simple majority to pass articles of impeachment, the impeachment process became a juggernaut that could not be stopped. Republican members of the House of Representatives were especially concerned that if they did not vote to impeach the president, they would risk opposition within their own party when they ran for reelection.

A third likely explanation as to why the Republicans persisted in the drive to impeach the president, even in the face of significant public opposition, can probably be traced to the fact that contemporary politicians have been schooled in a system in which politics is viewed as blood sport, and the pursuit of scandal is a natural and opportunistic political strategy. For example, Dick Armey, Republican House majority leader from 1995 to 2003, declared in a C-SPAN interview (cited in Richter, 1996, p. A9), "Politics is a mean business, and the Democratic Party is a very mean party. And our guys have to respond. . . . I'd like to live in a world where you didn't have all these politics. But I tell you, politics is a mean business."

Although it takes only a majority in the House of Representatives to impeach a president, it takes a two-thirds vote in the Senate to convict and remove a president from office. Given that Republicans outnumbered Democrats in the Senate by only 55 to 45, it was certain that they would need support from at least 12 Democrats to convict Clinton. Senators, unlike representatives, cannot be gerrymandered into "safe" seats. Even though there are some states that are "safe" for either Republicans or Democrats, it is far more likely that senators need to acquire the art of compromise and consensus to remain in power. Even though senators are elected to six-year terms and can hope that between elections the public will forget the votes that displeased them, senators cannot ignore the public will. No Democrat was willing to cross over and vote for impeachment; in fact, the Republicans lost five senators on the obstruction of justice charge (50–50) and ten on the perjury charge (55–45). Thus, both articles of impeachment failed, falling well short of the 67 votes needed for passage (Serrano & Lacey, 1999).

The American public was left feeling glad that the impeachment trial was over, but not that it had happened. A large majority expressed their disgust that the country's leaders had been distracted from issues of genuine significance by what amounted to a mere melodrama about immorality (Mehren, 1999).

Some members of Congress tried to reassure the public that some good had come out of this episode and that its outcome was evidence that the system worked. Henry Hyde, the Illinois Republican who had led the impeachment effort in the House, declared, for example, that "all Americans can take great comfort in knowing that by remaining faithful to this constitutional process, the Congress has strengthened, not weakened, the ties that bind our nation together" (Voices, 1999, p. A18). Trent Lott of Mississippi, who was then Senate majority leader, echoed this assessment and declared that Congress had merely "done its constitutional duty" (Voices, 1999, p. A19). Senator Larry Craig (R—Idaho) went even further and claimed that Republicans "can be proud of what we did" (Mehren, 1999, p. 19).* But even as the Republican leadership sought to claim that some good had come out of this dreary slugfest, the American public was left feeling more cynical and skep-

---

* Senator Craig (R—Idaho) found himself embroiled in his own sexual scandal during the summer of 2007. Craig was arrested and pled guilty to disorderly conduct for soliciting sex from an undercover police officer in a men's room at the Minneapolis–St. Paul airport. The story received relentless coverage in the media. Under intense pressure from his Republican colleagues in the Senate, Craig resigned his seat. He then had second thoughts and attempted to withdraw his guilty plea in an attempt to clear his name and salvage his career (Phillips, 2007). The court denied his petition to withdraw his guilty plea. Craig then decided not to resign from the Senate but did announce that he would not seek reelection.

tical than ever before about the mindless partisanship that characterized contemporary politics (Preston & Berger, 1999).

Although the Republicans tried to convince the public that the impeachment process was really a judicial and constitutional process, the
outcome of the impeachment effort starkly revealed that whatever the
legal issues at play are, impeachment is first and foremost a political
process, and no impeachment can succeed without bipartisan support.
It is noteworthy that in the wake of the Scooter Libby conviction, and
after Libby's sentence to a federal penitentiary was commuted by
President Bush, several Democratic House members called for impeachment proceedings to be undertaken against President Bush and Vice
President Cheney (Jackson: Bush actions, 2007). The Democratic leadership seems to have learned from the Clinton impeachment proceedings,
however, and they seem to understand that even though impeachment
hearings might mobilize the most partisan base within the Democratic
Party, they do not have the votes in the Senate to gain convictions.
Thus, these calls for impeachment have not been pursued.

THE LEGACY OF THE POLITICS OF SCANDAL

It is arguable that the relentless pursuit of scandals in the corridors of
power has been going on for so long that it may exhaust the public's interest, attention, and concern. In recent years, the public learned about so
many scandals involving politicians that it is difficult to distinguish
between the various charges and countercharges. It is much easier to conclude simply that all politicians are somehow corrupt. Such public perceptions would be a natural result of a political system in which ethical
investigations, charges, and countercharges have become so common that
all politicians and the political process itself have lost credibility. Congressional investigations have come and gone, with the partisans in each
party lining up to attack opponents and protect their own. Liberals defended Bill Clinton yet viciously attack George Bush. Conservatives
defend Bush but demonized Clinton. It is not surprising that the American
people, many of whom are increasingly disconnected from political news,
have a difficult time caring about alleged ethical improprieties or figuring
out the differences between major ethical lapses and minor or incidental
ones.

Some conservatives complained that the public did not support the
impeachment of President Clinton because ethics just do not matter as
much today as they used to or because the economy was so strong that

people were willing to overlook a certain amount of wrongdoing (see Abramson, 1997; Wines, 1996). But in an era in which political candidates routinely bash each other's honesty, integrity, and motivation in paid political advertisements, and the media relentlessly hound the candidates, probing deeply into their personal lives to gain information about their sexual histories, financial dealings, use of illegal drugs, tax records, medical records, and whether they ever hired an illegal alien to care for their children or mow their lawn, it should not surprise us that the public believes all politicians are unethical, self-interested sleazebags. Obviously, if that is the way the system works, the reasonable choices are either to withdraw from the process and not vote or ignore the alleged wrongdoing and vote for the sleazebag most likely to protect one's own interests.

The culture of scandal has not only made the public more cynical about politicians, but it has also made politicians more cynical about the public. As Brinkley (1997) argued:

> Aware of the suspicion with which the public views them and the speed with which any unpopular decision is likely to be linked to corruption, they become morbidly sensitive to swings in public opinion. Fearful that voters will not believe anything they say, they tailor their rhetoric to what they believe are the prevailing views—whether or not those views accord with reality. Nothing is more central to the anti-government ethos of our time than the widespread belief that politicians seldom tell the truth. (p. M6)

Although my argument is not that we should ignore corruption—which can clearly devastate confidence in any governmental system and that has been a factor in the fall of many governments—a preoccupation with political scandal and corruption can also be dangerous to the well-being of democratic rule. Dismantling this culture of scandal—which politicians in both parties have enthusiastically helped create and that the media seem to relish as an alternative to reporting other types of news that may require serious study and evaluation of complex policy alternatives yet lead to less dramatic news coverage—will be very difficult. This may be, however, one of the most important political challenges of our era (Brinkley, 1997).

Political candidates today, especially those seeking the presidency, must be prepared for the media spotlight to shine into their private lives. The media investigations into Clinton's sexual relationships led in the midst of this scandal to a series of other public stories about the extramarital affairs of many key players in the controversy, including Chairman of the House Judiciary Committee Henry Hyde (R—Illinois), Speaker

of the House Bob Livingston (R—Louisiana), and vocal Clinton antag-
onists Bob Barr (R—Georgia), Dan Burton (R—Indiana), and Helen
Chenowith (R—Idaho). Livingston resigned from Congress when it
became clear that his own past would become an issue in the impeachment debate (Pathway to peril, 1999). More recently, the public was
titillated by the news that conservative and pro–family values senator
David Vitter (R—Louisiana) had used the service of female escorts
provided by the notorious "D.C. Madam," who was herself facing pros-
ecution for running a prostitution ring (Murray, 2007). Although such
news stories appeal to our prurient interests and may even have some
probative value in helping the public ferret out hypocrisy and make
more accurate evaluations of candidates' characters, there is reason to
be concerned that strong candidates will choose not to enter politics
out of a sense of fear that their personal lives will become the subject
of scrutiny by the press and the public.

CONCLUSION

When the French philosopher and social critic Alexis de Tocqueville
visited the United States in the 1840s, he marveled at the success of
American democracy and at the institutions the young nation had created to sustain public political participation. In searching for the secrets
to the formation of successful democratic institutions in the United States
that might be exported to France, he noted that democracy required the
creation of laws, to be sure, but that laws alone would not be sufficient
to protect the rights of the citizenry and to prevent the emergence of ruling despots. In addition to laws, he said, the citizens of a democracy must
develop those customs of political participation that would allow people
to remain free. Specifically, he argued (Tocqueville, trans. 1945, p. 341),
"It is difficult to make people participate in the government, but it is still
more difficult to supply them with experience and to inspire them with
the feelings which they need in order to govern well."

If Tocqueville visited our shores today, it is doubtful that he would
be as impressed with our democracy as he was 160 years ago. We seem
no longer to celebrate those customs of electoral politics, or what
Bellah and his colleagues called those "habits of the heart" (Bellah et al.,
1985), that make effective democracy possible. We need to reinvent campaign politics in the United States to more effectively encourage citizens to participate in our democracy and restore public confidence in our
nation's political leadership and political institutions.

CHAPTER 12

The Crisis in American Democracy

In the first chapter of this book, I argued that political participation is one important measure of the health and vitality of a democracy and that voting is the purest and simplest measure of political participation. If that is the case, then the American democracy is in critical condition. In this chapter I describe the nature and extent of the problem, identify some of the causes, and finally, suggest some corrective actions that might reinvigorate our political system.

Voter turnout has long been a problem in the United States. The lowest turnout in presidential contests occurred in 1920 and 1924, when 44 percent of eligible voters went to the polls. Frustration over the Great Depression must have sparked public attention and interest in politics, for in 1932 the turnout rate climbed to 52 percent. Turnout then continued to increase for several years, peaking at 64 percent in 1964 and averaging 62 percent from 1952 through 1968 (Nardulli, Dalager, & Greco, 1996). Then voter turnout began to fall once again, dropping down to 49.1 percent in 1996. Although some have been encouraged by the fact that turnout was up in 2000, when 51.3 percent of eligible voters went to the polls, and in 2004, when 55.3 percent voted, these numbers are still well below those in other democracies (National voter turnout, 2007). In a study of voter participation in national elections held since 1945, the United States ranked 139th out of 172 nations, with an average turnout rate of 48.3 percent of eligible voters. In contrast, the average turnout in Western Europe was 77 percent, a significantly higher percentage than the United States has ever achieved. This study also indicated that the United States ranked behind every nation in Europe and most of the democratic nations in Asia. Even Latin America, which has experienced a long history of political instability, failed democracies, and military coups, has averaged a turnout rate of 53 percent in elections held since 1945 (Turnout in the world, 2007).

Turnout in presidential elections is low, but the rate is even worse for midterm elections. The lowest turnout in recent years was in 1998, when only 36.4 percent voted (National voter turnout, 2007). The turn-out in the most recent 2006 midterm elections was 41.4 percent (America goes to the polls, 2006). Voter turnout, especially in midterm elections, varies greatly from state to state. For example, in the 2006 midterm elections, the highest voter turnout was in Minnesota (60 percent), and the lowest voter turnout was in Louisiana (28 percent). It is perhaps likely that the turnout in Louisiana and Mississippi (30 percent turnout) was depressed by the disruption caused by Hurricane Katrina, which dis-placed many residents. The numbers in Texas (31 percent), District of Columbia (32 percent), and North Carolina and West Virginia (33 per-cent), however, suggest that the problem of low voter turnout is all too common in many other states (America goes to the polls, 2006).

Perhaps even more alarming is the small fraction of eligible voters who cast ballots in primary elections. For example, during the 2006 midterm elections—which selected Senate and House candidates as well as gubernatorial candidates in many states—turnout did not reach as high as 40 percent in any state. In most states, primary participation was in the 20 to 30 percent range. In Virginia, fewer than 4 percent of more than 4.5 million eligible voters turned out to select Senate nomi-nee Jim Webb in a race that had drawn significant national attention. Webb went on to defeat the Republican incumbent, Senator George Allen, in the general election in the fall (Kiely, 2006).

Turnout has historically been higher among well-educated citizens, but in recent elections it has declined across all levels of education. Although voter turnout is skewed in favor of better-educated citizens in all democracies, the gap seems to be especially wide in the United States. Census data going back to 1966 indicate that those with a high school diploma or less are 20 percent less likely to cast ballots than are college graduates, and this participation gap has continued to widen in the last thirty years (America goes to the polls, 2006). In the most recent midterm election, for example, 52 percent of eligible voters with a col-lege degree voted versus only 27 percent of eligible voters without a college degree, a turnout gap of 25 points (America goes to the polls, 2006).

Age is another key factor in predicting turnout. In the 2000 presi-dential election, 36 percent of 18- to 24-year-olds voted. This rate in-creased sharply to 47 percent in the 2004 election, giving many a reason to celebrate (Cook, 2007). It is estimated that some 2 million more young people turned out to vote in 2004 than had voted in 2000. Nonetheless, the rate of youth participation still trailed the rate of participation by persons age 25 and over by almost 19 percentage points (Shape the future, 2007). There may be some additional reason for optimism, however, in the fact that the number of young voters also increased in the 2006 midterm elections, when the youth share of the electorate went from 10 percent in 2002 to 12 percent, the largest gain for any age group (America goes to the polls, 2007). Level of education is an even more significant factor in youth voting than it is for older U.S. citizens. For example, in recent elections voter turnout among 18- to 24-year-olds with a bachelor's degree was approximately 70 percent, while voter turnout among those with less than a high school diploma was 20 percent, a 50-percentage-point gap (Civic youth, 2007). Given that nearly one in three high school students in the class of 2006 failed to graduate, it is difficult to be too optimistic about the prospects for a sharp increase in the number of young voters (Chaddock, 2006).

The low youth voter turnout will also be difficult to change because the percentage of young people in the United States who represent ethnic and racial minorities is increasing. Studies predict that by the year 2050, 50 percent of Americans will be members of minority groups and Hispanics and Asians will represent 61 percent of the growth in the U.S. population (Youth demographic trends, 2007). Unfortunately, members of minority groups in the United States, and especially Asians and Hispanics, have been far less likely to cast ballots. For example, in 2004, turnout rates for non-Hispanic whites were 67 percent, for African Americans 60 percent, for Asian Americans 44 percent, and for Hispanics (of any race) 47 percent. The voting participation from 2000 to 2004 increased by 5 percent for whites and by 3 percent for African Americans but did not change for either Asian or Hispanic citizens (U.S. voter turnout up, 2005).

Level of income also affects voter turnout in the United States. In 2004, for example, persons living in households earning less than $50,000 per year were 21 percent less likely to vote than those living in households earning $75,000 per year and over (America goes to the polls, 2007). These differences in who turns out to vote—in age, education, and race—are not insignificant. This skewing in voter participation has an impact on the nomination and election of candidates, the issues they see as important, the interests they serve, and the policies they enact.

Some noteworthy bright spots in terms of political participation, however, can be found. It does appear that if people become convinced that their interests and their lives are genuinely at stake in the political realm, they can be motivated to vote. For example, in 2004 the gay rights and gay marriage ballot initiatives under consideration in many states clearly mobilized gay voters. A recent study found that 92.5 percent of gay men voted in the 2004 presidential election and that almost 84 percent cast ballots in the 2006 midterm elections. The rate of participation for lesbians was almost as impressive as nearly 91 percent voted in 2004 and 78 percent cast ballots in 2006 (Frederick & Malcolm, 2007).

Although gay citizens may have become increasingly engaged in politics, the fact is that people generally, and especially young people, are not only failing to vote but in many cases are paying virtually no attention to political issues and have become discouraged about their government. Longo and Meyer (2006) wrote, "Among the greatest dangers for American democracy is that politics is becoming a spectator sport, an activity that relegates citizens to the sidelines. Perhaps nowhere is this crisis more dramatic than with our youngest generation." It is arguable that as pessimistic as it may seem, even the claim that citizens have become political spectators is an overstatement. As discussed in Chapter 5, fewer and fewer Americans may be paying any significant attention to politics. Newspaper readership is down, the audience for nightly TV newscasts is down, and although more people may be accessing some political news online, most seem not to be spending enough time on Internet sites to be able to consider themselves well informed about political candidates or issues.

It thus seems that fewer people are taking part in any form of election or political activity—reading newspapers, watching political debates, volunteering on campaigns, attending campaign events, or voting. As Thomas Patterson (2002) wrote:

> Few today pay even token tribute to presidential elections. In 1974, Congress established a fund to underwrite candidates' campaigns, financed by a check-off box on personal income tax returns that allowed citizens to assign $1 (later raised to $3) of their tax liability to the fund. Initially, one in three taxpayers checked the box. By the late 1980s, only one in five marked it. Now, only one in eight does so. (pp. 4–5)

POLITICAL CYNICISM IS COMMON

Recent studies suggest that the American people have become both extremely cynical about and estranged from their government. About a third (34 percent) agree with the statement "most elected officials care what people like me think," representing a ten-point drop since 2002 (Trends in political values, 2007). Some might argue that such negative political sentiments might be attributed, at least in part, to the fact that President George W. Bush had become increasingly unpopular as public opposition to the war in Iraq grew. For example, a New York Times/ CBS News poll in September 2007 found that only 30 percent of Americans surveyed approved of the president's job performance, 64 percent disapproved, and only 6 percent were unsure (President Bush—overall job rating, 2007). One might reasonably expect that the public unhappiness about the current occupant of the White House would affect attitudes about politics generally. It is noteworthy, however, that the Congress, which was controlled by the Democrats, was even more unpopular than the president.*

Polls taken during the summer of 2007 suggested that the U.S. Congress had an anemic job approval rating of about 25 percent (Holland, 2007). Perhaps these results should not be surprising, as another poll conducted in 2007 found that "most Americans believe that most Members of Congress will sell their vote for cash or a campaign contribution. Only 16 percent believe the legislators' votes are not for sale. By a nearly 5-to-1 margin, voters believe that Members of Congress are more interested in their own careers and agenda rather than the public good" (Why the Senate immigration bill failed, 2007). If Americans feel so strongly that Congress is filled with people who do not care about them and who would sell their votes in return for a campaign contribution, why do they not turn out to vote in greater numbers if only to throw the rascals out of office?

There seems to be a paradox here. Although the Congress narrowly changed from Republican to Democratic control in 2006, no great or dramatic shift occurred. Despite the public's expressed unhappiness with the job performance and the integrity of the Congress, incumbents still gain reelection. Indeed, over the past two decades incumbents have been reelected an astounding 95 percent of the time (Filling Rahm's shoes, 2007; A certain uncertainty, 2005). These results may suggest that although voters may be unhappy with the Congress as an institution, they may not necessarily be displeased with their own senator or representative (we discussed the benefits accrued by incum-

---

* The lack of public support for Congress was probably also influenced by the fact that even though the Democrats controlled both the Senate and the House, they lacked the sixty votes in the Senate necessary to end a Republican filibuster. As a result, the Republicans were able to defeat all Democrat-sponsored bills to curtail war spending or to set a specific deadline to bring the troops home from Iraq. It was strong public opposition to the war in Iraq that had allowed the Democrats to win control of Congress in the 2006 midterm elections.

bents in Chapter 10—fund-raising advantages and gerrymandered districts both come to mind). Another explanation may be that voters simply feel powerless and unconvinced that their vote matters because politics has become a cesspool (for example, see Political party poop, 2007; York, 2001).

Political psychologist Drew Westen (2007, pp. 35–36) argued that "in politics, when reason and emotion collide, emotion invariably wins. Although the marketplace of ideas is a great place to shop for policies, the marketplace that matters most in American politics is the marketplace of emotions." At the moment, the emotions that seem to be shaping Americans' view of politics and politicians are not conducive to increased levels of political participation. If there is to be an increase in public participation and enthusiasm about politics, we must change the negatively charged emotions that currently dominate political discussions.

THE CAUSES OF POLITICAL CYNICISM

In earlier chapters in this book, we described in some detail how political campaigns have evolved in the United States, how they have been covered in the media, and how they affect the ability of elected officials to effectively govern. As the preceding section suggests, the American people at the moment seem to be largely disconnected and disinterested in politics. Several factors have likely influenced the American public's increased cynicism and withdrawal from political activity. Although any single factor might not have been sufficient to create these current conditions, the cumulative effect has been significant and detrimental to the health of our democracy.

First, political campaigns and public discourse about politics have become more polarized and less civil. This book has argued that such negativity has actively discouraged political participation and confidence in governmental institutions. Why should voters believe that their government is working when during one electoral campaign after another they are barraged with negative messages that emphasize the failings of their political institutions and elected officials? It is one thing to express disagreement with a candidate's position on the issues. It is something altogether different to charge that the opposing candidate lacks integrity, is morally unfit for office, or is a threat to our security and well-being. Yet, these are precisely the kinds of claims that are now routinely made in election campaigns. A study by Patterson (2002, p. 51) reported that "75 percent of the respondents agreed with the statement 'political candidates are more concerned with fighting each other than with solving the nation's problems.' Respondents who held this belief were on the average day 12 percent less likely to discuss the campaign and 6 percent less likely to pay attention to news of it."

Second, the content and style of media coverage of political campaigns and political decision making have increased public cynicism. When citizens watch political discussion programs on television, they too often see either broadcasts that focus on campaign strategy and horse race coverage of who is ahead, who is behind, and who is meeting or failing to meet expectations; or they see sharply negative, critical, and increasingly polarizing programs. Confronted with dwindling audiences for news programs, news producers have begun to stage elaborate theatrical confrontations that encourage verbal combat between discussants. Politics on television has become a blood sport where all that matters are conflict, confrontation, and political gamesmanship. James Fallows (1996, p. 51) argued, "When ordinary citizens have a chance to pose questions to political leaders, they rarely ask about the game of politics. They want to know how the reality of politics will affect them—through taxes, programs, scholarship funds, wars." The natural instinct of the media, however, is to present public issues as if their real meaning is political in the narrowest sense of the term: "the attempt by parties and candidates to gain advantage over their rivals" (p. 51). Researchers have argued that this situation has deteriorated in recent years. For example, Lance Bennett (2005, p. 43), who has studied the content of news over the last several years, reported that he has observed that "a growing news trend is to portray unsympathetic, scheming politicians who often fail to solve problems, leaving disorder in their wake." Bennett further noted that today's media contain a "greater volume of criticism of government, politicians, and their policies, and less focus on the substance of policies" as well as a "higher journalistic tone of cynicism and negativity."

Third, the intensive use of political polling has created a form of politics that emphasizes motivating interest groups into action. We discussed the impact of new advances in polling on contemporary campaigns in Chapter 7. As that discussion indicated, candidates today realize that they do not need to make an attempt to convince all voters— or even most voters—to support their election or to endorse their policies. They only need a sufficient number of voters to secure more votes than their opponents, and they can achieve this goal by both urging peo-

ple to vote for them and discouraging them from voting for their opponents. The use of polling has also increased the focus on special interest constituencies who are so concerned about a handful of issues that
these become the litmus test that determines their votes. By activating
his or her special interest supporters, or by discouraging the opponents'
special interest supporters, a candidate can affect the outcome of elections. Candidates also use focus group polling techniques to test their
campaign messages. The result of all these polls is the creation of more
sharply polarized campaign discourse and perhaps the perception that
candidates do not genuinely believe in the arguments that they are advancing. Patterson (2002, p. 53) discovered that "81 percent of respondents agreed with the statement that 'most politicians will say almost
anything to get themselves elected.'" Patterson (2002, pp. 53–54) further reported that "respondents who believed candidates say whatever
it takes to get elected were 10 percentage points less likely to vote than
the other respondents. They were also less likely to pay attention to the
campaign."

Fourth, political polarization discourages political participation
because it decreases public confidence that their elected officials are
even interested in solving their problems. As discussed in Chapter 11,
political polarization often makes it more difficult for elected officials
to effectively govern once they gain office. The polarization of politics
discourages candidates and elected officials from reaching across the
political aisle to forge compromises or to pass complex but necessary
legislation. The consequence may well contribute to public perceptions
that our political system is largely ineffective or dysfunctional. It may
also contribute to a commonly held view that politicians willingly and
intentionally make promises that they fail to keep (Patterson, 2002).

Fifth, the flow of huge amounts of money into politics seems to
have undermined public confidence in politics and contributed to the
perception that politicians are only interested in their personal financial gain (in the worst case) or, in the best case, advancing the interests
of their wealthy contributors. As discussed in Chapter 10, those who
give the most money to political campaigns are able to gain access to
elected officials. Furthermore, these political contributions have influenced the passage of legislation and distorted policy making in the United
States. As indicated by the polling data cited earlier, many Americans
do not believe that their elected officials genuinely care about people
like them, and many believe that their elected officials are willing to
sell their votes to benefit the wealthy donors who help them cling to
power.

Sixth, it is not only participation in conventional electoral politics that has suffered from declining levels of public involvement; membership in almost all forms of civic associations is down. This argument was most articulately expressed by Harvard Professor of Public Policy Robert Putnam (2000) in his aptly entitled book *Bowling Alone: The Collapse and Revival of American Community*. Putnam takes his title from the fact that Americans today are more likely to bowl alone or with family members than they are on league teams. The book then discusses the dramatic decline in memberships in unions, parent-teacher associations (PTAs), and civic clubs (such as the Rotary Club, the Jaycees, and the Optimists Club). These organizations used to provide opportunities for citizens to come together, listen to guest speakers, discuss public issues, express their own political opinions, and have those opinions subjected to evaluation and dispute. The diminished opportunities for such interactions have dissolved important links between citizens and the political process. Instead of participating in these discussions, citizens are more likely to be politically passive (Schell, 1996). They may continue to receive political information through the media, but they have lost structured conversational settings that permitted them to disclose their opinions and to defend them against disagreements. The kinds of political discussions that may have once occurred in these settings either are not happening at all or may be happening in forums such as talk radio or cyberspace, where opinions can be expressed anonymously and therefore people are permitted to be far less accountable for what they say.

LIBERTY, CIVILITY, AND TRUST

Throughout history, Americans have had ambivalent feelings about their government. We celebrate and praise our political institutions with a patriotic fervor that many people from other nations find embarrassing, jingoistic, and shallow, yet we simultaneously express our dislike of and distrust for political insiders and for government intervention in our daily lives. The men who gathered at the Constitutional Convention in Philadelphia in 1787 debated vigorously over how to design a document that would balance the Founders' aspirations for personal and corporate liberty while simultaneously ensuring the creation of a nation that could withstand the as yet unforeseen political controversies that were sure to come. To achieve these goals, the delegates needed to reconcile the goals of ensuring sufficient authority for the government with maintaining liberty for themselves individually and collectively. Achieving these aims also meant creating a civic will of shared purpose and values (Smith, 1965).

The preservation of political liberty thus depends on the ability to preserve the fabric of political community. The health of a political community depends on citizens having a fundamental knowledge of public affairs, a sense of belonging, a concern for the whole, and a moral bond with the community whose fate is at stake. As Michael Sandel (1996) observed:

> To share in self-rule therefore requires that citizens possess, or come to acquire, certain civic virtues. But this means that republican politics cannot be neutral toward the values and ends that its citizens espouse. The republican conception of freedom . . . requires a formative politics, a politics that cultivates in citizens the qualities of character that self-government requires. (p. 58)

Sandel (p. 74) argued that the best hope for revitalizing civic virtue lies in finding ways to reinvigorate community at the level of the neighborhood, where people can most readily identify with fellow participants. In local communities people are most likely to know and trust each other, and in local communities people can more easily see themselves as responsible for one another's welfare. Thus, the vitality of the local community is essential to the preservation of democracy and to the creation of civic virtues that sustain the public good (Bellah et al., 1991).

Citizen involvement in public life is the foundation of a free society, but citizens must be encouraged to become involved in ways that permit them to see the effect that their participation has on society (Riley, Klumpp, & Hollihan, 1995). As the democratic theorist C. G. Benello (1992) observed:

> Attitudes, and thus beliefs, are formed and also changed at the level where people interact directly with one another—in cells, chapters, or groups. Groups must be created which function as therapeutic communities, where members are expected to live, not merely talk about the values of openness, honest cooperation, deriving from a less dystopian view of human nature, based on the primacy of the person. (p. 23)

Benello went on to say, "The problem is not how to influence politics but how to be politics—thus not how to get into power but how to transform and humanize it" (p. 27).

Democracy requires a great deal of trust, and trust in political institutions is at an all-time low in the United States and can no longer be taken for granted (Bellah et al., 1991). Nurturing and building trust will require effort and active participation by citizens, academics, the media, political consultants, and politicians. We must also set aside the political practices that focus on the game of politics, that engage in name calling and demonizing of our political adversaries, and that distract us from attempts to find solutions to our most vexing political problems.

We thus face many serious problems in our political system. Most acutely, we should seek to address the declining public interest in political participation, confidence in our government, and trust and respect for our elected officials. We need to reform campaign practices to give citizens greater confidence that the system is working and assure them that we are electing well-qualified, honest, creative, and courageous men and women to public office. Despite how negative much of this book may seem, I remain optimistic that politics can be reformed. Certainly the challenges that we face are significant, and the reforms will not come easily—too many people are gaining advantages from the system as it is currently operating not to acknowledge that there will be much resistance to any proposed reforms. Nonetheless, I believe that reforms are possible, and in the following section I provide several suggestions for accomplishing such reforms.

REINVENTING POLITICS IN AMERICA

To convince citizens that they should pay attention to politics and that it is worth their time and energy to become informed about political discussions, to vote, to volunteer their time for campaign activity, and perhaps even to submit their own names as candidates for office, we need to persuade them that their participation genuinely matters and that they can make a difference. If people feel that their participation does not matter, what can prompt them to become involved? Have things deteriorated to such a point that the system may be beyond redemption and repair? I do not believe this to be the case. Meaningful political reforms can be achieved if people can be convinced that they must exercise their voice to help shape political practices.

An active and engaged citizenry must demand political reform. Citizens must also demand a high standard of campaign discourse. It is a measure of respect for those who are asked to cast their ballots that they are provided with sufficient information to make intelligent and informed political choices. One measure of the quality of an argument is the quality of the audience that would adhere to it or become convinced by it. An engaged, informed, and reasoning citizenry requires and deserves that political campaigns focus on substantive issues. The responsibility for improving the quality of political discourse in the United States thus rests with all the participants in ongoing political conversations. Citizens must demand that their candidates provide them with clear information outlining their policy positions, not just with bland promises. In return, citizens must expend the energy to learn about the issues and must improve their notoriously short attention spans. Candidates must develop their positions, inform themselves on the issues, and engage in face-to-face public debates, not depend on vague promises, shallow slogans, and thirty-second negative political commercials. In return, candidates should have access to substantial media coverage and should be able to win public attention. The media must focus on the coverage of substantive political issues, avoid horse race poll-dominated reporting, and refrain from the conflict-focused political programming that now dominates the airwaves. In return, the media must have reasonable access to candidates in events that are not overly scripted and must also be able to attract patient, attentive, and interested audiences. Obviously, such changes in citizen, candidate, and media behaviors will not happen overnight. They will begin to occur only if all the players take deliberate and conscious steps to bring them about.

I believe that citizens must act individually and by joining forces with others to pressure their elected officials and governmental policy makers to adopt laws and policies aimed at reforming campaign practices. In addition, I think that concerted citizen effort can help shame political candidates into running more substantive campaigns and the news media into providing more helpful and informative coverage of the issues. As political philosopher Hannah Arendt noted (cited in Eliasoph, 1998, pp. 13–14), "Power springs up between men [or women] when they act together, and vanishes the moment they disperse." Politics in the United States must be reinvented. In the next section I discuss ways in which individual citizen actions can contribute toward this goal.

FINDING YOUR VOICE

One consequence of a situation in which increasing numbers of people have become politically detached and apathetic is that those who do participate and express their political viewpoints have much greater power and influence than might be suggested by their percentage in the population. I contend that those of us who are committed to renewing civic life and improving the political climate in the United

States need to use our voices to make a difference. The most obvious and essential step in this process is to become personally engaged and involved. Meaningful political participation begins at home as each of us becomes a committed agent for social change.

The participation that I envision can occur in many forms, at many levels, and in all kinds of institutional and organizational settings. Examples of places for meaningful civic participation include schools, student government groups, civic groups, volunteer organizations, political parties, workplaces, and, of course, local, state, and national governmental politics.

Schools

As discussed in Chapter 3 on political socialization, schools are important sites for the development of political knowledge, political attitudes, and values. Yet, many critics argue that our schools, especially at the elementary and secondary levels, do a poor job of providing civic education. John Patrick (2002), an education scholar who studied the effectiveness of civic education, concluded that currently "the outcomes are unsatisfactory." He went on to say the following:

> Most students in grades 4, 8, and 12 failed to reach the proficient level of achievement . . . which indicates competence in civics. Twenty-one percent of fourth-grade students, 21 percent of eighth-grade students, and 22 percent of twelfth-grade students reached the proficient level. Another way to look at the overall findings is to consider the large proportion of students that failed to reach the assessment's basic level of achievement: 31 percent of fourth-graders, 30 percent of eighth-graders, and 35 percent of twelfth-graders scored below the basic level.

Patrick (2002) further argued that the insufficient and superficial civic knowledge of young Americans is at least partially to blame for their low levels of political participation and civic engagement, their lack of understanding of democratic principles, and their poor citizenship skills. To address these deficiencies Patrick recommended increasing the number of required civics courses in the curriculum and incorporating a renewed focus on courses that teach critical thinking and public policy advocacy and analysis.

Although primary and secondary school students may not be able to affect the curriculums in their schools on their own, their parents and other interested citizens in the community can help foster such changes by encouraging individual teachers, principals, school boards, and state education officials to place more emphasis on civic education.

Furthermore, students should be taught to exercise their own voices in discussions with their classmates about significant social and political issues. The curriculum should encourage students to express their political opinions, and teachers should be trained to permit and value such student expression. Students should be permitted, even encouraged, to challenge their teachers and to ask questions as they critically evaluate the lessons they are taught. Evidence suggests that there is a positive relationship between a democratic school climate and the development of democratic civic dispositions and behaviors among students. Studies suggest that less authoritarian school climates encourage more democratic and tolerant political attitudes and behaviors (Baldi et al., 2001; Patrick, 2002).

Civic education should not stop when students graduate from high school. A study commissioned by the Intercollegiate Studies Institute's National Civics Literacy Board evaluated the political knowledge of college students and college graduates. The study found that college students and recent graduates had a woefully inadequate understanding of American history: 53.4 percent could not identify what century the colony of Jamestown was founded, more than half did not know that the Bill of Rights explicitly forbids the establishment of an official state religion in the United States, more than 75 percent did not know that the Monroe Doctrine was intended to prevent foreign influence in the Western Hemisphere, and fewer than half knew that the *Federalist Papers* were written in support of the passage of the U.S. Constitution. The most alarming finding in this study, however, was that the researchers discovered that student knowledge often dropped while they were enrolled in colleges or universities (The coming crisis in citizenship, 2006). In short, students took so few history or civics classes in college or learned so little from those that they did take that they often left college knowing less than they did when they left high school. The report also concluded that the most-prestigious universities in the United States fared no better in the study than did less-prestigious campuses. These depressing results underscore the need for more and better civic education, for as the report concluded (p. 7), "Students who demonstrated greater learning of America's history and institutions were more engaged in citizenship activities such as voting, volunteer community service, and political campaigns."

Active participation in student government is an excellent way to gain political experience and to begin to master some of the many skills involved in political advocacy. Participation in student government provides opportunities to speak in public, to consider and take positions on issues, and, perhaps most important, to form friendships and build political networks with like-minded fellow students. Forming good friendships is itself a move in the direction of nurturing good citizenship. As Eliasoph (1998, p. 12) noted, "Good friends are not just nice to each other; they also help each other to become good people. . . . Friends like these mutually raise each other to be good members of society."

Although student politics often seem trivial—and on many campuses are trivial and insignificant—the potential for student political action is great. There are numerous historical examples of how student activists affected political outcomes. For example, student political activists played a significant role in ending the U.S. military intervention in Vietnam and in helping win greater civil rights for minorities, women, and gay men and lesbians. More recently, student political activists have been very important in influencing public attitudes about the war in Iraq and in expressing their concerns about globalization and global warming. Throughout the world, student political activists have flexed their rhetorical muscles and have managed to win important political reforms. French students helped to bring about unparalleled political, economic, and social changes in their nation in the late 1960s, Taiwanese students won greater democratic changes in the 1970s, and South Korean students won important political reforms in the 1980s. Chinese students captured the attention of the entire world when they challenged the authority of the Communist Party in Tiananmen Square in Beijing in 1989. The power of organized student political movements is almost unparalleled. Even though other interest groups, economic classes, or occupational groups have also demonstrated their ability to shape political events once they have been mobilized (and in fact played an important role in all the movements just mentioned), students have probably had more impact than any other group and have transformed societies around the world.

My goal here is not to promote radical student protest movements. One does not have to emphasize radical student politics to envision the possibility for substantive student-inspired political change. Liberal, moderate, or conservative students can and should make themselves heard. Students have historically played an important role in mainstream Democratic and Republican party politics. Over the years, student chapters of the Democratic and Republican parties have been an important source of future party leadership. Student political activists meet ideologically like-minded friends and colleagues who can be of immense help for a lifetime of political involvement and participation. Students have also been an important source of support for many minor political parties in the United States, such as the Libertarians, the Greens, the Peace and Freedom Party, and the Reform Party. Once students acquire an interest in political issues and appropriate advocacy skills, it is likely that they will desire to apply those interests to other kinds of political situations.

Revitalizing the Political Parties

Those who want to express their political voice will find that the meetings of political parties provide important opportunities for influencing politics. Although most Americans declare themselves to be members of one party or another, in most instances this membership has little real meaning because they do not donate money, volunteer time, attend caucuses or conventions, or otherwise exercise their voice in helping shape their party's platform. Political parties are no longer mass-based political organizations. Instead, they have become nationally based fund-raising organizations whose primary purpose is raising money to purchase advertising, a form of communication that most Americans despise (Weir & Ganz, 1997).

I believe it is time for Americans to take back their political parties. I encourage direct participation in party meetings and functions. Join your local political party and attend its meetings. Meet the officeholders, committee members, convention delegates, and political candidates from your party, and tell them directly what you think the most important issues are and what positions you would like to see them take with regard to those issues. Volunteer your time, canvass your neighborhood, meet your neighbors and find out what they are thinking, solicit their opinions, encourage them to vote, and champion the issues, causes, and candidates that you support. These activities help improve communal bonds and foster the formation of a genuine civic community. Help your party by offering to solicit donations, circulate petitions, and organize letter or e-mail campaigns. Volunteer to serve on a committee, or get yourself nominated to serve as a convention delegate for a local, county, state, or national convention. Actively support and volunteer your time to the campaign for a candidate for office (local candidates in "minor" races especially need the help from volunteers). Even time spent doing minor chores for a campaign—answering phones, stuffing envelopes, driving voters to the polls on Election Day— will help you learn about politics, introduce you to the political leaders and candidates from your party, and increase the likelihood that your party and its candidates reflect your values and political views.

All political parties would appreciate and benefit from wider citizen support and participation. Certainly, some members of the party hierarchy might seem to discourage your direct involvement. Some of these folks may have been running the party to suit their interests and objectives for years, and they will not welcome change or alternative points of view. But it is not just *their* party; it is also *your* party. If you do not like your party's candidates or their stands on issues, it is up to you to get involved in the party and make your positions and preferences known. If the political parties are to energize political participation and involvement, they must mobilize citizens in specific communities and link them into larger networks capable of deliberating over, developing, and carrying out local, state, and national political strategies (Weir & Ganz, 1997).

Political Action Groups

Another opportunity for direct political involvement is through participation in interest groups and citizen action committees. Depending on your interests, many different such groups are available, including those focused on the environment, civil rights, peace, animal rights, and income disparities, to mention just a few. All offer opportunities for direct political participation. In an era when politicians closely monitor public opinion polls and listen to special interests, these groups have significant political power. With so many passive citizens in our midst, groups that deeply care about certain key issues can have a significant impact on how their legislators vote. Senators have indicated that there are few subjects in a given year on which they receive as many as two hundred or five hundred phone calls from constituents urging them how to vote. Senators listen to such messages and attend town hall meetings in their home districts because they know that such messages come from their most passionately committed and involved constituents who are almost certain to vote and who also tend to be opinion leaders in their communities (Drew, 1999b, pp. 270–271). Although legislators attend to (or at least keep tallies on the numbers of) all forms of constituent communication, well-written and succinct letters sent through the regular mail get the most attention because it is presumed that such letters require the most effort and therefore reflect the highest level of citizen engagement and commitment. To maximize the impact of your correspondence, customize your letter and avoid merely copying the "boilerplate text" often suggested by the advocacy groups. Be sure to include your mailing address. Your letter will be taken far more seriously if you are a political constituent.

One topic worth addressing in such communications with your congressional representatives is the need for political campaign reform. Later in this chapter, I propose some reforms that I believe would be useful in improving the quality and conduct of political campaigns and in increasing voter participation.

All Politics Are Local

Politicians have long been aware that all politics involve local issues and concerns. Citizens also need to be aware of the importance of local politics. As Weir and Ganz (1997, p. 151) argued, "Only through mobilization across localities and levels of government will citizens begin to develop broader understandings of common interests as well as the capacity for coordinated political action on behalf of those interests." It is obviously difficult for any of us as individual citizens to make a difference in the realms of national or global politics. It is, however, relatively easy to make a difference at the local level. Get to know the people on your floor, in your building, on your block, and in your neighborhood. Identify local issues of concern, and make your voice heard on such topics. Neighborhood watch groups; local school groups; committees seeking support for neighborhood libraries and parks; urban planning, zoning, or environmental groups—all provide opportunities for direct political participation and involvement. People who take the time to become engaged in such groups can indeed influence politics in their communities. In any city in America, the mayor or city council members would confirm that neighborhoods with the most active citizen groups have the most influence on political outcomes. Why do they locate new parks in affluent neighborhoods or new jails in poor neighborhoods? It is because affluent citizens are, in virtually all cities, more likely to become politically engaged and involved and as a result have greater influence on political decisions. More affluent citizens are more likely to have mastered the art of politics; they donate money to campaigns, they organize letters and phone calls to elected officials, and they are more likely to vote.

Many college students complain about the poor quality of municipal services offered in student neighborhoods. Countless students endure overpriced, inadequately regulated apartment housing because cities, especially those in college or university towns, are more sympathetic to the interests of landlords than they are to those of tenants. City politicians long ago learned that students pay little heed to local political issues and do not feel particularly invested in the communities in which they live while going to school. Many students, for instance, either do not vote at all or are registered to vote in their hometowns. Yet, political involvement by students could be a significant factor in local election outcomes, if only they bothered to vote and participated in local campaigns.

Civic and Community Groups

In addition to direct participation in local politics, another important opportunity for civic engagement that enhances political life is membership in civic and community groups. As Eliasoph (1998) argued:

> Such sociable gatherings can be fertile ground for public life. While not exclusively or even primarily politically motivated, these gatherings offer the familiarity that is a necessary precondition for some kinds of public life. Sociable familiar gatherings can create an infinitely nuanced stock of common sense and feeling, common knowledge and myths, common style and rhythm, and manners; background knowledge for how to act and how to be. . . . Whether for reading poetry aloud, debating playfully, playing music, joking, putting on plays, dancing, bowling, playing soccer, these usually unpolitical grounds for common life and meaning-making often make political life possible. (p. 12)

Many such groups exist, appealing to a wide range of interests and inclinations. For example, there are groups devoted to the promotion of business contacts and ethical standards, veterans' issues, library guilds, hospitals, food banks, homeless shelters, or child welfare or education issues. Consider becoming an active participant in your college's or university's alumni club. Participation in such groups helps you meet other people in the community and often accomplishes genuinely important social objectives and public works. In addition, local elected officials looking for the names of citizens to appoint to important civic commissions and boards often consult the membership rolls of these groups. Such forms of civic participation help you express your political beliefs and values and increase the likelihood that your opinions and political viewpoints will be heard.

Some critics of American political practices have warned that much of what currently passes for citizen activism is overly focused on individuals or groups of citizens who narrowly pursue their own special interests. The fear is that in worrying, for example, about the prison, freeway, or landfill that may be constructed near their own neighborhood, people lose sight of the broader public needs for such facilities (e.g., Wuthnow, 1991). These concerns are not without foundation. There is always the danger that citizens will adopt a NIMBY ("not in my backyard") attitude. But I submit that democratic political participation has always been, and will always be, inspired at least in part by a healthy dose of political self-interest. I hope that an improved climate for political discussion and debate, as well as a more engaged public, will make it easier rather than more difficult to craft a concern for the broader public interest from the rich texture of the enlivened political conversation. A reasoning and informed public should be capable of weighing political choices and acting to advance the interests of society as a whole. That kind of political deliberation is, after all, an underlying principle of our democracy. Problems occur when the political system short-circuits such debate or causes the playing field to become uneven because some citizens lack the intellectual or financial capital to understand the issues or to advocate their position.

Democratizing the Workplace

Another opportunity for meaningful democratic political participation exists in the workplace. This may sound surprising because many, perhaps even most, workplaces do not seem to function very much like democratic institutions. Yet, many workplaces do offer extensive opportunities for democratic political participation. This is obviously the case for organizations such as colleges or universities, which offer some semblance of faculty governance and participation in decision making. But other companies, too, are giving employees more extensive opportunities to participate in making important decisions. Many companies have adopted a team-based approach to working on projects. For example, many highly technical fields involving complex product design and manufacturing techniques (e.g., automobiles, computers and software, aircraft, and pharmaceuticals) have adopted participatory team-based management systems. Effective participation in such work teams often requires that employees possess more than technical expertise. To get ahead in such an environment, an employee must also demonstrate political wisdom and skill. Such skills always include the ability to advocate one's ideas in the organization, the willingness to listen to others, the ability to cooperate and compromise, and the ability to learn how to put one's own personal goals aside when necessary to promote the goals of the enterprise. These skills translate directly to the political sphere as well.

326 UNCIVIL WARS: POLITICAL CAMPAIGNS IN A MEDIA AGE

As more employees learn the skills of advocacy in workplace communication, they will demand more democratic and responsive employment practices in their companies. The presence of a participatory culture will likely become an important factor in recruiting and maintaining a highly skilled workforce. Workplaces that are more democratic are also likely to be more supportive and sympathetic to the interests of their employees. In a participatory workplace, workers' rights are likely to be respected. Such workplaces are likely to offer a supportive attitude on such issues as childcare (perhaps on-site daycare facilities), family leave (e.g., to care for a sick parent or child), employment security, employee stock ownership, and so on.

More democratic workplaces might also serve to give employees greater voice on issues such as product safety, environmental concerns, and the decisions of their companies to outsource new jobs or services. Greater employee participation in corporate decision making can also engage employees in conversations about corporate values and ethics. Such conversations can help improve corporate relationships with local communities and with other stakeholder groups. At the moment, most corporations are responsive to the concerns of their shareholders and of the financial markets but not always to their responsibilities to the broader community. These issues are more important than ever in an era of globalization where nation-states, the traditional sites for democratic participation, seem to be losing power while multinational corporations are gaining power and influence (Held, McGrew, Goldblatt, & Perraton, 1999; Hollihan, Klumpp, & Riley, 1999).

In some workplaces, political participation can also be expressed through membership in, or by playing an active role in, the union. Although unions frequently introduce a fiercely contentious style of political engagement into the workplace, they do provide workers with opportunities to forge connections with coworkers and satisfy their political objectives. It is likely that fewer companies would be unionized today had they created more opportunities for meaningful workplace political participation and demonstrated greater respect and concern for their employees in the past.

SUGGESTED POLITICAL REFORMS

The preceding sections have focused on ways that individuals can, through personal political participation, have a greater voice in politics, acquire important skills in political advocacy, enhance the bonds of civic commitment, and thereby help rehabilitate the American political system. Although I strongly believe that such individual action can be profoundly helpful, I also believe that structural, legal, and practical changes (i.e., changes embedded in a set of accepted practices) must occur if our political system is to be reinvented. As I have already pointed out, these reforms will not occur unless citizens demand them. Citizen activists must put pressure on their lawmakers and hold the lawmakers accountable for their votes and their conduct during their election campaigns.

Campaign Finance Reform

Perhaps more than any other single cause, the problems in contemporary campaigns can be blamed on the tremendous amount of money flowing to candidates and the political parties. Chapter 10 discussed in detail the emphasis on raising money and its corrosive effect on campaign politics. As noted earlier, every election costs more than the ones that came before, and the primary expenditures go to purchase television advertisements. Does it surprise us, given the tremendous profits to be earned from such advertising, that the broadcasters oppose laws that would require them to provide some free time to political candidates?

Although the Bipartisan Campaign Reform Act (BCRA) of 2002, popularly known as the McCain-Feingold Act, represented an attempt to correct some of the most significant problems in the area of campaign funding, significant loopholes remain, as noted in Chapter 10. Crafting legislation in this area is constitutionally difficult because of how the courts have interpreted the First Amendment to protect campaign donations. Nonetheless, citizen activists should continue to lobby Congress for legislation that would survive court challenges. For example, new legislation might limit the influence of lobbyists by preventing those who have recently left office to serve as lobbyists, prohibiting family members of legislators from serving as lobbyists, and placing more stringent limitations on gifts from lobbyists to elected officials. In addition, laws governing political action committees (PACs) should be more strictly enforced to prevent collusion between the advertising messages funded by PACs and those controlled by candidates.

Finally, limitations should be imposed on the ability of elected officials to form leadership PACs. These are PACs set up and maintained by congressional leaders, to which lobbyists are encouraged to donate funds. House and Senate leaders in both the Democratic and Republican parties maintain such funds. Leaders can use the funds donated to leadership PACs either to support their pet projects or, more likely, to redistribute the money to fellow members of Congress who are having difficulty raising campaign money on their own to ward off tough or well-funded challengers. Such gifts allow the leadership to hold onto power—the exchange suggests a quid pro quo agreement—and also help the parties maintain a semblance of discipline on highly contested bills (Phillips, 2006). Sometimes contributions to leadership PACs may be offered as gifts, such as donations to universities to fund professorships, research programs, or think tanks named after prominent politicians. Often, however, contributions to these PACs are used for elegant parties and receptions, to fund holidays (such as golf outings, ski lift tickets, charter boat cruises, or private jets), or to pay for lavish hotel suites in expensive resorts (Forsythe & Jensen, 2005). These PACs are an invitation for corruption or the appearance of corruption, as lobbyists are encouraged to make gifts to secure access to elected officials. Leadership PACs should be strictly limited or prohibited.

Decreasing the flow of money to candidates and the political parties will help limit the amount of polling and paid political advertising that they can purchase. It will cause them to spend less time raising money and more time serving their constituents. It might also make it easier for political challengers to mount successful campaigns against established incumbents and therefore make all elected officials more accountable.

Free Airtime

Citizens should demand that broadcasters make available free airtime to political candidates to get their messages to the public. This should not mean free time slots to run thirty-second political commercials but free opportunities to present policy positions, more extensive opportunities to debate opponents, and more press conferences and interviews with reporters. As noted earlier, broadcasters make a fortune off political candidates and thus are unlikely to give away what they are currently selling unless forced by law to do so. In that broadcasters operate their stations, however, on licenses granted by the federal government, and in that those airwaves have been declared to be public property, citizens have a legitimate and constitutional right to claim that they be operated in the public interest. The provision of time for a meaningful discussion of complex political issues certainly sounds like a public good to me.

Voting Made Easier

Throughout this book I have argued the importance of voting and political participation. We need to take steps to reduce the barriers to voting and to encourage citizens to go to the polls. Research has confirmed that if citizens are registered, they tend to vote. Yet, in many states and localities, the procedures for registering to vote are needlessly complicated. People in the United States move around often, but every time they change addresses, the law requires that they must reregister to vote. Increasingly, there have been moves to standardize voting registration procedures and to permit citizens to register by mail, at the post office, at the registry of motor vehicles, and so on. Yet, many people do not know how to register to vote. Public service announcements and broadcasts should be aired advising people how to register. Every high school in the United States should make it a point to register students on their eighteenth birthday. States should also be required to allow citizens to register to vote on the day of the election, at the polls themselves. Many oppose same-day registration, fearing potential voting fraud. Their concerns can be addressed by having such ballots held as "provisional." If the election is so close that it would be decided by the tally of the "provisional" ballots, the results can be withheld until these registrations can be verified by the Registrar of Voters.

In the United States, we almost always vote on a Tuesday, most often in November, where in some states the weather is starting to turn foul. This timing often acts as a deterrent to citizens who must get up early in the morning to go to work or who must work late to make up for the time taken to vote. People with young children may also find it difficult to vote on a weekday. We should consider following the example set by many other nations and allow citizens to vote on weekends. Or we could allow the polls to remain open for two or three consecutive days to enable citizens to vote. We should consider moving elections to summer months when weather is less likely to discourage turnout. Steps have been taken recently to make voting by absentee ballot easier, but still more could be done to make it convenient for citizens to cast their ballots. Some have even suggested the possibility of allowing people to vote via electronic mail or over the Web. Although there are serious security and voter fraud issues to be worked out before such voting is likely to be feasible, it does deserve our continuing interest and study. As computing technologies and message encryption systems improve, this may prove to be a very worthy alternative.

Revitalized Public Forums

One problem in politics today, as opposed to an earlier era, is that our cities, and indeed our nation, have grown large and our political system has become complex and bureaucratized. Democracy may be much easier to sustain in face-to-face settings where people know, understand, and trust their fellow citizens. Thus, the New England town hall meeting is frequently cited as the idealized democratic community. Although we cannot create the intimacy of the New England town meeting in New York, Los Angeles, or most other big cities surrounded by sprawling suburbs, we should look for opportunities to emulate the kinds of direct communicative opportunities that sustain such communities. Thus, it is important that school boards, city councils, county commissions, regulatory agencies, and the like host public forums in which citizens can express their concerns. Many cities have begun to create neighborhood councils where citizens can come together to discuss and present their opinions on civic issues. Certainly, such meetings can sometimes be unpleasant or distressing because the local cranks and crackpots who regularly attend these meetings often seize the microphones to rant and rave. But perhaps they behave this way because they do not know any other way to behave. After all, most of the "talking heads" they see on television also rant and rave, and the candidates and elected officials often berate each other. However, if citizens begin finding and utilizing new opportunities for deliberative political interactions, their advocacy skills and their demeanor will likely improve. As citizens develop greater respect for their elected officials and trust in their integrity, they may also begin to speak to them more respectfully. At any rate, even if such public forums are painful, they are important. We need to have more of them, and we need to do more to encourage citizens to attend them.

The possibility now exists to create "virtual" town meetings via the Internet, as discussed in Chapter 8. Although a virtual community does not equal a face-to-face community any more than virtual sex on the Internet equates with genuine human intimacy, we should continue to explore how the new technologies may be used to create meaningful political conversations and debate. Some very promising Web sites are now being created, such as the Democracy Network (http://www.democracynet.org), that are profoundly useful as sources of political information on local, state, and national races, and as sites for bulletin board discussions that invite individual citizens to participate and express their political opinions.

CONCLUSION

The twentieth century was often referred to as The American Century, because it was a period of dramatic change and accomplishment for the United States. The people of the United States populated a continent; built great cities; asserted an international presence through participation in foreign wars and conflicts; helped rebuild Western Europe and Japan after World War II; took a leadership role in the formation of the United Nations; created magnificent technological advances in transportation, communications, science, and medicine; and landed on the moon. In addition, Americans exported their culture, products, values, and, in many cases, social problems to other nations around the world. Largely as a result of America's influence through the export of media and entertainment programming, English became the lingua franca of the world. Despite all these achievements, however, the health and vitality of our democracy languished in the later years of the twentieth century. We proclaimed our commitment to spreading democracy around the world but did little to nourish it at home. Our challenge in the twenty-first century is to rehabilitate our democracy and to reclaim for our government both the respect and the participation of its citizenry, as we revitalize the public spirit through engaged political conversations. I believe that if citizens rise up to meet these new demands, mobilize for political action, and challenge themselves and their elected officials to learn new ways of solving our political problems, we will enjoy another century of greatness and achievement. If we fail to meet this task, I fear that historians will judge us harshly for having squandered the resources of economic, social, and intellectual capital that our parents, grandparents, and great-grandparents left us.

WORKS CITED

Abelson, J. (2005, June 12). The offer's in the mail. *Boston Globe.* http://www .boston.com/business/articles/2005/06/12/the_offers_in_the_mail/. Retrieved on September 6, 2007.

Abramowitz, A. I. (1995). It's abortion, stupid: Policy voting in the 1992 presidential election. *Journal of Politics, 57,* 176–186.

Abramson, J. (1997, January 20). Another day, another scandal. *Wall Street Journal,* p. R5.

Abramson, P. R., & Finifter, A. W. (1981). On the meaning of political trust: New evidence from items introduced in 1978. *American Journal of Political Science, 25,* 297–307.

Ackerman, K. D. (2005). *Boss Tweed: The rise and fall of the corrupt pol who conceived the soul of modern New York.* New York: Avalon.

Ackoff, R. L. (1994). *The democratic corporation.* New York: Oxford University Press.

Adamek, R. J. (1994). Public opinion and Roe vs. Wade: Measurement difficulties. *Public Opinion Quarterly, 58,* 409–418.

Air America Radio files for bankruptcy protection. (2006, October 13). Fox News. http://www.foxnews.com/story/0,2933,220507,00.html. Retrieved on August 31, 2007.

Alexander, H. E., & Corrado, A. (1995). *Financing the 1992 election.* Armonk, NY: M. E. Sharpe.

Allen's listening tour. (2006, August 14). YouTube. http://www.youtube.com/ watch?v=9G7gq7GQ71c. Retrieved on April 27, 2007.

Alvarez, L. (1999, February 13). A dispirited Hyde opposes indicting Clinton. *New York Times,* p. 1.

America goes to the polls: A report on voter turnout in the 2006 election. (2006). http://www.nonprofitvote.org/wp-content/uploads/AGttp.pdf. Retrieved on August 10, 2007.

Andersen, P. A., & Kibler, R. J. (1978). Candidate valence as a predictor of voter preference. *Human Communication Research, 5,* 4–14.

Anderson, R., Dardenne, R., & Killenberg, G. M. (1994). *The conversation of journalism: Communication, community, and news.* Westport, CT: Greenwood.

Ansolabehere, S., Behr, R., & Iyengar, S. (1993). *The media game: American politics in the television age.* New York: Macmillan.

Ansolabehere, S., Gerber, A. S., & Snyder, J. M. (2001). Does TV advertising explain the rise of campaign spending? A study of campaign spending and broadcast advertising prices in US House elections in the 1990s and the 1970s. http://econ-www.mit.edu/faculty/download_pdf.php?id=314. Retrieved on February 14, 2007.

Ansolabehere, S., & Iyengar, S. (1994). Riding the wave and claiming ownership over issues: The joint effects of advertising and news coverage in campaigns. *Public Opinion Quarterly, 58*, 335–357.

Ansolabehere, S., & Iyengar, S. (1995). *Going negative: How political advertisements shrink and polarize the electorate.* New York: Free Press.

Ansolabehere, S., Iyengar, S., & Simon, A. (1999). Replicating experiments using aggregate and survey data: The case of negative advertising and turnout. *American Political Science Review, 93*, 901–910.

Ansolabehere, S., Iyengar, S., Simon, A., & Valentino, N. (1994). Does attack advertising demobilize the electorate? *American Political Science Review, 88*, 829–839.

Anti-gay, bisexual, and transgender violence in 2004: A report of the national coalition on anti-violence programs. (2005). http://www.cuav.org/docs/2004hvreport.pdf. Retrieved on August 1, 2006.

Apple, R. W. (1998, December 19). With partisan rancor, a bitter House debates the president's impeachment. *New York Times*, p. 1.

Apple, R. W., Jr. (1996, September 1). For debate commission a predicament on Perot. *New York Times*, p. 1.

Armstrong, R. (1988). *The next hurrah: The communication revolution in American politics.* New York: Beech Tree Books.

Asher, H. (1992). *Polling and the public: What every citizen should know* (2nd ed.). Washington, DC: Congressional Quarterly Press.

Atkeson, L. R., & Rapoport, R. B. (2003). The more things change the more they stay the same: Examining gender differences in political attitude expression, 1952–2000. *Public Opinion Quarterly, 67*, 495–521.

Atkin, C. K., & Heald, G. (1976). Effects of political advertising. *Public Opinion Quarterly, 40*, 216–228.

Attitudes towards politics and public service: A national survey of college undergraduates. (2000). The Institute of Politics, Harvard University.

Auer, J. J. (1962). The counterfeit debates. In S. Kraus (Ed.), *The great debates: Kennedy vs. Nixon, 1960* (p. 146). Bloomington: Indiana University Press.

Auletta, K. (1993). On and off the bus: Lessons from campaign '92. In *1-800-president: The report of the Twentieth Century Fund Task Force on television and the campaign of 1992* (pp. 63–90). New York: Twentieth Century Fund Press.

Austin, E. W., & Pinkleton, B. E. (2001). The role of parental mediation in the political socialization process. *Journal of Broadcasting and Electronic Media, 45*, 221–240.

Ayidya, S. A., & McClendon, M. J. (1990). Response effects in mail surveys. *Public Opinion Quarterly, 54*, 229–247.

Ayres, B. D. (1999, August 19). Of hay and goats, and feet in mouths. *New York Times*, p. A16.

Babcock, C. R., & Weisman, J. (2005, November 29). Congressman admits taking bribes, resigns. *Washington Post*, p. A1.

Baker, P. (1998, October 21). Court hears Paula Jones appeal. *Washington Post*, p. A3.

Baldi, S., Perie, M., Skidmore, D., Greenberg, E., & Hahn, C. (2001). What democracy means to ninth-graders: U.S. results from the International IEA Civic Education Study. ERIC. ED 454152. http://www.eric.ed.gov/ERICWebPortal/ custom/portlets/recordDetails/detailmini.jsp?_nfpb=true&_&ERICExtSearch _SearchValue_0=ED454152&ERICExtSearch_SearchType_0=eric_accno &accno=ED454152. Retrieved on September 20, 2007.

Balthrop, V. W. (1989). W(h)ither the public sphere? An optimistic reading. In B. E. Gronbeck (Ed.), *Spheres of argument* (pp. 20–25). Fairfax, VA: Speech Communication Association.

Balz, D. (2005, March 29). Partisan polarization intensified in 2004 election. *Washington Post*, p. A4.

Bandow, D. (2003, December 1). Righteous anger: The conservative case against George W. Bush. *The American Conservative*. Cato Institute. http://www .cato.org/research/articles/bandow-031211.html. Retrieved on November 26, 2007.

Barkin, S. M. (1984). The making of a public in a political campaign: A participant observation study. *Political Communication and Persuasion*, *2*, 251–262.

Barlett, D. L., & Steele, J. B. (2000, February 7). How the little guy gets crunched. *Time*, 38–41.

Barrett, D. (2007, August 15). 9-11 health worries follow Giuliani. Associated Press. http://news.yahoo.com/s/ap/20070815/ap_on_el_pr/giuliani_ground_ zero. Retrieved on August 24, 2007.

Bartels, L. M. (1985). Expectations and preferences in presidential nominating campaigns. *American Political Science Review*, *79*, 805–815.

Bartels, L. M. (2005). Economic inequality and political representation. http://www .princeton.edu/~bartels/economics.pdf. Retrieved on June 26, 2007.

Bates, B., & Harmon, M. (1993). Do "instant" polls hit the spot? Phone in versus random sampling of public opinion. *Journalism Quarterly*, *70*, 369–380.

Bauman, S., & Herbst, S. (1994). Managing perceptions of public opinion: Candidates' and journalists' reactions to the 1992 polls. *Political Communication*, *11*, 133–144.

Baumgartner, J., & Morris, J. S. (2006). The *Daily Show* effect: Candidate evaluations, efficacy, and American youth. *American Politics Research*, *34*, 341–367.

Beck, P. A., & Jennings, M. K. (1991). Family traditions, political periods, and the development of partisan orientations. *Journal of Politics*, *53*, 742–763.

Belenkaya, V., Huff, R., & Siemaszko, C. (2006, April 5). Katie's "eye" to do $15 million. *New York Daily News*. http://www.nydailynews.com/news/gossip/ story/406403p-344078c.html. Retrieved on December 20, 2006.

Bell, D. (1962). *The end of ideology: On the exhaustion of political ideas in the fifties* (Rev. ed.). New York: Free Press.

Bellah, R. N., Madsen, R., Sullivan, W. M., Swindler, A., & Tipton, S. (1985). *Habits of the heart: Individualism and commitment in American life*. Berkeley: University of California Press.

Bellah, R. N., Madsen, R., Sullivan, W. M., Swindler, A., & Tipton, S. M. (1991). *The good society*. New York: Random House.

Benello, C. G. (1992). *From the ground up*. Boston: South End Press.

Benen, S. (2006, August 30). Is President Bush learning? *The American Prospect*. http://www.alternet.org/story/41015/. Retrieved on August 30, 2006.

Bennet, J. (1996, March 8). Despite defeats, Buchanan threatens to wield his "pitchfork" until convention. *International Herald Tribune*, p. 3.

Bennett, W. L. (1981). Assessing presidential character: Degradation rituals in political campaigns. *Quarterly Journal of Speech, 67*, 310–321.

Bennett, W. L. (1993). Constructing publics and their opinions. *Political Communication, 10*, 101–120.

Bennett, W. L. (1996). *The governing crisis: Media, money, and marketing in American elections* (2nd ed.). New York: St. Martin's Press.

Bennett, W. L. (2005). *News: The politics of illusion* (6th ed.). New York: Pearson Longman.

Benoit, P. J. (1997). *Telling the success story: Acclaiming and disclaiming discourse*. Albany: State University of New York Press.

Benoit, W. L., & Hansen, G. J. (2004). Presidential debate watching, issue knowledge, character evaluation, and vote choice. *Human Communication Research, 30*, 121–144.

Benoit, W. L., Hansen, W. G., & Hansen, G. J. (2001). Presidential debate questions and the public agenda. *Communication Quarterly, 49*, 130–141.

Benoit, W. L., Leshner, G., & Chattopadhayay, S. (2005). A meta-analysis of the effects of televised political advertising. Paper presented at the annual meeting of the International Communication Association, New York, NY.

Benoit, W. L., McKinney, M. S., & Holbert R. L. (2001). Beyond learning and persona: Extending the scope of presidential debate effects. *Communication Monographs, 68*, 259–273.

Benoit, W. L., Webber, D., & Berman, J. (1998). Effects of presidential debate watching and ideology on attitudes and knowledge. *Argumentation and Advocacy, 34*, 163–172.

Berke, R. L. (1996, May 5). Is age-bashing any way to beat Bob Dole? *New York Times*, p. E1.

Berke, R. L. (1996, July 14). Perot's back. But did the voters ask for an encore? *New York Times*, p. E1.

Berke, R. L. (1996, August 1). Clinton to sign welfare bill that ends U.S. aid guarantee and gives states broad power. *New York Times*, pp. A1, A8.

Berke, R. L. (1996, October 6). Dole camp looks to coming debates as a last chance. *New York Times*, pp. 1, 15.

Berke, R. L. (1999, August 22). Bush is the man. The issue is what he's made of. *New York Times*, sec. 4, p. 1.

Berke, R. L. (1999, May 30). Fitting Forbes for Oval Office is advertising man's assignment. *New York Times*, p. 1.

Berke, R. L. (2000). Debates seen as influential, even if few are tuning in. *New York Times*, p. Al.

Berke, R. L. (2000, February 2). McCain romps in first primary. *New York Times*, p. 1.

Berkowitz, D., & Beach, D. W. (1993). News sources and news context: The effect of routine news, conflict, and proximity. *Journalism Quarterly, 70*, 4–12.

Berlet, C. (2003, Summer). Religion and politics in the United States: Nuances you should know. *The Public Eye Magazine.* http://www.publiceye.org/magazine/v17n2/evangelical-demographics.html. Retrieved on August 16, 2006.

Big money at the conventions. (1996, September 1). *New York Times*, p. E8.

Bimber, B., & Davis, R. (2003). *Campaigning online: The Internet in US elections.* Oxford: Oxford University Press.

Birnbaum, J. H., & Edsall, T. B. (2004, November 6). At the end, pro-GOP "527s" outspent their counterparts. *Washington Post*, p. A6.

Bjork, R. (1992). *The Strategic Defense Initiative: Symbolic containment of the nuclear threat.* Albany: State University of New York Press.

Bligh, M. C., Kohles, J. C., & Pillai, R. (2005). Crisis and charisma in the California Recall Election. *Leadership, 1*, pp. 323–352.

Blumenthal, S. (1982). *The permanent campaign* (Rev. ed.). New York: Simon & Schuster.

Bock, A. (2007, May 4). Tommy Thompson on firing gays. *Orange County Register.* http://blogs.ocregister.com/orangepunch/archives/2007/05/tommy_thompson_on_firing_gays.html. Retrieved on May 16, 2007.

Bodenner, C. (2004, November 15). The undisputed champion of the 2004 campaign: The talking point. *CJR Daily.* http://www.cjrdaily.org/politics/the_undisputed_champion_of_the.php. Retrieved on March 30, 2007.

Borger, J. (2004, March 9). The brains. *The Guardian.* http://www.guardian.co.uk/uselections2004/story/0,13918,1165126,00.html. Retrieved on July 27, 2006.

Boulding, K. E. (1961). *The image.* Ann Arbor: University of Michigan Press.

Bowers, A. (2004, November 4). You Limey assholes. *Slate.* http://www.slate.com/id/2109217/. Retrieved on July 18, 2006.

Boyd, R. W. (1969). An explanation of voting defection. *American Political Science Review, 63*, 488–514.

Boyle, T. P. (2001). Intermedia agenda setting in the 1996 presidential election. *Journalism and Mass Communication Quarterly, 78*, 26–44.

Brehm, J. (1993). *The phantom respondents: Opinion surveys and political representation.* Ann Arbor: University of Michigan Press.

Brians, C. L., & Wattenberg, M. P. (1996). Campaign issue knowledge and salience: Comparing reception from TV commercials, TV news and newspapers. *American Journal of Political Science, 40*, 172–193.

Brinkley, A. (1997, November 2). The potent culture of scandal. *Los Angeles Times*, p. M1.

Broder, D. S. (1997, September 24). Lie, cheat—but don't show weakness. *Los Angeles Times*, p. B9.

Broder, D. S. (2004, December 12). The polarization express. *Washington Post*, p. B7.

Broder, D. S., & Balz, D. (2006, July 16). How common ground of 9/11 gave way to partisan split. *Washington Post*, p. A1.

Broder, J. M. (1996, March 14). Traveling Clinton has eye on U.S. audience. *Los Angeles Times*, p. A8.

Broder, J. M. (1996, August 1). Decision on welfare was difficult for Clinton, tough on Dole. *Los Angeles Times*, p. A16.

Broder, J. M., & Healy, P. (2007, January 22). Rush of entries gives 2008 race early intensity. *New York Times*, p. 1.

Brooks, D. J., & Geer, J. G. (2007). Beyond negativity: The effects of incivility on the electorate. *American Journal of Political Science, 51*, 1–16.

Brotherson, S. (2006, April). Keys to building attachment with young children. http://www.ag.ndsu.edu/pubs/yf/famsci/fs631w.htm. Retrieved on August 21, 2007.

Brownstein, R. (1998, September 14). Public's support of president found to remain strong. *Los Angeles Times*, p. 1.

Brownstein, R. (1999, August 10). Elizabeth Dole wears her résumé like a campaign button. *Los Angeles Times*, p. A7.

Brownstein, R., & Barabak, M. Z. (1999, August 16). More questions than answers in GOP straw poll. *Los Angeles Times*, p. 1.

Bryk, W. (2004, August 4). The conservative case against George W. Bush. *New York Press*. http://www.nypress.com/17/31/news&columns/WilliamBryk.cfm. Retrieved on November 26, 2007.

Buettner, R., & Perez-Pena, R. (2007, March 3). Noticeably absent from the Giuliani campaign: His children. *New York Times*. http://www.nytimes.com/2007/03/03/us/politics/03rudy.html?ex=1188100800&en=1f71cb946de504da&ei=5070. Retrieved on August 24, 2007.

Bumiller, E. (2003, May 16). Keepers of Bush image lift stagecraft to new heights. *New York Times*, p. A7.

Bunting, G. F. (1996, October 16). Dole lent clout to Gallo winery. *Los Angeles Times*, pp. 1, 8.

Bunting, G. F., & Frammolino, R. (1997, February 24). Cash-for-coffee events at White House detailed. *Los Angeles Times*, pp. 1, 12.

Bunting, G. F., & Frammolino, R. (1997, March 2). Democratic Party lacks funds to repay donors. *Los Angeles Times*, p. 1.

Burger, T. J. (2006, January 6). Disgraced congressman wore a "wire." *Time*. http://www.time.com/time/nation/article/0,8599,1146700,00.html. Retrieved on May 21, 2007.

Burke, K. (1937/1959). *Attitudes toward history*. Berkeley: University of California Press.

Burke, K. (1954/1964). *Permanence and change* (2nd ed.). Berkeley: University of California Press.

Burke, K. (1966). *Language as symbolic action*. Berkeley: University of California Press.

Bush approval falls to 33%, Congress earns rare praise. (2006, March 15). The Pew Research Center for the People and the Press. http://people-press.org/reports/display.php3?ReportID=271. Retrieved on August 31, 2006.

Bush fell short on duty at Guard: Records show pledges unmet. (2004, September 8). *Boston Globe*. http://www.boston.com/news/nation/articles/2004/09/08/bush_fell_short_on_duty_at_guard/. Retrieved on August 29, 2006.

By the numbers. (2000, February 22). *Los Angeles Times*, p. A12.

Caldwell, L. M. (2007, August 6). Rudy Giuliani's daughter is supporting Barack Obama. *Slate*. http://slate.com/id/2171730/. Retrieved on August 24, 2007.

Campaign '08: Analysis of key voter groups. (2007, April 26). Pew Research Center for the People and the Press. http://pewresearch.org/pubs/463/campaign-2008-voter-groups. Retrieved on September 12, 2007.

Campaign contributions by tobacco interests (2006, September). Common Cause. http://tobaccofreeaction.org/contributions/september2006/september2006.pdf. Retrieved on June 10, 2007.

Campaigns spin debate advantage. (2004, September 30). CNN.com. http://www.cnn.com/2004/ALLPOLITICS/09/29/debate.main/index.html. Retrieved on May 16, 2007.

Campbell, A., Converse, P. E., Miller, W. E., & Stokes, D. E. (1960). *The American voter*. New York: John Wiley & Sons.

Campbell, D. E., & Munson, J. Q. (2005). *The religion card: Gay marriage and the 2004 election*. http://www.nd.edu/~dcampbe4/RELIGION%20CARD.pdf. Retrieved on August 16, 2006.

Candidates start early in Iowa for 2008 presidential race (2005, November 3). Fox News.com. http://www.foxnews.com/story/0,2933,174366,00.html. Retrieved on July 19, 2006.

Cannon, C. M. (2007, January/February). Untruth and consequences. *The Atlantic Monthly*. http://www.theatlantic.com/doc/prem/200701/cannon-lying. Retrieved on July 27, 2007.

Cantlupe, J. (2006, August 11). Report details the way Cunningham made deals. *San Diego Union Tribune*, p. 1.

Cantril, A. H. (1991). *The opinion connection: Polling, politics, and the press*. Washington, DC: Congressional Quarterly Press.

Cappella, J. N., & Jamieson, K. H. (1997). *Spiral of cynicism: The press and the public good*. New York: Oxford University Press.

Carey, J. W. (1975). A cultural approach to communication. *Communication, 2*, 1–22.

Carey, J. W. (1989). *Communication as culture: Essays on media and society*. Boston: Unwin Hyman.

Carey, J. W. (2002). American journalism, on, before, and after September 11. In B. Zelizer & S. Allan (Eds.), *Journalism after September 11*. New York: Routledge.

Carlin, D. B. (1989). A defense of the "debate" in presidential debates. *Journal of the American Forensic Association, 25*, 208–213.

Carlin, D. B. (2005). Debate watch: Creating a public sphere for the unheard voices. In M. S. McKinney, L. L. Kaid, D. G. Bystrom, & D. B. Carlin (Eds.), *Communicating politics: Engaging the public in democratic life*. New York: Peter Lang.

Carlin, D. B., Howard, C., Stanfield, S., & Reynolds, L. (1991). The effects of presidential debate formats on clash: A comparative analysis. *Argumentation and Advocacy*, *27*, 126–136.

Carlin, D. B., & McKinney, M. S. (Eds.). (1994). *The 1992 presidential debates in focus*. Westport, CT: Praeger.

Carter, S. L. (1998). *Civility: Manners, morals, and the etiquette of democracy*. New York: Harper Perennial.

Carter, S., Fico, F., & McCabe, J. A. (2002). Partisan and structural balance in local television election coverage. *Journalism and Mass Communication Quarterly*, *79*, 41–53.

Cassel, C. A. (1993). A test of Converse's theory of party support. *Journal of Politics*, *55*, 664–681.

Castells, M., Fernandez-Ardevol, M., Qiu, J. L., & Sey, A. (2007). *Mobile communication and society: A global perspective*. Cambridge: MIT Press.

Causin, T., Howard, P., & Miller, M. (2005, December 6). Projecting US Senate campaign expenditures in 2006. Center for Communication and Civic Engagement Working Paper #2005-2. http://www.campaignaudit.org. Retrieved on February 14, 2007.

A certain uncertainty. (2005). Center for Politics and Public Affairs, Franklin and Marshall University. http://www.fandm.edu/x8135.xml. Retrieved on September 14, 2007.

Chace, J. (2004). *1912: Wilson, Roosevelt, Taft and Debs—the election that changed the country*. New York: Simon & Schuster.

Chaddock, G. R. (2006, June 21). US high school dropout rate: High, but how high? *Christian Science Monitor*. http://www.csmonitor.com/2006/0621/p03s02-ussc.html. Retrieved on September 13, 2007.

Chadwick, A. (2006). *Internet politics: States, citizens, and new communication technologies*. Oxford: Oxford University Press.

Chaffee, S. H. (1981). Mass media in political campaigns: An expanding role. In R. E. Rice & W. J. Paisley (Eds.), *Public communication campaigns* (pp. 181–198). Beverly Hills, CA: Sage.

Chaffee, S. H., Ward, L. S., & Tipton, L. P. (1970). Mass communication and political socialization. *Journalism Quarterly*, *47*, 647–666.

Church, G. J. (1996, August 12). Ripping up welfare. *Time*, 16–22.

Chyi, H. I., & McCombs, M. (2004). Media salience and the process of framing: Coverage of the Columbine school shootings. *Journalism and Mass Communication Quarterly*, *81*, 22–35.

Citizens, meeting in community forums around the country, see free air time as best way to check money in politics (2001, November/December). *The Political Standard*, *4*, 1.

Civic and policy engagement of youth. (2006). National Conference of State Legislatures. http://www.ncsl.org/programs/cyf/engagement.htm. Retrieved on August 1, 2006.

Civic education of American youth: From state policies to school district practices. (1999). Lyndon B. Johnson School of Public Affairs, University of Texas at Austin, Policy Research Project Report, Number 133.

Civic youth. (2007). The Center for Information and Research on Civic Learning and Engagement. http://www.civicyouth.org/staff_advisory/index.htm. Retrieved on September 13, 2007.

Clark, J. (2006, September 29). YouTube in me world. *In These Times*. http://www.inthesetimes.com/article/2836/. Retrieved on April 27, 2007.

Clark, W. K. (2006, March 13). A petty Hitler. *Wall Street Journal*, p. A18.

Clinton, B. (1996, May 12). Gratitude, like love, never ends. *Los Angeles Times*, p. M5.

Clinton, J. D., & Lapinski, J. S. (2004). "Targeted" advertising and voter turnout: An experimental study of the 2000 presidential election. *Journal of Politics*, *66*, 69–96.

Cloud, D. S. (2006, August 30). Rumsfeld says war critics haven't learned lessons of history. *New York Times*, p. A4.

Cohen, B. C. (1963). *The press and foreign policy*. Princeton, NJ: Princeton University Press.

Coleman, N. (2007, May 17). Here's a name for the next hit list: Rachel Paulose. *Minneapolis Star & Tribune*. http://www.startribune.com/coleman/story/1191198 .html. Retrieved on July 16, 2007.

Colford, P. D. (1996, March 31). News weeklies hold big sway over campaigns. *Minneapolis Star & Tribune*, p. A20.

The coming crisis in citizenship: Higher education's failure to teach America's history and institutions. (2006). Intercollegiate Studies Institute: American Civic Literacy Program. http://www.americancivicliteracy.org/report/pdf/09-26-06/civic_literacy_report.pdf. Retrieved on September 20, 2007.

Common Cause and Democracy 21 file comments with FEC on financing of presidential nominating conventions. (2003, May 23). *Democracy 21*. http://www.democracy21.org/index.asp?Type=B_PR&SEC=%7BC052F433-38ED-467D-8F7B-E64DE8CBC314%7D&DE=%7B3C7A4C54-02BD-4552-8274-5380BE8192DB. Retrieved on June 21, 2007.

Connell, R. W. (1972). Political socialization in the American family: The evidence reexamined. *Public Opinion Quarterly*, *36*, 323–333.

Conover, P. J., & Feldman, S. (1984). How people organize the political world: A schematic model. *American Journal of Political Science*, *28*, 93–126.

Conrad, C. (1993). Political debates as televisual form. *Argumentation and Advocacy*, *30*, 62–76.

Converse, P. E. (1976). *The dynamics of party support*. Beverly Hills, CA: Sage.

Cook, C. E. (2004, June 28). Nader, although weaker, may reprise spoiler role. Spokesman-Review.com. http://www.spokesmanreview.com/breaking/story .asp?ID=2426. Retrieved on August 17, 2007.

Cook, W. (2007, April 23). 18–24-year-olds choose Obama & Giuliani. *Campus Report* Online.net. http://www.campusreportonline.net/main/articles.php?id=1630. Retrieved on September 13, 2007.

Cooper, R. T. (1996, August 8). Dole carved from Kansas bedrock. *Los Angeles Times*, p. A1.

Cooperman, A. (2004, November 4). Same-sex bans fuel conservative agenda. *Washington Post*, p. A39.

Corley, M. (2006). Your massive election guide to 2008 prez campaign staffs. http://www.tpmcafe.com/blog/electioncentral/2006/dec/21/your_massive_election_central/_guide_to_2008_presidential_campaign_staffs. Retrieved on March 26, 2007.

Cornelius, R. M. (2007). W. J. Bryan and the Scopes trial. http://www.bryan.edu/803.html. Retrieved on August 16, 2007.

Cornfield, M. (2004). The Internet and campaign 2004: A look back at the campaigners. http://www.pewinternet.org/pdfs/cornfield_commentary.pdf. Retrieved on April 23, 2007.

Corrado, A., Mann, T. E., & Potter, T. (2003). *Inside the campaign finance battle: Court testimony on the new reforms.* Washington, DC: Brookings Institution Press.

Crespi, I. (1980). The case of presidential popularity. In A. H. Cantril (Ed.), *Polling on the issues* (pp. 28–51). Cabin John, MD: Seven Locks Press.

Crime and victims statistics (2006). U.S. Department of Justice. http://www.ojp.usdoj.gov/bjs/cvict.htm. Retrieved on July 12, 2006.

Cronin, B. (2001). The paradox of hegemony: America's ambiguous relationship with the United Nations. *European Journal of International Relations, 7,* 103–130.

Crosbie, V. (2004, March 4). What newspapers and their web sites must do to survive. *Online Journalism Review.* http://www.ojr.org/ojr/business/1078349998.php. Retrieved on July 27, 2006.

Crouse, T. (1972). *The boys on the bus.* New York: Random House.

Crowley, B. E. (2006, October 1). Who is Mark Foley? *Palm Beach Post.* http://www.palmbeachpost.com/blogs/content/shared-blogs/palmbeach/floridapolitics/entries/2006/10/01/who_is_mark_foley.html. Retrieved on October 4, 2006.

Cundy, D. T. (1986). Political commercials and candidate image. In L. L. Kaid, D. Nimmo, & K. R. Sanders (Eds.), *New perspectives on political advertising* (pp. 210–247). Carbondale: Southern Illinois University Press.

Curtin, R., Presser, S., & Singer, E. (2005). Changes in telephone survey nonresponse over the past quarter century. *Public Opinion Quarterly, 69,* 87–98.

Dahl, R. A. (1972). *Democracy in the United States: Promise and performance* (2nd ed.). Chicago: Rand McNally.

Dao, J. (2000, January 30). Analysts question wisdom of Bradley's new aggressiveness. *New York Times,* p. A18.

Dauber, C. (1989). Debate as empowerment. *Journal of the American Forensic Association, 25,* 205–207.

Daves, R. P., & Newport, F. (2005). Pollsters under attack: 2004 election incivility and its consequences. *Public Opinion Quarterly, 69,* 670–681.

Davis, D. K. (1981). Issues, information, and connotation in candidate imagery: Evidence from a laboratory experiment. *International Political Science Review, 2,* 461–479.

Davis, R. H. (2004, March 21). The anatomy of a smear campaign. *Boston Globe.* http://www.boston.com/news/politics/president/articles/2004/03/21/the_anatomy_of_a_smear_campaign/. Retrieved on March 29, 2006.

The dawn of e-life. (1999, September 20). *Newsweek*, 38–41.

Dawson, R. E., Prewitt, K., & Dawson, K. S. (1977). *Political socialization* (2nd ed.). Boston: Little, Brown.

The debate effect: How the press covered the pivotal period, the major stories. (2004, October 27). Journalism.org. http://journalism.org/node/198. Retrieved on September 28, 2006.

Delia, J. G., & Grossberg, L. (1977). Interpretation and evidence. *Western Journal of Speech Communication, 41*, 32–42.

Delli Carpini, M. X. (1994). Scooping the voters? The consequences of the networks' early call of the 1980 presidential race. *Journal of Politics, 46*, 866–885.

Delli Carpini, M. X. (2005). An overview of the state of citizens' knowledge about politics. In M. S. McKinney, L. L. Kaid, D. G. Bystron, & D. B. Carlin (Eds.), *Communicating politics: Engaging the public in democratic life* (pp. 27–40). New York: Peter Lang.

Delli Carpini, M. X., & Keetzer, S. (1993). Measuring political knowledge: Putting first things first. *American Journal of Political Science, 37*, 1179–1206.

Dennis, J., Chaffee, S. H., & Choe, S. Y. (1978). Impact on partisan, image, and issue voting. In S. Kraus (Ed.), *The great debates: Carter vs. Ford, 1976* (pp. 314–330). Bloomington: Indiana University Press.

Denton, R. E. (2006). *Moral leadership and the American presidency*. Lanham, MD: Rowman & Littlefield.

Denton, R. E., & Woodward, G. C. (1990). *Political communication in America* (2nd ed.). New York: Praeger.

Derbyshire, J. (2003, October 20). Third-party peril. *National Review*. http://www.nationalreview.com/derbyshire/derbyshire200310200831.asp. Retrieved on August 17, 2007.

Dervin, B. (1981). Mass communication: Changing conceptions of the audience. In R. E. Rice & W. J. Paisley (Eds.), *Public communication campaigns* (pp. 71–87). Beverly Hills, CA: Sage.

Devitt, E. G., Jr. (1997). Framing politicians: The transformation of candidate arguments in presidential campaign news coverage, 1980, 1988, 1992, and 1996. *American Behavioral Scientist, 40*, 1139–1160.

Devlin, L. P. (1986). An analysis of presidential television commercials, 1952–1984. In L. L. Kaid, D. Nimmo, & K. R. Sanders (Eds.), *New perspectives on political advertising* (pp. 21–54). Carbondale: Southern Illinois University Press.

Devlin, L. P. (1995). Political commercials in American presidential elections. In L. L. Kaid & C. Holtz-Bacha (Eds.), *Political advertising in western democracies: Parties and candidates on television* (pp. 186–205). Thousand Oaks, CA: Sage.

DHinMI (2005, March 31). Whither political advertising? *The next hurrah*. http://thenexthurrah.typepad.com/the_next_hurrah/2005/03/advertising.html. Retrieved on February 7, 2007.

Diamond, E., & Bates, S. (1992). *The spot: The rise of political advertising on television* (3rd ed.). Cambridge, MA: MIT Press.

Did Democrats page Mark Foley? (2006). *Yahoo News.* http://news.yahoo.com/ s/ibd/20061002/bs_ibd_ibd/2006102issues01. Retrieved on October 4, 2006.

Dillman, D. A., Sinclair, M. D., & Clark, J. R. (1993). Effects of questionnaire length, respondent-friendly design, and a difficult question on response rates for occupant addressed census mail surveys. *Public Opinion Quarterly, 57,* 289–304.

Dionne, E. J. (1991). *Why Americans hate politics.* New York: Touchstone Books.

Dionne, E. J. (1996). *They only look dead: Why progressives will dominate the next political era.* New York: Simon & Schuster.

Djerejian, G. (2006, April 21). The tragedy of George W. Bush. *The Belgravia Dispatch.* http://www.belgraviadispatch.com/2006/04/the_tragedy_of_george _w_bush_1.html. Retrieved on July 17, 2006.

Dobbs, M. (2004, August 22). Swift boat accounts incomplete: Critics fail to disprove Kerry's version of Vietnam War episode. *Washington Post,* p. A1.

Dohmen, T. J., Falk, A., Huffman, D., & Sunde, U. (2006, October). The intergenerational transmission of risk and trust attitudes. IZA Discussion Paper No. 2380 Available at SSRN: http://ssrn.com/abstract=941116. Retrieved on August 21, 2007.

Dole-Kemp truth watch (1996, October 10). http://www.politicsnow.com/news/ Oct96/10/pn1010dkrebut/. Retrieved on October 11, 1996.

Don't look now. (1996, November 18). *Newsweek,* 106–110.

Donald, D. H. (1995). *Lincoln.* New York: Simon & Schuster.

Dowd, M. (1999, August 18). White noise. *New York Times,* p. A25.

Downs, A. (1957). *An economic theory of democracy.* New York: Harper & Row.

Drew, D., & Weaver, D. (1998). Voter learning in the 1996 presidential election. Did the media matter? *Journalism and Mass Communication Quarterly, 75,* 292–301.

Drew, E. (1999a, July/August). And for the dollar. *The Political Standard, 2,* 2.

Drew, E. (1999b). *The corruption of American politics: What went wrong and why.* Secaucus, NJ: Birch Lane Press.

Druckman, J. N. (2003). The power of television images: The first Kennedy-Nixon debate revisited. *Journal of Politics, 65,* 559–571.

Dube, J. (2006, November 6). A dozen tips for writing news online. Committee of Concerned Journalists. http://www.concernedjournalists.org/node/470. Retrieved on April 26, 2007.

Dubose, L. (2001, February 15). Bush's hit man. *The Nation.* http://www.thenation .com/doc/20010305/dubose. Retrieved on July 26, 2006.

Duncan, H. D. (1965). Introduction to K. Burke, *Permanence and change* (2nd ed.). Boston: Beacon Press. (Original work published 1954.)

Dwyer, P. (1999, August 30). Why Washington won't clean up its act. *Business Week,* 19.

Dyson, E. (2004). Election 2004: Lessons for the future. Personal Democracy Forum. http://www.personaldemocracy.com/nod. Retrieved on April 4, 2007.

Edelman, M. (1988). *Constructing the political spectacle.* Chicago: University of Chicago Press.

Edsall, T. B. (2004, May 14). In boost for Democrats, FEC rejects proposed limits on small donors. *Washington Post*, p. A9.

Edsall, T. B., & Cillizza, C. (2006, March 11). Money's going to talk in 2008. *Washington Post*, p. A1.

Eggen, D., & Solomon, J. (2007, March 13). Firings had genesis in White House. *Washington Post*, p. A1.

Election results. (2004). http://www.cnn.com/ELECTION/2004/pages/results/states/US/P/00/epolls.0.html. Retrieved on July 26, 2007.

Eliasoph, N. (1998). *Avoiding politics: How Americans produce apathy in everyday life*. Cambridge: Cambridge University Press.

Elliott, W. R., & Sothirajah, J. (1993). Post debate analysis and media reliance: Influences on candidate image and voting probabilities. *Journalism Quarterly*, *70*, 321–335.

Ellsworth, J. W. (1965). Rationality and campaigning: A content analysis of the 1960 presidential campaign debates. *Western Political Quarterly*, *18*, 794–802.

Emrich, C. G., Brower, H. H., Feldman, J. M., & Garland, H. (2001). Images in words: Presidential rhetoric, charisma, and greatness. *Administrative Science Quarterly*, *46*, 527–557.

Engle, M. A. (2001). Can new technology beat the old campaign finance system? *Capital Eye*, *8*. http://www.opensecrets.org/newsletter/ce75/technology.asp. Retrieved on April 15, 2007.

Entman, R. (1993). Framing: Toward clarification of a fractured paradigm. *Journal of Communication*, *43*, 51–58.

Epstein, L. D. (1986). *Political parties in the American mold*. Madison: University of Wisconsin Press.

Erikson, R. S., Panagopoulos, C., & Wlezien, C. (2004). Likely (and unlikely) voters and the assessment of campaign dynamics. *Public Opinion Quarterly*, *68*, 588–601.

Fallows, J. (1996, February). Why Americans hate the media. *The Atlantic Monthly*, 45–64.

Fein, S., Goethals, G. R., & Kugler, M. B. (2007). Social influence on political judgments: The case of presidential debates. *Political Psychology*, *28*, 165–192.

Fico, F., & Freedman, E. (2001). Setting the news story agenda: Candidates and commentators in news coverage of a governor's race. *Journalism and Mass Communication Quarterly*, *78*, 437–449.

Filling Rahm's shoes. (2007, February 14). *The Hill*. http://thehill.com/editorials/filling-rahms-shoes-2007-02-14.html. Retrieved on September 14, 2007.

Finder, A. (1996, August 25). Welfare clients outnumber jobs they might fill. *New York Times*, pp. 1, 10.

Fineman, H. (1996, February 5). Last Call. *Newsweek*, 24.

Fineman, H. (1999, February 22). The survivor. *Newsweek*, 20.

Fineman, H. (1999, June 21). Here comes the son. *Newsweek*, 24.

Fineman, H. (1999, September 20). Pressing the flesh online. *Newsweek*, 50–53.

Fineman, H., & Isikoff, M. (1997, March 10). Strange bedfellows. *Newsweek*, 22–28.

Finkel, S. E., Guterbock, T. M., & Berg, M. J. (1991). Race-of-interviewer effects in a pre-election poll. *Public Opinion Quarterly, 55*, 313–330.

Finnegan, M. (2006, May 18). Westly stumbles in the mud. *Los Angeles Times,* p. 1.

Finnigan, M., & Saladay, R. (2005, November 9). All four of Schwarzenegger's ballot measures defeated. *Los Angeles Times*, p. 1.

Fiorina, M. P. (1992). An era of divided government. *Political Science Quarterly, 107*, 387–410.

Fisher, W. R. (1970). A motive view of communication. *Quarterly Journal of Speech, 56*, 131–139.

Fisher, W. R. (1987). *Human communication as narration.* Columbia: University of South Carolina Press.

Fiske, W. (2006, December 8). Allen speaks out for first time on last month's loss. *The Virginian-Pilot.* http://content.hamptonroads.com/story.cfm?story=115688&ran=82762. Retrieved on April 27, 2007.

527s in 2004 shatter previous records for political fundraising. (2004). Center for Public Integrity. http://www.publicintegrity.org/527/report.aspx?aid=435. Retrieved on June 25, 2007.

Flanagan, C. A., & Tucker, C. J. (1999). Adolescents' explanations for political issues: Concordance with their views of self and society. *Developmental Psychology, 35*, 1198–1209.

Flanagan, C. A., Gallay, L. S., Gill, S., Gallay, E., & Nti, N. (2005). What does democracy mean? Correlates of adolescents' views. *Journal of Adolescent Research, 20*, 193–218.

Forsythe, M., & Jensen, K. (2005, October 10). McCrery, Oxley, DeLay use contributions for jets, resorts, golf. Bloomberg.com. http://www.bloomberg.com/apps/news?pid=10000103&sid=a.wihIcOy2Sw&refer=us. Retrieved on September 28, 2007.

Foster, D., & Levinson, A. (1995, May 21). The anger rebellion: Anti-government mania on the march, paramilitary: Bombing awakens a shocked nation to a fury in its midst. *Los Angeles Times*, p. 1.

Fox, S. (2007, March 14). Latinos online. http://www.pewinternet.org/pdfs/Latinos_Online_March_14_2007.pdf. Retrieved on April 15, 2007.

Frammolino, R., & Fritz, S. (1997, February 26). Clinton led move for donors to stay night in White House. *Los Angeles Times*, pp. 1, 12.

Frana, A. W. (1989). Characteristics of effective argumentation. *Journal of the American Forensic Association, 25*, 200–202.

Frank, R. (2003). "These crowded circumstances": When pack journalists bash pack journalism. *Journalism, 4*, 4–41.

Frankovic, K. A. (2005). Reporting "the polls" in 2004. *Public Opinion Quarterly, 69*, 682–697.

Frederick, D., & Malcolm, A. (2007, August 12). Gay and lesbian power. *Los Angeles Times*, p. A27.

Frederick, D. & Malcolm, A. (2007, September 9). Red click, blue click. *Los Angeles Times*, p. A36.

Freedman, E., & Fico, F. (2004). Whither the experts? Newspaper use of horse race and issue experts in coverage of open governors' races in 2002. *Journalism and Mass Communication Quarterly, 81*, 498–510.

Freedman, P. W., & Lawton, D. (1999). Dos and don'ts of negative ads: What voters say. *Campaigns and Elections, 20*, 20–25.

Fremstad, S. (2004, January 30). Recent welfare reform research findings. Center on Budget and Policy Priorities. http://www.cbpp.org/1-30-04wel.htm.http://www.cbpp.org/1-30-04wel.htm. Retrieved on July 19, 2007.

Freud, S. (1932). Lecture XXXV: A philosophy of life. http://www.marxists.org/reference/subject/philosophy/works/at/freud.htm. Retrieved on August 22, 2007.

Freyman, R., & McGoldrick, B. (2000). *Neglection 2000 final report and conference: They pretend to talk to us, we pretend to vote: Candidates and young adults in Campaign 2000 and beyond.* Sponsored by the Third Millennium Project. (Released December 5, 2000.)

Friedenberg, R. V. (1979). "We are present here today for the purpose of having a joint discussion": The conditions requisite for political debates. *Journal of the American Forensic Association, 16*, 1–9.

Friedenberg, R. V. (1997). *Communication consultants in political campaigns.* New York: Praeger.

Friedman, H. S., Mertz, T. I., & DiMatteo, M. R. (1980). Perceived bias in the facial expressions of television news broadcasters. *Journal of Communication, 30*, 103–111.

Fritsch, J. (1996, July 6). Democrats as well as GOP profit from tobacco. *New York Times*, pp. 1, 8.

Frontline: The choice '96. (1996). http://www.pbs.org/wgbh/pages/frontline/shows/choice/. Retrieved on August 29, 2006.

Froomkin, D. (2007, July 9). Bush tries moving the goal posts. Washington Post.com. http://www.washingtonpost.com/wp-dyn/content/linkset/2005/04/11/LI2005041100879.htm. http://www.washingtonpost.com/wp-dyn/content/linkset/2005/04/11/LI2005041100879.html. Retrieved on July 9, 2007.

Fry, S. (2003). *Let's read about George W. Bush.* New York: Scholastic Press.

Fuller, J. (1996). *News values: Ideas for the information age.* Chicago: University of Chicago Press.

Funding clean elections (2007, March). U.S. Public Interest Research Group. http://www.uspirg.org/uploads/ox/GP/OxGPaTOMJTpkdsxgW7vlHiw/Funding_Clean_Elections.pdf. Retrieved on December 4, 2007.

The future of network TV news. (2006, July 10). Journalism.org. http://www.journalism.org/node/943. Retrieved on December 6, 2006.

Gailey, P. (1996, September 22). Commentary: Perot has a place at debates. *Detroit News.* http://www.detnews.com/1996/menu/stories/66214.htm. Retrieved on September 23, 1996.

Gamson, W. A. (1996). Media discourse as a framing resource. In A. N. Crigler (Ed.), *The psychology of human communication* (pp. 111–131). Ann Arbor: University of Michigan Press.

Ganly, G. (1991). Power to the people via personal electronic media. *Washington Quarterly*, pp. 5–22.

Garofoli, J. (2007, July 24). YouTube steals the Dem debate. *San Francisco Chronicle*. http://sfgate.com/cgi-bin/article.cgi?file=/c/a/2007/07/24/YOUDEBATE .TMP. Retrieved on September 25, 2007.

Garramone, G. M. (1984). Voter responses to negative political ads. *Journalism Quarterly*, *61*, 250–259.

Garramone, G. M. (1985). Effects of negative political advertising: The roles of sponsor and rebuttal. *Journal of Broadcasting and Electronic Media*, *29*, 147–159.

Geer, J. G. (2006). *In defense of negativity: Attack ads in presidential campaigns.* Chicago: University of Chicago Press.

Germond, J. W. (1999). *Fat man in a middle seat: Forty years of covering politics.* New York: Random House.

Gerstenzang, J., & Gold, M. (2000, January 30). Gore explains change in abortion stand. *Los Angeles Times*, p. A19.

Gertzen, J. (2006, April 15). Stem-cell rules criticized: Federal policies restrict funding. *Kansas City Star*. http://www.kansascity.com/mld/kansascity/ 14346712.htm. Retrieved on August 17, 2006.

Ghorpade, S. (1986). Agenda setting: A test of advertising's neglected function. *Journal of Advertising Research*, *25*, 23–27.

Gibbs, N. (1997, February 24). Cash-and-carry diplomacy. *Time*, 22–25.

Gillman, H. (2001). *The votes that counted: How the Court decided the 2000 presidential election.* Chicago: University of Chicago Press.

Gimpel, J. G. (2003). *Cultivating democracy: Civic environments and political socialization in America.* Washington, DC: Brookings Institution Press.

Gitel, S. (2007, August 16). Biden chides competitors on foreign policy experience. *New York Sun*. http://www.nysun.com/article/60618. Retrieved on August 24, 2007.

Gitlin, T. (1980). *The whole world is watching.* Berkeley: University of California Press.

Gitlin, T. (1995). *The twilight of common dreams: Why America is wracked by culture wars.* New York: Metropolitan Books.

Givhan, R. (2007, July 20). Hillary Clinton's tentative dip into new neckline territory. *Washington Post*, p. C01.

Glass, J., Bengston, V. L., & Dunham, C. C. (1986). Attitude similarity in three generational families: Socialization, status inheritance, or reciprocal influence? *American Sociological Review*, *51*, 685–698.

Gobetz, R. H., & Chanslor, M. (1999). A content analysis of CNN "Inside Politics" Adwatch coverage of high-profile, nonpresidential races. In L. L. Kaid & D. G. Bystrom (Eds.), *The electronic election: Perspectives on the 1996 campaign communication* (pp. 113–121). Mahwah, NJ: Lawrence Erlbaum.

Golan G., & Wanta, W. (2001). Second-level agenda setting in the New Hampshire primary: A comparison of coverage in three newspapers and public perceptions of candidates. *Journalism and Mass Communication Quarterly*, *78*, 247–259.

Gold, E. R. (1978). Political apologia: The ritual of self-defense. *Communication Monographs, 45*, 306–316.

Goldberg, S. (2000). *Attachment and development.* Hillsdale, NJ: Analytic Press.

Goldstein, K., & Freedman, P. (2002). Campaign advertising and voter turnout: New evidence for a stimulation effect. *Journal of Politics, 64*, 721–740.

Goldstein, K., & Ridout, T. N. (2004). Measuring the effects of televised political advertising in the United States. *Annual Review of Political Science, 7*, 205–226.

Goodnight, G. T. (1982). The personal, technical, and public spheres of argument: A speculative inquiry into the art of public deliberation. *Journal of the American Forensic Association, 18*, 214–227.

Goodnight, G. T. (1991). Controversy. In D. W. Parson (Ed.), *Argument in controversy* (pp. 1–13). Fairfax, VA: Speech Communication Association.

Goodnough, A. (1999, August 21). An on-air mayor gives his city an earful. *New York Times*, p. A1.

GOP tightens hold on Senate, defeats top Demo Daschle. (2004, November 3). MSNBC. http://www.msnbc.msn.com/id/6381429/. Retrieved on July 26, 2006.

Gould, L. L. (2005, October 30). Stop the campaigning: The Bush White House is in trouble because of its disdain for governing. *Washington Post*, p. B1.

Graber, D. A. (1987). Framing election news broadcasts: News context and its impact on the 1984 presidential election. *Social Science Quarterly, 68*, 552–568.

Graber, D. A. (1993). *Mass media and American politics* (4th ed.). Washington, DC: Congressional Quarterly Press.

Graff, G. M. (2005, December 20). Online campaigns 2005: Reflections from NYC, VA and CA. *Personal Democracy Forum.* http://www/personaldemocracy.com/node/778. Retrieved on April 5, 2007.

Green, J. (2004, June). Playing dirty. *The Atlantic Monthly.* http://www.theatlantic.com/doc/200406/green. Retrieved on July 11, 2007.

Green, J. (2007, September). The Rove presidency. *The Atlantic Monthly*, 52–72.

Greenberg, E. S. (1986). *Workplace democracy: The political effects of participation.* Ithaca, NY: Cornell University Press.

Greenberg, S. B. (2004). *The two Americas: Our current political deadlock and how to break it.* New York: St. Martin's Press.

Greene, K. E., & Hernson, P. S. (2002). Running against a stacked deck? Candidate assessments of campaign politics and political reform. *Campaigns and Elections.* http://findarticles.com/p/articles/mi_m2519/ is_4_23/ai_86517. Retrieved on June 27, 2007.

Greenhouse, L., & Kirkpatrick, D. D. (2007, June 26). Justices loosen ad restrictions in campaign law. *New York Times*, pp. A1, A18.

The greening of America. (1996, February 12). *U.S. News & World Report*, pp. 34–39.

Grenzke, J. (1990). Money and congressional behavior. In M. L. Nugent & J. R. Johannes (Eds.), *Money, elections, and democracy* (pp. 143–164). Boulder, CO: Westview Press.

Grieve, T. (2004, August 31). The passion of the Rudy. Salon.com. http://dir.salon .com/story/news/feature/2004/08/31/rnc_day_one/index.html. Retrieved on August 25, 2006.

Grimes, C. (1999, February). Whither the civic journalism bandwagon? Discussion paper, Joan Shorenstein Center for Press, Politics, and Public Policy. Cambridge, MA: Harvard University.

Gronbeck, B. E. (1992). Negative narratives in 1988 presidential campaign ads. *Quarterly Journal of Speech, 78,* 333–346.

Grunig, J. E. (1989). Publics, audiences and market segments: Segmentation principles for campaigns. In C. T. Salmon (Ed.), *Information campaigns: Balancing social values and social change* (pp. 199–228). Newbury Park, CA: Sage.

Grunwald, M. (2007, June 20). Bloomberg's independent streak. *Time.* http://www .time.com/time/nation/article/0,8599,1635129,00.html. Retrieved on June 27, 2007.

Grunwald, M., & Cillizza, C. (2006, October 8). Foley consuming GOP as election draws near. *Washington Post,* p. A1.

A guide to reaching young voters (2004). The Institute of Politics, Harvard University.

Habermas, J. (1989). *The structural transformation of the public sphere: An inquiry into a category of bourgeois society* (T. Burger, Trans.). Cambridge: MIT Press. (Original work published 1962.)

Hahn, D. (2002). *Political communication: Rhetoric, government and citizens* (2nd ed.). State College, PA: Strata Publishing.

Hallin, D. C. (1992). Sound bite news: Television coverage of elections, 1968–1988. *Journal of Communication, 42,* 5–24.

Halpin, J., Heidbreder, J., Lloyd, M., Woodhull, P., Scott, B., Silver, J., & Turner, S. D. (2007). The structural imbalance of political talk radio. Center for American Progress. http://www.americanprogress.org/issues/2007/06/talk _radio.html. Retrieved on August 30, 2007.

Halstead, T. (1999, August). A politics for Generation X. *The Atlantic Monthly,* 33–42.

Hansen, S. (2001, March 30). Let them spend millions. Salon.com. http://archive .salon.com/books/int/2001/03/30/smith/index.htm. Retrieved on June 27, 2007.

Harden, B. (1996, May 13). But how does Bob Dole's dialect play in Peoria? *Los Angeles Times,* p. E3.

Harp, S. (2006, July 19). Coining "neochristianity." *The Daily Texan.* http:// www.dailytexanonline.com/media/storage/paper410/news/2006/07/19/ Opinion/Coining.neochristianity2132828.shtml?norewrite200608247944& sourcedomain=www.dailytexanonline.com. Retrieved on August 24, 2006.

Harris, J. F. (2004, September 2). Cheney calls Kerry unfit: Democrat joins Vice President in barrage against challenger. *Washington Post,* p. A1.

Harrison, T. M., Stephen, T. D., Husson, W., & Fehr, B. J. (1991). Image versus issues in the 1984 presidential election. *Human Communication Research, 18,* 209–227.

Hart, R. P. (1987). *The sound of leadership: Presidential communication in the modern age*. Chicago: University of Chicago Press.

Hart, R. P. (1999). *Seducing America: How television charms the modern voter*. Thousand Oaks, CA: Sage.

Hart, R. P. (2000). *Campaign talk: Why elections are good for us*. Princeton, NJ: Princeton University Press.

Harvey, M. (2003). The nuts and bolts of college writing. http://nutsandbolts .washcoll.edu/plagiarism.html. Retrieved on August 30, 2006.

Harwood, J. (2004, October 27). As a final gambit, parties are trying to damp turnout. *Wall Street Journal*, p. 1.

Hawkins, R. P., & Pingree, S. (1982). Television's influence on social reality. In D. Pearl, L. Bouthilet, & J. Lazar (Eds.), *Television and behavior: Vol. 2*. Rockville, MD: U.S. Government Printing Office.

Held, D., McGrew, A., Goldblatt, D., & Perraton, J. (1999). *Global transformations: Politics, economics, and culture*. Stanford, CA: Stanford University Press.

Hellweg, S. A. (1979). An examination of voter conceptualizations of the ideal political candidate. *Southern Speech Communication Journal, 44*, 373–385.

Hellweg, S. A. (1995). Campaigns and candidate images in presidential elections. In K. L. Hacker (Ed.), *Candidate images in presidential elections* (pp. 1–18). Westport, CT: Praeger.

Herbst, S. (1995). On the disappearance of groups: 19th century and early 20th century conceptions of public opinion. In T. L. Glasser & C. T. Salmon (Eds.), *Public opinion and the communication of consent* (pp. 89–104). New York: Guilford Press.

Herman, K. (2007, April 25). McCain running a "little different" campaign. Cox Newspapers. http://www.coxwashington.com/hp/content/reporters/stories/ 2007/04/25/BC_MCCAIN_ANNOUNCES25_1STLDCOX.html. Retrieved on August 24, 2007.

Herr, N. (2001). *The sourcebook for teaching science: Television and health*. http:// www.csun.edu/science/health/docs/tv&health.html. Retrieved on July 27, 2006.

Herrera, K. (2006, January 12). New year produces a new Schwarzenegger. Pacific News Service. http://news.pacificnews.org/news/view_article.html? article_id=fc028eb67bfb43bfcb43a7c9753b4ad1. Retrieved on July 17, 2006.

Hibbing, J., & Theiss-Morse, E. (1995). *Congress as public enemy*. Cambridge: Cambridge University Press.

Hibbing, J., & Theiss-Morse, E. (2002). *Stealth democracy*. Cambridge: Cambridge University Press.

Hill, D. B., & Luttbeg, N. R. (1983). *Trends in American electoral behavior* (2nd ed.). Itasca, IL: F. E. Peacock.

Hillary Clinton is first First Lady in Senate. (2000, November 7). *BBC on this day*. http://news.bbc.co.uk/onthisday/hi/dates/stories/november/7/newsid _4385000/4385582.stm. Retrieved on January 26, 2007.

Hillary Clinton's campaign song: A job for Bachman Turner Overdrive. (2007, May 17). *Rolling Stone*. http://www.rollingstone.com/rockdaily/index.php/2007/ 05/17/hillary-clintons-campaign-song-a-job-for-bachman-turner-overdrive/. Retrieved on September 6, 2007.

Hillygus, D. S., & Shields, T. (2007). The persuadable voter: Strategic candidates and wedge issues. http://www.people.fas.harvard.edu/~hillygus/chapter1.pdf. Retrieved on August 24, 2007.

Hinck, E. A. (1988). Enacting the presidency: Political debates and dramatic enactment of presidential character. Paper presented at the Speech Communication Association Convention, New Orleans, LA.

Hinds, L. B., & Windt, T. O. (1991). *The Cold War as rhetoric: The beginnings, 1945–1950.* New York: Praeger.

Hinich, M. J., & Munger, M. C. (1994). *Ideology and the theory of political choice.* Ann Arbor: University of Michigan Press.

Hirschfeld, L. (1997). The conceptual politics of race: Lessons from our children. *Ethos, 25,* 63–92.

Hofstetter, R. C., Zukin, C., & Buss, T. F. (1978). Political imagery and information in an age of television. *Journalism Quarterly, 55,* 562–569.

Hogan, J. M. (1989a). Managing dissent in the Catholic Church: A reinterpretation of the pastoral letter on war and peace. *Quarterly Journal of Speech, 75,* 400–415.

Hogan, J. M. (1989b). Media nihilism and the presidential debates. *Journal of the American Forensic Association, 25,* 220–225.

Holbert, R. L., Benoit, W. L., Hansen, G. J., & Wen, W. (2002). The role of communication in the formation of an issue-based citizenry. *Communication Monographs, 69,* 296–310.

Holland, S. (2007, July 10). Unpopular US Congress enduring tough times. Reuters. http://www.netscape.com/viewstory/2007/07/11/congress-popularity-below-bushs/?url=http%3A%2F%2Fwww.alertnet.org%2Fthenews%2Fnewsdesk%2FN09237000.htm&frame=true. Retrieved on September 13, 2007.

Hollihan, T. A. (2006). Sí, se puede!: An engaged look at the Villaraigosa mayoral campaign. In P. Riley (Ed.), *Engaging argument* (pp. 333–341). Washington, DC: National Communication Association.

Hollihan, T. A., & Baaske, K. T. (2005). *Arguments and arguing: The products and process of human decision making* (2nd ed.). Prospect Heights, IL: Waveland Press.

Hollihan, T. A., Klumpp, J. F., & Riley, P. (1999). Public argument in the post-mass media age. In F. H. van Eemeren, R. Grootendorst, J. A. Blair, & C. A. Willard (Eds.), *Proceedings of the fourth international conference of the International Society for the Study of Argumentation* (pp. 365–371). Amsterdam: Sic-Sat.

Hollihan, T. A., & Riley, P. (1981). The 1980 presidential debates: An analysis of argument types, issues, and perceptions of the candidates. Paper presented at the International Communication Association Convention, Minneapolis, MN.

Hollihan, T. A., & Riley, P. (1993). Rediscovering ideology. *Western Journal of Communication, 57,* 272–277.

Hollihan, T. A., Riley, P., & Klumpp, J. F. (1993). Greed versus hope, self-interest versus community: Reinventing argumentative praxis in post-free marketplace America. In R. E. McKerrow (Ed.), *Argument and the post-modern challenge* (pp. 332–339). Fairfax, VA: Speech Communication Association.

Hook, J., & Brownstein, R. (2006, October 4). Foley case shakes GOP. *Los Angeles Times*, p. A1.

Hook, J., & Chen, E. (1997, March 7). Fund-raising is routine at Capitol, lobbyists say. *Los Angeles Times*, pp. 1, 18.

Horrigan, J. B. (2006, March 22). Online news: For many home broadband users, the Internet is a primary news source. *Pew Internet and American life project.* http://www.pewinternet.org/pdfs/PIP_News.and.Broadband.pdf. Retrieved on April 26, 2007.

House winners raised a record average of $1.1 million. (2006, November 8). *The Campaign Finance Institute.* http://www.cfinst.org/pr/prRelease.aspx?releaseID=102. Retrieved on February 14, 2007.

Howard, P. N. (2006). *New media campaigns and the managed citizen.* New York: Cambridge University Press.

How broadcasters' ad revenues rise while audiences shrink (2001, July). *The Political Standard, 4*, p. 3.

Howell, D. (2007, July 29). A column prompts a dressing-down. *Washington Post*, p. B6.

Howell, S. E., & McLean, W. P. (2001). Performance and race in evaluating minority mayors. *Public Opinion Quarterly, 65*, 321–343.

How Gore caters to the press. (2000, February 7). *Newsweek*, 4.

How to become a top banana. (2000, February 7). *Time*, 42–55.

Huckfeldt, R., Plutzer, E., & Sprague, J. (1993). Alternative contexts of political behavior: Churches, neighborhoods, and individuals. *Journal of Politics, 55*, 365–381.

Hulse, C., & Zeleny, J. (2006, October 3). Pressure grows for Republicans over Foley case. *New York Times*, p. A1.

Hurtado, A. (1994). Does similarity breed respect? Interviewer evaluations of Mexican-descent respondents in a bilingual survey. *Public Opinion Quarterly, 58*, 77–95.

Husson, W., Stephen, T., Harrison, T. M., & Fehr, B. J. (1988). An interpersonal communication perspective on images of political candidates. *Human Communication Research, 14*, 397–421.

Hutchings, V. L., Valentino, N. A., Philpot, T. S., & White, I. K. (2004). The compassion strategy: Race and the gender gap in campaign 2000. *Public Opinion Quarterly, 68*, 512–541.

Hyman, H. H. (1969). *Political socialization: A study in the psychology of political behavior.* Glencoe, IL: Free Press.

Immigrant union members: Numbers and trends. (2004, May). Migration Policy Institute. http://www.migrationpolicy.org/pubs/7_Immigrant_Union_Membership.pdf. Retrieved on July 20, 2006.

Immigration: Polling Report.com. (2007). http://www.pollingreport.com/immigration.htm. Retrieved on July 23, 2007.

In the public interest? A content study of early coverage of the 2000 campaign. (2000, Feb. 3). Journalism.org. http://journalism.org/node/397. Retrieved on September 28, 2006.

Iorio, S. H., & Huxman, S. S. (1996). Media coverage of political issues and the framing of personal concerns. *Journal of Communication, 46*, 97–115.

Iowa Politics.com Report. (2006, June 14). http://iowapolitics.com/index.iml? Content=119. Retrieved on July 19, 2006.

Irwin, G. A., & van Holsteyn, J. J. M. (2002). According to the polls: The influence of opinion polls on expectations. *Public Opinion Quarterly, 66*, 92–104.

Isikoff, M. (1999). *Uncovering Clinton: A reporter's story.* New York: Crown.

Iyengar, S. (1996). Framing responsibility for political issues. *Annals of the American Academy of Political and Social Science, 456*, 59–70.

Jackson: Bush actions "crime against constitution." (2007, July 2). CBS2Chicago .com. http://cbs2chicago.com/homepage/local_story_183225657.html. Retrieved on July 27, 2007.

Jacobs, L. R., & Page, B. I. (2003). Who influences U.S. foreign policy over time? Paper presented at the Inequality and American Democracy Conference, Princeton, NJ. http://www.princeton.edu/~csdp/events/pdfs/JacobsPage.pdf. Retrieved on June 27, 2007.

Jacobs, L. R., & Shapiro, R. Y. (1994). Issues, candidate image, and priming: The use of private polls in Kennedy's 1960 presidential campaign. *American Political Science Review, 88*, 527–540.

Jacobson, G. C. (2006). *A divider, not a uniter: George W. Bush and the American people.* New York: Pearson-Longman.

Jamieson, K. H. (1986). The evolution of political advertising in America. In L. L. Kaid, D. Ninno, & K. R. Sanders (Eds.), *New perspectives on political advertising* (pp. 1–20). Carbondale: Southern Illinois University Press.

Jamieson, K. H. (1992). *Dirty politics: Deception, distraction, and democracy.* New York: Oxford University Press.

Jamieson, K. H. (1992). *Packaging the presidency: A history and criticism of presidential campaign advertising* (2nd ed.). New York: Oxford University Press.

Jamieson, K. H. (1993). The subversive effects of a focus on strategy in news coverage of presidential campaigns. In *1-800-president: The report of the Twentieth Century Fund Task Force on Television and the campaign of 1992* (pp. 35–62). New York: Twentieth Century Fund Press.

Jamieson, K. H. (1996). *Packaging the presidency: A history and criticism of presidential campaign advertising.* (3rd ed.). New York: Oxford University Press.

Jamieson, K. H. (1999). *Campaigns for sale: A newsroom guide to political advertising.* A publication of the Political Coverage Project, The Radio and Television News Directors Foundation. http://www.rtnda.org/resources/politics/cfs.PDF. Retrieved on March 5, 2007.

Jamieson, K. H., & Adasiewicz, C. (2000). What can voters learn from election debates? In S. Coleman (Ed.), *Televised election debates: International perspectives* (pp. 25–42). New York: St. Martin's Press.

Jamieson, K. H., & Birdsell, D. S. (1988). *Presidential debates: The challenge of creating an informed electorate.* New York: Oxford University Press.

Jennings, M. K. (1992). Ideological thinking among mass publics and political elites. *Public Opinion Quarterly, 56*, 419–441.

Johnson, T. J. (1993a). Filling out the racing form: How the media covered the horse race in the 1988 primaries. *Journalism Quarterly, 70*, 300–310.

Johnson, T. J. (1993b). The seven dwarfs and other tales: How the networks and select newspapers covered the 1988 Democratic primaries. *Journalism Quarterly, 70*, 311–320.

Johnston, D. C. (2007, March 29). Income gap is widening, data shows. *New York Times.* http://www.nytimes.com/2007/03/29/business/29tax.html?ex=1332820800&en=fb472e72466c34c8&ei=5088&partner=rssnyt&emc=rss. Retrieved on July 19, 2007.

Jones, D. (2004, September 3). Ad wars and the search for truth. Counterbias .com. http://www.counterbias.com/109.html. Retrieved on March 2, 2007.

Joseph Biden's plagiarism; Michael Dukakis' attack video — 1988. (1998). Washington Post.com. http://www.washingtonpost.com/wp-srv/politics/special/clinton/frenzy/biden.htm. Retrieved on August 30, 2006.

Joslyn, R. A. (1981). The impact of campaign spot advertising on voting defections. *Human Communication Research, 7*, 347–360.

Joslyn, R. A. (1986). Political advertising and the meaning of elections. In L. L. Kaid, D. Nimmo, & K. R. Sanders (Eds.), *New perspectives on political advertising* (pp. 139–183). Carbondale: Southern Illinois University Press.

Just, M. R., Crigler, A. N., & Wallach, L. (1990). Thirty seconds or thirty minutes: What viewers learn from spot advertisements and candidate debates. *Journal of Communication, 40*, 120–133.

Kaid, L. L., & Chanslor, M. (1995). Changing candidate images: The effects of political advertising. In K. L. Hacker (Ed.), *Candidate images in presidential elections* (pp. 83–97). Westport, CT: Praeger.

Kaldenberg, D. O., Koenig, H. F., & Becker, B. W. (1994). Mail survey response rate patterns in a population of the elderly. *Public Opinion Quarterly, 58*, 68–76.

Kamber, V. (1997). *Poison politics: Are negative campaigns destroying democracy?* New York: Insight Books.

Kamieniecki, S. (1985). *Party identification, political behavior, and the American electorate.* Westport, CT: Greenwood.

Kane, P., & Murray, S. (2007, August 28). GOP senator pleaded guilty after restroom arrest. *Washington Post*, p. A1.

Kaplan, J. (1996, June 19–26). The politics of rage: Militias and the future of the far right. *The Christian Century*, pp. 657–662.

Kaplan, M. (2003). Local TV news coverage of politics and the obligations of broadcasters. The Lear Center Local News Archive. http://www.learcenter .org/pdf/SenateTestimony.pdf. Retrieved on October 24, 2006.

Kaplan, M., Goldstein, K., & Hale, M. (2005). Local news coverage of the 2004 campaigns: An analysis of nightly broadcasts in eleven markets. The Lear Center Local News Archive, Annenberg School for Communication, University of Southern California. http://www.localnewsarchive.org/pdf/LCLNA Final2004.pdf. Retrieved on December 5, 2006.

Kaplan, S. (1996, May/June). Tobacco Dole. *Mother Jones.* http://www.motherjones .com/news/special_reports/1996/05/kaplan.html. Retrieved on March 30, 2007.

Kapoor, S., & Kang, J. G. (1993). Political diversity is alive among publishers and opinion page editors. *Journalism Quarterly, 70,* 404–411.

Karlgaard, R. (2006, June 23). Should we lift North Korean sanctions? Forbes.com. http://www.typepad.com/t/trackback/5175567. Retrieved on July13, 2006.

Katz, C., & Baldassare, M. (1992). Using the "L-word" in public: A test of the spiral of silence in conservative Orange County, California. *Public Opinion Quarterly, 56,* 232–235.

Katz, J. (1996). The age of Paine. http://www.hotwired.com/wired/3.05/features/paine.html. Retrieved on November 2, 1997.

Kaye, K. (2005). Political Sims: Interactive games do serious politics. Personal Democracy Forum. http://www.personaldemocracy.com/node/500. Retrieved on April 5, 2007.

Keeter, S. (1987). The illusion of intimacy: Television and the role of candidate personal qualities in voter choice. *Public Opinion Quarterly, 51,* 344–358.

Keeter, S. (2006). The impact of cell phone noncoverage bias on polling in the 2004 presidential election. *Public Opinion Quarterly, 70,* 88–98.

Kelley, M. (2004). Debating the debates. http://www.law.harvard.edu/news/2004/09/15_debates.php. Retrieved on May 14, 2007.

Kellner, D. (1990). *Television and the crisis of democracy.* Boulder, CO: Westview Press.

Kelly, S., Jr. (1960). *Political campaigning.* Washington, DC: Brookings Institution Press.

Kempster, N. (1997, May 1). Chinese minister assures Clinton on Hong Kong rights. *Los Angeles Times,* p. 10.

Kendall, K. E., & Paine, S. C. (1995). Political images and voting decisions. In K. L. Hacker (Ed.), *Candidate images in presidential elections* (pp. 19–35). Westport, CT: Praeger.

Kendall, K. E., & Yum, J. O. (1984). Persuading the blue collar voter: Issues, images, and homophily. In R. N. Bostrom (Ed.), *Communication Yearbook 8* (pp. 707–722). Beverly Hills: Sage.

Kennamer, J. D., & Chaffee, S. H. (1982). Communication of political information during early presidential primaries: Cognition, affect, and uncertainty. In M. Burgoon (Ed.), *Communication Yearbook 5* (pp. 627–650). New Brunswick, NJ: Transaction Books.

Kennedy, R. F., Jr. (2006, June 1). Was the 2004 election stolen? *Rolling Stone.* http://www.rollingstone.com/news/story/10432334/was_the_2004_election_stolen. Retrieved on August 18, 2007.

Kenney, K., & Simpson, C. (1993). Was coverage of the 1988 presidential race by Washington's two major dailies biased? *Journalism Quarterly, 70,* 345–355.

Kenski, K., & Stroud, N. J. (2005). Who watches presidential debates? A comparative analysis of presidential debate viewing in 2000 & 2004. *American Behavioral Scientist, 49,* 213–228.

Ketupa.net. Media profiles Bloomberg. (2007). http://www.ketupa.net/bloomberg.htm. Retrieved on June 27, 2007.

Kharif, O. (2006, May 31). Social networking goes mobile. *BusinessWeek online*. http://www/businessweek.com/print/technology/content/may2006. Retrieved on March 19, 2007.

Kid gloves. (1996, November 18). *Newsweek*, 112–117.

Kiely, K. (2006, July 17). Growing number of voters ignore primary elections. *USA Today*. http://www.usatoday.com/news/washington/2006-07-16-primary-turnouts_x.htm. Retrieved on August 11, 2007.

Kinder, D. R. (2006, June 30). Politics and the life cycle. *Science*, 1905–1908.

King, E. G. (1990). Thematic coverage of the 1988 presidential primaries: A comparison of *USA Today* and the *New York Times*. *Journalism Quarterly*, *67*, 83–87.

King, J. D., & McConnell, J. B. (2003). The effect of negative campaign advertising on vote choice: The mediating influence of gender. *Social Science Quarterly*, *84*, 843–857.

Kiolbassa, J. (1996). *Local TV news goes to Washington: The 1992 election in Los Angeles*. Unpublished dissertation, University of Southern California, Los Angeles.

Kiousis, S., McDevitt, M., & Xu, W. (2005). The genesis of civic awareness: Agenda setting in political socialization. *Journal of Communication*, *55*, 756–774.

Kirkpatrick, D. D. (2007, January 23). Death knell may be near for public election funds. *New York Times*, p. 1.

Kirkpatrick, D. D. (2007, January 29). Feeding frenzy for a big story, even if it's false. *New York Times*, p. 1.

Kirkpatrick, D. D. (2007, April 3). Romney leads G.O.P. in money, tapping Wall St. and Mormons. *New York Times*, p. A1.

Kirkpatrick, D. D. (2007, June 7). Alaskan gets campaign cash; Florida road gets U.S. funds. *New York Times*, pp. 1, 29.

Klein, J. (2006). *Politics lost: How American democracy was trivialized by people who think you're stupid*. New York: Doubleday.

Klein, R. (2007, February 28). Kennedy, McCain try again on immigration. Boston.com. http://www.boston.com/news/nation/washington/articles/2007/02/28/kennedy_mccain_try_again_on_immigration/. Retrieved on July 24, 2007.

Klinenberg, E. (2005). Convergence: News production in a digital age. *The Annals of the American Academy of Political and Social Science*, *597*, 48–64.

Klinenberg, E. (2007, March/April). Breaking the news. *Mother Jones*. http://www.motherjones.com/news/feature/2007/03/breaking_the_news.html. Retrieved on July 11, 2007.

Klumpp, J. F., Riley, P., & Hollihan, T. A. (1995). Argument in the post-political age: Reconsidering the democratic lifeworld. In F. H. van Eemeren, R. Grootendorst, J. A. Blair, & C. A. Willard (Eds.), *Special fields and cases* (pp. 318–328). Amsterdam: Sic-Sat.

Koch, W. (2006, December 12). Poll: Washington scandals eating away at public trust. *USA Today*, p. 1.

Koprowski, G. J. (2006, January 18). Digital divide separates rural, urban Internet users. *Technewsworld.* http://www.technewsworld.com/rsstory/48190.html. Retrieved on April 19, 2007.

Kornblutt, A. E. (2007, April 2). Clinton shatters fund-raising record. *Washington Post*, p. A1.

Kovach, B., Rosenstiel, T., & Mitchell, A. (2006). State of the news media: An annual report on American journalism. Journalism.org. http://www.state ofthemedia.com/2006/printable_newspapers_audience.asp?media=1&cat=1. Retrieved on July 2, 2007.

Kranish, M. (2006, January 28). Family ties spark concern in lobby debate: Watchdogs want Congress to act. *Boston Globe.* http://www.boston.com/news/nation/ articles/2006/01/28/family_ties_spark_concern_in_lobby_debate/. Retrieved on December 5, 2007.

Kraus, S. (1988). *Televised presidential debates and public policy.* Hillsdale, NJ: Lawrence Erlbaum.

Krauthammer, C. (1997, February 28). A thousand friends. *Washington Post*, p. A21.

Kubiak, G. D. (1994). *The gilded dome.* Norman: University of Oklahoma Press.

Kuhnhenn, J. (2006, December 11). Legislator's win complicates ethics matters for Democrats. *Boston Globe.* http://www.boston.com/news/nation/articles/2006/ 12/11/legislators_win_complicates_ethics_matters_for_democrats. Retrieved on May 21, 2007.

Kuhnhenn, J. (2007, May 11). Romney's estimated wealth in millions. http://www .foxnews.com/wires/2007May11/0,4670,RomneyWealth,00.html. Retrieved on June 27, 2007.

Kuran, T. (1995). *Private truths, public lies: The social consequences of preference falsification.* Cambridge, MA: Harvard University Press.

Kurtz, H. (2004, November 24). Dan Rather to step down at CBS. *Washington Post*, p. A1.

LaGanga, M. L., & Broder, J. (1996, September 20). Dole's tumble sends his aides spinning. *Los Angeles Times*, p. A20.

LaGanga, M. L., & Shogren, E. (1996, October 19). Dole lashes out at Clinton over foreign donors. *Los Angeles Times*, pp. 1, 17.

Lambro, D. (2003, July 12). Republicans draw Hispanic voters from Democrats. *Washington Times.* http://www.washtimes.com/national/20030712-104208- 8767r.htm. Retrieved on August 24, 2006.

Lambro, D. (2006, July 13). A polarizing figure in a polarized age. Townhall.com. http://www.townhall.com/columnists/column.aspx?UrlTitle=a_polarizing _figure_in_a_polarized_age&ns=DonaldLambro&dt=07/13/2006&page= full&comments=true. Retrieved on August 24, 2007.

Lamoureux, E. R., Entrekin, H. S., & McKinney, M. S. (1994). Debating the debates. In D. B. Carlin & M. S. McKinney (Eds.), *The 1992 presidential debates in focus* (pp. 55–67). Westport, CT: Praeger.

Lanoue, D. J. (1991). The "turning point": Viewers' reactions to the second 1988 presidential debate. *American Politics Quarterly*, *19*, 80–95.

Lasswell, H. D. (1941). *Democracy through public opinion.* New York: George Banta.

Lau, R. R. (1994). An analysis of the accuracy of "trial heat" polls during the 1992 presidential election. *Public Opinion Quarterly, 58*, 2–20.

Lau, R. R., & Pomper, G. M. (2001). Effects of negative campaigning on turnout in U.S. Senate elections, 1988–1998. *Journal of Politics, 63*, 804–819.

Lau, R. R., & Pomper, G. M. (2002). Effectiveness of negative campaigning in U.S. Senate elections. *American Journal of Political Science, 46*, 47–66.

Lau, R. R., Sigelman, L., Heldman, C., & Babbit, P. (1999). The effects of negative political advertisements: A meta-analytical assessment. *American Political Science Review, 93*, 851–876.

Lawrence, J. (2006, August 8). Congress full of fortunate sons—and other relatives. *USA Today*, p. 1.

Layman, G. C., Carsey, T. M., & Horowitz, J. M. (2006). Party polarization in American politics: Characteristics, causes, and consequences. *Annual Review of Political Science, 9*, 83–110.

Leavey, P. (2007, February 23). '08 fallout: Vilsack announces that he's out. *The Democratic Daily*. http://blog.thedemocraticdaily.com/?p=5361. Retrieved on March 24, 2007.

LeClaire, J. (2006, February 27). Internet subscriber growth may be stalling, report suggests. *Technewsworld*. http://www.technewsworld.com/story/49079.html. Retrieved on April 19, 2007.

Leibovich, M. (2006, July 11). 'Pit Bull' of the House latches on to immigration. *New York Times*. http://www.nytimes.com/2006/07/11/washington/11sensenbrenner.html. Retrieved on July 13, 2006.

Lengel, A., & Barakat, M. (2006, May 22). Bribery allegedly caught on tape: Court filing says congressman hid cash in freezer. *Boston Globe*. http://www.boston.com/news/nation/washington/articles/2006/05/22/bribery_allegedly_caught_on_tape/. Retrieved on May 21, 2007.

Leon, M. (1993). Revealing character and addressing voters' needs in the 1992 presidential debates: A content analysis. *Argumentation and Advocacy, 30*, 88–105.

Levey, N. N., & Schmitt, R. B. (2006, October 4). Foley a victim of sex abuse, attorney says. *Los Angeles Times*, p. A18.

Lewis, N. A. (2007, March 6). Libby guilty of lying in C.I.A. leak case. *New York Times*, p. 1.

Lichter, S. R. (1988, July–August). How the press covered the primaries. *Public Opinion*, pp. 45–49.

Lieberman again claims "No freedom from religion" in Notre Dame address: Cites Judeo-Christian roots of America. (2000, October 26). *American Atheists*. http://www.atheists.org/flash.line/elec21.htm. Retrieved on August 15, 2006.

Lieberman losing ground in Senate race. (2006, July 20). http://www.abcnews.go.com/Politics/wireStory?id=2215760. Retrieved on July 25, 2006.

Lightman, D. (2007, February 2). The billion-dollar '08 campaign. *Chicago Tribune*. http://newsblogs.chicagotribune.com/news_theswamp/2007/02/the_billiondoll.html. Retrieved on February 14, 2007.

Lin, C. A. (1993). Modeling the gratification-seeking process of television viewing. *Human Communication Research, 20*, 224–244.

Lincoln campaign parade torch. (2007). Civil War@Smithsonian. http:// civilwar .si.edu/lincoln_torch.html. Retrieved on February 7, 2007.

Lind, B. (2000). The origins of political correctness: An accuracy in academia address. http://www.academia.org/lectures/lind1.html. Retrieved on August 22, 2007.

Lindeman, M., & Brady, R. (2006). Behind the controversy: A primer on U.S. presidential exit polls. http://www.publicopinionpros.com/from_field/2006/jan/ lindeman_1.asp. Retrieved on April 2, 2007.

Lipton, E. (2000, May 13). Giuliani decision on Senate expected in days. *New York Times*, p. B1.

Longo, N. V., & Meyer, R. P. (2006, May). College students and politics: A literature review. The Center for Information and Research on Civic Learning and Engagement. CIRCLE Working Paper 46. http://www.civicyouth.org/PopUps/ WorkingPapers/wp46LongoMeyer.pdf. Retrieved on September 18, 2007.

Louden, A. D. (1990). *Image construction in political spot advertising: The Hunt/Helms Senate campaign, 1984.* Unpublished dissertation, University of Southern California, Los Angeles.

Madden, M. (2006, April). Pew Internet and American life project. http://www .perinternet.org/pdfs/PIP Internet Impact.pdf. Retrieved on April 15, 2007.

Madsen, A. (1991). Partisan commentary and the first 1988 presidential debate. *Argumentation and Advocacy, 27,* 100–113.

Magleby, D. (2004). 527s had a substantial impact on the ground and air wars in 2004, will return: Swift Boat Veterans 527 played historic role. Center for the Study of Elections and Democracy. http://72.14.253.104/search?q=cache: w85u2WzwPgAJ:csed.byu.edu/PressReleases/Dec%2520%252016% 2520CSED%2520Press%2520Release%2520(2).pdf+527s+had+a+ substantial+impact+on+the+ground+and+air+wars&hl=en&ct=clnk&cd= 1&gl=us. Retrieved on June 25, 2007.

Maisel, L. S. (2007). *American political parties and elections: A very short introduction.* New York: Oxford University Press.

Mankinson, L. (2002). Where the money is: The geography of political fundraising. http://www.opensecrets.org/newsletter/ce71/02geog.asp. Retrieved on June 26, 2007.

Marable, M. (2004). How our children learn racism. *The Free Press.* http://www .freepress.org/columns/display4/2004/896. Retrieved on August 21, 2007.

Maraniss, D. (1996, August 12–18). How Bob Dole thinks. *Washington Post National Weekly Edition*, pp. 6–11.

Marcus, G. E. (1988). The structure of emotional response: 1984 presidential candidates. *American Political Science Review, 82,* 737–761.

Margolis, M., & Mauser, G. A. (1989). Public opinion as a dependent variable: A framework for analysis. *Political Communication and Persuasion, 6,* 87–108.

Markus, G. B. (1979). The political environment and the dynamics of public attitudes: A panel study. *American Journal of Political Science, 23,* 338–359.

Martin, J. (2002). *The education of John Dewey: A biography.* New York: Columbia University Press.

Matasar, A. (1986). *Corporate PACs and federal campaign financing laws*. New York: Quorum Books.

Mattei, F., & Neimi, R. G. (1991). Unrealized partisans, realized independents, and the intergenerational transmission of partisan identification. *Journal of Politics, 53*, 161–173.

Mauser, G. A., & Kopel, D. B. (1992). "Sorry, wrong number": Why media polls on gun control are often unreliable. *Political Communication, 9*, 69–92.

McAllister, I., & Studlar, D. T. (1991). Bandwagon, underdog, or projection? Opinion polls and electoral choice in Britain, 1979–1987. *Journal of Politics, 53*, 720–741.

McCall, J. M. (1984). The panelists as pseudo-debaters: An evaluation of the questions and questioners in the presidential debates of 1980. *Journal of the American Forensic Association, 21*, 97–104.

McClain, T. B. (1989). Secondary school debate pedagogy. *Journal of the American Forensic Association, 25*, 203–204.

McCombs, M. E. (1976). Agenda setting research: A bibliographic essay. *Political Communication Review, 1*, 1–7.

McCombs, M. E., & Shaw, D. L. (1972). The agenda-setting function of mass media. *Public Opinion Quarterly, 36*, 176–185.

McCombs, M. E., & Shaw, D. L. (1993). The evolution of agenda-setting research: Twenty-five years in the marketplace of ideas. *Journal of Communication, 43*, 58–67.

McDermott, M. L., & Frankovic, K. A. (2003). Horserace polling and survey method effects: An analysis of the 2000 campaign. *Public Opinion Quarterly, 67*, 244–264.

McDevitt, M., & Chaffee, S. H. (2000). Closing gaps in political communication and knowledge: Effects of a school intervention. *Communication Research, 27*, 259–292.

McDevitt, M., & Chaffee, S. H. (2002). From top-down to trickle-up influence: Revisiting assumptions about the family in political socialization. *Political Communication, 19*, 281–301.

McGee, M. C. (1975). In search of "the people": A rhetorical alternative. *Quarterly Journal of Speech, 61*, 235–249.

McIntire, M., & Wayne, L. (2007, August 30). Clinton donor under a cloud in fraud case. *New York Times*. http://www.nytimes.com/2007/08/30/us/politics/30bundler.html. Retrieved on September 15, 2007.

McKinney, M. S. (2005). Engaging citizens through presidential debates. In M. S. McKinney, L. L. Kaid, D. G. Bystrom, & D. B. Carlin (Eds.), *Communicating politics: Engaging the public in democratic life* (pp. 209–221). New York: Peter Lang.

McKinney, M. S., & Carlin, D. B. (2004). Political campaign debates. In L. L. Kaid, (Ed.), *Handbook of political communication research* (pp. 203–234). Mahwah, NJ: Lawrence Erlbaum.

McKinnon, L. M., & Kaid, L. L. (1999). Exposing negative campaigning or enhancing advertising effects: An experimental study of adwatch effects on voters' evaluations of candidates and their ads. *Journal of Applied Communication Research, 27*, 217–236.

McKinnon, L. M., Tedesco, J. C., & Kaid, L. L. (1993). The third 1992 presidential debate: Channel and commentary effects. *Argumentation and Advocacy, 30*, 106–118.

McLeod, J. M., & Detenber, B. H. (1999). Framing effects of television news coverage of social protest. *Journal of Communication, 49*, 3–23.

Meadow, R. G. (1980). *Politics as communication.* Norwood, NJ: Ablex.

Medved, M. (2006, September 27). Beating back the TV takeover. *Townhall.com.* http://www.townhall.com/columnists/MichaelMedved/2006/09/27/beating _back_the_tv_takeover. Retrieved on October 23, 2006.

Mehren, E. (1999, February 13). Glad it's over, but not glad it happened. *Los Angeles Times*, p. 1.

Memmott, M. (2004, September 26). Voters in Ohio give political ads a thumbs down. *USA Today.* http://www.usatoday.com/news/politicselections/nation/ president/2004-09-26-ad-meter_x.htm. Retrieved on March 30, 2007.

Memmott, M., & Lawrence, J. (2007, June 27). Ann Coulter vs. Elizabeth Edwards: Sparks fly after Coulter remark on terrorist assassination of John Edwards. *USA Today.* http://blogs.usatoday.com/onpolitics/2007/06/ann-coulter-vs- .html. Retrieved on July 18, 2007.

The mendacity index: Which president told the biggest whoppers? You decide. (2003, September). *Washington Monthly.* http://www.washingtonmonthly .com/features/2003/0309.mendacity-index.html. Retrieved on July 19, 2007.

Mendelsohn, H. (1973). Some reasons why information campaigns can succeed. *Public Opinion Quarterly, 37*, 50–61.

Merolla, J. L., Ramos, J. M., & Zechmeister, E. J. (2007). Crisis, charisma and consequences: Evidence from the 2004 U.S. presidential election. *Journal of Politics, 69.* http://www.journalofpolitics.org.art69_1.html.#a3. Retrieved on August 27, 2007.

Merry, M. S. (2007). Patriotism, history and the legitimate aims of American education, educational philosophy and theory (OnlineEarly Articles). doi:10.1111/ j.1469-5812.2007.00363.x. Retrieved on August 22, 2007.

Michael, G. (2003). *Confronting right-wing extremists and terrorism in the U.S.* New York: Routledge.

Milbank, D. (2004, September 10). Secret Service not coddling hecklers. *Washington Post*, p. A8.

Miller, A. H., & MacKuen, M. (1978). Informing the electorate: A national study. In S. Kraus (Ed.), *The great debates: Carter vs. Ford, 1976* (pp. 269–297). Bloomington: Indiana University Press.

Miller, M., Andsager, J. L., & Riechert, B. P. (1998). Framing the candidates in presidential primaries: Issues and images in press releases and news coverage. *Journalism and Mass Communication Quarterly, 75*, 312–324.

Miller, P. V. (1995). The industry of public opinion. In T. L. Glasser & C. T. Salmon (Eds.), *Public opinion and the communication of consent* (pp. 105–131). New York: Guilford Press.

Miller, T. C. (2006). *Blood money: Wasted billions, lost lives, and corporate greed in Iraq.* New York: Little, Brown.

Moehringer, J. R. (1999, April 29). Littleton killings strike at the heart of U.S. *Los Angeles Times*, p. A1.

Molyneux, G. (1996, March 3). It's still the economy, stupid. *Los Angeles Times*, p. 1.

Monica makes history, again. (1999. March 4). http://www.abcnews.go.com/onair/ 2020/2020_990304http://www.abcnews.go.com/onair/2020/2020_990304. Retrieved on April 8, 1999.

Moore, D. (1999). Daily tracking polls: Too much "noise" or revealed insights? *Public Perspective, 10,* 27–32.

Moore, D. W. (1987). Political campaigns and the knowledge gap hypothesis. *Public Opinion Quarterly, 51,* 186–200.

Morain, D. (2007, July 2). Raising $32.5 million, Obama far outpaces rivals, sets record. *Los Angeles Times,* pp. A1, A12.

Morain, D. (2007, July 4). Romney loans way to lead in GOP funding. *Los Angeles Times*, p. A13.

More comments on the Internet and the '06 elections. (2006). *Personal Democracy Forum.* http://www.personaldemocracy.com/node/1085. Retrieved on Apil 5, 2007.

Morris, D. (1998, December 7). The bogeyman unmasked: TV in the '98 Senate races. *Washington Post.* http://www.washingtonpost.com/wp-srv/politics/ campaigns/money/money.htm. Retrieved on February 7, 2007.

Mosk, M. (2007, February 7). In campaign 2008, candidates starting earlier, spending more. Washington Post.com. http://www.washingtonpost.com/wp-dyn/ content/article/2007/02/06/AR2007020601598_pf.html. Retrieved on February 14, 2007.

Mulloy, D. (2004). *American extremism: History, politics and the militia movement.* New York: Routledge.

Murray, B. (2006, January 5). Covering Latino political behavior and trends. *Facsnet.* http://www.facsnet.org/issues/faith/latino_voting.phphttp://www .facsnet.org/issues/faith/latino_voting.php. Retrieved on September 26, 2007.

Murray, S. (2007, July 10). Senator's number on "madam" phone list. *Washington Post*, p. A3.

Murray, S. K., & Howard, P. (2002). Variation in White House polling operations: Carter to Clinton. *Public Opinion Quarterly, 66,* 527–558.

Mutz, D. C. (1994). Contextualizing personal experience: The role of the mass media. *Journal of Politics, 56,* 689–714.

My fellow non-Americans. (2004, October 13). *The Guardian.* http://www .guardian.co.uk/uselections2004/story/0,13918,1326033,00.html. Retrieved on July 18, 2006.

Myers, S. L., & Shenon, P. (2007, August 27). Embattled attorney general resigns. *New York Times,* p. 1.

Nagourney, A. (2007, February 1). Biden unwraps his bid for '08 with an oops! *New York Times,* p. 1.

Nagourney, A. (2007, April 5). News analysis; Early '08 fund-raising has clear blue tint. *New York Times*, p. A7. http://query.nytimes.com/gst/fullpage.html?res =9C02E1DA163FF936A35757C0A9619C8B63. Retrieved on June 8, 2007.

Nagourney, A., & Thee, M. (2007, June 27). Young Americans are leaning left, new poll finds. *New York Times*, p. 7.

Nardulli, P. F., Dalager, J. K., & Greco, D. E. (1996). Voter turnout in U.S. elections: An historical view and some speculation. *PS: Political Science and Politics*, 481–490. http://www.jstor.org/view/10490965/ap020036/02a00140/0?frame =noframe&userID=807dee70@usc.edu/01cce4405c00501c91eee&dpi=3& config=jstor. Retrieved on September 13, 2007.

Natchez, P. B., & Bupp, I. C. (1968). Candidates, issues, and voters. *Public Policy*, 17, 409–437.

National voter turnout in federal elections: 1960–2004. (2007). http://www.infoplease .com/ipa/A0781453.html. Retrieved on August 11, 2007.

Neimi, R. G., & Jennings, M. K. (1991). Issues and inheritance in the formation of party identification. *American Journal of Political Science*, 35, 970–988.

Nesbitt, J. (2001, September 26). Many American right-wing radical extremists applaud September 11 attacks. Newhouse News Service. http://watch.winds of change.net/0924_0930.htm. Retrieved on November 20, 2007.

Network TV: State of the news media (2005). Journalism.org. http://www.state ofthenewsmedia.org/2005/narrative_networktv_audience.asp?cat=3&media =4. Retrieved on May 9, 2007.

New millennium survey: American youth attitudes on politics, citizenship, government and voting. (2006). National Association of Secretaries of State. http://www.stateofthevote.org/survey/sect5.htm. Retrieved on July 31, 2006.

Newport, F. (2004, October 18). Bush gains after debates: Race remains close in key swing states. The Gallup Organization. http://www.gallup.com/poll/ content/login.aspx?ci=13657. Retrieved on February 4, 2005.

News audiences increasingly politicized. (2004). The Pew Research Center for the People and the Press. http://people-press.org/reports/display.php3?PageID =834. Retrieved on August 31, 2007.

Newspaper Association of America. (2006). http://www.naa.org/thesource/14 .asp#number. Retrieved on October 4, 2006.

Nielsen Media Research. (2002). http://www.r-vcr.com/~television/DMA.htm. Retrieved on February 14, 2007.

Nihart, T., Lersch, K. M., Sellers, C. S., & Mieczkowski, T. (2005). Kids, cops, parents, and teachers: Exploring juvenile attitudes toward authority figures. *Western Criminology Review*, 6, 79–88.

Nimmo, D. (1974). *Popular images of politics*. Englewood Cliffs, NJ: Prentice-Hall.

Nimmo, D. D., & Combs, J. E. (1990). *Mediated political realities* (2nd ed.). New York: Longman.

Novak, M. (1974). *Choosing our king*. New York: Macmillan.

O'Keefe, G. J. (1989). Strategies and tactics in political campaigns. In C. T. Salmon, (Ed.), *Information campaigns: Balancing social values and social change* (pp. 259–284). Newbury Park, CA: Sage.

Obama downplays campaign's racial factor. (2007, May 13). *USA Today*. http://www.usatoday.com/news/politics/2007-05-13-3921336696_x.htm. Retrieved on August 24, 2007.

The Obamas are tired of the blackness question. (2007, August 14). Washington Post.com. http://www.washingtonpost.com/wp-dyn/content/article/2007/08/13/AR2007081300965.html. Retrieved on August 24, 2007.

Oldendick, R. W., & Link, M. W. (1994). The answering machine generation. *Public Opinion Quarterly, 58*, 264–273.

Oliphant, J. (2007, September 20). Clinton donor Hsu indicted in New York. *Baltimore Sun*. http://weblogs.baltimoresun.com/news/politics/blog/2007/09/clinton_donor_hsu_indicted_in.html. Retrieved on September 25, 2007.

1.6 billion reasons for campaign reform. (1996, October 21). *Los Angeles Times*, p. B4.

Online papers modestly boost newspaper readership: Maturing Internet news audience broader than deep. (2006, July 30). The Pew Research Center for the People and the Press. http://people-press.org/reports/display.php3?ReportID=282. Retrieved on April 26, 2007.

Opensecrets.org. (2000). http://www.opensecrets.org/2000elect/index/P00003335.htm. Retrieved on June 11, 2007.

Ostrom, C. W., Jr., & Simon, D. M. (1989). The man in the Teflon suit? *Public Opinion Quarterly, 53*, 353–387.

Otis, M. D., & Loeffler, D. N. (2005). Changing youth's attitudes toward difference: A community-based model that works. *Social Work with Groups, 28*, 41–64.

Owen, D. (1991). *Media messages in American presidential elections*. New York: Greenwood.

Page, S. (2004, June 2). Churchgoing closely tied to voting patterns. *USA Today*. http://www.usatoday.com/news/nation/2004-06-02-religion-gap_x.htm. Retrieved on August 16, 2006.

Paletz, D. L. (1999). *The media in American politics: Contents and consequences*. New York: Longman.

Parenti, M. (1993). *Inventing reality: The politics of the news media*. New York: St. Martin's Press.

Pathway to peril. (1999, January 31). *Los Angeles Times*, p. S1.

Patrick, J. J. (1977). Political socialization and political education in schools. In S. A. Renshon (Ed.), *Handbook of political socialization* (pp. 190–222). New York: Free Press.

Patrick, J. J. (2002). Improving civic education in schools. *ERIC Digest*. ED470039. http://www.ericdigests.org/2003-3/civic.htm. Retrieved on September 20, 2007.

Patterson, T. E. (1980). *The mass media election: How Americans choose their president*. New York: Praeger.

Patterson, T. E. (2002). *The vanishing voter: Public involvement in an age of uncertainty*. New York: Alfred A. Knopf.

Patterson, T. E. (2004). *Young voters and the 2004 election*. Paper released by the Joan Shorenstein Center on the Press, Politics, and Public Policy. John F. Kennedy School of Government, Harvard University.

Patterson, T. E. (2005). Of polls, mountains: U.S. journalists and their use of election surveys. *Public Opinion Quarterly, 69,* 716–724.

Patterson, T. E., & McClure, R. D. (1976). *The unseeing eye: The myth of television power in national elections.* New York: Putnam Press.

Payola pioneering: Exposing the Bush Pioneer/Ranger networks. (2004). http://www.tpj.org/pioneers/pioneers04/who_all.html. Retrieved on May 17, 2007.

Pear, R. (2007, July 15). A million faxes later, a little-known group claims victory on immigration. *New York Times,* p. 13.

Peer, L., & Nesbitt, M. (2004). An analysis of content in 52 U.S. daily newspapers: Summary report. http://www.readership.org/new_readers/data/content_analysis.pdf. Retrieved on October 19, 2006.

Perloff, R. M. (1998). *Political communication: Politics, press and public in America.* Mahwah, NJ: Lawrence Erlbaum.

Perloff, R. M., & Kinsey, D. (1992). Political advertising as seen by consultants and journalists. *Journal of Advertising Research, 32,* 53–60.

Perot launches third-party presidential bid. (1996, August 18). *CNN All Politics.* http://www-cgi.cnn.com/ALLPOLITICS/1996/news/9608/18/reform.party/. Retrieved on August 17, 2007.

Peters, J. D. (1995). Historical tensions in the concept of public opinion. In T. L. Glasser & C. T. Salmon (Eds.), *Public opinion and the communication of consent* (pp. 3–32). New York: Guilford Press.

Pfau, M. (1983). Criteria and format to optimize political debates: An analysis of South Dakota's "Election '80 Series," *Journal of the American Forensic Association, 19,* 205–214.

Pfau, M., Diedrich, T., Larson, K. M., & Van Winkle, K. M. (1995). Influence of communication modalities on voters' perceptions of candidates during presidential primary campaigns. *Journal of Communication, 45,* 122–133.

Pfau, M., & Eveland, W. P. (1994). Debates versus other communication sources: The pattern of information and influence. In D. B. Carlin & M. S. McKinney (Eds.), *The 1992 presidential debates in focus* (pp. 155–173). Westport, CT: Praeger.

Pfau, M., Houston, J. B., & Semmler, S. M. (2007). *Mediating the vote: The changing media landscape in U.S. presidential campaigns.* Lanham, MD: Rowman & Littlefield.

Pfau, M., & Kang, J. G. (1991). The impact of relational messages on candidate influence in televised political debates. *Communication Studies, 42,* 114–128.

Pfau, M., & Parrott, R. (1993). *Persuasive communication campaigns.* Needham Heights, MA: Allyn & Bacon.

Phillips, K. (2006, November 2). Campaign cash: Leadership PACs. *New York Times.* http://thecaucus.blogs.nytimes.com/2006/11/02/campaign-cash-leadership-pacs/. Retrieved on September 28, 2007.

Phillips, K. (2007, September 27). Senator Craig to stay in Senate, for now. *New York Times.* http://thecaucus.blogs.nytimes.com/2007/09/26/senator-craig-to-stay-in-senate-for-now/. Retrieved on September 27, 2007.

Phillips, K. P. (1969). *The emerging Republican majority.* New Rochelle, NY: Arlington House.

Piazza, T. (1993). Meeting the challenge of answering machines. *Public Opinion Quarterly, 57,* 219–231.

Pillai, R., & Williams, E. A. (1998). Does leadership matter in the political arena? Voter perceptions of candidates' transformational and charismatic leadership and the 1996 U.S. presidential vote. *Leadership Quarterly, 9,* 397–416.

Pillai, R., Williams, E. A., Lowe, K. B., & Jung, D. I. (2003). Personality, transformational leadership, trust, and the 2000 U.S. presidential vote. *Leadership Quarterly, 14,* 161–192.

Pious, R. M. (1996). *The presidency.* Boston: Allyn & Bacon.

Plumer, B. (2007, January 30). How rich people control politics. *The New Republic.* http://www.tnr.com/doc.mhtml?i=w070129&s=plumer013007. Retrieved on June 26, 2007.

Pointed questions. (2000, February 14). *New York Times,* p. A16.

Political party poop. (2007). Blogtoplist.com. http://www.blogtoplist.com/politics/blogdetails-1986-2.html. Retrieved on September 14, 2007.

Political sites gain, but major news sites still dominant: Modest increase in Internet use for campaign 2002. (2003, January 5). The Pew Research Center for the People and the Press. http://people-press.org/reports/display.php3?ReportID=169. Retrieved on April 25, 2007.

Poll: Americans say nation is off-track. (2007, July 1). CBS News Polls. http://www.cbsnews.com/stories/2007/06/30/opinion/polls/main3002337.shtml. Retrieved on July 17, 2007.

Pollay, R. W. (1989). Campaigns, change and culture: On the polluting potential of persuasion. In C. T. Salmon (Ed.), *Information campaigns: Balancing social values and social change* (pp. 185–196). Newbury Park, CA: Sage.

Pollock, F. (1976). Empirical research into public opinion. In P. Connerton (Ed.), *Critical sociology* (pp. 225–236). New York: Penguin Books.

Polyani, M. (1983). *The tacit dimension.* Gloucester, MA: Peter Smith. (Original work published 1966).

Pooley, E. (1996, September 2). Who is Dick Morris? *Time.* http://www.time.com/time/magazine/article/0,9171,985043-7,00.html. Retrieved on September 7, 2007.

Pooley, E. (2000, February 14). How conservative is McCain? *Time,* 40–42.

Popkin, S. L. (1994). *The reasoning voter* (2nd ed.). Chicago: University of Chicago Press.

Popular votes for H. Ross Perot. (1996). StateMaster.com. http://www.statemaster.com/graph/pre_1996_pop_vot_for_h_ros_per_of_tot-votes-h-ross-perot-total. Retrieved on August 17, 2007.

Pratte, R. (1998*).* Civic education in a democracy. *Theory into Practice, 27,* 303–308.

President Bush—overall job rating. (2007). PollingReport.com. http://www.pollingreport.com/BushJob.htm. Retrieved on September 13, 2007.

President results by state. (2004). http://www.usatoday.com/news/politicselections/vote2004/nationalelectionresultsbystate.aspx?oi=P&rti=G&cn=1&tf=1. Retrieved on August 17, 2007.

Presidential campaign finance. (2004). http://www.gwu.edu/action~/2004/presfin04
.html. Retrieved on June 25, 2007.

Presidential campaign slogans. (2005). http://www.presidentsusa.net/campaign
slogans.html. Retrieved on February 7, 2007.

Preston, J., & Berger, J. (1999, February 13). Republican stronghold bears scars.
New York Times, p. A7.

Public agenda: 20 questions journalists should ask about poll results. (2007). http://
www.publicagenda.org/polling/polling_20q.cfm. Retrieved on March 23, 2007.

Purdum, T. S. (1996, May 19). Facets of Clinton. *Los Angeles Times Magazine*,
p. 34.

"Push polling" takes center stage in Bush-McCain South Carolina fight. (2000, February 10). http://www.cnn.com/2000/ALLPOLITICS/stories/02/10/campaign.
wrap/index.html. Retrieved on February 10, 2000.

Putnam, R. (2000). *Bowling alone: The collapse and revival of American community*. New York: Simon & Schuster.

Radcliff, B. (2005). Class organization and subjective well-being: A cross-national
analysis. *Social Forces, 84*, 513–530.

Raine, L., Cornfield, M., & Horrigan, J. (2005, March 6). The Internet and campaign
2004. The Pew Internet and American Life Project. http://www.pewinternet
.org/pdfs/PIP_2004_campaign.pdf. Retrieved on August 30, 2007.

Rampton, S., & Stauber, J. (2006). *The best war ever: Lies, damned lies, and the
mess in Iraq*. New York: Penguin Books.

Randolph, E., & Boyarsky, B. (1996, August 30). Tabloid's story on strategist
was timed for "maximum effect." *Los Angeles Times*, p. A19.

Raney, J. (2007, August 10). Iowa works at being first and foremost. *Los Angeles Times*. http://www.latimes.com/news/nationworld/nation/la-na-iowaside10
aug10,1,1927304.story?track=rss. Retrieved on July 16, 2007.

Raney, R. F. (1998, November 6). Former wrestler's campaign got a boost from the
Internet. *New York Times*. http://www.politicsonline.com/coverage/nytimes2/
06campaign.html. Retrieved on April 17, 2007.

Reed, D. C. (2007). Why the methods matter: The effectiveness of party contact-
ing since the 1950s. Paper presented at the annual meeting of the Midwest
Political Science Association, Chicago, IL.

Reeher, G. (2006, February 28). Log on, tune off? The complex relationship
between Internet use and political activism. *Personal Democracy Forum*.
http://www/personaldemocracy.com/node/836. Retrieved on April 5, 2007.

Reeves, R. (2005). *President Reagan: The triumph of imagination*. New York:
Simon & Schuster.

Reich, R. B. (1997). *Locked in the cabinet*. New York: Alfred A. Knopf.

Reiche, F. P. (1990). Weakness of the FEC. In M. L. Nugent & J. R. Johannes
(Eds.), *Money, elections, and democracy: Reforming congressional campaign finance*. Boulder, CO: Westview Press.

Reid, S., Stohl, M., & Stauffer, A. (2006). Effects of political knowledge, interest and efficacy on college voter turnout. Paper presented at the annual meeting of the International Communication Association, Dresden, Germany.

Religion and the presidential vote: Bush's gains broad-based. (2004, December 6). The Pew Research Center for the People and the Press. http://people-press .org/commentary/display.php3?AnalysisID=103. Retrieved on August 16, 2006.

Religious practices in the US: Poll results. (2000). Religious tolerance.org. http://www.religioustolerance.org/chr_prac.htm. Retrieved on August 17, 2006.

Riccards, M. P. (1973). *The making of the American citizenry.* New York: Intext Educational Publishers.

Rich, F. (2000, January 29). Wake me when it's almost over. *New York Times,* p. A29.

Richter, P. (1996, April 19). Armey cites "politics" of Whitewater. *Los Angeles Times,* p. A9.

Riley, P., & Hollihan, T. A. (1981). The 1980 presidential debates: A content analysis of the issues and arguments. *Speaker and Gavel, 18,* 47–59.

Riley, P., Hollihan, T. A., & Cooley, D. M. (1980). The 1976 presidential debates: An analysis of the issues and arguments. Paper presented at the Central States Speech Communication Association Convention, Chicago, IL.

Riley, P., Klumpp, J. F., & Hollihan, T. A. (1995). Democratizing the lifeworld of the 21st century: Evaluating new democratic sites for argument. In S. Jackson (Ed.), *Argumentation and values* (pp. 254–260). Fairfax, VA: Speech Communication Association.

Roberts, C. L. (1981). From primary to the presidency: A panel study of images and issues in the 1976 election. *Western Journal of Speech Communication, 45,* 60–70.

Roberts, D. F., Hawkins, R. P., & Pingree, S. (1975). Watergate and political socialization: The inescapable event. *American Politics Quarterly, 3,* 406–422.

Rogers, E. M., Dearing, J. W., & Bregman, D. (1993). The anatomy of agenda setting research. *Journal of Communication, 43,* 68–84.

Rokeach, M. (1968). *Beliefs, attitudes, and values.* San Francisco: Jossey-Bass.

Ronfeldt, D. (1991). *Cyberocracy, cyberspace, and cyberology: Political effects of the information revolution.* Santa Monica, CA: RAND.

Rosenbaum, D. E. (1981, March 17). Reagan's "safety net" proposal: Who will land, who will fall; news analysis. *New York Times.* http://query.nytimes.com/ gst/fullpage.html?sec=health&res=9E05EEDC1239F934A25750C0A96794 8260. Retrieved on July 19, 2007.

Rosenbaum, D. E. (1996, March 17). Now this message from our tormentor. *New York Times,* p. E3.

Rosenberg, S. W., & McCafferty, P. (1987). The image and the vote. *Public Opinion Quarterly, 51,* 31–47.

Rosenstiel, T. (2004, September 12). The end of "network news." Journalism.org. http://www.journalism.org/node/304. Retrieved on December 14, 2006.

Rosenstiel, T. (2005). Political polling and the new media culture: A case of more being less. *Public Opinion Quarterly, 69,* 698–715.

Rosenstone, S. J. (1983). *Forecasting presidential elections.* New Haven: Yale University Press.

Ross, B., & Sauer, M. (2006, October 3). New Foley instant messages; Had Internet sex while awaiting House vote. http://blogs.abcnews.com/theblotter/2006/10/new_foley_insta.html. Retrieved on October 3, 2006.

Rowland, R. (1986). The substance of the 1980 Carter-Reagan debate. *Southern Speech Communication Journal, 51*, 142–165.

Royko, M. (1984, May 9). Chicago is still the land of opportunity. *Los Angeles Times*, p. B7.

Rucinski, D. (1993). Rush to judgment? Fast reaction polls in the Anita Hill–Clarence Thomas controversy. *Public Opinion Quarterly, 57*, 575–592.

Rutenberg, J., & Zernike, K. (2004, August 25). Bush campaign's top outside lawyer advised veterans group. *New York Times*. http://www.nytimes.com/2004/08/25/politics/campaign/25swift.html?ex=1251086400&en=750d293f0962cc04&ei=5090&partner=rssuserland. Retrieved on June 25, 2007.

Saad, L. (2007, April 25). Most Americans favor giving illegal immigrants a chance. The Gallup Poll. http://www.galluppoll.com/content/?ci=27307. Retrieved on July 24, 2007.

Saad, L. (2007, August 2). Gallup finds increase in independents, typical of off-years. The Gallup Poll. http://www.galluppoll.com/content/?ci=28279. Retrieved on August 16, 2007.

Sabato, L. J. (1981). *The rise of political consultants.* New York: Basic Books.

Sabato, L. J. (1989). *Paying for elections: The campaign finance thicket.* New York: Priority Press.

Sabato, L. J. (1992). Open season: How the news media cover presidential campaigns in the age of attack journalism. In M. D. McCubbins (Ed.), *Under the watchful eye: Managing presidential campaigns in the television era* (pp. 127–152). Washington, DC: Congressional Quarterly Press.

Sailer, S. (2000, November 22). In 2000, Bush won 19 states with highest white birthrates. United Press International. http://www.isteve.com/2000_Bush_Won_19_States_with_Highest_White_Birthrates.htm. Retrieved on September 26, 2007.

Sandel, M. J. (1996, March). America's search for a new public philosophy. *The Atlantic Monthly*, 55–74.

Sather, J. (2006). TV: How much is too much? *MSN Encarta*. http://encarta.msn.com/encnet/departments/elementary/default.aspx?article=toomuchtv. Retrieved on August 17, 2006.

Sauer, M., & Schecter, A. (2006, October 1). GOP staff warned pages about Foley in 2001. http://blogs.abcnews.com/theblotter/2006/10/gop_staff_warne.html. Retrieved on October 4, 2006.

Savage, D. G. (2007, June 26). Rules on political ads eased. *Los Angeles Times*, pp. A1, A10.

Scheer, R. (1996, August 27). Good Clinton loses out to bad Clinton. *Los Angeles Times*, p. B7.

Schell, J. (1996, August). The uncertain leviathan. *The Atlantic Monthly*, 70–78.

Schenck-Hamlin, W., Procter, D., & Rumsey, D. (2000). The influence of negative advertising frames on political cynicism and politician accountability. *Health Communication Research, 26*, 53–74.

Schmidt, S., & Grimaldi, J. V. (2006, January 4). Abramoff pleads guilty to three counts. *Washington Post*, p. A1.

Schmitt, R. B. (2007, July 27). FBI chief seems to contradict Gonzales. *Los Angeles Times*, p. 1.

Schmuhl, R. (1998). Creating civic connections. In M. Salvador & P. M. Sias (Eds.), *The public voice in a democracy at risk* (pp. 11–22). Westport, CT: Praeger.

Schram, S. F. (1991). The post-modern presidency and the grammar of electronic electioneering. *Critical Studies in Mass Communication, 8*, 210–216.

Schubert, J. N. (1988). Age and active-passive leadership style. *American Political Science Review, 82*, 763–772.

Schudson, M. (1978). *Discovering the news: A social history of American newspapers*. New York: Basic Books.

Schudson, M. (2003). *The sociology of news*. New York: W. W. Norton.

Scott, B. T., & Sieber, A. W. (1992). Remaking *Time*, *Newsweek*, and *U.S. News & World Report*. In P. S. Cook, D. Gomery, & L. W. Lichty (Eds.), *The future of news: Television, newspapers, wire services, newsmagazines* (pp. 191–205). Washington, DC: Woodrow Wilson Center Press.

Scully, M. (2007, September). Present at the creation. *The Atlantic Monthly*, 77–88.

Searing, D. D., Schwartz, J. J., & Lind, A. E. (1973). The structuring principle: Political socialization and belief systems. *American Political Science Review, 67*, 415–432.

Sears, D. O. (1969). Political behavior. In G. Lindsey & E. Aronson (Eds.), *The handbook of social psychology* (pp. 315–458). Reading, MA: Addison-Wesley.

Sears, D., & Chaffee, S. (1978). Uses and effects of the 1976 debates: An overview of empirical studies. In S. Kraus (Ed.), *The great debates: Carter vs. Ford, 1976* (pp. 233–261). Bloomington: Indiana University Press.

Section by section summary of McCain-Feingold. (2007). The Brookings Institution. http://www.brookings.org/gs/cf/debate/MF_summary.htm#sec101. Retrieved on June 22, 2007.

Seelye, K. Q. (1999, May 22). Clintons take sudden notice of New York vacation spots. *New York Times*, p. 1.

Seelye, K. Q. (2007, June 13). New presidential debate site? Clearly YouTube. *New York Times*. http://www.nytimes.com/2007/06/13/us/politics/13cnd-youtube.html. Retrieved on September 25, 2007.

Seelye, K. Q. (2007, July 20). Women supportive but skeptical of Clinton, poll says. *New York Times*. http://www.nytimes.com/2007/07/20/us/politics/20poll.html?ex=1188360000&en=374722057b847b24&ei=5070. Retrieved on August 27, 2007.

Seper, J., & Dinan, S. (2006, May 27). "Amnesty" jams compromise bill. *Washington Times*, p. 7.

Serrano, R. A., & Lacey, M. (1999, February 13). Clinton acquitted: Votes fall far short of conviction. *Los Angeles Times*, p. 1.

Setting the record straight. (1996, October 10). http://www.politicsnow.com/news/Oct96/10/pn1010cgrebut/. Retrieved on October 11, 1996.

Shah, D. V., Watts, M. D., Domke, D., & Fan, D. P. (2002). News framing and cueing of issue regimes: Explaining Clinton's public approval in spite of scandal. *Public Opinion Quarterly, 66,* 339–370.

Shamir, B. (1994). Ideological position, leaders' charisma, and voting preferences: Personal vs. partisan elections. *Political Behavior, 16,* 265–287.

Shape the future: Vote. (2007). http://www.shapethefuture.org/features/youthvote .asp. Retrieved on August 11, 2007.

Shapiro, A. L. (1999). *The control revolution: How the Internet is putting individuals in charge and changing the world we know.* New York: A Century Foundation Book.

Shaw, D. (1996, April 19). Critics of media cynicism point a finger at television. *Los Angeles Times,* pp. A1, A21, A22.

Shaw, J. (1996). Environmentalism: The new socialism. Ecoworld.com. http:// www.ecoworld.com/home/articles2.cfm?tid=409. Retrieved on August 22, 2007.

Shea, N. (2006, May 22). This is a Saudi textbook. (After the intolerance was removed.) *Washington Post,* p. A7.

Shear, M. D. (2007, May 3). California primary's new clout. *Seattle Times.* http://seattletimes.nwsource.com/html/nationworld/2003691003_calif03.html. Retrieved on May 7, 2007.

Shear, M. D., & Kane, P. (2007, May 23). McCain turns focus to his fundraising. *Washington Post,* p. A4.

Shelley, C. (1996). Rhetorical and demonstrative modes of visual argument: Looking at images of human evolution. *Argumentation and Advocacy, 33,* 53–68.

Shelley, M. C., II, & Hwang-Du, H. (1991). The mass media and public opinion polls in the 1988 presidential election: Trends, accuracy, consistency, and events. *American Politics Quarterly, 19,* 59–79.

Sherman, A. K., & Kolker, A. (1987). *The social bases of politics.* Belmont, CA: Wadsworth.

Sherwell, P. (2007, January 29). Hillary Clinton turns to Chelsea in a bid to soften her image. *Daily Telegraph.* http://www.telegraph.co.uk/news/main.jhtml?xml=/ news/2007/01/28/whills28.xml. Retrieved on August 27, 2007.

Shields, S. A., & MacDowell, K. A. (1987). Appropriate emotion in politics: Judgment of a televised debate. *Journal of Communication, 37,* 78–89.

Shilts, R. (1987). *And the band played on: Politics, people, and the AIDS epidemic.* New York: St. Martin's Press.

Shogan, R. (1996, June 18). GOP mounts broad attack on president's character. *Los Angeles Times,* p. A1.

Shogan, R. (1999). *The double-edged sword: How character makes and ruins presidents, from Washington to Clinton.* Boulder, CO: Westview Press.

Shyles, L. (1986). The televised political spot advertisement. In L. L. Kaid, D. Nimmo, & K. R. Sanders (Eds.), *New perspectives on political advertising* (pp. 107–138). Carbondale: Southern Illinois University Press.

Sigel, R. S., & Hoskin, M. B. (1981). *The political involvement of adolescents.* New Brunswick, NJ: Rutgers University Press.

Sigelman, L., & Kugler, M. (2003). Why is research on the effects of negative campaigning so inconclusive? Understanding citizens' perceptions of negativity. *Journal of Politics, 65*, 142–160.

Singel, R. (2004, February 2). Net politics down but not out. *Wired News.* http://www.wired.com/politics/law/news/2004/02/62123. Retrieved on April 24, 2007.

Sinopoli, R. (1995). Thick-skinned liberalism: Redefining civility. *American Political Science Review, 89*, 612–620.

16% say government reflects the will of the people. (2006, December 21). *Rasmussen Reports.* http://www.rasmussenreports.com/public_content/politics/top_stories__1/16_say_government_reflects_the_will_of_the_people. Retrieved on July 9, 2007.

Skalaban, A. (1988). Do the polls affect elections? Some 1980 evidence. *Political Behavior, 10*, 136–150.

Skelton, G. (1996, October 31). Anti-209 ad takes the lowest road. *Los Angeles Times*, p. 3.

Smith, D., & Whereatt, R. (1998, November 4). Ventura elected governor. *Minneapolis Star and Tribune*, p. 1.

Smith, D. G. (1965). *The convention and the Constitution: The practical ideas of the founding fathers.* New York: St. Martin's Press.

Smith, R. A. (2006). *Money, power and elections: How campaign finance reform subverts American democracy.* Baton Rouge: Louisiana State University Press.

Smith, R. J. (2005, September 29). DeLay indicted in Texas financial probe. *Washington Post*, p. A1.

Smith, S. L., & Wilson, B. J. (2002). Children's comprehension of and fear reactions to television news. *Media Psychology, 4*, 1–26.

Smith, T. W. (1990). The first straw? A study of the origins of election polls. *Public Opinion Quarterly, 54*, 21–36.

Sniderman, P. M., Glaser, J. M., & Griffin, R. (1990). Information and electoral choice. In J. A. Ferjohn & J. J. Kuklinski (Eds.), *Information and democratic processes.* Urbana: University of Illinois Press.

Snyder, J. M., & Ting, M. M. (2002). An informational rationale for political parties. *American Journal of Political Science, 46*, 90–110.

Solomon, N. (2005). *War made easy: How presidents and pundits keep spinning us to death.* Hoboken, NJ: John Wiley.

Somin, I. (2006, November 7). The politics of ignorance: Election Day reflections. *Jurist.* http://jurist.law.pitt.edu/forumy/2006/11/politics-of-ignorance-election-day.php. Retrieved on August 27, 2007.

Sorauf, F. J. (1984). *Party politics in America* (5th ed.). Boston: Little, Brown.

Sourcebook on criminal justice statistics. (2002). http://www.albany.edu/sourcebook/pdf/sb2002/sb2002-section2.pdf. Retrieved on July 12, 2006.

Sparks fly in one and only California governor debate. (2006, October 8). http://www.nbc11.com/politics/10025575/detail.html. Retrieved on July 11, 2007.

Spillman, B. (2006, January 23). Conservatives meet in valley, mum on agenda.

The Desert Sun. http://www.thedesertsun.com/apps/pbcs.dll/article?AID=/20060123/NEWS0301/601230318/1006. Retrieved on July 18, 2006.

Squire, P. (1988). Why the 1936 *Literary Digest* poll failed. *Public Opinion Quarterly, 52,* 125–133.

Stacey, B. (1977). *Political socialization in Western society.* New York: St. Martin's Press.

Starr says Foster did commit suicide. (1998, October 13). *Capitol Hill Blue.* http://207.153.2312/July1997/starrjul16.htm. Retrieved on July 12, 1997.

State of the news media 2004: An annual report on American journalism. Journalism.org. http://www.stateofthenewsmedia.org/narrative_newspapers_content analysis.asp?cat=2&media=2. Retrieved on October 19, 2006.

State of the news media 2006: An annual report on American journalism, magazines. (2006). http://www.stateofthenewsmedia.org/2006/narrative_magazines_audience.asp?cat=3&media=8. Retrieved on October 20, 2006.

Steen, J. A. (2006). *Self-financed candidates in congressional elections.* Ann Arbor: University of Michigan Press.

Steinhauer, J. (2007, August 2). California struggles to end budget deadlock. *New York Times,* p. A10.

Stempel, G. H., III. (1994). Print media and campaign coverage. In G. H. Stempel III (Ed.), *The practice of political communication* (pp. 40–49). Englewood Cliffs, NJ: Prentice-Hall.

Stengel, R. (2006, July 3). Why history matters. *Time,* 8.

Stephanopoulos, G. (1999). *All too human.* Boston: Little, Brown.

Stuckey, M. E. (1991). *The president as interpreter in chief.* Chatham, NJ: Chatham House.

Sudman, S. (1986). Do exit polls influence voting behavior? *Public Opinion Quarterly, 50,* 331–339.

Sullivan, A. (2003, June). Do the Democrats have a prayer? To win in '04 the next nominee will need to get religion. *Washington Monthly.* http://www.washingtonmonthly.com/features/2003/0306.sullivan.html. Retrieved on August 24, 2006.

Sunstein, C. (2001). *Republic.com.* Princeton, NJ: Princeton University Press.

Suro, R. (1997, December 3). Reno decides against independent counsel to probe Clinton, Gore. *Washington Post,* p. A1.

Suro, R., & Escobar, G. (2006, July 13). Pew Hispanic Center Report. *2006 National survey of Latinos: The immigration debate.* http://www.pewhispanic.org. Retrieved on July 13, 2006.

Sussman, G. (2005). *Global electioneering: Campaign consulting, communications, and corporate financing.* Lanham, MD: Rowman & Littlefield.

Tannen, D. (1990). *You just don't understand: Men and women in conversation.* New York: HarperCollins.

Tannenbaum, P. H., Greenberg, B. S., & Silverman, F. R. (1962). Candidate images. In S. Kraus (Ed.), *The great debates* (pp. 271–288). Bloomington: Indiana University Press.

Tarde, G. (1898). Opinion and conversation. An unpublished translation by R. Morris. The French original was first published in the *Revue de Paris*, 1898.

Taylor, P. (2001, July). Holding an election on the cheap would spare candidates from lots of fundraisers. *The Political Standard, 4*, 2.

Taylor, P., & Ornstein, N. (2002). The case for free air time: A broadcast spectrum fee for campaign finance reform. http://newamerica.net/files/archive/pub_file_876_1.pdf. Retrieved on February 7, 2007.

Television history—The first 75 years. (2006). http://www.tvhistory.tv/facts-stats.htm. Retrieved on February 13, 2007.

Tenpas, K. D. (2003, March 23). Words vs. deeds: President George W. Bush and polling. The Brookings Institution. http://www.brookings.edu/press/review/summer2003/tenpas.htm. Retrieved on March 25, 2007.

Tenpas, K. D., & Hess, S. (2002). The Bush White House: First appraisals. *Presidential Studies Quarterly, 32*, 577–585.

Thomas, E. (1999, February 22). Why Clinton won. *Newsweek*, 25.

Thompson, D. (1970). *Democratic citizen*. Cambridge: Cambridge University Press.

Tocqueville, A. (1945). *Democracy in America* (P. Bradley, Trans.). New York: Vintage Books.

Tollerson, E. (1996, March 14). Forbes planning on dropping out of GOP campaign. *New York Times*, p. 1.

Tony Snow labels Foley's sex messages to teens "simply naughty e-mails." (2006, October 2). *Editor and Publisher*. http://www.editorandpublisher.com/eandp/news/article_display.jsp?vnu_content_id=1003189765. Retrieved on October 4, 2006.

Toobin, J. (1999). *A vast conspiracy: The real story of the sex scandal that nearly brought down a president*. New York: Random House.

Toobin, J. (2001). *Too close to call: The thirty-six-day battle to decide the 2000 election*. New York: Random House.

Toobin, J. (2007). *The nine: Inside the secret world of the Supreme Court*. New York: Doubleday.

Top 20 countries with the highest number of Internet users. (2007). *Internet World Stats*. http://www.internetworldstats.com/top20.htm. Retrieved on April 19, 2007.

Top zip codes. (2006). http://www.opensecrets.org/bigpicture/topzips.asp?cycle=2004. Retrieved on June 26, 2007.

Traugott, M. W. (2001). Assessing poll performance in the 2000 campaign. *Public Opinion Quarterly, 65*, 389–419.

Traugott, M. W., & Lavrakas, P. J. (2006). Polling, the news media, and politics. http://www.publicopinionpros.com/inprint/2006/jan/traugott.asp. Retrieved on March 29, 2007.

Trends in political values and core attitudes: 1987–2007, political landscape more favorable to Democrats. (2007, March 22). http://www.pewtrusts.org/ideas/ideas_item.cfm?content_item_id=4044&content_type_id=18&issue_name=&issue=0&page=18&name=Public%20Opinion%20Polls%20and%20Survey%20Results. Retrieved on August 14, 2007.

Trent, J. S., & Friedenberg, R. V. (1995). *Political campaign communication: Principles and practices* (3rd ed.). Westport, CT: Praeger.

Trent, J. S., Short-Thompson, C., Mongeau, P. A., Nusz, A. K., & Trent, J. D. (2001). Image, media bias, and voter characteristics: The ideal candidate from 1988–2000. *American Behavioral Scientist, 44*, 2101–2124.

Trippi, J. (2004). *The revolution will not be televised: Democracy, the Internet, and the overthrow of everything.* New York: Regan Books.

Tucker, R. (Ed.). (1978). *The Marx-Engels reader* (2nd ed.). New York: W. W. Norton.

Tumulty, K. (2006, August 28). Ready to run. *Time,* 26–34.

Turnout in the world: Country by country performance. (2007). International Institute for Democracy and Electoral Assistance. http://www.idea.int/vt/survey/voter_turnout_pop2.cfm. Retrieved on August 11, 2007.

TV host Bill Maher suggests Dick Cheney's death would save lives. (2007, March 5). Fox News. http://www.foxnews.com/story/0,2933,256650,00.html. Retrieved on July 19, 2007.

TV versus print. (2000). Project for Excellence in Journalism. http://www.journalism.org/electionfeb6.html. Retrieved on October 6, 2001.

TV viewers tune out debate. (1996, October 7). http://www.politicsnow.com/news/Oct96/07/pn1007ratings.

Urofsky, M. I. (2005). *Money and free speech: Campaign reform and the courts.* Lawrence: University Press of Kansas.

U.S. Electoral College. (2007). http://www.archives.gov/federal-register/electoral-college/faq.html#takeall. Retrieved on July 17, 2007.

U.S. News' Barone accused Dem pollster Greenberg of "blood libel" for saying 1988 Willie Horton ads were race-baiting. (2004, November 17). *Media Matters for America.* http://mediamatters.org/items/200411170006?offset=20&show=1. Retrieved on September 7, 2007.

U.S. voter turnout up in 2004. (2005, May 26). U.S. Census Bureau. http://www.census.gov/Press-Release/www/releases/archives/voting/004986.html. Retrieved on September 13, 2007.

U.S.: Study finds that most young Americans do not consume the news. (2007, July 16). *The editor's weblog.* http://www.editorsweblog.org/print_newspapers/2007/07/us_study_finds_that_most_young_americans.php. Retrieved on July 17, 2007.

Van Ausdale, D., & Feagin, J. R. (2001). *The first R: How children learn race and racism.* Lanham, MD: Rowman and Littlefield.

Vanderford, M. L. (1989). Vilification and social movements: A case study of pro-life and pro-choice rhetoric. *Quarterly Journal of Speech, 75,* 166–182.

The vanishing voter: A project to study and invigorate the American electoral process. (2004, November 11). http://www.ksg.harvard.edu/presspol/vanishvoter/Releases/release11110shtml. Retrieved on July 17, 2007.

Vargas, J. A. (2007, March 30). Grass roots planted in cyberspace. *Washington Post,* p. C01.

Verba, S., Burns, N., & Schlozman, K. L. (2004). Unequal at the starting line: Creating participatory inequalities across generations and among groups. In

I. L. Horowitz (Ed.), *Civil society and class politics: Essays on the political sociology of Seymour Martin Lipset* (pp. 69–106). New Brunswick, NJ: Transaction Publishers.

Viale, R. (2001). Truth, science, and politics: An analysis of social epistemology. In R. Viale (Ed.), *Knowledge and politics* (pp. 1–61). Heidelberg: Physica-Verlag.

Voices. (1999, February 13). *Los Angeles Times*, p. 18.

Voss, D. S., Gelman, A., & King, G. (1995). Pre-election survey methodology: Details from eight polling organizations, 1988 & 1992. *Public Opinion Quarterly, 59*, 98–132.

Wald, K. D., Owen, D. E., & Hill, S. S. (1990). Political cohesion in churches. *Journal of Politics, 52*, 197–215.

Walker, D., & Dubitsky, T. M. (1994). Why liking matters. *Journal of Advertising Research, 34*, 9–18.

Wallace, J. (2006, September 30). Representative Mark Foley quits in disgrace. Herald-Tribune.com. http://www.heraldtribune.com/apps/pbcs.dll/article?AID=/20060930/NEWS/609300536. Retrieved on October 4, 2006.

Wallsten, P. (2006, August 15). Conservatives put faith in church voter drives. *Los Angeles Times*, p. Al.

Walsh, B., & Alpert. B. (2007, June 4). Jefferson indicted for bribery, racketeering. NoLa.com. http://blog.nola.com/updates/2007/06/jefferson_indicted_for_bribery.html. Retrieved on June 8, 2007.

Waters, E., Hamilton, C. E., and Weinfield, N. S. (2000). The stability of attachment security from infancy to adolescence and early adulthood: General introduction. *Child Development, 71*, 678–683.

Wattenberg, M. (2005). Elections: Turnout in the 2004 presidential election. *Presidential Studies Quarterly, 35*, 138–146.

Wattenberg, M., & Brians, C. (1999). Negative campaign advertising: Demobilizer or mobilizer? *American Political Science Review, 93*, 891–900.

Wayne, L. (1996, October 20). Hunting cash, candidates follow the bright lights. *New York Times*, p. E5.

Wayne, S. J. (1980). *The road to the White House*. New York: St. Martin's Press.

Weaver, D., & Drew, D. (2001). Voter learning and interest in the 2000 presidential election: Did the media matter? *Journalism and Mass Communication Quarterly, 78*, 787–798.

Weaver, D., McCombs, M. E., & Spellman, C. (1975). Watergate and the media: A case study of agenda-setting. *American Politics Quarterly, 3*, 458–472.

The Web and the Net. (1998). *Campaign Web Review*. http://www.campaignwebreview.net/issues/11181998/3.shtml. Retrieved on November 19, 1998.

Webb, V. J., & Marshall, C. E. (1995). The relative importance of race and ethnicity on citizen attitudes toward the police. *American Journal of Police, 14*, 45–65.

Weiler, M. (1989). The 1988 electoral debates and debate theory. *Journal of the American Forensic Association, 25*, 214–219.

Weiner, T. (1997, March 2). Money, money, money. *New York Times*, pp. 1, 14.

Weinraub, B. (2000, January 19). Elections barometer: Barbs of late-night TV. *New York Times*, p. A16.

Weir, M., & Ganz, M. (1997). Reconnecting people and politics. In S. B. Greenberg & T. Skocpol (Eds.), *The new majority: Toward a popular progressive politics* (pp. 149–171). New Haven: Yale University Press.

Weisman, J. (2006, August 8). Embattled Rep. Ney won't seek reelection: Abramoff ties led GOP to urge his withdrawal. *Washington Post,* p. A1.

Weiss, P. (1997, February 23). Clinton crazy. *New York Times Magazine,* 34.

Weissman, J., & Cillizza, C. (2006, April 4). DeLay to resign from Congress. *Washington Post*, p. A1.

Weissman, S. R., & Ryan, K. D. (2007). Soft money in the 2006 election and the outlook for 2008: The changing nonprofits landscape. The Campaign Finance Institute. http://www.cfinst.org/pr/prRelease.aspx?ReleaseID=132. Retrieved on June 25, 2007.

We know Bart, but Homer is Greek to us. (2006, August 15). *Los Angeles Times*, p. A14.

West, D. M. (2000). *Checkbook democracy: How money corrupts political campaigns*. Boston: Northeastern University Press.

West, P. (2007, April 26). Debate season opens tonight. *Orlando Sentinel.* http://www.orlandosentinel.com/news/elections/bal-te.debate26apr26,0,392250.story?coll=orl-elections-utility. Retrieved on May 9, 2007.

Westen, D. (2007). *The political brain: The role of emotion in deciding the fate of the nation*. New York: Public Affairs.

What is NPR? (2007). NPR.org. http://www.npr.org/about/. Retrieved on August 31, 2007.

Where voters get information. (1996, November 6). *USA Today*, p. 1.

White, J., & Tyson, A. S. (2006, February 3). Rumsfeld offers strategies for current war. *Washington Post*, p. A8.

White, N. (2004). Conflicting values and conflicting virtues. In P. Baumann & M. Betzler (Eds.), *Practical conflicts: New philosophical essays* (pp. 223–243). Cambridge: Cambridge University Press.

Why did you vote for Bush? (2004, November 11). BBC News. http://news.bbc.co.uk/L/hi/talking_point/2981669.stm. Retrieved on November 20, 2007.

Why the Senate immigration bill failed. (2007, June 8). *Rasmussen Reports News Letter.* http://www.rasmussenreports.com/public_content/politics/why_the_senate_immigration_bill_failed. Retrieved on September 13, 2007.

Wilhelm, A. G. (2000). *Democracy in the digital age: Challenges to political life in cyberspace*. New York: Routledge.

Wilkinson, M. (2004, July 31). John Kerry, reporting for duty. *The Sydney Morning Herald.* http://www.smh.com.au/articles/2004/07/30/1091080442645.html?from=storylhs. Retrieved on August 29, 2006.

Wines, M. (1996). A scandal? What's the sound bite? *New York Times*, p. E3.

Winfield, B. H., & Friedman, B. (2003). Gender politics: News coverage of the candidates' wives in campaign 2000. *Journalism and Mass Communication Quarterly*, *80*, 548–566.

Wing, B. (2003). The color of election 2000: A look at the resurgence of electoral racism. *Urban Habitat*. http://urbanhabitat.org/node/974. Retrieved on July 26, 2007.

Winkler, C. K., & Black, C. F. (1993). Assessing the 1992 presidential and vice presidential debates: The public rationale. *Argumentation and Advocacy, 30,* 77–87.

Witte, J., & Howard, P. N. (2002). The future of polling: Relational inference and the development of Internet survey instruments. In J. Manza, F. L. Cook, & B. I. Page (Eds.), *Navigating public opinion: Polls, policy and the future of American democracy* (pp. 272–289). New York: Oxford University Press.

Wlezien, C. & Erikson, R.S. (2002). Patterns of poll movement. Oxford University Politics Research Paper. http://72.14.253.104/search?q=cache: VquKEP41EE8J:www.nuffield.ox.ac.uk/Politics/papers/2002/w27/wlezien. pdf+tracking+poll+results+can+differ+dramatically+from+day+to+day&hl= en&ct=clnk&cd=2&gl=us. Retrieved on September 10, 2007.

Wlezien, C., & Erikson, R. S. (2005). Post-election reflections on our pre-election predictions. *PS: Political Science and Politics, 38,* 25–26.

Women office holders: Fact sheets and summaries. (2008, January). Center for American Women and Politics. http://www.cawp.rutgers.edu/Facts.html. Retrieved on August 17, 2008.

Woodward, B. (2006). *State of denial: Bush at war, Part III.* New York: Simon & Schuster.

Worley, B. (2001). Comment: Nader's traders vs. state regulators: Examining the controversy over Internet vote swapping in the 2000 presidential election. *North Carolina Journal of Law and Technology, 2,* 32–66.

Wray, L., & Flanagan, C. (2006). Value development and civic engagement. http:// www.apa.org/pi/cyf/values.pdf. Retrieved on July 31, 2006.

Wuthnow, R. (1991). *Acts of compassion.* Princeton, NJ: Princeton University Press.

Xinshu, Z., & Chaffee, S. H. (1995). Campaign advertisements versus television news as sources of political issue information. *Public Opinion Quarterly, 59,* 41–65.

Yamamura, K. (2007, August 5). Electoral system initiative worries Dems. *Sacramento Bee,* p. A3.

Yamane, D. (2003). Non-Hispanic Catholics. *Religion in the news.* http://www .trincoll.edu/depts/csrpl/RINVol6No3/2004%20Election/non%20hispanic %20catholics.htm. Retrieved on August 23, 2007.

Yardley, J. (2000, February 14). Calls to voters at center stage in G.O.P. race. *New York Times,* pp. A1, A16.

Yeric, J. L. (2001). *Mass media and the politics of change.* Itasca, IL: F. E. Peacock Publishers.

York, A. (2001, June 7). Los Angeles' dirty little election. Salon.com. http://dir .salon.com/politics/feature/2001/06/07/hahn/index/html?sid=10. Retrieved on July 7, 2005.

York, A. (2001, June 12). All aboard the party switching express. Salon.com. http:// archive.salon.com/politics/red/2001/06/12/blue/index.htmlhttp://archive.salon

.com/politics/red/2001/06/12/blue/index.html. Retrieved on September 14, 2007.

Youth demographic trends. (2007). http://education.stateuniversity.com/pages/2556/Youth-Demographic-Trends.html. Retrieved on September 13, 2007.

Youth voting trends. (2004). CIRCLE (the Center for Information and Research on Civic Learning and Engagement). http://www.civicyouth.org/quick/youth_voting.htm. Retrieved on July 26, 2006.

Zarefsky, D. (2006). The U.S. and the world: The unexpressed premises of American exceptionalism. Paper presented at the 6th International Conference on Argumentation, Amsterdam, The Netherlands.

Zernike, K. (2006, May 28). Kerry pressing Swift Boat case long after loss. *New York Times*, p. 1.

Zhao, X., & Chaffee, S. H. (1995). Campaign advertisements versus television news as a source of political issue information. *Public Opinion Quarterly, 59*, 41–65.

Zhu, J., Milavsky, J. R., & Biswas, R. (1994). Do televised debates affect image perception more than issue knowledge? A study of the first 1992 presidential debate. *Human Communication Research, 20*, 302–333.

Zito, S. (2006, June 26). Making hay in Iowa. *Pittsburgh Tribune-Review.* http://www.pittsburghlive.com/x/pittsburghtrib/opinion/columnists/zito/s_459301.html. Retrieved on July 19, 2006.

Index

ABC, 282
ABC News, 108, 110, 123, 124
Abelson, J., 150
abortion, 176–77
Abraham Lincoln aircraft carrier, 113, 276
Abramoff, Jack, 118, 240–41
Abramowitz, A. I., 176
Abramson, J., 304
Abramson, P. R., 58
absentee ballots, 329
Ackerman, K. D., 33, 34
Ackoff, R. L., 238
Adamek, R. J., 176
Adams, John, 137, 155, 295–96
Adams, John Quincy, 170, 295–96
Adasiewicz, C., 230
ADI (area of dominant influence), 147
adolescents. *See also* young people
    authority and, 57–58
    family influence, 58–60
    political socialization of, 56–57
advertising. *See* negative advertising; newspaper advertising; political advertising; radio advertising; television advertising
ad watch programs, 164–65
affective components, of attitudes, 21
AFL-CIO, 257
African Americans
    Obama and, 82–83
    party affiliation of, 32
    prejudice against, 157*n*
    voting behavior, 291, 308
age
    of candidates, 96–98
    Internet access and, 200
    partisanship and, 69

radio listenership and, 114
television news viewing habits and, 108
voter turnout and, 307–8
agenda setting
    debates and, 230
    defined, 71, 116
    by news media, 116–24
    "priming," 119–20
Agnew, Spiro T., 156
AIDS, 119
Air America Radio, 115
Alexander, H. E., 251, 270
Alexander, Lamar, 89
alienation, 279
Alito, Samuel A., Jr., 61, 256
Allen, George, 29, 212, 307
Alliance for Better Campaigns, 110
all-news radio stations, 114
Alpert, B., 242
Al Qaeda, 17
Alvarez, L., 300
Amazon.com, 219
America Coming Together, 258, 259
American Association for Public Opinion Research, 178–79
American Century, 331
American Civil Liberties Union, 257
American exceptionalism, 26–27, 66–67
American Idol, 61
American Museum of the Moving Image, 143*n*
American Society of Newspaper Editors, 135
American Telephone & Telegraph, 251
amnesty, for illegal immigrants, 15
Anderson, P. A., 85

Anderson, R., 102, 103, 192, 193
Andreas, Dwayne O., 245–46,
    248–49, 251
Andsager, J. L., 119
Angelides, Phil, 157
Annenberg Foundation, 135
Ansolabehere, S., 47, 51, 106,
    146–47, 152, 153, 154,
    159–60, 161n, 162, 165, 279,
    281n
apathy, 273
appearance, of candidates, 94–95
Apple, R. W., 176n, 225
Arbitron, 114
Archer-Daniels-Midland, 249, 251
Arendt, Hannah, 317
Armey, Dick, 301
Armstrong, R., 147
Arnall, Roland, 259
Arsenio Hall Show, The, 134
Asher, H., 173, 174n, 180, 181, 185
Asian Americans, 247, 291, 308
Asner, Ed, 150
Associated Press, 105
Association for Education in
    Journalism and Mass
    Communication, 135
Association of Trial Lawyers of
    America, 251
Atkin, C. K., 153
Atlanta Constitution, 105
attack advertising. See negative
    advertising
attitudes, 21
Audacity of Hope, The (Obama), 82
Auer, J. J., 227
Auletta, K., 129
Austin, E. W., 58, 135
authority
    attitudes toward, 57–58
    language and, 14
Ayidya, S. A., 180

B2 stealth bombers, 251
Baaske, K. T., 17
Babbit, P., 162
Babcock, C. R., 240
Baker, P., 298n

Baldassare, M., 79
Baldi, S., 319
Balthrop, V. W., 217
Baltimore Sun, 105
Balz, D., 292
Bandow, D., 43
banners
    for candidates, 137
    "Mission Accomplished," 113, 276
Barabak, M. Z., 89
Barakat, M., 241
Barkin, S. M., 196
Barlett, D. L., 251–52
Barr, Bob, 305
Barrett, D., 80
Bartels, L. M., 193, 265
Bartlett, Dan, 235
Bassik, Michael, 227
Bates, B., 131
Bates, S., 14, 155, 156
Bauman, S., 169
Baumgartner, J., 89, 134
Bayh, Evan, 29
Beach, D. W., 125, 126
Bechtel Corporation, 267
Beck, P. A., 66
Becker, B. W., 181
behavioral components, of attitudes,
    21
Behr, R., 51, 106, 146–47
Belenkaya, V., 124
belief systems, 21
Bell, D., 72, 73
Bellah, R. N., 216, 217, 305, 315
Benello, C. G., 315
Benen, S., 91
Bengston, V. L., 58
Bennet, J., 11
Bennett, W. L., 102, 145, 196, 236,
    250, 279, 280, 312
Benoit, Pamela, 76
Benoit, W. L., 152, 228, 230
Berg, M. J., 185, 186
Berger, J., 303
Berke, R. L., 76–77, 88, 97, 224,
    234, 270, 287
Berkowitz, D., 125, 126
Berlet, C., 68

Berman, J., 230
Bernstein, Carl, 118
bias. *See* also partisanship
  in newspapers, 126–27
Biden, Joseph, Jr., 1
  image of, 90–91, 92
  media coverage of, 134
  2008 presidential campaign, 242
billboards, 138
Bill of Rights, 66
Bimber, B., 203
Bing, Stephen, 259
Bipartisan Campaign Finance
      Reform Act (McCain-Feingold
      Act), 82, 243–44, 253–63
  constitutionality of, 255–57
  electioneering communications,
    255
  First Amendment and, 255–57,
    327
  501(c)(4) organizations and,
    261–62
  527 organizations and, 258–62
  individual contribution limits, 255
  PAC contribution limits, 255
  recommended reforms, 327–28
  soft money, 254–57
Birdsell, David, 226
Birnbaum, J. H., 260
Biswas, R., 230–31
Bjork, R., 67
Black, C. F., 232
blastfaxing, 199
Bligh, M. C., 98
blogs, 207
Bloomberg, Michael, 46, 270–71
Blumenthal, Sydney, 45
Bock, A., 236
Bodenner, C., 189
Boehner, John A., 248
Borger, J., 48
Boston Globe, 105
Boulding, Kenneth E., 75
Bowers, A., 23
Bowling Alone (Putnam), 314
Boxer, Barbara, 150, 202
Boyarsky, B., 130
Boyd, R. W., 83

Boyle, T. P., 152
Boys on the Bus, The (Crouse), 125
Bradley, Bill, 19, 120–21, 203
Brady, R., 191
Braun, Carol Moseley, 134
Bregman, D., 124
Brehm, J., 177, 182
Breyer, Stephen, 256, 257
Brians, C. L., 152, 161*n*
bribery, 241–42
Brinkley, A., 296, 297, 304
broadcast technology, 113
Broder, D. S., 97, 278, 285, 291, 292
Broder, J. M., 2, 53, 236
Brooks, D. J., 282–83
Brotherson, S., 55
Brower, H. H., 98
Brownback, Sam, 1, 29
Brownstein, R., 44, 89, 123, 301
Bryan, William Jennings, 28, 138
Bryk, W., 43
Buchanan, Patrick J., 11, 65–66
Buckley v. Valeo, 255, 256
Buettner, R., 81
bumper stickers, 138
bundling, 268
Bunting, G. F., 247, 248
Bupp, I. C., 83
Burger, T. J., 240
Burke, Kenneth, 5, 11, 13, 74
Burmiller, E., 275–76
Burns, N., 58, 59
Burton, Dan, 299, 305
Bush, George H. W.
  election of, 39
  focus groups and, 188
  image of, 96
  narrative fidelity and, 16
  negative campaign advertising by,
    157–58
  1984 election campaign, 231
  political scandals and, 296
  public opinion polls and, 172, 175
Bush, George W.
  advisors, 274–77
  approval ratings, 2, 39, 52–53, 91,
    208, 243, 310
  bundling and, 268

Bush, George W. (*continued*)
   campaign financing, 46, 249–50,
      259, 268–69
   campaign messages, 11
   dishonesty of, 298
   election of, 6, 39–40, 258
   evangelical Christians and, 68
   focus groups and, 188–89
   humor about, 89
   image of, 20, 25, 76–77, 79, 80, 85,
      87–88, 91, 92, 95, 101, 113
   immigration policy and, 14–15,
      288–90
   impeachment and, 303
   interest groups and, 43
   Iraq war and, 3, 52–53, 107, 113,
      310
   Latino voters and, 291
   McCain-Feingold bill and, 254
   media and, 125, 131, 132–33, 134
   military records, 87
   negative campaign advertising
      and, 163, 178
   patronage and, 35
   polarization and, 6
   public opinion polls and, 169–70,
      197
   push polling and, 178–79
   Saudi Arabia and, 63
   special investigations and, 297
   summer reading list, 91
   terrorism and, 24
   2000 presidential campaign, 6,
      138, 189–90, 203, 203n, 225,
      249–50, 268, 278, 291
   2004 presidential campaign, 47,
      81, 87, 112–13, 140, 208,
      226, 233–35, 259, 260,
      268–69
Bush, Jeb, 190
Bush family, 3
Buss, T. F., 152

cable news shows, 112, 124–25
Caddell, Patrick, 172
California
   electoral votes, 40n
   gubernatorial campaigns, 157, 278
   1994 Senate election, 270

campaign consultants. *See* political
      consultants
campaign debates. *See* debates
campaign finance reform, 243–44,
      271–73. *See also* Bipartisan
      Campaign Finance Reform
      Act (McCain-Feingold Act)
   recommendations, 327–28
campaign financing, 240–73
   Bipartisan Campaign Finance
      Reform Act and, 253–63
   campaign costs and, 267
   Congress and, 267–69
   contribution controversies, 245–53
   cynicism and, 313
   federal matching funds, 250
   illegal contributions, 241
   Internet and, 204–8
   large donors, 246–53
   national political conventions and,
      252
   political corruption and, 242–45
   reporting requirements, 245–46
   soft money, 249, 250–62
   2008 presidential campaign and,
      242–44
campaigns
   advertising stages, 151
   candidate involvement in, 28
   continuous, 222, 277
   costs of, 242
   criticism of, 4
   cultural identity and, 22–23
   cynicism and, 26, 277–83
   debates and, 222–29
   direct mail advertising in, 148
   funding, 46
   history of, 25–26, 28–30
   image-dominated, 79–83
   Internet and, 201–9
   media coverage of, 36, 109,
      120–21, 124–32
   role of, 5
   state visits during, 29–30
   television coverage of, 109–13
   values and, 21–22
   in wartime, 3
   world interest in, 23
campaign songs, 137

campaign strategy
  communication technology and,
    198–99, 201–9, 213–15
  governing behavior and, 274–75
  media coverage of, 312
  national unity and, 290–93
  public opinion polls and, 172–73
Campbell, A., 33
Campbell, D. E., 68
Camus, Albert, 91
candidates
  affluent, 4, 270–71
  age of, 96–98
  appearance of, 94–95
  banners for, 137
  branding, 88
  buttons for, 138
  campaigning on own behalf,
    28–29
  campaign messages, 10–11
  caricatures of, 95
  challengers, 268, 269
  character of, 94, 231–32
  charisma of, 98–99
  communication by, 4, 9
  criticism of each other, 19
  drinking parties for, 136–37
  evaluation of, 71
  free airtime for, 272–73, 328
  front-runners, 84
  gaffes of, 235–36
  images of, 19–20, 24–25, 30,
    76–101
  incumbents, 267–68, 269
  leadership style, 97–98
  media and, 24–25, 109–10, 125,
    127, 133–35
  nonverbal behavior of, 94–96
  parades for, 136–37
  political ideologies of, 21–22
  political party assistance to, 41
  positions on issues, 21–22
  slogans for, 137–38
  "small-town origins" image of,
    85–86
  songs for, 137
  state visits by, 29–30
  trustworthiness of, 92–94, 99
  underdogs, 232

Cannon, Carl, 298
Cantril, A. H., 174, 174n, 175, 182,
    187, 188
Cappella, J. N., 52, 133
Carey, J. W., 102, 104
caricatures, of candidates, 95
Carlin, D. B., 224, 226, 227, 228,
    232, 233, 234, 237
Carsey, T. M., 292
Carter, Billy, 296
Carter, Jack, 4
Carter, Jimmy
  advisors to, 275
  caricatures of, 95
  exit polls and, 189
  family political involvement, 4
  image of, 80
  1980 presidential campaign, 225,
    229, 232
  1976 presidential campaign, 225,
    229, 231, 235–36
  political scandals and, 296
  public opinion polls and, 171–72
Carter, S., 126
Carter, S. L., 281, 282
Cassel, C. A., 58, 60
Castells, M., 213–14
Catholic Church, 67–68
caucuses
  Iowa, 2, 29, 111, 146, 206
  political participation and, 37
Causin, T., 146
CBS News, 87, 108, 110, 124, 178
CBS News poll, 279–80
celebrity journalists, 124–25
cell phones, 183, 212, 213–14
Center on Budget Priorities, 286
Center for Media Literacy, 207n
Center for Public Integrity, 244, 258
Center for Responsive Politics, 250–51
Chace, J., 29
Chaddock, G. R., 308
Chadwick, A., 71, 201, 204, 205,
    207, 236
Chaffee, S. H., 60, 65, 70, 151, 152,
    153, 164, 231, 233
Chamberlain, Neville, 17
Chanslor, M., 92, 165
character, 295, 296, 298–300

character assassination, 296–97
charisma, 98–99
Chase, Chevy, 95
Chattopadhayay, S., 152
checkbook democracy, 269
Chen, E., 248
Cheney, Dick, 48, 267, 282, 297, 303
   fund-raising by, 206
   humor about, 89
   image of, 85–86
"Cheney Challenge," 206
Chenowith, Helen, 305
Chicago
   political machines, 33–34
   welfare policy, 286
Chicago Tribune, 105
China, People's Republic of, 247
Chiquita Bananas, 252
Choe, S. Y., 231
Church, G. J., 285
church and state, 66–69
Churchill, Winston, 17n
Chyi, H. I., 124
Cillizza, C., 41, 129, 242
citizens. *See also* political
      participation
   candidate interest in issues of,
      10–11
   communication by, 9–10
   personal interests of, 13
   political influences on, 17–18
city bosses, 33–36
civic education, 60–66. *See also*
      education
   in college, 63, 319
   content of, 64–65
   effectiveness of, 318
   Internet and, 221
   purposes of, 63
   recommendations for, 318–21
   in Saudi Arabia, 62–63
   student government and, 319–20
civic groups, 324–25
civil loyalty, 61
civil rights movement, 37
civil service requirements, 35
Civil War, 7–8

Clark, J. R., 181
Clark, W. K., 16, 212–13
Clark, Wesley, 29
Clay, Henry, 31, 170
Cleveland, Grover, 137
Clinton, Bill, 3, 17n, 45, 46, 301
   advisors to, 275, 276
   character attacks against, 157–58,
      298–300
   FEC nomination, 272
   fund-raising by, 242, 246–49, 251,
      252, 253
   humor about, 89
   image of, 25, 78, 85, 86–87, 86n,
      94, 95, 97, 167–68, 299
   impeachment of, 49, 176, 256n,
      299–303
   media coverage of, 128–29, 130,
      134
   negative advertising against, 163
   1996 presidential campaign, 138,
      201–2, 226, 230–31, 234,
      246–49, 292–93
   1992 presidential campaign, 39,
      128–29, 225, 230
   political consultants and, 49, 167n
   political scandals and, 296, 298,
      304–5
   public discourse and, 100
   public opinion polls and, 169, 172
   Republican Party and, 301
   sexual conduct of, 120, 122, 128,
      129, 296, 298, 298n,
      299–300, 304–5
   2004 presidential campaign and,
      150
   welfare reform and, 285, 286–87
Clinton, Chelsea, 92, 246
Clinton, Hillary
   attitudes toward, 93, 299
   as front-runner, 169
   fund-raising by, 242, 253
   humor about, 89
   image of, 78, 92–93, 167–68
   media coverage of, 128–29
   2008 presidential campaign, 1, 3,
      44, 46, 130, 137, 154, 208,
      242, 253

2000 Senate campaign, 81
  Web site, 208
Clinton, J. D., 162
Cloud, D. S., 16
Club for Growth, 261
CNN, 112, 122, 210
cognitive components, of attitudes, 21
cognitive misers, 83
Cohen, B. C., 71
Colbert, Stephen, 89
Colbert Report, The, 134
Coleman, Norm, 225, 275
colleges and universities. *See also* education
  civic education in, 63, 319
  liberal attitudes and, 63
  local issues and, 323–24
  voting behavior and, 64
Colmes, Alan, 112
Columbine High School, 63*n*
Combs, J. E., 18, 79
Comedy Central, 89–90, 134
comedy news programs, 89–90, 134
Commission on Presidential Debates (CPD), 224, 225, 227
Common Cause, 252–53
communal thinking, 217–18
communication. *See also* political communication
  civic education and, 63
  gender differences, 59
  interpretation and, 13, 17–18
  language use and, 13–14
  role of, 9–22
  shared symbolism in, 11
  speeches, 100–101
communication technology, 198–221. *See also* Internet
  campaign strategy and, 198–99, 201–9, 213–15
  online news, 209–15
  public opinion polls and, 171
  pull vs. push, 209
  virtual town meetings and, 330
community groups, 324–25
computer-assisted telephone calls, 149–50

computer databases, 198–99
Congress
  approval ratings, 267, 310
  Democratic control of, 310
  earmarks and, 294–95
  election of members, 30
  impeachment of Clinton and, 300–301
  political corruption in, 240–42
  political polarization in, 292
  special interests and, 267–69
Congressional Record, 99
Connell, R. W., 58
Conover, Pamela Johnston, 83
Conrad, C., 229
conservatives
  image interpretation by, 77
  image of, 79
  moral issues and, 68–69, 300–301
  party affiliation and, 39
  polarization and, 292
  political attacks by, 8–9
  radio listening habits, 115
  scandals and, 303
Constitution, U.S., 5–6, 30
Constitutional Convention, 314–15
Constitutional Rights Foundation, 61*n*
"continuous campaigning," 277
Converse, P. E., 33, 60
Cook, C. E, 40
Cook, W., 307
cookies, 219
Cooley, D. M., 229
Coolidge, Calvin, 137, 140
Cooper, Anderson, 124
Cooper, R. T., 86
Cooperman, A., 43
Corley, M., 170
Cornelius, R. M., 28
Cornfield, M., 106, 205–6
corporate donors, 246–53
Corrado, A., 251, 254, 270
corruption. *See* political corruption
Coulter, Ann, 282, 283
Counterbias Web site, 163
Couric, Katie, 24, 124
cover photos, news magazines, 107–8

Craig, Larry, 123*n*, 302, 302*n*
Crawford, William H., 170
Crespi, I., 194
Crigler, A. N., 152
crime
    beliefs about, 11–12
    media coverage of, 12–13
    television coverage of, 109
    in urban areas, 11–12
Cronin, B., 27
Crosbie, V., 51
Crouse, T., 127
Crowley, B. E., 122
C-SPAN, 301
cultural identity
    American exceptionalism, 26–27
    presidential elections and, 22–23
Cunningham, Randy "Duke," 240
Curtin, R., 182
cynicism
    alienation and, 279
    campaign financing and, 313
    campaigns and, 26, 277–83
    causes of, 311–14
    comedy news programs and,
        89–90
    deliberately created, 277
    effects of, 135
    elected officials and, 52
    family influence on, 58
    government and, 52–53, 58
    media coverage and, 312
    negative advertising and, 278–81,
        281*n*
    news media and, 132–35
    polarization and, 311–12, 313
    public opinion polls and, 197,
        312–13
    scandals and, 295, 304
    spread of, 309–11

Dahl, R. A., 215
Daily Show with Jon Stewart, The,
    89–90, 134
"Daisy Spot" ad, 155–56, 280*n*
Dalager, J. K., 306
Dallas Morning News, 105
D'Amato, Alfonse, 286
Dao, J., 19

Dardenne, R., 102, 103, 192, 193
Daschle, Tom, 42, 268
Dauber, C., 227
Daves, R. P., 197
Davis, D. K., 80
Davis, Gray, 19
Davis, John W., 140
Davis, R., 203
Davis, R. H., 179
Dawson, K. S., 54, 65, 66
Dawson, R. E., 54, 65, 66
"D.C. Madam," 305
Dean, Howard, 41, 204–8, 236
Dearing, J. W., 124
debates, 222–39
    agenda-setting effects of, 230
    artificialness of, 99
    authenticity of, 227–29
    candidate expectations for, 234–35
    content of, 227, 229
    critics of, 228
    effects of, 224, 230–34
    format of, 227
    history of, 223–24
    information provided by, 231–34,
        238
    marketplace of ideas and, 217
    media coverage of, 235–37
    moderators, 228
    participation in, 224–25
    participatory democracy and,
        238–39
    partisanship of, 231
    political strategy and, 278
    rationality and, 237–39
    spin and, 234–37
    voting behavior and, 222–23,
        232–34
Debs, Eugene, 28
deceptive advertising, 149
Declaration of Independence, 72
DeLay, Tom, 41, 118, 241, 268
Delia, J. G., 17
deliberation, 219
Delli Carpini, M. X., 71, 117, 189
democracy
    debates and, 238–39
    equality and, 5–7
    Internet and, 215–21

legitimacy of, 7–8, 9
marketplace of free ideas and, 215–17
political campaigns and, 5
political participation and, 305, 306, 314–16
political parties and, 30–31
preservation of, 9, 314–16, 331
shared interests and, 9
stability of, 7–8
trust and, 315–16
in workplace, 325–26
young people and, 56
Democracy Network, 330
Democratic Leadership Council, 79
Democratic National Committee, 41, 246–48
Democratic Party
African Americans and, 32
campaign contributions and, 246–48, 251
Congress and, 310
debates and, 224
"democratization" of, 37
establishment of, 31
groups identifying with, 32, 56
immigrants and, 33
Iowa caucuses, 29
leadership of, 40–41
national conventions, 37, 82–83, 86, 199, 222, 252
negative advertising and, 159
polarization and, 292
political consultants and, 46
political corruption and, 241
presidential campaign of 2008 and, 208–9, 243
radio and, 114–15
South and, 32–33
special interest groups and, 43, 263
telephone polling and, 182, 184
urban political machines and, 33–35
weekly radio addresses, 142
welfare reform and, 285, 287
young people and, 38–39
Dennis, J., 231
Denton, R. E., 23, 170, 171, 172, 187

Derbyshire, J., 39
Dervin, B., 150
Detenber, B. H., 121
Detroit, 286
Devitt, E. G., 121
Devlin, L. P., 155
Dewey, John, 103, 216
DHinMI, 136
Diamond, E., 14, 155, 156
Diedrich, T., 110
digital divide, 200
Dillman, D. A., 181
DiMatteo, M. R., 95
Dinan, S., 15
Dionne, E. J., 52, 162, 197
direct mail advertising, 147–49
dishonesty, 90–91, 297–98
District of Columbia Appropriations Act, 246
Djerejian, G., 20
Dobbs, Lou, 112
Dobbs, M., 159
Dobson, James C., 68
Dodd, Christopher, 1, 242
Dohmen, T. J., 55
Dole, Bob, 3
    campaign messages, 11
    fund-raising by, 248
    image of, 85, 86, 86n, 94, 95, 97
    negative advertising against, 270
    1996 presidential campaign, 201–2, 226, 234, 236, 248, 292–93
Dole, Elizabeth, 3, 44
Donald, D. H., 28, 29
"Do Not Call" registry, 150, 182
door-to-door campaigning, 147
Dowd, M., 77
Downs, A., 292
Dreams from My Father (Obama), 82
Drew, D., 130, 152
Drew, E., 41, 245, 322
drinking parties, 136–37
Druckman, J. N., 83
Drudge Report, 130
Drunkard's Search, 84–85
Dube, J., 211
Dubitsky, T. M., 154
Dubose, L., 47

Dukakis, Michael
   focus groups and, 188
   image of, 96
   negative advertising against, 157
   public opinion polls and, 175
Duke, David, 186
Duncan, Hugh Dalziel, 13–14
Dunham, C. C., 58
Dwyer, P., 41
Dyson, E., 202
dystopians, 218

earmarks, 294–95
eco-terrorism, 8
Edelman, Murray, 14
Edsall, T. B., 242, 258, 260
education. *See also* civic education;
      colleges and universities
   Internet access and, 200
   voter turnout and, 307
Edwards, Elizabeth, 282
Edwards, John, 1
   Coulter's attack against, 282, 283
   fund-raising by, 242, 243
   image of, 11, 85
   social networking sites and, 214
   2008 presidential campaign, 2,
      209, 214, 242, 243
   2004 presidential campaign, 208
   Web site, 209
Eggen, D., 35
Eisenhower, Dwight D., 73, 138,
      143, 171
Eisner, William, 88
elderly citizens, 13
elected officials. *See also*
      government
   communication by, 9–10
   cynicism about, 52, 275
   online access to, 215
   political consultants for, 275–77
   spin and, 277
electioneering communications, 255
Electoral College, 30, 40, 40n, 189,
      191
elementary schools, 61n
Eliasoph, N., 317, 320, 324
Elliot, W. R., 236

Ellsworth, J. W., 229
e-mail
   for campaign messages, 199, 202
   distributing humor clips with, 90
   online news, 211
   rapid-response, 202–3
emotion, 85
Emrich, C. G., 98
"enemies list," 281–82
Engle, M. A., 204
Entman, R., 121
Entrekin, H. S., 228
environmental policy, 8, 119
Environmental Protection Agency
      (EPA), 251
Epstein, L. D., 37, 83
equality
   democratic elections and, 6–7
   freedom and, 73
   U.S. Constitution and, 5–6
equal time rules, 140n
Erikson, R. S., 169, 184, 187
Escobar, G., 15
ethics scandals. *See* scandals
ethnicity, 55. *See also* minority
      groups
European Union, 252
evangelical Christians
   McCain and, 82
   as percentage of U.S. residents, 68
   political activism by, 68–69
   2004 presidential election and, 43
Eveland, W. P., 230
exit polls, 189–91
"experts" interviews, 111, 125–26

Face the Nation, 133
fairness doctrine, 140n
Falk, A., 55
Fallows, James, 312
Falwell, Jerry, 82
family, 54–60
   nuclear, decline of, 64
   police attitudes and, 57–58
   political attitudes and, 58–60
   social contract and, 56–57
   social identity and, 58
   trust and, 55

farmers, 13
Farrakhan, Louis, 178
fax machines, 199
Federal Communications
        Commission, 140*n*
Federal Election Campaign Act, 261
Federal Election Commission (FEC),
        2, 224, 242, 258, 261, 272
federal matching funds, 250
Fehr, B. J., 91–92, 93
Fein, S., 237
Feingold, Russell, 29, 244, 253–55,
        258
Feinstein, Dianne, 150, 270
Feldman, H. H., 98
Feldman, Stanley, 83
Fernandez-Ardeol, M., 213–14
Ferraro, Geraldine, 44
Fico, F., 119, 126, 130
financial services industry, 251
Finder, A., 286
Fineman, H., 46, 94, 176, 201, 203,
        246
Finifter, A., 58
Finkel, S. E., 185, 186
Finnegan, M., 157
Finnigan, M., 19
Fiorina, M. P., 83
fireside chats, 141
First Amendment
    Bipartisan Campaign Finance
        Reform Act and, 255–57, 327
    equality and, 73
First Family, 25
First National Bank v. Bellotti, 255
Fisher, Walter R., 15, 20, 92, 104
Fiske, W., 212
Fitzgerald, Patrick, 297
501(c)(4) organizations, 261–62
527 organizations, 258–62
flags, for candidates, 137
flag salute, 60
Flanagan, C. A., 56–57
flash mobs, 214
flat tax, 88
Florida
    Everglades cleanup, 249
    Nader supporters in, 204

2000 presidential election and, 6,
        39–40
Florida Supreme Court, 190
Flowers, Gennifer, 128, 129
Flynn, Ed, 34
focus groups, 188–89, 313
"Focus on the Family," 69
Foley, Mark, 122–23, 129
Followthemoney.org, 204, 272
Forbes, Steve, 16, 46, 88, 270
Forbes magazine, 89
Ford, Gerald
    image of, 95
    1976 presidential campaign, 225,
        229, 231, 235–36
    public opinion polls and, 171
foreign policy, 16, 252
Forsythe, M., 328
Foster, D., 8
Foster, Vince, 299
Fox, S., 200
Fox News, 112, 237
framing, 121–24
    negative, 133–35
Frammolino, R., 246, 247
Frana, A. W., 228
Frank, Barney, 269
Frank, R., 128
Franken, Al, 115
Frankovic, Kathleen, 170, 175, 179,
        193–94, 196
Frederick, D., 209, 309
free airtime, 272–73, 328
Freedman, E., 119, 126, 130
Freedman, P., 160–61
Freedman, P. W., 279
freedom
    equality and, 73
    of the press, 102
    religious, 66–67
Fremstad, S., 286
Freud, Sigmund, 72*n*
Freyman, R., 38
Friedenberg, R. V., 45, 138, 223
Friedman, Barbara, 25
Friedman, H. S., 95
Friendster, 206*n*
fringe groups, 8–9, 18

Fritsch, J., 249
Fritz, S., 246
Frontline (PBS), 86n
front-runners, 84
Froomkin, D., 275
Fry, S., 62
Fuller, J., 102
fundamentalists, 67–69
Fundrace.org, 272

Gailey, P., 225
Gallo family, 248
Gallup, George H., Jr., 171, 197
Gallup poll, 169, 183, 197
Gamson, W. A., 121
Ganly, G., 201
Ganz, M., 321, 322, 323
Garland, H., 98
Garofoli, J., 227
Garramone, G. M., 157
Gates, Bill, 7
gay marriage, 43, 68
gay rights, 308–9
gays and lesbians
    violence against, 63n
    voting behavior, 309
gay sex scandals, 123n, 129
Geer, J. G., 280, 280n, 281n, 282–83
gender
    communication differences, 59
    personal image and, 93
    politics of, 44
    voting behavior and, 56
Generation Xers, 38. *See also* young
        people
Germond, J. W., 96
Gerstenzang, J., 19
Gertzen, J., 69
get-out-the-vote (GOTV) efforts,
        250, 254, 261, 278
Ghorpade, S., 152
Gibbons, Dawn, 4
Gibbs, N., 247
Gibson, Charles, 228
Gillespie, Ed, 258
Gimpel, J. G., 67
Gingrich, Newt, 29, 192

Ginsburg, Ruth Bader, 256, 257
Gitel, S., 83
Gitlin, S., 66, 120, 121
Giuliani, Andrew, 81
Giuliani, Caroline, 81
Giuliani, Rudolph W. (Rudy), 1
    fund-raising by, 243, 244
    image of, 80–81
    Senate campaign, 81
    2008 presidential campaign, 81,
        169, 209, 243, 244
    Web site, 209
Givhan, Robin, 92
Glaser, J. M., 83
Glass, J., 58
global warming, 119
Gobetz, R. H., 165
Goethals, G. R., 237
Golan, G., 121
Gold, E. R., 96
Gold, M., 19
Goldberg, S., 58
Goldblatt, D., 326
Goldstein, K., 110–11, 136, 153,
        160–61
Goldwater, Barry, 138, 156
Gonzales, Alberto, 275, 297
Good Morning America, 282
Goodnight, G. T., 217
Goodnough, A., 81
Gore, Al
    Bradley and, 19
    fund-raising by, 249–50, 253
    global warming and, 119
    humor about, 89
    image of, 11, 48, 77–78, 85, 94
    media and, 125
    1996 reelection campaign, 247, 248
    2000 presidential campaign, 6,
        39–40, 120, 132–33, 189–90,
        203, 203n, 204, 234, 249–50,
        278, 291
    2008 presidential campaign and, 192
gossip, as news, 129
Gould, L. L., 277
government. *See also* elected officials
    attitudes toward, 314

cynicism about, 52–53, 58
former employees as lobbyists,
    293–94
legitimacy of, 7–8
online access to, 215
power hierarchies in, 4–5
spending concerns, 13, 52
trust in, 53
Graber, D. A., 103, 121, 127, 140*n*
Graff, G. M., 214
Grant, Ulysses S., 295
Gravel, Mike, 1
Great Britain, 17, 23
Greco, D. E., 306
Green, J., 43, 278
Greenberg, B. S., 94
Greenberg, E. S., 32, 33, 238
Greene, K. E., 267, 268
Greenhouse, L., 256, 257
Green Party, 39–40, 203, 225
Grenzke, J., 251
Grieve, T., 81
Griffin, R., 83
Griffin, Tim, 278
Grimes, C., 102
Gronbeck, B. E., 155
Grossberg, L., 17
Ground Zero, 80
group think, 126, 126*n*
Grunig, J. E., 153
Grunwald, M., 129, 270
Guardian (London), 23
"guest worker" program, 289–90
Gulf War, 16
Guterbock, T. M., 185, 186

Habermas, Jurgen, 103, 195, 217
Hahn, D., 54
Hahn, James, 95, 158
Hale, M., 110–11
Halliburton Company, 266–67
Hallin, D. C., 110, 111
Halpin, J., 114, 115
Halstead, T., 65
Hamilton, C. E., 58
Hannity, Sean, 112
Hannity and Colmes, 133

Hanover, Donna, 81
Hansen, G. J., 152, 228
Hansen, S., 272
Hansen, W. G., 228, 230
Hardball, 133, 282
Harden, B., 101
Harding, Warren G., 137, 295
Harmon, M., 131
Harp, S., 79
Harris, Katherine, 190
Harrisburg Pennsylvanian, 170
Harrison, T. M., 91–92, 93
Harrison, William H., 137
Harris poll, 169, 183
Hart, Gary, 128
Hart, Roderick, 24, 51, 70, 98, 100,
    101, 128, 156
Harvey, M., 90
Harwood, J., 278
Hastert, Dennis, 99–100, 123
Hawkins, R. P., 70, 116
Hayes, Rutherford B., 296
Heald, G., 153
Healy, P., 2, 53
Heiferman, Scott, 204
Held, D., 326
Heldman, C., 162
Hellweg, S. A., 80, 94
Helms, Jesse, 167*n*
Herbst, Russell, 20
Herbst, S., 169
Herman, K., 82
Hernson, P. S., 267, 268
Herr, N., 51
Herrera, K., 20
Hess, S., 277
Hicks, Taylor, 61
high schools, 12, 62
Hill, D. B., 58
Hill, S. S., 67, 68
Hillygus, D. S., 83
Hinck, E. A., 228
Hinds, L. B., 18, 22
Hinich, M. J., 292
Hirschfeld, L., 55
Hispanics. *See* Latinos
Hitler, Adolf, 16–17

Hofstetter, R. C., 152
Hogan, J. M., 67, 227, 235
Holbert, R. L., 152, 230
Holland, S., 310
Hollihan, T. A., 17, 72, 95, 158, 217, 218, 229, 315, 326
homophily, 85–88
honesty, 90–94, 99, 297–98
Hook, J., 123, 248
Hoover, Herbert, 137
Horowitz, J. M., 292
Horrigan, J. B., 106, 210–11
"horse race" stories, 126, 130, 196
Horton, William ("Willie"), 157, 157n, 188
Hoskin, M. B., 58
House of Representatives, 30
Houston, J. B., 210
Howard, C., 227
Howard, P., 146, 172
Howard, P. N., 198–99, 203, 209, 219–20
Howell, Deborah, 93
Howell, S. E., 186n
Hsu, Norman, 253
Huckabee, Mike, 1, 29
Huckfelt, Robert, 67, 69
Huff, R., 124
Huffington, Michael, 270
Huffman, D., 55
Hulse, C., 123
human rights, 72
humor
    of candidates, 94
    comedy news programs, 89–90, 134
    sex scandals and, 299
Humphrey, Hubert, 156, 223n, 225
Hunter, Duncan, 1
Hurricane Katrina, 119, 307
Hurtado, A., 185
Hussein, Saddam, 16, 17, 52, 113, 196, 266
Husson, W., 91–92, 93
Huxman, S. S., 121
Hwang-Du, H., 187
Hyde, Henry, 302, 304
Hyman, H. H., 58
hyperrealism, 24

identity
    family influence on, 58
    ideologies and, 74
    political party and, 60
ideologies, 21, 71–74
ideologues, 72–73
illegal immigration, 14–15, 95, 287–90. See also immigration policy
image, 75–101
    candidate personality and, 81–83
    conflicting, 76–79
    creating, 76–85
    development, 75
    homophily and, 85–88
    persistence of, 75–76
    personal, 91–94
    political, 91–94
    political advertising and, 76, 79, 153
    political attitudes and, 85
    of political parties, 79
    redefining, 88–91
    small-town origins, 85–86
    video images, 113
    voting behavior and, 83–85
image-dominated campaigns, 79–83
immigrants
    illegal, 14–15, 95, 287–90
    Internet access and, 200
    newspaper readership by, 106
    political party affiliation of, 33
    welfare policy and, 285
immigration policy, 14–15, 112, 287–90
impeachment
    Bush, George W., and, 303
    of Clinton, 49, 176, 256n, 299–303
    Congress and, 300–301
    Nixon and, 175–76
    political scandals and, 296
    public opinion polls and, 175–76, 176n
Imus, Don, 299
inclusiveness, Internet and, 219
income
    awareness of, 58
    of candidates, 270–71

gap between rich and poor, 221,
    287
Internet access and, 200
party identification and, 36–37, 59
political participation and, 264–66,
    265
voting behavior and, 265, 291, 308
Inconvenient Truth, An (Gore), 119
incumbents, 267–68, 269
Independence Party of Minnesota,
    197
independents
    family influence on, 59
    increase in, 83
    negative advertising and, 159–60,
        162
    young people as, 38
influential citizens, 7
information, news media and, 102–3
Insight, 130
Intercollegiate Studies Institute, 319
Internet, 199–221. *See also* e-mail;
        online news
    blogs, 207*n*
    broadband (high-speed) connec-
        tions, 201, 210–11
    campaign financing and, 204–8
    civic education and, 221
    concerns about, 218–21
    democracy and, 215–21
    marketplace of free ideas and,
        215–21
    news sources, 130, 209–15
    political campaigns and, 201–9
    political expression on, 8
    political news on, 106, 115–16
    political participation and, 217–21
    polls, 184–85
    privacy issues, 215–21
    usage rates, 200
    uses of, 199–201
    voter targeting and, 212–13
interpretation
    of communication, 13, 17–18
    credibility of, 18
interviews
    with candidates, 24–25
    with "experts," 111, 125–26

payment for, 129–30
as public opinion polls, 185–86
telephone, 181–84
television, 24–25
Iorio, S. H., 121
Iowa caucuses, 2, 29, 111, 146, 206
Iran-Contra scandal, 296
Iraq, 17
    Gulf War, 16
    reconstruction of, 266–67
Iraq war
    news media and, 107, 117
    presidential campaign and, 3–4
    public trust and, 52–53, 276
    student involvement and, 320
    video images of, 113
Irwin, G. A., 168, 193
Isikoff, M., 49, 246
issues
    candidate positions on, 21–22
    evaluation of, 71
    image-dominated campaigns and,
        79–80
    media coverage of, 130–32
Iyengar, S., 12, 47, 51, 106, 121,
        146–47, 152, 153, 154,
        159–60, 161*n*, 162, 165, 277,
        279, 281*n*

Jackson, Andrew, 31, 127
Jackson, Jesse, 134
Jacobs, L. R., 79, 266
Jacobson, G. C., 6
Jamieson, K. H., 28–29, 47, 50, 52,
        127, 131–32, 133, 136, 137,
        140, 141, 157*n*, 165, 226, 230
Jefferson, Thomas, 137, 155
Jefferson, William, 241
Jeffersonian Party, 31
Jennings, M. K., 55, 66, 193
Jennings, Peter, 124
Jensen, K., 328
"Jesse-Net" Web site, 202
Johnson, Brooks, 272
Johnson, Lyndon B., 32, 155, 280*n*,
        296
Johnson, T. J., 130–31
Johnston, D. C., 287

Jones, Dennis, 163
Jones, Paula, 298*n*
Joslyn, R. A., 154, 155
journalists. *See also* media coverage;
    news media
  bias and, 126, 127
  candidate relationships with, 125
  celebrity, 124–25
  ethical responsibilities of, 135
  for newspapers, 106
  public opinion polls and, 168–69
  strategies for, 135
Journeys with George, 77, 125
Judaism, 68
Jung, D. I., 98
Just, M. R., 152

Kaid, L. L., 92, 165, 231
Kaldenberg, D. O., 181
Kamber, V., 282
Kamieniecki, S., 33, 59, 67
Kane, P., 123*n*, 244
Kang, J. G., 127, 230, 231
Kansas City, 33
Kaplan, J., 8, 177–78
Kaplan, Martin, 109, 110–11
Kapoor, S., 127
Karlgaard, R., 16
Katz, C., 79
Katz, J., 218
Kaye, K., 221
KBR, 266–67
Keeter, S., 92, 183
Keetzer, S., 117
Kelley, M., 226
Kellner, D., 164
Kelly, S., Jr., 280*n*
Kempster, N., 247
Kendall, K. E., 83, 85, 94
Kennamer, J. D., 151
Kennedy, Anthony, 256
Kennedy, Edward (Ted), 288–90
Kennedy, Jacqueline, 144
Kennedy, John F.
  Clinton and, 87
  debates, 223, 229
  1960 presidential campaign, 225,
    229

  public opinion polls and, 171
  television campaign advertising,
    144
Kennedy, Robert F., Jr., 6
Kennedy-McCain bill, 289
Kennedy-Nixon debates, 144
Kenney, K., 127
Kenski, K., 233
Kerry, John F.
  focus groups and, 189
  fund-raising by, 259
  humor about, 89
  image of, 78, 87–88, 189, 259–61
  media and, 134
  military records, 87
  negative campaign advertising
    against, 159, 163
  public opinion polls and, 183
  2004 presidential campaign, 43,
    87, 140, 150, 191, 205, 208,
    226, 233–35, 259–61, 291
Kharif, O., 214
Kibler, R. J., 85
Kids Voting USA, 64
Kiely, K., 307
Killenberg, G. M., 102, 103, 192,
    193
Kim Jong Il, 16, 17
Kinder, D. R., 59, 69
King, E. G., 130
King, J. D., 157
King, Larry, 24, 124
King, Rodney, 57*n*
Kinnock, Neil, 90
Kinsey, D., 154, 155
Kiolbassa, J., 109
Kiousis, S., 70
Kirkpatrick, D. D., 2, 130, 243, 256,
    257, 294–95
Klan Watch, 9
Klein, J., 46, 48, 80, 289
Klein, R., 287, 289
Klineberg, E., 106
Klumpp, J. F., 217, 218, 315, 326
Koch, W., 267
Koenig, H. F., 181
Kohles, J. C., 98
Kolker, A., 54, 58, 73

Kopel, D. B., 175
Koprowski, G. J., 201
Korean Reunification Church, 127
Kovach, B., 106
Kranish, M., 294
Kraus, S., 225, 227, 232
Krauthammer, C., 246
Kubiak, G. D., 269
Kucinich, Dennis, 1, 154
Kugler, M., 161
Kugler, M. B., 237
Kuhner, Jeffrey T., 130
Kuhnhenn, J., 241, 270
Kuran, T., 54, 186
Kurtz, H., 87
Kuwait, 16

labor unions
    attack ads by, 19
    campaign contributions by, 251
    501(c) organizations, 262
    immigration policy and, 288
    party affiliation and, 33
    political participation and, 326
    political power of, 36
Lacey, M., 302
bin Laden, Osama, 16, 17
LaGanga, M. L., 236, 248
Lambro, D., 79, 92
Lamoureux, E. R., 228
Lance, Bert, 296
Landon, Alfred M., 171, 174
language, 13–14, 22
Lanoue, D. J., 233
"lapdog" journalism, 132
lapel buttons, 138
Lapinski, J. S., 162
Larson, K. M., 110
Lasswell, H. D., 194
*Late Show with David Letterman,
    The,* 134
Latinos
    appealing to, 86, 144
    discrimination against, 15
    immigration policy and, 15, 95
    negative advertising and, 158
    telephone polling and, 181
    voting behavior, 291, 308

Lau, R. R., 155, 162, 182, 192
Lauer, Matt, 24
Lavrakas, P. J., 182
Lawrence, J., 4, 282, 283
Lawton, D., 279
Layman, G. C., 292
leadership style, 97–98
League of Women Voters, 224, 227
Leavey, P., 169
LeClaire, J., 200
Lehrer, Jim, 228
Leibovich, M., 15
Lengel, A., 241
Leno, Jay, 89, 92, 134, 247
Leon, M., 231
Lersch, K. M., 57
lesbians. *See* gays and lesbians
Leshner, G., 152
Let's Read about George W. Bush, 62
Letterman, David, 92, 134, 247
Levey, N. N., 123
Levinson, A., 8
Lewinsky, Monica, 49, 256n, 296,
    298, 299–300
Lewis, Charles, 244
Lewis, N. A., 297
Lewis, Peter, 259
Lexis-Nexis, 193
Libby, I. Lewis "Scooter," 48, 297, 303
liberals
    colleges and, 63–64
    image interpretation by, 77
    image of, 79
    party affiliation and, 39
    polarization and, 292
    scandals and, 303
Lichter, S. R., 130
Lieberman, Joe, 38, 66–67
Liebling, A. J., 218
Lightman, D., 146
Limbaugh, Rush, 115, 130, 299
Lin, C. A., 117
Lincoln, Abraham, 136, 137
    African Americans and, 32
    presidential campaign, 28
    re-election campaign, 3
    refusal to vote, 29
    Southern response to, 7

Lincoln-Douglas debates, 228
Lind, A. E., 55
Lind, Bill, 63
Lindeman, M., 191
Lindner, Carl, 252
Link, M. W., 182
Lipton, E., 81
Literary Digest straw polls, 170–71,
    173–74
"Living Room Candidate, The,"
    143*n*
Livingston, Bob, 305
lobbyists. *See also* special interest
        groups
    campaign finance reform and, 327
    former government employees as,
        293–94
    open government and, 293
    political corruption and, 240–41
    press coverage of, 118
    public policy and, 293–95
    role of, 42–43
local issues, 323–24
local television news, 108–9
Lockhart, Joe, 234–35
Loeffler, D. N., 63
Lohuizen, Jan van, 170
Longo, N. V., 309
Los Angeles
    direct mail advertising in, 148–49
    mayoral elections, 158
    media market, 147
    negative advertising in, 148
    political contributions from, 264
    yard signs, 138–39
Los Angeles Times, 47, 104, 128,
    139, 248
Los Angeles Times/Bloomberg poll,
    287
Lott, Trent, 251, 302
Louden, A. D., 154
Lowe, K. B., 98
low-income persons
    immigration policy and, 15
    telephone polling and, 181
low information rationality, 84
Luttbeg, N. R., 58
lying, 297–98

MacDowell, K. A., 231
MacKuen, M., 231, 232, 233
Madden, M., 200
Madsen, A., 236
Madsen, Phil, 201
"magic hour light," 276
Magleby, D., 260, 261
Maher, Bill, 282
mail surveys, 179–80
Maine, 40*n*
Maisel, L. S., 33
Malcolm, A., 209, 309
management, participatory, 325–26
Mankinson, L., 263–64, 266
Mann, T. E., 254
Maplight.org, 272
Marable, M., 55
Maraniss, D., 86
Marcus, G. E., 85
Margolis, M., 194
marketplace of free ideas, 215–21
Markus, G. B., 55
Marshall, C. E., 57
Martin, J., 216
Marx, Karl, 72
mass media. *See* news media
Matasar, A., 255
Mattei, F., 59
Mauser, G. A., 175, 194
McAllister, I., 193
McCabe, J. A., 126
McCafferty, P., 95
McCain, Bridget, 179
McCain, Cindy, 179
McCain, John, 1, 90
    campaign finance reform and,
        253–55, 258
    evangelical Christians and, 82
    fund-raising by, 243–44, 250
    image of, 81–82
    immigration policy and, 288–90
    negative campaigning against, 47,
        178
    push polling and, 178–79
    2000 presidential campaign, 225,
        250
    2008 presidential campaign,
        243–44

McCain-Feingold bill. *See* Bipartisan Campaign Finance Reform Act (McCain-Feingold Act)
McCall, J. M., 227
McClain, T. B., 227
McClellan, George, 3, 137
McClendon, M. J., 180
McClure, R. D., 152
McCombs, Maxell, 71, 116, 118, 121, 124
McConnell, J. B., 157
McConnell, Mitch, 256
McCurry, Mike, 246
McDermott, M. L., 175, 196
McDevitt, M., 60, 65, 70
McGee, M. C., 195
McGoldrick, B., 38
McGovern, George, 125
McGrew, A., 326
McIntire, M., 253
McKinley, William, 28, 137, 138
McKinney, M. S., 165, 224, 226, 228, 230, 231, 233, 234
McLean, W. P., 186*n*
McLeod, J. M., 121
McVeigh, Timothy, 8
Meadow, R. G., 64, 70, 71
media coverage, 50–53. *See also* news media
  biases in, 126–27
  of campaigns, 36, 120–21, 124–32
  of campaign strategy, 312
  of crime, 12–13
  cynicism and, 132–35, 312
  of debates, 235–37
  ethics of, 135
  "expert" interviews, 111, 125–26
  framing, 121–24
  "horse race" stories, 126, 130
  influence of, 17
  interpretation of, 13, 17–18
  of issues, 130–32
  "lapdog" journalism, 132
  negative, 132–35
  newspapers, 50–51, 104–7, 109, 126–27
  pack journalism, 127–28
  political advertising and, 152, 164
    presidential dishonesty and, 298
    of public opinion polls, 131–32, 193–94
    radio, 50, 114–15, 142
    reporting strategies, 135
    of sex scandals, 298–99, 304–5
    substantive issues, 317
    television, 50–52, 108–13
    "watchdog" journalism, 132
media-focused campaigns, 168
Media Fund, The, 258
Medved, M., 108
Meehan, Martin, 254
Meet the Press, 133
Meetup.com, 204–5, 208
Mehren, E., 302
Memmott, M., 189, 282, 283
Mendelsohn, H., 153
Merolla, J. L., 98
Merry, M. S., 65
Mertz, T. I., 95
Metzger, Tom, 8
Mexico, 6
Meyer, R. P., 309
Miami Herald Publishing Company v. Tornillo, 140*n*
Michael, G., 8
Michaels, Jim, 16
Microsoft, 7
middle school, 62
midterm elections
  exit polls and, 191
  Internet and, 202
  television advertising, 146
  voter suppression in, 278
  voter turnout, 306–7
  wedge issues in, 284
Mieczkowski, T., 57
Milavsky, J. R., 230–31
Milbank, D., 113
military actions, 16
Miller, A. H., 231, 232, 233
Miller, Mrs. Alex, 171
Miller, M., 119, 146
Miller, P. V., 192
Miller, T. C., 266–67
Miller, W. E., 33
Milosovic, Slobodan, 16, 17, 17*n*

Minneapolis Star Tribune, 197
Minnesota gubernatorial elections,
    202
Minnesota News Council, 197
minority groups. *See also* African
        Americans; Latinos
    personal interviews and, 185–86,
        186*n*
    political party identification of, 56
    voting behavior, 291, 308
Minuteman Project, 288
"Mission Accomplished" banner,
    113, 276
Mitchell, A., 106
Moehringer, J. R., 64*n*
Molyneux, G., 11
Mondale, Walter, 96, 226
Moore, D., 187
Moore, D. W., 164
Morain, D., 243, 244, 270
Morales, Dan, 177–78
moral issues
    public opinion polls and, 175–76
    public policy and, 302
    voting behavior and, 69
Morris, D., 136
Morris, Dick, 129–30, 167–68, 167*n*,
    285
Morris, J. S., 89, 134
mothers, 58–59
MoveOn.org, 140, 258, 259, 261
MSNBC, 91, 112, 224
    Web site, 210
Mulloy, D., 8
Munger, M. C., 292
Munson, J. Q., 68
Murrah, Alfred P., Federal Building,
    Oklahoma City, 8
Murray, B., 291
Murray, S., 123*n*, 305
Murray, S. K., 172
Mutz, Diana, 117, 291
Myers, S. L., 275
MySpace, 206*n*, 214

Nader, Ralph, 39–40, 203–4, 203*n*,
    225
Nagourney, A., 39, 134, 208, 242, 243

name recognition, 143
Napoleon, 72
Nardulli, P. F., 306
narrative fidelity, 15, 16
narrative probability, 15–16
narrative rationality, 15
Natchez, P. B., 83
National Civics Literacy Board, 319
National Conference of State
        Legislatures, 61
national conventions. *See also*
        Democratic Party; Republican
        Party
    history of, 136–37
    political contributions and, 252
    uncommitted delegations, 33
National Guard, 87
National Public Radio (NPR),
        114–15, 142
National Rifle Association, 257
national television news, 108–9
national unity, 290–93
Native Americans, 291
NATO, 16
natural rights, 72
Nazi Germany, 16–17
NBC News, 52, 108, 110
Nebraska, 40*n*
negative advertising, 47, 155–66. *See
        also* political advertising
    campaign stage and, 151
    cynicism and, 278–81, 281*n*
    defense of, 280–81
    direct mail, 148
    effects of, 157–66
    history of, 155–57
    incivility and, 282–83
    national unity and, 290–93
    opposition research and, 278
    personal attacks, 282–83
    polarization and, 163, 283
    sponsors of, 158–59
    on television, 145
    voting behavior and, 278–80
negative message framing, 133–35
Neimi, R. G., 55, 59
neo-futurists, 218
Nesbitt, J., 9

Nesbitt, M., 105, 105*n*
Nessen, Ron, 95
network news programs, 108–9, 112–13
New England town meetings, 330
New Hampshire
  presidential primary, 2, 110, 111, 121
  voter suppression in, 278
Newport, F., 197, 233–34
news magazines, 107–8
news media, 50–53, 102–35. *See also* media coverage; news magazines; newspapers; radio; television
  agenda-setting functions of, 116–24
  competitiveness of, 126
  information and, 102–3
  negative coverage by, 132–33
  online news, 209–15
  political attitudes and, 69–71
  political consultants and, 45
  power of, 71, 119
  role of, 102–4, 132
  sources of political news, 104–16
  Web sites, 210–11
newspaper advertising, 139–40, 164, 281*n*
Newspaper Association of America, 50–51, 104
newspapers, 50–51, 104–7
  candidate endorsements by, 127
  large dailies, 104–5
  number of, 106
  partisanship of, 126–27, 140
  political news in, 105, 106–7, 109
  readership, 105–6
  reporters, 106
news programs
  comedy, 89–90, 134
  local, 108–9
  national, 108–9
  television, 108–9
news services, 104–5
Newsweek, 107
New York
  image of, 80–81
  political contributions from, 264

political machines, 33–34
welfare policy, 286
New York Times, 15, 76, 88, 104, 113, 139, 178, 197, 310
  Web site, 210
New York Times/CBS Poll, 93
Ney, Robert W., 118, 240
Nicaraguan Contras, 296
Nielsen Media Research, 146
Nihart, T., 57
Nimmo, Dan, 18, 75, 79
Nixon, Richard M., 95
  debates, 223, 229
  "enemies list," 281–82
  image of, 295
  impeachment survey, 175–76
  media and, 125
  1960 presidential campaign, 223, 225, 229
  1968 presidential campaign, 223*n*
  resignation of, 118
  Southern Strategy and, 32–33
  television campaign advertising, 144, 156
  Watergate and, 118, 176, 245–46
nonverbal behavior, 94–96
Noriega, Manuel, 16, 17
North American Free Trade Agreement (NAFTA), 11
North Korea, 16, 17
No Spin Zone, 237
Novak, Michael, 23

Obama, Barack
  African Americans and, 82–83
  campaign attacks against, 130
  as front-runner, 169
  fund-raising by, 242–43
  social networking sites and, 214
  on *Time* cover, 107
  2008 presidential campaign, 1, 46, 81, 82–83, 208, 214, 242–43
  Web site, 208
"Obama Girl," 213
O'Brien, Conan, 92
O'Connor, Sandra Day, 256
Ohio, 6, 23, 43
O'Keefe, G. J., 142

Olbermann, Keith, 112
Oldendick, R. W., 182
Oliphant, J., 253
online news, 209–15. *See also*
    Internet
  exposure to, 219–21
  quality of, 210
  rich-poor information gap and, 221
  usage patterns, 210–12
online polling, 184–85
Opensecrets.org, 204, 250, 272
opposition research, 278
Orange Revolution (Ukraine), 6
O'Reilly Factor, The, 133
Ornstein, N., 136, 166
Ostrom, C. W., Jr., 94
Otis, M. D., 63
Owen, D., 71
Owen, D. E., 67, 68

pack journalism, 127–28
Page, B. I., 266
Page, S., 69
Paine, S. C., 83, 94
Paine, Thomas, 218
Paletz, D. L., 142, 242
Panagopoulos, C., 184
Panama, 16, 17
parades, 136–37
Parenti, M., 126
Parrott, R., 150–51
participatory democracy. *See*
    democracy
participatory team-based manage-
    ment, 325–26
partisanship
  age and, 69
  of debates, 231
  "red" states vs. "blue" states, 292
  scandals and, 299
Pataki, George, 29
Patrick, John, 64, 317–18
patriotic history, 64–65
patronage jobs, 35
Patterson, Thomas, 7, 58, 65,
    132–33, 152, 155, 196, 236,
    282, 309, 312, 313
Paul, Ron, 1

Pear, R., 290
Peer, L., 105, 105*n*
Pelosi, Nancy, 99, 191, 241
Pendergast, Thomas J., 296
Penn, Mark, 167
Penthouse, 128
Pérez-Peña, R., 81
Perloff, R. M., 47, 109, 120, 124,
    154, 155
Perot, Ross, 39, 46, 224–25, 231,
    232, 270
Perraton, J., 326
Perry, Bob, 259
personal attacks, 282–83
personal digital assistants (PDAs), 214
personal image, 91–94. *See also*
    image
Peters, J. D., 195
Pew Charitable Trusts, 135
Pew poll, 169
Pew Research Center, 91, 106
Pfau, M., 110, 117, 150–51, 210,
    227, 230, 231
Philadelphia, 286
Philip Morris, 249, 251
Phillips, K., 302*n*, 327
Phillips, Kevin, 32–33
phone-in polls, 131
Piazza, T., 182
Pickens, T. Boone, 259
Pillai, R., 98
Pingree, S., 70, 116
Pinkleton, B. E., 58, 135
Pious, R. M., 34
plagiarism, 90–91
Plame, Valerie, 47–48, 297
Pledge of Allegiance, 60
Plumer, B., 264–65
pluralist society, 62
Plutzer, Eric, 67, 69
polarization
  campaign strategy and, 290–93
  cynicism and, 311–12, 313
  negative advertising and, 163, 283
  public policy and, 292–93
  "red" states vs. "blue" states, 292
police, 57–58
police brutality, 57*n*

political action committees (PACs),
        254, 255, 327
political action groups, 322–23
political activists, 68–69
political advertising, 136–66. *See
        also* negative advertising
    ad content, 164
    ad watch programs, 164–65
    in battleground states, 259
    campaign stages and, 150–51
    criticism of, 4
    direct mail advertising, 147–49
    expenditures on, 136
    free airtime, 272–73
    image and, 76, 79, 153
    impacts of, 152–55
    improving, 166
    media coverage and, 152, 164
    negative, 47, 155–66
    newspaper display, 139–40
    polarization and, 291
    questions to ask about, 165
    radio, 140–43
    strategies for, 150–51
    symbols in, 154
    telephone, 149–50
    television, 143–47
    types of, 138–39
    voter recall of, 153
political alienation, 58
political attitudes
    family influence on, 58–60
    image and, 85
    mass media and, 70–71
    school shootings and, 63n
political campaigns. *See* campaigns
political candidates. *See* candidates
political caucuses. *See* caucuses
political communication, 10. *See also*
        communication
political consultants, 44–50
    for elected officials, 275–77
    impacts of, 45–46, 49–50
    interests of, 45–46
    mass media and, 45
    negative effects of, 48–50
    worldwide use of, 27
political correctness, 63

political corruption
    appearance of, 242
    bribery, 241–42
    campaign financing and, 242–45,
        328
    in Congress, 240–42
    lobbyists and, 240–41
    redistricting and, 241
    soft money and, 250–53
political discussion programs, 112
political image, 91–94. *See also*
        image
political influence
    inequality in, 7
    political parties and, 30–31
political news. *See also* media cover-
        age; news media
    importance of, 102–4
    interest in, 106–7
    legitimization by media, 116–18
    newspaper coverage of, 105,
        106–7, 109
    sources of, 104–16
    television coverage of, 108–13
political parades, 136–37
political participation
    in community groups, 324–25
    debates and, 238–39
    decline in, 314
    democracy and, 305, 306, 314–16
    encouraging, 316–17
    importance of, 27
    income and, 264–66
    Internet and, 217–21
    in local issues, 323–24
    negative advertising and, 160–62
    personal involvement, 317–18
    in political action groups,
        322–23
    in political parties, 321–22
    primary contests and, 37
    public forums and, 330
    public opinion and, 195
    schools and, 318–21
    skepticism and, 7
    voting reform and, 329
    in the workplace, 325–26
    by young people, 64, 309, 319

political parties, 30–42. *See also*
    Democratic Party; Republican
    Party
  African Americans and, 32
  campaign finance reform and,
    327–28
  Constitution and, 30
  crossing party lines, 32
  identification with, 31–33, 36–39,
    58
  images of, 79
  influence of, 33, 35–37
  involvement in, 321–22
  labor unions and, 36
  leadership of, 40–41, 44–45
  party discipline, 41
  political loyalty, 33
  political platforms of, 31–32
  popular democracy and, 30–31
  prospective candidates and, 41
  regulations affecting, 37
  revitalizing, 321–22
  role of, 31–32
  student involvement in, 320–21
  suburban development and, 36
  urban political machines and,
    33–36
  women and, 36, 44
  young people and, 38–39
political patronage, 35
political platforms, 31
political pluralism, 63
political positions, 21–22
political power, 4–9
political reform, 316–17, 326–30
political socialization, 54–74
politics
  as communication, 9–22
  confidence in, 7
  cultural values and, 22
  importance to individuals, 5
  interest in, 58
  religion and, 67–69
Pollay, R. W., 154
Pollock, F., 193–94
Polyani, M., 54
Pomper, G., 155, 162
Pooley, E., 167*n*, 244

Popkin, Samuel, 84, 92, 152
populism, 11
"pork" projects, 294
posters, 139
postmodern presidency, 24
Potok, Mark, 9
Potter, T., 254
poverty, 13–14
power hierarchies, 4–5
powerlessness, 279
Poynter Institute, 135
Pratte, R., 64
praxis, 73
predictive dialing software, 149–50
presidency, 22–25
  dishonesty of, 297–98
  national identity and, 23
  postmodern, 24
  speeches, 100–101
presidential campaign of 1824, 170
presidential campaign of 1924,
    170–71
presidential campaign of 1936,
    170–71
presidential campaign of 1952,
    143–44
presidential campaign of 1960, 144,
    223, 225, 229, 230
presidential campaign of 1964,
    155–56
presidential campaign of 1968, 223*n*
presidential campaign of 1976, 225,
    229, 230, 231, 235–36
presidential campaign of 1980,
    225–26, 229, 230
presidential campaign of 1984, 226
presidential campaign of 1988
  debates, 226
  focus groups and, 188
  negative advertising in, 157
  newspaper coverage of, 105
presidential campaign of 1992
  debates, 230–31
  negative advertising in, 157–58
presidential campaign of 1996
  debates, 226, 230, 234, 236
  Internet and, 202–3
  voter suppression in, 278

presidential campaign of 2000
 campaign contributions and,
   249–50
 debates, 223, 224, 226
 election results, 6
 exit polls, 189–90
 image in, 77–78, 94
 Internet and, 203–4
 Nader and, 39–40
 opposition research and, 278
 political advertising and, 153
 public opinion polls and, 172–73
 push polling in, 177–79
 voter polarization in, 291
 vote swapping, 203–4
presidential campaign of 2004
 debates, 223, 234–35
 evangelical Christians and, 43
 exit polls, 191
 gaffes, 236
 image in, 77
 Internet and, 204
 negative advertising in, 159, 163
 Ohio votes and, 6
 polarization and, 291–92
 political advertising and, 153
 public opinion polls and, 173
 voting behavior, 279
presidential campaign of 2008
 candidate diversity and, 1
 candidate wealth and, 270–71
 debates, 223–24, 227
 financing, 2, 242–43
 gaffes, 236
 Internet and, 208–9
 Iraq war and, 3–4
 length of, 1–2
 political advertising, 154
 political contribution controversies, 253
 primaries, 2
 public opinion polls and, 169, 170
 public scrutiny of, 2
 race and, 186
 television advertising and, 147
 terrorism and, 3
presidential campaigns. See campaigns
presidential election, Mexico, 6

press. See also news media
 freedom of, 102
Presser, S., 182
Preston, J., 303
Prewitt, K., 54, 65, 66
primary elections
 date changes, 2
 direct mail advertising in, 148
 front-runners, 84
 media coverage of, 120–21
 political participation and, 37
 television coverage of, 110, 111
 voter turnout, 307
"priming," 119–20
privacy issues, 215–21
private concerns, public interest and,
   215–17
Procter, D., 155
Progressive Party, 28
progressive reform movements, 35
Project for Excellence in Journalism,
   111
Protestants, 67
pseudocertainty principles, 84
public assistance programs, 14. See
   also welfare programs
Public Citizen's Congress Watch,
   294
public discourse, 99–101
public forums, 330
Publicintegrity.org, 272
public interest, private concerns and,
   215–17
public opinion
 mandate of, 195–97
 measurement of, 45
 public opinion polls and, 193
public opinion polls, 167–97
 accuracy of, 173–74
 campaign strategy and, 172–73
 candidate uses of, 167–68
 conducting, 179–91
 cynicism and, 197, 312–13
 exit polls, 189–91
 focus groups, 188–89
 history of, 170–72
 impeachment and, 175–76, 176n
 Internet polls, 184–85

public opinion polls (*continued*)
　interpreting, 192–93
　mail surveys, 179–80
　media coverage of, 131–32,
　　　193–94
　media use of, 168–69
　personal interviews, 185–86
　phone-in, 131
　public opinion and, 193
　public policy and, 284
　push polling, 177–80
　sampling, 173–74
　scientific, 171
　survey construction, 175–77
　telephone interviews, 180–84
　tracking polls, 186–87
Public Opinion Strategies, 177, 260
public policy, 283–90
　earmarks and, 294–95
　environmental policy, 8, 119
　foreign policy, 16, 252
　immigration policy, 14–15, 112,
　　　287–90
　lobbyists and, 293–95
　moral issues and, 302
　polarization and, 292–93
　"pork" projects and, 294
　public opinion polls and, 284
　special interest groups and,
　　　293–95
　wedge issues and, 284–85
　welfare reform, 284–87
pull technologies, 209
push polling, 177–80, 282
push technologies, 209
Putnam, Robert, 314

Qiu, J. L., 213–14
Quayle, Dan, 77, 90, 236
Quayle, Marilyn, 77

race
　personal interviews and, 185–86
　push polling and, 178
　self-identification, 55
　voting behavior and, 56
Raciot, Marc, 258

racism
　Hispanics and, 15
　institutionalization of, 55–56
Radcliff, B., 59
radical politics, 8
radio, 50, 114–15. *See also* Web
　　　radio
　all-news stations, 114
　campaigning and, 141
　listenership, 114–15, 142
　talk radio, 115
　weekly broadcasts, 141–42
radio advertising, 140–43
　advantages of, 142
　costs of, 142
　disadvantages of, 142–43
　finances of, 145–47
　targeting voters with, 142
Raine, L., 106
Ramos, J. M., 98
Rampton, S., 52
Randolph, E., 130
Raney, J., 29*n*, 201
"rapid-response" e-mails, 202–3
Rasmussen poll, 169
Rather, Dan, 87
Reagan, Ronald, 43
　advisors to, 275
　exit polls and, 189
　health of, 96–97, 113
　image of, 25, 113
　1980 presidential campaign, 225,
　　　229, 232
　1988 presidential campaign, 226
　public opinion polls and, 172
　radio broadcasts, 141
　television campaign advertising,
　　　145
　welfare reform and, 284–85, 287
reality, construction of, 18
Real Time with Bill Maher, 282
redistricting, 241
Red Lion Broadcasting Co. v.
　　　Federal Communications
　　　Commission, 140*n*
Reed, D. C., 150
Reeher, G., 215

Reform Party, 39, 202, 224–25, 232
reframing, 124
Rehnquist, William, 256
Reich, R. B., 285
Reiche, R. P., 272
Reichert, B. P., 119
Reid, S., 232
religion, 66–69, 175
Reno, Janet, 247–48
reporters. *See* journalists
Republican Party
    campaign contributions and, 248–49
    establishment of, 31
    groups favoring, 32
    image of, 79
    impeachment of Clinton and, 301
    Iowa caucuses, 29
    leadership of, 40–41
    national conventions, 199, 214,
        222, 252
    negative advertising and, 159
    polarization and, 292
    political corruption and, 241
    presidential campaign of 2008
        and, 208–9, 243
    soft money and, 249
    special interest groups and, 43, 263
    telephone polling and, 182
    urban political machines and, 33
    voter suppression by, 278
    welfare reform and, 285–87
Reuters, 105
Reynolds, L., 227
Riccards, M. P., 55
Rice, Donna, 128
Rich, Frank, 88–89
Richards, Ann, 47
Richardson, Bill, 1, 29, 242, 243
Richter, P., 301
Ridout, T. N., 136, 153
"rigged trees," 196
right-wing extremist organizations,
    8–9
Riley, P., 72, 217, 218, 229, 315, 326
Roberts, C. L., 93
Roberts, D. F., 70
Roberts, John, 256, 257

Rock the Vote, 64
Rogers, E. M., 124
Rokeach, Milton, 21
"rolling average," 187
Roman Catholics, 33
Romney, Mitt
    campaign financing, 243, 244, 270
    personal wealth of, 46
    2008 presidential campaign, 1, 29,
        169, 209, 243
    Web site, 209
Ronfeldt, D., 218
Roosevelt, Franklin Delano, 32, 141,
    171, 174
Roosevelt, Theodore, 28–29
Roper Organization poll, 169, 174
Rosenbaum, D. E., 11, 285
Rosenberg, S. W., 95
Rosenstiel, T., 106, 112, 183
Rosenstone, S. J., 171
Ross, B., 122
Ross, Richie, 47
Rove, Karl, 47–48, 91, 170, 274–75
Rowland, R., 232
Royko, Mike, 33
Rucinski, D., 192
Rumsey, D., 155
Rumsfeld, Donald, 16
rural areas, Internet access in,
    200–201
Rutenberg, J., 259
Ryan, K. D., 261–63

Saad, L., 37, 288
Sabato, L. J., 45, 47, 127, 132, 156,
    242, 268
Sailer, S., 291
Saladay, R., 19
sample ballots, 148–49
sampling, 173–74
Sandel, Michael, 315
Sather, Jeanne, 70
Saturday Night Live, 95
Saudi Arabia, 62–63
Sauer, M., 122
Savage, D. G., 257
Scalia, Antonin, 256

scandals, 293–305
    cynicism and, 295, 304
    ethics, 118
    historical, 294–96
    impeachment, 296
    legacy of, 303–5
    partisanship and, 299
    search for, 296–97
Scarborough, Rick, 91
Schecter, A., 122
Scheer, R., 287
Schell, J., 168, 196, 314
Schenck-Hamlin, W., 155
Schieffer, Bob, 228
Schlozman, K. L., 58, 59
Schmitt, R. B., 123, 297
Schmuhl, R., 103
Schnur, Dan, 90
schools. *See also* civic education;
        education
    shootings, 12, 13, 63n
Schram, S. F., 24, 98–99
Schubert, J. N., 97
Schudson, M., 109
Schwartz, J. J., 55
Schwarzenegger, Arnold, 19–20, 46,
        134, 157, 278
scientific polling, 171
Scott, B. T., 107
Scully, M., 47
Searing, D. D., 55
Sears, D., 231, 233
Sears, D. O., 83
Seelye, K. Q., 168, 227
Sellers, C. S., 57
Semmler, S. M., 210
Senate, 30, 99
sensational news stories, 299
Sensenbrenner, F. James, 15
Seper, J., 15
September 11 terrorist attacks, 8–9,
        10, 24
Serbia, 16, 17
Serrano, R. A., 302
sex scandals
    Clinton, Bill, 120, 122, 128, 129, 298
    Craig, Larry, 123n, 302n
    Foley, Mark, 122
    media coverage of, 298–99, 304–5

Sey, A., 213–14
Shamir, B., 98
Shapiro, A. L., 217
Shapiro, R. Y., 79, 80
Sharpton, Al, 134
Shaw, D., 52, 59
Shaw, Donald, 71, 116, 121
Shay, Christopher, 254
Shays-Meehan bill, 254
Shea, N., 62
Shear, M. D., 224, 244
Shelley, C., 281n
Shelley, M. C., 187
Shenon, P., 275
Sherman, A. K., 54, 58, 73
Sherwell, P., 92
Shields, S. A., 231
Shields, T., 83
Shiltz, R., 119
Shogan, R., 158
Shogren, E., 248
Shultz, George, 267
Shyles, L., 164
Sieber, A. W., 107
Siemaszko, C., 124
Sierra Club, 261
Sigel, R. S., 58
Sigelman, L., 161, 162
Silverman, F. R., 94
Simon, A., 161n, 281n
Simon, D. M., 94
Simon, Paul, 269
Simpson, C., 127
Sinclair, M. D., 181
Singel, R., 206, 207
Singer, E., 182
Sinopoli, R., 282
60 Minutes, 128
Skalaban, A., 130
Skelton, George, 47, 128
skepticism, 7, 242
slogans, 137–38, 205
small-town origins, 85–86
Smith, Bradley, 272
Smith, D., 225
Smith, D. G., 315
Smith, R. A., 245
Smith, R. J., 241
Smith, S. L., 70

Smith, T. W., 170
Sniderman, P. M., 83
Snow, Tony, 91, 122
Snow White, 61
Snyder, J. M., 39, 41
social class
    awareness of, 58
    equality principle and, 5
    political party identification and, 36
    religion and, 68
social contract, 56–57
social interaction, 314
Socialist Party, 28
social networking sites, 205–6, 206n,
    214–15
Society of Professional Journalists,
    135
soft money
    Bipartisan Campaign Finance
        Reform Act and, 254–63
    defined, 250
    527 organizations and, 258–62
    political corruption and, 250–53
    Republican Party and, 249
Solomon, J., 35
Solomon, N., 16, 17n
Somin, I., 99–100
Sorauf, F. J., 30, 31, 83
Soros, George, 258–59
Sothirajah, J., 236
sound bites, 51–52, 96, 110
source-originated news, 125–26
Souter, David, 256, 257
South, Democratic Party and, 32–33
South Carolina primary, 2
South Central Los Angeles riots, 57n
Southern Strategy, 32–33
Spanish-speaking residents, 200, 203
Spanos, Alexander, 259
Speaker of the House of
    Representatives, 99–100
special interest groups, 42–43,
    263–69. *See also* lobbyists
    Congress and, 267–69
    political parties and, 263
    public policy and, 293–395
special investigations, 297
speeches, 100–101
speech writers, 101

Spellman, C., 71, 121
Spillman, B., 20
spin, 234–37, 277
Sprague, John, 67, 69
Squier, Bob, 107–8
Squire, P., 174
Stacey, B., 55, 57, 59
Stanfield, S., 227
Starr, Kenneth, 256, 256n, 299, 300
State of Denial: Bush at War, Part III
    (Woodward), 107
statistical weighting, 174
Stauber, J., 52
Stauffer, A., 232
Steele, J. C., 251–52
Steen, J. A., 271
Steeper, Fred, 170
Steinhauer, J., 20
Stempel, G. H., III, 105
Stengel, Richard, 22–23
Stephanopoulos, George, 276, 278
Stephen, T. D., 91–92, 93
Stevens, John Paul, 256, 257
Stevenson, Adlai, 143–44
Stewart, Jon, 89, 92
St. George, Andrew, 281
Stockdale, James, 232
Stohl, M., 232
Stokes, D. E., 33
stratified sampling, 173–74, 174n
straw polls, 170–71
Stroud, N. J., 233
Stuckey, Mary, 24
student government, 62, 319–20
students, 13. *See also* civic educa-
    tion; young people
Student Voices Project, 61n
Studlar, D. T., 193
suburban development, 36
Sudman, S., 189
Sullivan, A., 79
Sunde, U., 55
Sunstein, C., 210
Superfund Recycling Equity, 252
Supreme Court
    campaign finance regulations and,
        256–57, 271
    citizen knowledge about, 61
    equal time rules, 140n

Supreme Court (*continued*)
  presidential election of 2000 and,
    190
Suro, R., 15, 248
Sussman, Gerald, 147–48
Sutton, Willie, 264
Swift Boat Veterans for Truth, 87,
    140, 159, 259–61
"swing states," 146, 173
symbolism, 11, 16–17, 18, 154
synthesizing ideologies, 73

tabloid press, 129–30, 167*n*
Taft, William Howard, 28–29
"talking heads," 111, 145, 330
talking points, 188, 199
talk radio, 6, 115
Tammany Hall (New York), 33–34
Tancredo, Tom, 1
Tannen, D., 59
Tannenbaum, P. H., 94
Tarde, G., 239
targeting voters
  computer databases for, 199
  Internet and, 212–13
  with radio advertising, 142
  with telephone advertising,
    149–50
Task Force on Inequality and
    Democracy, 265
Taylor, P., 136, 146, 166
Teamsters Union, 251
technorealists, 219
Tedesco, J. C., 231
telephone advertising, 149–50
telephone interviews, 180–84
television, 50–52, 108–13
  broadcast technology, 113
  cable news shows, 112
  comedy news programs, 89–90
  crime coverage, 109
  "experts" on, 111
  free airtime, 272–73, 328
  intimacy of, 98, 109–10
  network news, 112–13
  ownership trends, 144–45
  personal interviews, 24–25
  political attitudes and, 70–71

political discussion programs,
    112
  reliance on, 85
  sound bites, 110
  subjectivity of, 111
  time spent watching, 70
  viewing habits, 108
television advertising, 138, 143–47
television stations, 146
Tenpas, K. D., 170, 277
terrorism, 3, 16, 24
Thatcher, Margaret, 97
Thee, M., 39
thin citizens, 219–20
third-party candidates, 39–40,
    224–25
Thomas, Clarence, 256
Thomas, E., 176
Thompson, D., 280*n*
Thompson, Fred, 1, 209
Thompson, Tommy, 1, 236
Thune, John, 42
Tilden, Samuel J., 296
Time magazine, 77, 107
Times Mirror, 129
Ting, M. M., 39, 41
Tipton, L. P., 70
tobacco industry, 177, 248, 249
Tocqueville, Alexis de, 215–16, 305
Toner, Michael, 2
Toobin, J., 191*n*, 297
town meetings, 330
toxic waste cleanup, 246–47
tracking polls, 187–88
Tracy, Destutt de, 72
transgendered people, 63*n*
Traugott, Michael W., 169, 179–80,
    182, 188
Trent, J. S., 94, 138
"trial heat" surveys, 192
"trickle-up" influence, 60
Trippi, Joe, 204, 206
Truman, Harry S, 296
trust
  candidate appeal and, 92–94
  democracy and, 315–16
  family and, 55, 58
  plagiarism and, 90–91

presidential elections of 2000 and 2004 and, 6
Tucker, C. J., 57
Tucker, R., 72
Tumulty, Karen, 78
Tweed, William "Boss," 34
20/20, 298
Tyson, A., 16

Ukraine, 6
underdog candidates, 232
United Nations, 27
"unit rule," 33
Unruh, Jesse, 242
urban areas
    crime rates in, 11–12
    Internet access in, 200–201
    political machines, 33–36
Urofsky, M. I., 256
USA Today, 189
    Web site, 210
USA Today/Gallup poll, 287
U.S. Chamber of Commerce, 257
U.S. Justice Department, 11, 275
U.S. News & World Report, 107

Valentino, N., 281*n*
values
    civic education and, 64–65
    formation of, 21
    political campaigns and, 21–22
    political rhetoric and, 22
    symbolic communication and, 18
    traditional values voters, 129
Vanderford, M. L., 67
van Holsteyn, J. J. M., 168, 193
Van Winkle, K. M., 110
Vargas, J. A., 214
Ventura, Jesse, 201, 225
Verba, S., 58, 59
Viale, R., 54
video feeds, 211–12
video images, 113
Vietnam War
    Democratic Party and, 37
    government legitimacy and, 8
    opposition to, 18
    student involvement and, 320

2004 presidential campaign and, 87–88
Villaraigosa, Antonio, 95, 158
Vilsack, Tom, 1, 29, 168–69
violence, 126
viral marketing, 206, 206*n*
Virginia Tech University, 12, 13
Vitter, David, 305
Voss, Gelman, King, 181, 182, 183–84
Voter/Consumer Research, 178
Voter News Service, 39–40
voter suppression, 277–78
vote swapping, 203–4
voting
    Constitution and, 30
    fraud, 191, 329
    political advertising and, 153
    political parties and, 31
    reforms, 329
    registration, 217
voting behavior
    age and, 307–8
    cognitive misers and, 83
    college attendance and, 64
    debates and, 222–23, 232–34
    education and, 307
    of gays and lesbians, 308–9
    gender and, 56
    of Generation Xers, 38
    image and, 83–85
    income and, 265, 291, 308
    of minority groups, 291, 308
    moral issues and, 69
    negative advertising and, 160–66, 278–80
    polarization and, 291–92
    radio advertising and, 142
    turnout, 217, 306–9
    voting reform and, 329
    of young people, 61, 64, 309

Wald, K. D., 67, 68
Walker, D., 154
Wallace, George, 223*n*
Wallace, J., 122
Wallach, L., 152
Wallsten, P., 68

Wall Street Journal, 127
Walsh, B., 242
Walters, Barbara, 298
Wanta, W., 121
Ward, L. S., 70
wartime campaigns, 3
Washington, D.C., 264
Washington, George, 136, 298
Washington Monthly, 284
Washington Post, 92–93, 104, 107,
    117, 139
    Web site, 210
Washington Times, 127, 130
wasteful government spending, 52
"watchdog" journalism, 132
Watergate scandal, 80, 117, 132,
    245–46, 249, 297
Waters, E., 58
Wattenberg, M. P., 152, 161*n*, 226
Wayne, L., 253, 266
Wayne, S. J., 32
Weaver, D., 71, 121, 130, 152
Webb, Jim, 307
Webb, V. J., 57
Webber, D., 230
Web radio, 143
Web sites
    for candidates, 208–9
    for news media, 210–11
wedge issues, 284–85
Weiler, M., 227
Weiner, T., 247
Weinfield, N. S., 58
Weinraub, B., 89, 90
Weir, M., 321, 322, 323
Weiss, P., 299
Weissman, J., 41, 118, 240
Weissman, S. R., 261–63
Weld, Bill, 235
welfare programs, 14
welfare reform, 284–87
Weltanschauung, 72, 72*n*, 74
Wen, W., 152
West, D. M., 269
West, P., 224
Westen, D., 260, 285, 311
Westly, Steve, 157
Whereatt, R., 225

Whig Party, 31
White, J., 16
White, N., 73
White Aryan Resistance, 8–9
White House Press Office, 141
Wilder, Douglas, 186
Wilhelm, A. G., 218–19
Wilkinson, M., 87
Will, George F., 77
Williams, E. A., 98
Wilson, B. J., 70
Wilson, Charles E., 73
Wilson, Joseph, 48
Wilson, Woodrow, 28, 29
Windt, T. O., 18, 22
Wines, M., 304
Winfield, Betty, 25
Wing, B., 291
Winkler, C. K., 232
wire services, 105
Wisconsin Right to Life Committee,
    257
Witte, J., 199
Wlezien, C., 169, 184, 187
women. *See also* gender
    Clinton, Hillary, and, 93–94
    party identification of, 36, 44, 56
Woodward, Bob, 107, 118
Woodward, G. C., 170, 171, 172, 187
workplace participation, 325–26
Worley, B., 203
Wray, L., 57
Wuthnow, R., 325
Wynette, Tammy, 129

Xinshu, Z., 164
Xu, W., 70

Yamamura, K., 40*n*
Yamane, D., 67
Yardley, J., 179–80
yard signs, 138–39
Yeric, J. L., 153, 155, 156
York, A., 95, 158
Young, Don, 294–95
young people. *See also* adolescents
    Democratic Party and, 38–39
    local issues and, 323–24

newspaper readership by, 106
political participation by, 64, 309,
    319–21
political parties and, 38–39, 320–21
telephone polls and, 183
voting behavior, 61, 64, 308, 309
YouTube, 90, 206*n*, 211–12, 213,
    227, 278
Yum, J. O., 85

Zarefsky, D., 26, 66
Zechmeister, E. J., 98
Zeleney, J., 123
Zernike, K., 87, 259
Zhao, X., 152
Zhu, J., 230–31
Zito, S., 29
Zogby International poll, 61, 169
Zukin, C., 152